Historical Archaeology

Charles E. Orser, Jr.
Illinois State University

Brian M. Fagan
University of California, Santa Barbara

Acquisitions Editor/Executive Editor: Alan McClare
Cover Design: Larry Pezzato
Photo Researcher: Mira Schachne
Electronic Production Manager: Angel Gonzalez
Publishing Services: Ruttle, Shaw & Wetherill, Inc.
Electronic Page Makeup: Ruttle, Shaw & Wetherill, Inc.
Printer and Binder: R. R. Donnelley and Sons Company
Cover Printer: The Lehigh Press, Inc.

Historical Archaeology

Library of Congress Cataloging-in-Publication Data

Lindbriar Corporation and Orser, Charles E.
    Historical Archaeology/Charles E. Orser, Jr., Brian M. Fagan.
  p. cm.
    Includes bibliographical references (p.255) and index.
    ISBN 0-673-99094-X
    1. Archaeology and history. I. Fagan, Brian M. II. Title.
    CC77.H5077 1995   94–18994
    930.1' 09—dc20   CIP

95 96 97 98   9 8 7 6 5 4 3 2 1

To Janice

Contents

Preface

We're all familiar with archaeologists, or think we are. TV depicts them as bold adventurers, scientists digging in the shadow of lofty pyramids, poring over clay tablets and incredibly ancient stone tools. We marvel at high technology brought to bear on tiny seeds and broken animal bones, at X-rays of Egyptian Pharaohs and 20,000-year-old cave art painted during the late Ice Age. Yes, archaeology can be an adventure, but it is also a highly sophisticated multidisciplinary science that covers the entire spectrum of the human past from human origins to late twentieth-century urban landfills. This book explores part of the world of modern archaeology in all its fascinating diversity, not remote human beginnings or the earliest civilizations, but the archaeology of the recent past. As such, it is somewhat unusual.

"Historical Archaeology," the archaeological study of people documented in recent history, has expanded dramatically in recent years, creating a need for a basic text on the subject. So we joined forces to write this short volume. One of us, Charles E. Orser, Jr., is a working historical archaeologist with experience on many kinds of historical sites, the other, Brian M. Fagan, is an archaeologist with a broad experience of excavations on sites of the prehistoric and historical past, and author of several basic texts on archaeology. Our book covers the basic methods and concepts of historical archaeology. The first three chapters describe basic principles, the history of the subject, and fundamental definitions. From there we move on to the methods of historical archeology, to such topics as time and space, historical artifacts, survey, and excavation. We also consider some basic theory and explore some of the archaeology that is being conducted across the globe. We end with a look at career prospects in historical archaeology and at ways in which individuals—like you—can help to save the past for future generations. References for more detailed readings are given at the end of the book. No previous experience in archaeology is needed, for technical terms are kept to a minimum, and those that are used are defined both in the text and in a short Glossary.

We hope that this brief volume will give you insights into the fascinating world of historical archaeology. Good luck with your adventures in the past!

Charles E. Orser, Jr.
Brian M. Fagan

Acknowledgments

We are grateful to all those who have assisted in the arduous task of writing this book, especially the many colleagues who have answered questions, supplied information, or provided illustrations. The following academic reviewers of the manuscript provided invaluable advice: Mary Carolyn Beaudry, Boston University; Charles Ewen, University of Arkansas; Richard A. Fox, University of South Dakota; Donald Hardesty, University of Nevada-Reno; Kenneth Lewis, Michigan State University; Randall McGuire, SUNY-Binghamton; Rochelle A. Marrinan, Florida State University; and Robert Paynter, University of Massachusetts-Amherst.

We also wish to extend our most heartfelt thanks to Janice L. Orser, who assisted with editing, reading, and many other much-needed tasks, and to Jeanne M. Schultz, who helped with the illustrations. Lastly, our thanks to our editor, Alan McClare, who encouraged us all along the way, and to the talented production staff at HarperCollins, who turned a much amended manuscript into a book, especially Michael Kimball, Mira Schachne, and Suzanne Van Cleve. Thank you one and all!

CHAPTER

I

What Is Historical Archaeology?

"Archaeology has revolutionized history"

V. Gordon Childe, 1944

In the year 1781, Thomas Jefferson, the future president of the United States, retired to the peace of his country estate at Monticello, Virginia, where he indulged a passion for academic research. Surrounded by "his family, his farm, and his books," Jefferson sat down to compile a lengthy discourse, which he entitled *Notes on the State of Virginia*. He wrote of laws and money, of products "animal, vegetable, and mineral," and of the native tribes of his beloved state. Inevitably, too, he wondered about their origins. Many of his contemporaries asked who had built the silent earthen mounds that dotted the landscape of the eastern United States—in some places majestic and flat-topped, in others small and rounded. Were the Mound Builders a vanished race of non-Indians who had migrated to the New World, perhaps from as far away as the Holy Land, and then constructed the great mounds after battling and subjugating the Native Americans around them? Or were the mysterious earthworks built by the forebears of the scattered Native American groups, who still lived in eastern North America? But Jefferson was cautious, and would not take a stand on the Mound Builders. The debate raged for years among Jefferson's friends in the coffee shops of Philadelphia and among other antiquarians. But Jefferson was one of the few people who then bothered to excavate to search for more information.

Thomas Jefferson, early American archaeologist.

Jefferson chose an earthwork near the Rivanna River, a small mound that was a "repository of the dead." In 1784, his slaves dug a perpendicular trench through the tumulus, "so that I might examine its internal structure." He recorded layers of human bones at different depths, lying in complete confusion, "so as, on the whole, to give the idea of bones emptied promiscuously from a bag or basket." The story of America's first scientific archaeological excavation, one of the earliest in the world, is well known. Jefferson was the first scientist to identify the Mound Builders as Native Americans. In the history of archaeology he stands as the first person to make a careful and, for his day, scientific, excavation of a Native American burial mound.

What Jefferson would never have guessed, however, was that he and his contemporaries—the slaves who actually performed the digging into the mound, the carriage driver who drove him to the earthwork, and the merchant who sold him the paper on which he would make his careful and pioneering notes—would one day themselves become the subject of archaeological study (Figure 1.1). Little would Jefferson suspect that two centuries later his own era would be put under the

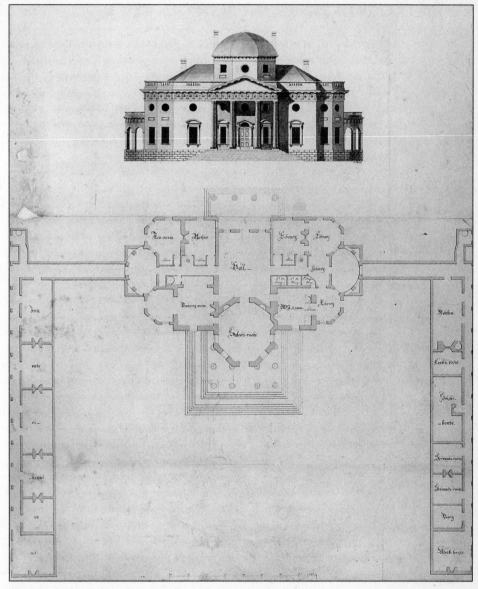

Figure 1.1 *Floor plan of Monticello, Jefferson's home.*

microscope of scientific archaeology. Perhaps he would be amused to learn that the many common, and to him, uninteresting, objects that he and his contemporaries used in their daily lives would be unearthed with the same care, interest, and wonder as he felt toward the smoking pipes and copper ornaments used by the ancient North American Mound Builders. Today, archaeology is as much a part of the study of history as the historic building, crabbed document, or government archive.

ARCHAEOLOGY OF THE RECENT PAST

Eccentric pith-helmeted professors, ragged adventures overcoming all to retrieve a priceless relic, excavations in the shadow of great pyramids—these are some of the popular images of archaeology. Most people know that archaeology deals with ancient history and with old things. Agatha Christie, the famed mystery writer and wife of well-known British archaeologist, Sir Max Mallowan, once remarked that she liked being married to an archaeologist because the older she became, the more he liked her! Many people assume that archaeology focuses on the old and the venerated, and the older the better.

Nothing could be further from the truth. Today's archaeologists study the entire range of human history, from our origins in East Africa more than 2.5 million years ago, to Victorian railroad stations and nineteenth-century Western mining towns. Some archaeologists even spend their careers researching modern urban garbage dumps and landfills, both as a way of interpreting ancient rubbish heaps, and as a dispassionate means of studying contemporary waste management systems. Modern archaeology is not treasure hunting, nor is it a fantasy search for lost worlds; *it is the systematic study of humanity in the past.* This general definition covers not only ancient technology and human behavior, but social organization, religious beliefs, and every aspect of human culture.

Archaeologists and historians often divide the enormous span of human existence into *prehistoric* and *historical* times. *Prehistory* is *that portion of human history that extends back before the time of written documents and archives.* Prehistoric archaeologists deal with a very long time scale, for prehistoric archaeology is the primary source of information on 99% of human history. Prehistoric archaeologists investigate how early societies all over the world came into being, how they differed from one another, and, in particular, how they changed through time. Their researches are, for example, the primary source of information on the development of Native American societies over the past 15,000 years.

"Historical times" is a generic term that refers to *that portion of human history that begins with the appearance of written records and continues until today.* It is the history of literate societies, which first appeared in Mesopotamia and in the Nile Valley in about 3,250 B.C. Not that writing appeared simultaneously in all parts of the world, for prehistory continued much later in other regions. Literate civilization developed in northwest India in about 2,000 B.C., in northern China by about the same time, and among the Maya of Central America about the time of Christ. Many parts of the world entered written history with the arrival of European explorers after the fifteenth century A.D. Some parts of Central Africa, New Guinea, and the Amazon Basin remained effectively in prehistoric times until this century.

Many of the world's most spectacular discoveries come from the archaeological record of the earliest civilizations. The royal library of Assyrian King Assurbanipal from Nineveh, the gold-rich tomb of Egyptian pharaoh Tutankhamun, the terra-cotta regiment buried by the tomb of Chinese emperor Xuang Ti in the second century B.C.—all come from historical times. They can be characterized as *text-aided archaeology, archaeology carried out with the aid of historical documentation that throws light on human life at the time.*

There are many specialties within text-aided archaeology, the archaeology of historical times. Assyriologists, Egyptologists, Mayanists, and Sinologists (specialists in Chinese civilization) are just a few of the highly specialized archaeologists who focus on single societies, or even minute details of a single period. Then there are Classical archaeologists, who study the classical civilizations of Greece and Rome. Many of them concentrate on architecture and changing art styles, rather than on the minute economic and social problems that absorb archaeologists working on earlier periods. Finally, there is *historical archaeology, the archaeological study of people documented in recent history*—like Jefferson and his contemporaries—the subject of this book.

Historical archaeology is the archaeology of a more recent past. It is a past that includes both the colonial and early modern American and the world history that most people learn in school, as well as the well-remembered history that has unfolded in living people's lifetimes. The latter is of vital importance. For historical archaeologists, the history that people carry around in their heads, their own personal experiences, is often as important, and sometimes more so, than the "official" histories appearing in books. Historical archaeology breathes life into arid histories made up of serried dates and dusty personages, and animates the people who lived in it. It treats not only kings and queens, statesmen and the rich and famous, but the common folk, the anonymous heroes of history. The historical archaeologist studies European colonists, African-American slaves, Native American fur traders, Chinese railroad laborers, German immigrant farm wives, early Australian convicts, and all those people who made the "modern" world, all too often the people without documented history. Historical archaeology provides a unique opportunity for studying changing gender roles in the past or changing human societies from a truly multicultural perspective.

Historical archaeology is important not only because it is a means of studying the past, but because it has the potential to teach us about ourselves. We may not be able to relate to the circumstances faced by people who lived many centuries ago, but we can achieve an understanding of the long-forgotten and often compelling histories of once anonymous folk, whose direct descendants are alive today. British archaeologist Stuart Piggott once described archaeology as the "science of rubbish." He is partially right, for archaeologists spend much of their time delving into ancient garbage heaps and abandoned dwellings. Therein lies the importance of historical archaeology, for the dispassionate eye of the archaeologist can conjure up prosaic details of day-to-day history that never appear in government archives. In recent years, for example, excavations at Red Bay, Labrador, have revealed astoundingly comprehensive information on sixteenth-century Basque whaling in the Strait of Belle Isle off northeastern Canada, a chapter of European history virtually absent from the history books. The enslavement of Africans centuries ago has direct relevance to many present-day problems faced by people of African descent in the United States, many parts of Africa, South America, and the Caribbean. Historical archaeology studies African enslavement from the humble artifacts and discarded food remains found in slave quarters and plantations. One can even trace the survival of traditional African beliefs through telltale artifacts found in such sites, beliefs never mentioned in documents kept by their masters. Archaeologists and their trowels add an engrossing dimension to African-American history accessible by no other means. Similarly, the archaeology of early modern consumerism sheds light on current patterns of purchasing, and helps to demonstrate in clear, tangible ways how so many people in the world came to depend so strongly on the mass, global market of today.

Prehistoric archaeology documents the emerging biologic and cultural diversity of humankind. It shows us how our earliest ancestors faced and solved the challenges of daily existence. Many of these problems, except for their antiquity, are not all that different from the dilemmas of survival faced by much of humanity today. In contrast, historical archaeology, because of its more recent focus, holds a mirror directly before the face of the contemporary world and reflects precisely the complex roots of our own increasingly diverse society. This unique reflection of our recent past is a vital tool in our achieving a better understanding of ourselves. Small wonder the rapidly maturing discipline of historical archaeology is becoming a vital tool for social scientist and historian alike. This book describes this exciting field of modern archaeology and how it came into being.

THREE PAST DEFINITIONS OF HISTORICAL ARCHAEOLOGY

Historical archaeology has strong roots in the historical preservation movement. In its earliest days, historical archaeology was a full partner in often herculean efforts to interpret sites of national importance for an eager public. In the United States, archaeology at places like Jamestown and Colonial Williamsburg provided many of the architectural details that made historic homes and their yards come alive for modern visitors. These preservation efforts made it clear that real men and women, once-living individuals, had to be inserted into the reconstructed buildings and landscapes. Modern historical archaeology came from this realization. The new discipline has evolved as something different from prehistoric archaeology, even if both share the same basic excavation techniques and many similar analytical approaches. It has developed as a rich diverse field of inquiry that defies precise definition, as the focus of research has changed. Let us examine some definitions that have stood the test of time.

Historical Archaeology as the Study of a Period

When the Conference on Historic Sites Archaeology—the first professional historical archaeology organization founded in the United States—was organized in 1960 at the University of Florida, its expressed purpose was to focus on the "historical" period, a period that was clearly defined as "post-prehistoric." Soon afterward, archaeologist Robert Schuyler defined historical archaeology simply as "the study of the material remains from any historic period," an equivalent to prehistoric archaeology. This viewpoint envisages human history as a layer cake, the bottom, thickest layer being prehistoric times; the thin top layer, the historical period. In reality, however, the frontier between "prehistory" and "history" is usually blurred. For example, Colonial New England flourished within historical times, whereas the surrounding Native American groups were technically still in prehistory. Some experts think in terms of transition periods, sometimes referred to as "protohistory," literally primitive history. The noted British prehistorian Grahame Clark speaks of three archaeological periods: "autonomous prehistory," "secondary prehistory," and "history."

Under Schuyler's definition, a broadly defined historical archaeology based simply on not being prehistoric is composed of numerous subfields: classical archaeology, medieval archaeology, postmedieval archaeology, historic sites archaeology, industrial archaeology, and "a series of mainly unnamed areas of research such as the study of literate civilizations in India and the Islamic world." These subfields are firmly rooted in different time periods. Classical archaeology focuses on a period beginning with the Minoans around 3,000 B.C. and ending with the Later Roman Empire at about A.D. 527; medieval archaeology concentrates on the period from about A.D. 400 to 1400; postmedieval archaeology focuses on the period from A.D. 1450 to 1750; historic sites archaeology considers the period from A.D. 1415 to industrialization; and industrial archaeology studies the world's complex technologies after about A.D. 1750. These subfields also are tied to various parts of the world: Classical archaeology is associated with the Mediterranean and Europe, medieval and postmedieval archaeology with Europe, historic sites archaeology with the world colonized by Europe, and industrial archaeology with Europe and the European postcolonial world. These periods of emphasis for the subfields of historical archaeology are somewhat arbitrary—for example, the postmedieval period in Scotland is considered to extend from 1488 to 1609—but their usage demonstrates how historical archaeology can be seen to focus on a broadly conceived period.

What ties all of these subfields together, and what makes them "historical," is the central idea that the "historical" period encompasses all those periods for which written information is available. Archaeologist James Deetz, for example, argues that "the literacy of the people it studies is what sets historical archaeology apart from prehistory." In this sense, then, we may take the word "historical" to mean "literate," and the word "prehistoric" to mean "nonliterate." Clark's "secondary prehistory" is that time during which literate peoples came into contact with and wrote about nonliterate peoples. Using this idea, an archaeologist digging a sixteenth-century Portuguese settlement in Brazil would be engaged in the study of the "historical" period; an archaeologist studying a site once inhabited by a group of nonliterate Tupinambá Indians described by the French friar André Thevet would be researching the "protohistorical" period; and an archaeologist investigating a Tupinambá site that shows no evidence of foreign contact and predates Portuguese involvement in Brazil would be studying "prehistoric" time.

Definitions of archaeology that divide time into two large periods make sense because "history" is, after all, widely understood as that part of the past for which documentation exists. In the Western tradition, we may imagine the historical period to begin with the Greeks and to continue, perhaps unevenly in places, until the present. In contrast, prehistory is literally that period *before* history. We may imagine that historical archaeology may be viewed as studying a period that extends from the focus of Classical archaeology (from 1,000 B.C.) on the earliest end to industrial archaeology (from A.D. 1750) at the most recent.

One can apply the same prehistoric-historical division to non-Western culture areas, like China. The Chinese past can be divided into "prehistory"—composed of Paleolithic (Old Stone Age: about 600,000–7,000 B.C.) and Neolithic ("New Stone Age": about 7,000–1,600 B.C.) periods—and "history," beginning with the Shang civilization, around 1,600 B.C. The earliest writings in China, appearing as "oracle bones"—shoulder blades of oxen used to foretell the future and inscribed with royal divinations—serve to mark the beginning of Chinese "history." These inscriptions, corroborated by the later writings of the historian Ssu-ma Ch'ien in the first century B.C., document the uninterrupted development of Chinese writing since about 1,000 B.C. In this sense, then, we may say that historical archaeology in China focuses on sites dating from any time since the Shang Dynasty.

Historical Archaeology as a Method

A second, common definition of historical archaeology focuses on the methodological aspects of the field. This approach seeks an equal combination of "historical" and "archaeological" materials in the study of the past. For William Adams, who used this approach in his study of the late nineteenth- and early twentieth-century town of Silcott, Washington, historical archaeology is not restricted to a particular time, but rather rests on the use of diverse sources of information in any study that has archaeology as a major component. Adams used written documents, archaeological findings, and even recollections of living informants to interpret the history and culture of the people who once lived at Silcott. Adams learned, for example, that the pickers in the town's bountiful fruit orchards referred to their boss, Hiram Werst, as "Hiram Fire Em." It was said that he would fire a man because he did not like the cut of his hair. Even though Hiram could "curse for twenty minutes without repeating himself once," he did not hold a grudge for long and would usually rehire the fired man. Adams also learned from his informants that when two other Silcott residents, Weldon and Jennie Wilson, decided to build a new home to store-bought plans, they adamantly refused to place the bathroom next to the kitchen. They were dead set against an indoor toilet, so they converted the room into a pantry!

In Adams' view, such fields of research as Mayan civilization, Classical archaeology, and Egyptology are all historical archaeology. The periods are different in each instance, but each field allows archaeologists to combine "nonarchaeological" materials with archaeological data, in essence working both as a historian and as an archaeologist.

Definitions that focus on methodology give written records precedence over chronology. Thus, they include all literate cultures in the field. Under this rubric, we may consider that Heinrich Schliemann's use of Homer's texts in his excavations at Troy in 1871 represented an example of historical archaeology. So do archaeologist Neville Chittick's excavations at the fourteenth-century Swahili town of Kilwa on the East Africa coast in the 1960s. Chittick combined Islamic chronicles with archaeology. By the same token, Robin Birley has recovered letters written on thin wood slivers from the Roman frontier fort at Vindolanda on Hadrian's Wall in northern Britain. They provide priceless information on Roman garrison life in the first century A.D. Under this definition, the dates of the sites are not important. What takes precedence is the presence of some form of written text—transcribed on paper, clay, stone, or whatever—that may be used by archaeologists in their efforts to interpret the past. In the late nineteenth century, British Classical archaeologist David G. Hogarth distinguished between "literary documents" (that is, writings) and "material documents" (artifacts) in an effort to explain how archaeologists use "nonarchaeological" pieces of information in their research. The combined interpretation of these different kinds of "documents" defines how historical archaeology can be viewed as a methodology.

The methodological definition can be drawn even wider, by including some alternate but valuable sources of historical information obtained from ethnohistory and oral history.

Ethnohistory is *the study of the past using non-Western, indigenous historical records, and especially oral traditions.* Like historical archaeology, ethnohistory also rests on the combined use of different sources of information. Ethnohistory often focuses on people that are known to have existed in history but who are known largely through the writings of outsiders. Ethnohistory became important in the United States with the creation of the Indian Claims Commission in August 1946. Both native groups and governmental bodies needed expert testimony about the documented history of native people. Anthropologists began to work as historians in archives and other documentary repositories, and historians started to work as anthropologists as they researched the histories of nonliterate peoples and used ethnological language. For example, for the case *Sac and Fox Tribe of Indians, et al.* v. *The United States,* filed in 1955, the Native Americans, defendants, hired ethnohistorians to prepare several reports about their history and culture. Defendant's Exhibit 97 is entitled "An Anthropological Report on the Indian Occupancy [of land] Ceded to the United States by the United Tribes of Sac and Fox under the Treaty of November 3, 1804." Some of these legal documents can be painfully dry reading. For instance, Defendant's Exhibit 57, "An Account of the Manners and Customs of the Sauk Nation of Indians," begins: "The original and present name of the Sauk Indians proceeds from the compound word Saw-kie alias A-saw-we-kee literally Yellow Earth. The Fox Indians call themselves Mess-qua-a-kie alias Mess-qua-we-kie literally Red Earth." Although dense reading, Claims Commission reports are crammed with valuable ethnohistorical information about Native American history and culture, ranging from games and dances to cosmology and language. They demonstrated the power of ethnohistorical interpretation, and pushed the study of oral sources to the cutting edge of both anthropology and history.

When Hernán Cortés and his conquistadors entered the Aztec capital, Tenochtitlán, in 1519, they marveled at a sophisticated, cosmopolitan city with a market larger than that of Constantinople (today known as Istanbul). Cortés overthrew the Aztec rulers in 1521, bringing centuries of Indian civilization to an end. Fortunately for science, Dominican friar Bernardino de Sahagun later developed a passion for Aztec culture and devoted his lifetime to recording their history. He assembled informants at strategic missions and took down many details of a culture that were transmitted with picture signs and oral recitations. Sahagun's *History of the General Things of New Spain* was considered so heretical by his priestly superiors that it was not published until the nineteenth century. But it is a mine of priceless ethnohistorical information for twentieth-century archaeologists and historians. When Mexican archaeologist Eduardo Matos Moctezuma excavated the Templo Mayor (Great Temple) of the Aztec gods Huitzilopochtli and Tlaloc from beneath modern Mexico City, he found that many details of the structure and its history were corroborated by both Spanish accounts and Sahagun's informants.

Ethnohistory is a powerful tool for historical archaeologists, especially when combined with archaeological and conventional historical sources. It is a truly multidisciplinary form of research.

Oral history is *historical tradition, often genealogies, passed down from generation to generation by word of mouth.* It is transitory history in the sense that it is retained in the memory, destined to vanish if not written down or passed on to the next generation. It is for this reason that much oral history is genealogy, for tracing ties back to ancestral kin amounts to a major concern in many societies, including our own. Maya lords were obsessed with genealogy, with establishing their royal legitimacy back to divine ancestors. Many Africans think of the past in terms of generations, of links to the ancestors who are intermediaries with the spiritual world and the land. But oral traditions treat of far more than genealogies. They retain vivid memories of major events like solar eclipses, wars, and famines, of nineteenth-century family migrations from Ohio out west, and so on. It is only in recent years that we have fully appreciated the value of the historical memories of old people, who often pass on without handing down their priceless legacy of historical information.

The study of oral history has achieved great sophistication in sub-Saharan Africa, which is rich in eighteenth- and nineteenth-century oral traditions, many of them recorded early in this century, when memories were still vivid. Such traditions are a historical minefield, for they require careful critical analysis before they can be accepted as accurate reflections of the past. When archaeologist Peter Schmidt studied the ancient Buhaya kingdoms in East Africa, he combined oral traditions with data from archaeological and historical sources. Schmidt found that he had to spend two to four hours with each of his informants. In doing so, he learned the art of extracting relevant information from men who had acquired a lifetime's experience of local oral traditions. He had to learn how to evaluate the Buhaya's rich mythology, the myths of the people's cultural origins and early migrations, then correlate them with the archaeological sites he had discovered. Rather than just looking at the sites as isolated habitations occupied at different dates, he used the myths to tie them together, combining archaeology with oral history.

Oral history is a vital tool in more recent American history, especially when studying the experiences of ethnic groups and working class families. It began as a kind of local history focused on what people could remember about themselves and their times. In researching a particular region or place, like an urban neighborhood, some historians realized that much "documentation" of recent history was not written down, but was nevertheless remembered by still-living people. Tracking down such oral traditions required drawing on the field experience of anthropologists and folklorists, who had a long history of collecting and interpreting oral information. During his time in Tanzania, Schmidt heard several stories of the founding of the Buhaya kingdoms and many accounts of their royal lineages. In one tale, he learned how the king Rugomora Mahe traveled through his domains. Eventually he arrived at a place where some people were smelting iron, a prehistoric technology documented by Schmidt's research. "They failed to welcome Rugomora, who, then, out of pique, changed their clan name to *Bahuge*, or 'the dull ones.'" After traveling further Rugomora saw more people making iron tools, whereupon "he drew up a plan to build a tower to the heavens to see what they looked like." Schmidt's informant told him that he knew the precise spot where the iron for Rugomora's tower was smelted.

Thinking of historical archaeology as a methodology brings out a critical point. Like prehistoric archaeology, our field is a multidisciplinary enterprise. The prehistoric archaeologist draws on the researches of botanists, chemists, and zoologists, to mention only a few. The historical archaeologist does exactly the same, but uses an even greater diversity of sources, everything from documents to oral traditions, minute details of sixteenth-century art to the technology of nails in 1890. It is truly multidisciplinary detective work, the only limit being the creativity and ingenuity of the researcher in locating additional sources.

Historical Archaeology as the Study of the Modern World

A third definition focuses not only on chronology and on methodology, but on a specific historical topic. In a now-classic definition, James Deetz defines historical archaeology as "the archaeology of the spread of European culture throughout the world since the fifteenth century and its impact on indigenous peoples." Although Deetz's definition contains an element of time—"since the fifteenth century"—his main idea is that historical archaeology is the archaeology of a specific subject, namely the spread of Europeans and European culture and institutions throughout the world by adventurers, explorers, merchants, and traders. As these Europeans traveled outward from their homelands and into Africa, the Far East, the New World, and the Pacific, they carried with them the ideas, perceptions, and material things with which they were familiar. Scholars sometimes refer to the interconnected network of European outposts, trading ports, and towns as a "world system." Historical archaeology is unique as the archaeology that studies this system and the spread of ideas and people that were part of it.

This definition assumes that historical archaeology is a combined anthropological and historical study of the modern world. By "modern world," historical archaeologists mean the world that contained the earliest elements of our own world, such as large-scale urbanization, complex industrial production, mercantilism and capitalism, widespread literacy, long-distance travel, and contacts between large numbers of people from vastly different cultures. If there is one overriding assumption behind Deetz's definition, it is that of interconnectedness between different Western nations, and between these nations and the non-Western world.

This interconnectedness between far-flung human societies is nothing new, for it dates back to the beginnings of early civilizations in the Near East, and even earlier. By 2,500 B.C., long-distance trade networks connected Mesopotamia with

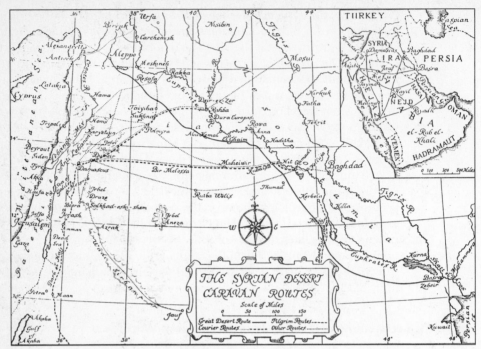

Figure 1.2 *Trade routes through the Near East.*

the Mediterranean and the Persian Gulf with northwest India (Figure 1.2). By 200 B.C., coasting routes around the Indian Ocean connected the Red Sea with India, Sri Lanka with China, East Africa with Arabia. The European Age of Discovery between the fifteenth and twentieth centuries expanded international trade routes to every corner of the world. In archaeological terms, these burgeoning connections are reflected in artifacts like, for example, Ming porcelain from China or majolica ware from Spain that were traded over enormous areas of the world. With trade and voyaging went ideas and spiritual beliefs, and common cultures and goals. Historical archaeologists can study Portuguese colonial settlements in central Africa, Brazil, and India, or English outposts in Virginia, South Africa, and Australia, with the understanding that each nation's settlements were part of the same global "system." In this way, many objects found by archaeologists at colonial sites in Massachusetts, and in contemporary towns in South Africa and southern England, can be expected to look similar or to be identical, because the people who made, used, and discarded them were members of the same cultures, who for historical reasons lived in different parts of the globe. Deetz calls the archaeological interest in these large-scale, modern connections the "comparative international perspective" because this approach is a conscious attempt to examine the spread of Europeans across historically changing national boundaries.

Anyone who attempts to study any global issue automatically discovers what geographer Peter Haggett learned when he said that the "problem posed by any subject which aims to be global is simple and immediate: the earth's surface is so

Sixteenth-century drawing of the Khoi Khoi.

staggeringly large." To which we should add, "and its people so diverse." The use of an overt international perspective means that historical archaeologists face a formidable task, not only because of the complexity of their data, but also because they are researching complex interactions between rapidly changing societies. When Portuguese explorer Bartolemeu Diaz rounded the Cape of Good Hope at the southern tip of Africa in 1488, he anchored in a bay with low hills where Khoi Khoi herders grazed their cattle. Two centuries later, Dutch colonists settled at the Cape and took over lands used by the Khoi Khoi for centuries, disrupting the herders' lifeways catastrophically. These disruptions continued for more than a century. Thus, an archaeologist excavating a seventeenth-century Colonial Dutch settlement has not only to achieve an understanding of European history and material culture, but also to be sensitive to the complex dynamics that governed indigenous cattle herding in the area.

These dynamics may be reflected in servants' artifacts, for example, for many Khoi Khoi were forced off their lands and became indentured servants. As was the case with African-American slaves, the anonymous servants came from a radically different physical and spiritual world that did not include the Dutch. Did they per-petuate these beliefs, or adopt the alien faith of their masters? Did they perceive advantage in adopting a European diet, or did they maintain contacts with their own group still living elsewhere? Sometimes, an acute excavator can acquire an-swers to these questions. To even begin, he or she would need to know something about the complex history of at least two disparate peoples, the Dutch and the Khoi Khoi, the ever-changing nature of their cultural contacts, the material cultures used by both, and the ways in which each group exploited the natural environment (see Chapter 11).

As a result of the historical interactions of culturally distinct peoples from Eu-rope and elsewhere, historical archaeologists see the study of the modern world as constituting the study of a process. What keeps the various colonial settlements of each nation from being identical copies of cities at home is the often significant in-fluence of indigenous peoples on the various Europeans who left Europe in search of wealth, power, or religious converts. Non-Westerners reacted to, embraced, re-jected, and fought against the Spanish, Dutch, English, Portuguese, and French cultures in many complex ways, depending on their individual circumstances, cul-tural traditions, and outlooks (Figure 1.3). Thus, even though Deetz tends to focus on European cultures in his definition, most historical archaeologists give equal weight to the actions and reactions of the many non-Westerners who accepted and rejected European social mores, economic ideas, political organizations, and reli-gious beliefs and traditions. Using this definition, a historical archaeologist may wish to study a particular settlement of native North Americans, not because these people lived in the "historical" or "modern" period, but because they constitute part of the history of the modern world. The actions, beliefs, and attitudes of these native peoples throughout the world are as important to the telling of world history as were the actions, beliefs, and attitudes of the powerful nation-states that are the usual stuff of basic history courses.

DEFINING TODAY'S HISTORICAL ARCHAEOLOGY

It is important to understand some of the complexities subsumed by these three de-finitions, for historical archaeologists have grappled with them for more than a generation. Today, we have a better understanding of the special strengths of his-torical archaeology, of the ways in which it can enhance our understanding of the recent past. Current definitions of the field combine elements of the three earlier formulations. They can be summarized: *historical archaeology is a multidisciplinary field that shares a special relationship with the formal disciplines of anthropology and history, focuses its attention on the post-prehistoric past, and seeks to understand the global nature of modern life.* Each clause in this definition is particularly important to framing a clear understanding of the nature and direction of contemporary historical archaeology. Let us dissect it a little further.

Figure 1.3 *The massacre at Cholula by the Spanish, according to the Aztecs.*

Historical Archaeology Is Multidisciplinary

All modern archaeology can be said to be multidisciplinary because all archaeologists, regardless of specialization, routinely use information from a series of related fields, including anthropology, botany, geography, geology, sociology, and zoology. What makes historical archaeology unique is that it is *by nature* multidisciplinary. It is virtually impossible for a historical archaeologist to conduct any serious research without consulting a wide range of other disciplines, most notably history and cultural anthropology. With feet firmly planted in history and anthropology, historical archaeologists regularly draw on the letters, maps, diaries, and governmental records that would be used by any modern historian, and the culture histories, ethnographies, and concepts of the cultural anthropologist, as well as the site plan maps, soil profile drawings, and artifacts that are common to all archaeological research.

Historical archaeology is text-aided archaeology, to the point that documents are a primary source for the field. Documents and texts of all kinds support and supplement archaeological information to such an extent that historical archaeologists must be as adroit at archival research and documentary interpretation as they are at site research and artifact analysis. They must be adept at locating and dissecting historical sources, just as historians are, but with the added dimension of relating these sources to the archaeological evidence. They must decide whether a set of documents are an independent source of information on their site or region, or whether they are purely a supplement to the archaeological evidence. If their assessment is that the sources are entirely independent, then the two sources, one archaeological, the other documentary, will throw light on the same problems, with each having equal weight. If, however, the documentary sources are supplementary, then the archaeological and the historical information may shed light on the same issue in slightly different ways: one written, and one based on artifacts, but the archaeological evidence will be more revealing. Sometimes there are real tensions between archaeological and historical data, which can only be resolved by meticulous critical analysis.

Suppose we are involved in the excavation of a plantation slave cabin in the American South, dating to about the year 1800. We have excavated the cabin and found that it has a limestone foundation measuring 12 by 16 feet (3.7 by 4.8 m), and that it contains numerous artifacts—glass bottle fragments, ceramic dish pieces, buttons, and so forth. We also have access to a series of letters written by the plantation's owner. In one or two of these letters the owner describes the slaves' cabins and mentions some of the articles the occupants used in their daily lives. We decide that they are an important supplementary source of information. Depending on the data at hand, we may consider the letters to supplement what we have learned from the archaeological remains, or our finds to amplify what we have learned from the documents. In either case, each of the two sources of information can be viewed as complementing the other. The letters help us to understand the material remains of the excavated slave cabin. The physical remains are tangible amplification of the owner's comments about the slaves on his plantation.

Imagine for a moment that we decide the archaeological data and the letters are completely independent sources, each providing a different view of the actual

Excavation of a slave cabin in Virginia.

historical reality of slave experience. By their activities the slaves created the archaeological deposits found at the cabin site. This creative process was probably not exactly a conscious one. When a dish was broken, a button lost, or a hog bone discarded, the slaves were only living their daily lives, not seeking to leave a record of their lives for future generations. It was almost accidental that the artifacts became part of the archaeological record. The plantation owner, who was generally a descendant of a different culture than his slaves (even though there were African-American slaveowners), *was* consciously attempting to create a record of life at his plantation in his letters. The owner may have misrepresented the lives of his slaves—either purposefully or through his own misunderstanding of them—or he may have written about what he hoped their lives would be like based on his plans for his estate. In this case, we decide that the archaeological and the documentary sources of information are not supplementary but are actually quite distinct. Each was created by a different sort of person for a unique reason, and each reflects the past in a disparate way.

This kind of interpretive controversy is important for historical archaeology because it forces us to continue exploring various ways of incorporating nonarchaeological materials into our research. That most of the nonarchaeological sources used by historical archaeologists derive from the formal discipline of history means that text-aided archaeology has a special relationship with that field, a relationship whose boundaries must be continually tested by new ideas and approaches.

This part of our definition draws on the idea that historical archaeology provides a useful method for examining the past, a method that combines "historical"

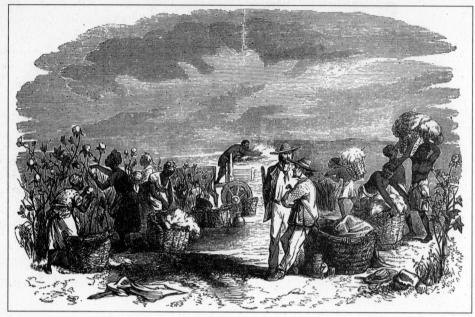

African-American slaves at work on a plantation in the eighteenth century.

and "archaeological" sources of information. The basic assumption is that historical archaeologists have many sources of information available to them and the failure to use them is simply bad historical archaeology.

Historical Archaeology Focuses Its Attention on the Post-prehistoric Past

This part of our definition assumes that historical archaeology focuses on historical times, not prehistory. Most historical archaeology described in this book concentrates on the "modern age"—the age many historians say began in A.D. 1415 with Portugal's successful capture of Ceuta in North Africa. This event was the catalyst for Prince Henry the Navigator's African explorations and the Age of Discovery that took Portuguese and other Western navigators throughout the globe. 1415 is, of course, a purely arbitrary date, for many institutions of what can loosely be called the "modern age" developed much earlier. For instance, some elements of modern mercantilism, for instance, may be found in the ways in which Europe's Knights Templars—the powerful religious-military organization of the Middle Ages—trafficked in fabrics, wool, spices, dyes, porcelain, and glass. Although the link between these medieval entrepreneurs and modern industrial capitalists may be weak indeed, historical archaeologists understand that the practices of modern peoples can have long traditions that extend backward in time beyond A.D. 1415. In this sense, then, we may expect some overlap between historical archaeology and European medieval archaeology based not solely on a similarity of method—although both make extensive use of written records—but on a similarity of subject matter.

Nonetheless, the use of the term *post-prehistoric* signifies that historical archaeology finds much of its subject matter in those places that Europeans visited and colonized. Thus, the term *post-prehistoric* stands in contrast to *prehistoric,* and is meant to suggest that the world was a different place after Europeans took Western culture to various places on the globe.

In this part of our definition we accept the special place of literacy in helping to transform the modern world, but we do not give literacy a primary role in shaping recent history. The adoption in the West of a movable type printing press in 1451, after centuries of use in China, made knowledge available to more people than simply the elites of society. The effects of printed books and increasing literacy eventually did change the world, but many of the individual Europeans who went into the non-Western world were illiterate. The actions of these people and the ideals of the nations that drove them forward were more important than whether they could read and write.

Historical Archaeology Seeks to Understand the Global Nature of Modern Life

Perhaps the most important facet of historical archaeology is its focus on modern life. No matter where we choose to set the beginning of "the modern world," the fundamental point is that the world of the late twentieth century was shaped in considerable part by compelling historical forces. The exploration of the New World, the African slave trade, the Industrial Revolution, the invention of the steamship and the railroad—these are but a few of the developments that have crafted the late twentieth-century world. Many of them affected hundreds of diverse human societies throughout the world. The invention of the steamship alone sparked human migrations on a hitherto unheard-of scale in the nineteenth century. For this reason, historical archaeology is a global field that shuns often arbitrary political boundaries in favor of understanding the large-scale events and broad processes that held people and groups together by their involvement in a common enterprise (such as colonial settlement or economic trade) or by common, historical circumstances (such as slavery or membership in a social class). But for all this global perspective, historical archaeologists work on a small scale, on forts, mining villages, and colonial towns, on slave cabins and isolated shipwrecks. They focus on the minute and the particular, on the humblest of artifacts, and on the usually anonymous people who made them. And from these small-scale researches come new insights into the larger issues of world history.

Europe was not a monolithic empire during the Age of Discovery. It was an ever-changing mosaic of competing nation-states, each with their own goals, histories, and traditions. Each had their own agenda, their own ambitions and values. Each was affected by the actions and technological achievements of societies across the world. For example, the technological innovations that helped to make it possible for Portugal to become a major world power in the sixteenth century included the astrolabe from the Near East and the magnetic compass from China. Thus, in using the term *international,* historical archaeologists generally refer both to a rising internationalism within Europe, and a globalization that took Europeans into the world. This openly international focus means that historical archaeologists frequently study issues of vital concern today: multiculturalism, gender roles, the effects of European exploration and settlement on native peoples and environments, racism, ethnicity, social inequality, consumerism, and the rise of the global mass market.

The prominence of these contemporary issues in our field means that historical archaeologists constantly negotiate between the past and the present. Many archaeologists now acknowledge that archaeology, although it studies the past, is part of the contemporary world. As a result, our interpretations of the past are always bound within, and somewhat restricted by, our perceptions and attitudes about both the past and the present. This point is currently the subject of much debate within prehistoric archaeology, for there are those who argue that white archaeologists with a Western cultural perspective, however well trained, cannot legitimately interpret Native American or African history from their excavations. The situation is somewhat different with historical archaeology, where it is obvious that our current perceptions of the recent past are shaped by our own histories and ideas. For example, the history of consumerism that historical archaeology documents is still being played out, and we are all actors in this continuing drama. In a real sense, the past studied by historical archaeology is still unfolding and, thus, historical archaeologists find it difficult to argue that the past they study is long dead and too remote to be of relevance to the present.

The conscious internationalism of historical archaeology means that the field studies a vast array of people. Rather than focusing on an archaeological record that is essentially anonymous—as prehistorians must do because of prehistoric archaeology's inability to focus on specific individuals—historical archaeology has the ability to concentrate on named, known people in history. Thus, a great deal of archaeology has been conducted at Monticello, Jefferson's stately mansion, and on the properties of other people well known in history. More importantly, historical archaeology also has the ability to document the lives of people whose general histories may be known, but whose daily lives remain a mystery. We can explore the daily lives of slaves, factory workers, public works laborers, farmers, colonists, and fur traders by excavating their humble abodes, workplaces, and artifacts. Archaeology writes the history not only of the rich and famous, but also of common folk. As such, it makes a priceless contribution to human history.

Douglas Armstrong's excavations at Drax Hall, Jamaica, provide a perfect case in point. Drax Hall was built on St. Ann's Bay, on the north coast of the island (Figure 1.4). This bay is where Columbus and his crew were marooned for a year and five days after his ship became infested with borers during his fourth voyage to the New World. During his survey of the plantation estate lands, Armstrong found some 60 possible house locations lying behind the mansion. These dwellings were variously the residences of slaves (1760–1810), transitional laborers (1810–1840), and fully freed slaves (1840–1925). Rather than focus specifically on the mansion,

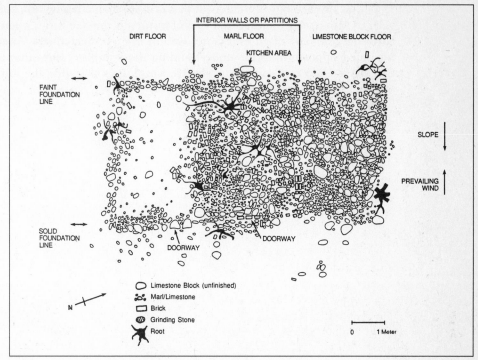

Figure 1.4 *House remains at Drax Hall, Jamaica.*

as some earlier historical archaeologists might have done, Armstrong sought to give voice to the laborers, the people who actually provided the wealth of the William Drax family. Here, archaeology looked on both sides of the social fence, at the rich and the poor, the literate and the nonliterate.

This means, too, that the archaeologist has a vital role to play in the fostering of national identity, of ethnic pride. Archaeologists have uncovered black cemeteries under New York and Philadelphia, documented the survival of traditional African beliefs in Southern slave communities, and chronicled daily life at Catholic missions in the Southwest. Humble, day-to-day artifacts, food remains, houses, and myriad other seemingly insignificant finds come together in complicated jigsaw puzzles of forgotten history as compelling as any document or faded nineteenth-century photograph. It is from such palimpsests of finds that the historical archaeologist restores a fabric of history to those whose past has been ignored, pushed aside, or just plain forgotten.

Historical archaeology is far more than historic preservation and the reconstruction of stately colonial homes. It shines like a searchlight into the recent past, clothing the deeds of common people with historical perspective, studying changing gender roles, ethnic communities, and technological innovation over generations and centuries.

The archaeology of the recent past is more than a fascinating curiosity, it provides us with a truly multifaceted view of history during centuries when everyone on earth became part of an ever-closer web of interconnectedness. As such, it offers unrivaled opportunities for understanding the complex, and often subtle, forces that shaped our own ever more diverse world. It is changing the way we perceive our ancestors and ourselves.

CHAPTER
2

A Brief History of Historical Archaeology

"A good half of all we see is seen through the eyes of others"

Marc Bloch, 1953

In 1855 a Jesuit father named Félix Martin traveled westward from Montréal, Canada, to the eastern edge of Georgian Bay in what is today Ontario. Carrying with him an official commission from the Canadian government, Father Martin planned to explore and excavate the site known as Sainte Marie I, a location as important as any in early Canadian history (Figure 2.1). It was at this tiny mission, deep in the country of the Huron Indians, that the Jesuit fathers had established themselves in 1639, with the hope of bringing these powerful people to the altar of Christianity. The Jesuits had built this mission with promise and hope, but only a decade later they abandoned and burned it. Devastating smallpox epidemics and constant attacks by the more powerful Iroquois, who lived to the southeast, decimated the Huron as a people and forced the missionaries to evacuate Sainte Marie. Father Martin journeyed to Georgian Bay, as had his religious forebears 216 years earlier, but instead of going there to save souls, Father Martin went to record history. He drew a map of the famous mission's remains and documented the presence of the Jesuits at Georgian Bay.

The following year, similar activities were underway further south in the United States. Civil engineer James Hall decided to excavate the home of his ancestor, Miles Standish, famed leader of the Pilgrims from the *Mayflower*. Hall was a trained engineer, so he made careful excavations of Standish's home, faithfully

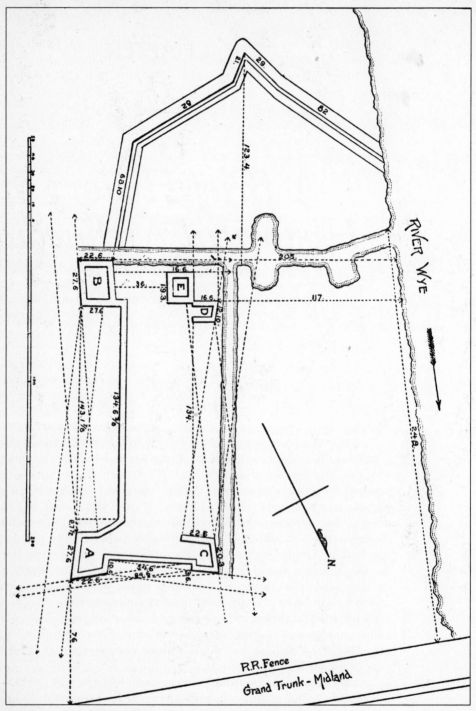

Figure 2.1 *Plan of Ste. Marie I, Ontario, drawn by Félix Martin.*

recorded the soil layers, mapped the stone foundation, and even plotted the locations of several artifacts found during the dig on a site plan.

These nineteenth-century investigations are the first known examples of historical archaeology in North America. This kind of archaeology has a relatively short history, compared with relatively scientific Classical and prehistoric archaeology, which began somewhat earlier. This chapter describes the early history of historical archaeology, and some of the general trends of the field, as it developed in the United States and Canada. Our focus on North America is simply one of convenience. As archaeologists living in the United States, the history of historical archaeology in this continent is more accessible to us. We expect that the broad trends outlined here also appear in other countries, such as Australia, that also have a strong tradition of historical archaeology.

THE IMPORTANT AND THE FAMOUS (1855 TO THE 1960s)

The excavations made by Martin in Canada and Hall in the United States more than a century ago did not meet the rigorous methodological standards of today's scientific archaeology. They worked hastily by modern yardsticks, paying little attention to those kinds of minute details like food remains that often disclose startlingly important information. These early excavations nonetheless are significant, not simply because they represent the first historical archaeology in North America, but also because they define neatly the scope of much of the historical archaeology that was conducted before the mid-twentieth century. In general, the pioneer excavators tended to work on sites associated with famous people or with events important in American or Canadian national history. In the United States, this kind of historical archaeology was sanctioned by the Historic Sites Act of 1935, which declared it national policy "to preserve for public use historic sites, buildings, and objects of national significance for the preservation and benefit of the people of the United States." This act came five years after the Canadian National Parks Act, which stipulated the same protection for historical landmarks and objects having "national importance."

The writers of the 1935 Act were undoubtedly aware that archaeology was already underway at some sites having national significance. Jamestown, Virginia, was the first permanent English settlement in America (1607), the seat of the country's first legislative assembly (1619), and the locale of Bacon's Rebellion (1676–1677). In 1930 President Herbert Hoover proclaimed Jamestown to be a Colonial National Monument. The first systematic excavations began there only four years later. Before World War II, the excavation was conducted with support from two governmental public works agencies active during the Depression: the Emergency Conservation Work group, and the Civilian Conservation Corps. In 1938 the government went so far as to build an archaeological field laboratory and a storage building at Jamestown. Excavations resumed in 1954, as part of a larger plan to celebrate the town's 350th anniversary in 1957.

The archaeology at Jamestown was always about interpreting and presenting the site to visitors. When archaeologists unearthed iron hinges and door locks, white clay ceramics etched with blue pigments to add color, or the foundations of the glasshouse, they used these finds to help in interpreting the history and daily life of the town. The excavated remains, coupled with carefully accurate reconstructions of buildings, enabled visitors to Jamestown to experience a little of what it meant to live in the seventeenth century.

Jamestown's archaeology focused on the people who built and lived in the settlement as a group, even though we often read about the village in terms of the famous people we know from there—John Smith, Pocahontas, and John Rolfe. Jamestown is certainly famous because these people lived there, but the archaeology was more about how the *entire* Jamestown community built, and lived, in the settlement.

During this period, however, a number of historical archaeologists did focus their attention on sites associated with famous people in American history. When archaeologist Richard Hagen first thought of excavating Abraham Lincoln's two-story frame house in Springfield, Illinois, he went immediately to a reliable historical source: Lincoln's insurance policy, written by the Hartford Insurance Company on February 8, 1861. This policy protected "Abraham Lincoln of Springfield Illinois against loss or damage by fire to the amount of . . . Three Thousand and Two Hundred Dollars." Three thousand dollars protected the house, the remainder covered the carriage house and the privy. Armed with this document, which carefully described Lincoln's home just in case the company had to replace it, Hagen began his excavation. He searched specifically for objects related to Mr. Lincoln himself, but he was not able to relate any particular object to the man himself. For example, Hagen unearthed an 1857 penny and a large brass key. He imagined excitedly that the penny fell from Lincoln's pocket or that some careless member of the family had lost the key, but he was cautious. He could "hypothesize the Lincolns' temporary distress at being locked out!" but Hagen realized that his research could not provide the evidence for Lincoln's behavior. The best contribution he could make was to provide architectural details for use in interpreting the house. Using excavation, he provided information about the size, shape, and location of Lincolns' carriage house and woodshed. He also showed what kinds of artifacts were used by the Lincoln family by illustrating the objects recovered from the two privies he excavated.

During this period of historical archaeology, several archaeologists interested in Canadian history investigated a major early industry—the fur trade. Starting in 1938, archaeologist Emerson Greenman studied the river-borne fur trade between the French and the Native Americans who lived in the Georgian Bay region of Ontario. The Ottawa River provided a convenient highway for canoes traveling from Montreal to Lake Huron, passing close to Old Birch Island, a tiny island in Georgian Bay. Greenman used several written sources to document the presence of both European fur traders and Native American groups in this area. The *Jesuit Relations*—letters and reports Jesuit fathers sent home to Rome to explain their missionary activities—relate much of the history of the region between 1608 and 1760. Using these documents as a guide and resource, Greenman conducted a field survey of the island. He found a Native American cemetery that included the remains of 16 individuals in 12 graves. The discovery of brass pails, iron butcher knives, and brightly colored glass beads in the graves of these deceased men and women told Greenman that this group of Native Americans had indeed conducted commerce

Figure 2.2 *Artist's reconstruction of Kipp's Post, North Dakota.*

with French traders who came from Montreal. The objects also told him that the Native Americans had adopted at least some European artifacts and technology into their traditional way of life.

The Flood Control Act of 1944 mandated the construction of a series of dams along the Missouri River in North and South Dakota. These projects spurred the investigation of several archaeological sites that were important in the history of the American West. Agents of the powerful Columbia Fur Trading Company built "Kipp's Post"—sometimes called "Fort Kipp"—on the Missouri River in the fall and winter of 1826–1827. The post, about 50 miles (80 km) east of present-day Williston, North Dakota, was named for its builder, James Kipp, a Canadian fur trader of German descent who traded with the Assiniboine Indians at this site. Traders occupied Kipp's Post until about 1828, when the larger, more important Fort Union was constructed nearby. Kipp's Post was then abandoned. Historians of the fur trade knew that Kipp's Post had been built, but they knew little else. European-American traders only occupied the post for a short time, and they left painfully few records about their activities there. As a result, the archaeology conducted at the site provided a rare opportunity to learn about life at an important outpost of the frontier fur trade.

Archaeologists Alan Woolworth and Raymond Wood excavated Kipp's Post in July and August 1954 (Figure 2.2). Their careful research presents otherwise unknown architectural details about the post. They learned, for instance, that the stockade around the post was 96 feet (29.3 m) a side, with a rectangular bastion extending 5 feet (1.5 m) beyond the northeastern corner of the enclosure. The posts of the walls were badly rotted, but the dark postholes in the ground showed they were about 6 inches (15.2 cm) in diameter. The entrance to the post was on the south side and measured 9.5 feet (2.9 m) across. Four buildings of various sizes were found inside the stockade, along its back wall facing the gate. For defense, the traders apparently had a cannon that could fire balls weighing 1 pound (453.6 g). Apparently, the gun exploded, for Woolworth and Wood found several cannon fragments around the fort.

The excavations also documented the daily life and trade commodities imported to the post. The traders themselves ate from plain, white plates and drank from glass tumblers and white cups, but their stores contained a far wider range of artifacts that were bartered for furs—white clay smoking pipes, pieces of gold braid, small brass bells, and brass arrowheads. Then there were tiny green, amber, blue, black, and white glass beads, spherical brass beads, and delicate, conical-shaped, silver ear bangles.

Through their extensive research, Woolworth and Wood were able to present a wonderfully detailed picture of this one small trading post on the Missouri River. Kipp's Post is but a footnote to the larger story of the fur trade in the American West, but the two archaeologists' pioneer researches added remarkable detail to local history.

Even though much of the historical archaeology conducted during the field's formative years was directed toward sites of national importance, some archaeologists did turn to the study of sites that were associated with less prominent people. For example, in 1943, Adelaide and Ripley Bullen excavated the home of Lucy Foster, an African-American slave who lived in Andover, Massachusetts. The Bullens published a short statement of their research in 1945, but in 1978 a larger report was presented under the authorship of archaeologist Vernon Baker. As is true of most people who are neither prominent in the community nor wealthy, little documentary information exists about Lucy Foster. Baptismal records on file at the Andover South Parish Congregational Church include the following brief note: "July 14, 1771, Sarah, a child given to Job Foster and Lucy, a Negro, Child was baptized." These few words place Lucy Foster in Massachusetts in the 1770s. Lucy was apparently freed sometime in the early 1800s, and lived for 30 years in her cabin. In her later years, she survived in desperate poverty until her death of asthma in November 1845.

When the Bullens excavated Lucy's home, they discovered that the house had burned and that someone had apparently rummaged through the rubble looking for something, perhaps useful building materials. The archaeology of the cellar foundation, made of dry-laid fieldstone, showed that Lucy's house was small, only 10.5 to 11.5 feet (3.2–3.5 m) on a side (Figure 2.3). Baker thinks this size may represent an African-American building tradition, because folklorists have demonstrated that the narrow, long houses built in West Africa, Haiti, and in the American South—called "shotgun" houses—generally have 12-foot dimensions. The Bullens also excavated a shallow well, an oval pit about 3.6 feet (1.1 m) deep, and a trash dump, located just west of the cellar. When Baker compared the ceramic vessels from these archaeological features with those from a slave cabin at Cannon's Point Plantation, Georgia (see Chapter 10), he made a startling discovery. The percentages of vessel forms from the slave cabin matched those from Lucy's house. At the plantation there were 44% serving bowls; at Lucy's there were 41%. The slave cabin had 49% serving flatware (like plates), and Lucy's home had 51%. Both sites also had a low percentage of other shapes. Lucy's site had 8%, the slave cabin, 7%.

Figure 2.3 *Artist's reconstruction of Lucy Foster's Home in Massachusetts.*

Baker was justifiably unable to determine whether the similarity was caused by the African-American heritage of the residents of both sites, or whether it resulted from a condition of extreme poverty (see Chapter 10). In any case, the Bullens' pioneering research, like that at Kipp's Post, showed the great potential of archaeology for attacking basic historical problems.

Theoretical Foundations for Early Research

A number of archaeologists provided the theoretical foundation for much of the historical archaeology of the early period by arguing that historical archaeology was a historical pursuit. As early as 1910, archaeologist Carl Russell Fish, in a paper presented before the Wisconsin Archaeological Society, observed that "Nearly every historian should be something of an archaeologist, and every archaeologist should be something of an historian." Fish knew about the discoveries that archaeologists had made in Egypt and Assyria, and was impressed by recent research on the Roman colonization of Britain. He believed that the same attention should be given to American history: "we have monuments which are worthy of preservation, and which can add to our knowledge of our American ancestors."

Forty years later, J.C. Harrington, famous for his excavations at Jamestown, defined historical archaeology as an "auxiliary science to American history." He vigorously argued that the archaeology of the historical period was an "important historical tool" that should be developed and used by historians. In the early 1960s, Ivor Noël Hume, the famed excavator of Colonial Williamsburg, referred to historical archaeology as "the handmaiden of history." All these authorities stressed that historical archaeology is an important kind of archaeology that can be used to contribute unique and tangible information to the study of history.

The idea that archaeology could provide information for historians rather than for anthropologists made historical archaeology unique but not truly unusual. In fact, the view that historical archaeology is about "history" was generally consistent with the way in which prehistoric archaeologists conducted their research during this period. They thought of themselves as a "special kind of anthropologist," directing most of their efforts toward the construction of cultural chronologies. These chronologies were actually broad-brush histories of nonliterate peoples based on artifacts—stone tools and clay vessels—and other archaeological evidence, rather than on written documents. Under this "culture historical approach," archaeological cultures were defined on the basis of the artifacts collected from a certain number of key sites of the same approximate age. For instance, a specific archaeological culture might be defined on the basis of pottery incised with an "S" pattern, copper ornaments, and the use of small, conical burial mounds. Another archaeological culture might be identified on the basis of undecorated pottery, shell ornaments, and the use of large, flat-topped burial mounds. To this day, prehistorians still construct their culture histories of prehistoric Native American societies largely by using the artifacts these peoples left behind.

The creation of cultural chronologies forms the foundation of much archaeological research, whether historical or prehistoric, but the situation for historical archaeology is slightly different. The societies studied by historical archaeologists usually do not require construction by means of stratified artifacts. Their histories are generally known from documentary sources. For example, Father Martin knew that his Jesuit forebears traveled to the country of the Hurons, that in 1639 they built Sainte Marie Mission, and that in 1649 they abandoned and burned it. Martin did not need to establish these historical facts because they were well documented in Jesuit records. Martin's archaeological research, however, was important. He could use the archaeology to substantiate the facts and to add flesh to them. How large was the mission? How did the Jesuits actually build it? Did they place the chapel in the center or near the gate? What kinds of religious objects did the Jesuits give to the Huron men, women, and children who visited the mission?

Let us use two brief case studies to show the way in which historical archaeology was conceived of before the mid-1960s—J.C. Harrington's research at Fort Necessity, Pennsylvania, and Edward B. Jelks' excavations at Signal Hill, Newfoundland.

Fort Necessity, Pennsylvania

The history of Fort Necessity began in 1754 when George Washington, then a Lieutenant Colonel in the Virginia militia, took about 160 poorly trained men to what is today southwestern Pennsylvania. Washington was sent to this area because of French encroachments on land "notoriously known to be the property of the Crown of Great Britain." The French paid no heed to the warnings of the British because they too had established forts at strategic locations in North America; they were as eager as the British to control this territory. Washington's orders were to reinforce the English force at today's city of Pittsburgh and to improve the trail to the British stronghold. He did not plan to construct a fort originally, but after his troops attacked a small French detachment in the vicinity of Great Meadow, south of today's Pittsburgh, and killed their leader, he decided that a small fortification was needed. Fort Necessity was constructed, and so began the French and British struggle for North America.

Although the location of the fort was known, its exact shape was a mystery. In 1816, a professional surveyor drew the fort as triangular, but a local historian in 1830 described it as shaped like a diamond or flattened square (Figure 2.4). The fort's precise shape became important when the National Park Service decided to reconstruct it in 1932. Harrington said that when the National Park Service began

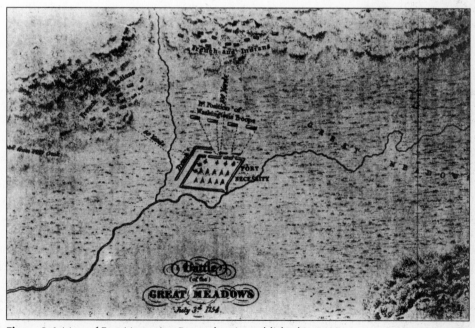

Figure 2.4 *Map of Fort Necessity, Pennsylvania, published in 1837.*

their historical study of the fort, they realized that few documents existed that could explain the difference. Thus, they found "it necessary to supplement the scanty documentary information by archaeological exploration." When excavations finally got underway in 1952—after the Great Depression and World War II had considerably slowed the historic preservation movement—the objectives were "1. to settle, once and for all, the 'triangle versus square' controversy, 2. to establish the 1754 location of the stream bed, and 3. to secure additional objects for museum display."

J. C. Harrington's excavations showed that the fort consisted of two elements: a diamond-shaped earthwork with a circular stockade inside it. The charred posts of the stockade were still visible in the soil of the old fortification trench. Inside lay a log storehouse. Harrington combined his archaeological findings with a deposition by John Shaw, a member of Washington's regiment, which explains the way the fort was built. Although this document had great relevance to the reconstruction of the fort, it was not taken seriously until the archaeological findings demonstrated its accuracy. In this way, then, Harrington used archaeology and historical documents to establish the size and shape of Washington's strategic frontier fort.

Signal Hill, Newfoundland

Like Fort Necessity, Signal Hill figured in the history of the French and British campaigns. Situated on a strategic point overlooking the Atlantic Ocean and the harbor leading to St. John's and Fort William (established shortly before 1700), the hill was used from 1750 to the mid-nineteenth century as a signal station that identified arriving ships. In 1762, the British lost the area to the French and then quickly regained it. Signal Hill, for all its strategic importance, did not have any fortifications built on it until 1795. For several years after 1795, various plans were made to build fortifications on the hill, but many of these ideas were changed or never carried out. During its greatest period of activity—from 1795 until the mid-nineteenth century—three batteries, or cannon stations, and numerous other buildings were built on Signal Hill. The hilltop is also famous as the place where the wireless pioneer Guglielmo Marconi made his first trans-Atlantic Morse code transmission on December 12, 1901. His message, simply the letter "s," sent all the way from Cornwall, England, showed that ships could communicate with each other and with the shore for at least 2,000 miles (3,200 km).

The number and locations of buildings on the hill became extremely important when the Canadian government decided to build an interpretive center for the new Signal Hill National Historic Park. When archaeologist Edward Jelks was commissioned to conduct the excavations in 1958, his objectives were to dig in the area of the interpretive center to ensure that no archaeological remains would be destroyed by construction, to determine the development potential of the park for future visitors, and to recover "artifacts and other data of general value to archaeological studies of British colonial sites."

Jelks' excavations were successful because he was able to document the complex construction sequence at Signal Hill and to locate numerous buttons, bottles, coins, and other objects used by the soldiers who occupied the hill. Without these excavations, the story of what happened at Signal Hill would be less well known.

HISTORICAL ARCHAEOLOGY OF PEOPLE (1960 TO TODAY)

Archaeologists have used archaeology for many years to construct the broad culture histories of past peoples, but this approach was not always accepted by everyone as all that archaeology could contribute to knowledge about the past. Some historical archaeologists, having been trained, as most archaeologists were and still are, in departments of anthropology, began to imagine in the early 1960s that archaeology could be like cultural anthropology in the sense that it could provide information about people's daily lives. Some archaeologists began to see themselves as anthropologists of the past, working to reconstruct people's ways of life instead of simply the broad elements of their histories.

Ideas such as these were voiced in 1962 by Lewis Binford in his essay "Archaeology as Anthropology." Binford argued that instead of simply following paths that lead only to broad cultural histories based on the identification of "archaeological cultures," archaeologists could be pathfinders who could lead the way to understanding past cultures. Instead of viewing culture as something static and represented in a collection of artifacts, Binford adopted an anthropologist's view that culture represents a changing adaptation to an environment. Like anthropologists, archaeologists could provide information about economics, kinship, religion, social interaction, and almost all other elements of daily life. They would study the processes of cultural change and explain major developments in the prehistoric past. Binford used as an example the Old Copper Culture in Wisconsin (3,000–500 B.C.). Wisconsin archaeologists refer to this period as the "Archaic," or "Old Copper," a time when the people of the Great Lakes region developed considerable cultural complexity, because game and plant foods were readily available in the environmentally rich boreal forests. Using the copper that occurred naturally in the northern Great Lakes region, Old Copper people hammered out axes, knives, fishing hooks, awls, and large spear points, which they traded far south into the Midwest. Binford was well aware that an anthropological approach would serve historical archaeology well. He had served as a field assistant during the 1959 excavation at Fort Michilimackinac, an eighteenth-century French and British military post in Michigan.

Theoretical Foundations

The impact of Binford's article was immense. Prehistorian Paul Martin proclaimed that Binford had created a "revolution" in archaeology, an entire new theoretical paradigm for the study of the past. This soon became the so-called "new archaeology," an attempt to introduce greater scientific and theoretical rigor into field and laboratory research. Inevitably, the furor over the study of cultural process spilled over into historical archaeology. A year after the publication of "Archaeology as Anthropology," a number of archaeologists held a symposium entitled "The Meaning of Historic Sites Archaeology," at the annual meeting of the Society for American Archaeology in Boulder, Colorado. Binford was a panelist for this symposium, but the chair was Bernard Fontana. Fontana, an anthropologist who had conducted historical archaeology in Arizona, was inspired by the session and wrote an essay entitled "On the Meaning of Historic Sites Archaeology," which appeared in 1965.

Artifacts of the Old Copper Culture.

As an anthropologist, Fontana understood the important role that non-Europeans played in creating the modern world. As a result, he designed a classification of historical sites that stressed the amount of Native American influence on a site. His scale extended from a "protohistoric" site (one occupied after 1492 and that may contain some European artifacts, but that predates actual face-to-face contact between Native Americans and Europeans) to a "nonaboriginal" site (one that had little or no Native American influence). Robert Schuyler reinforced Fontana's overt anthropological message in his paper "Historical and Historic Sites Archaeology as Anthropology: Basic Definitions and Relationships," published in 1970. Schuyler proposed that historical archaeology had much to offer to anthropology and that historical archaeology was not simply a way to reinforce or to substantiate historical facts.

By the early 1970s, many historical archaeologists had realized that their theoretical foundation should be within anthropology. The question of whether anthropologists or historians should conduct historical archaeology became the subject of considerable debate. The controversy revolved around two central issues: first, whether the subject matter of historical archaeology was "history"—the realm of historians—or "culture"—the realm of anthropologists; and second, whether artifacts were historical documents—because they "told" about the past—or whether documents were really artifacts—defined as anything made or modified by conscious human effort. Traditional wisdom of the day held that historians study written documents and archaeologists study artifacts.

Both sides tended to caricature the other in the debate. Historians were sometimes described as narrow-minded scholars who wore tweed jackets and rummaged through dusty documents while oblivious to the outside world. Archaeologists were sometimes portrayed as adventurers who would go to any lengths to obtain a rare artifact and who had no knowledge of documents. In 1962, Bernard Cohn published an article entitled "An Anthropologist Among the Historians: A Field Study." In this seemingly tongue-in-check study, Cohn said that "Historians are older than anthropologists." He also said that "A historian is usually regular in his work habits. The archives are open only certain hours." Conversely, "An anthropologist often works in great bursts." As a final salvo at his anthropological colleagues, Cohn wrote that "A historian usually studies a topic which, even if somewhat obscure, is intrinsically important." However, "An anthropologist may study intrinsically insignificant things"!

In hindsight, the history-or-anthropology debate raised a false issue by attempting to draw too fine a line between two closely related fields. Some of its participants promoted stereotyped characterizations of historians and anthropologists, and misunderstood the theoretical bases of both history and anthropology. The debate was important, however, because it forced historical archaeologists to consider seriously the theoretical foundations of their field.

At about the same time that historical archaeologists were debating history-or-anthropology, many professional historians "discovered" anthropology and began to employ concepts and ideas from ethnography in their historical interpretations. Rhys Isaac, for example, won a Pulitzer Prize in history for his very anthropological *The Transformation of Virginia, 1740–1790.* Isaac's first word in his "historical" book is "Anthropologists." He was specifically interested in explaining how society in Tidewater Virginia changed from 1740 to 1790, or before and after the American Revolution. During this half century, Virginia's social hierarchy had become more rigid, for reasons that were hard to discern. Rather than focus on politics or economics, Isaac studied such "anthropological" topics as architecture, interior design, furniture, silverware, dance, dress, manners, and the use of space (Figure 2.5). From these lines of evidence, Isaac drew two conclusions. First, he said that rich planters made common cause with poorer whites to claim independence from England and to forge a new government. This conclusion is not entirely new, but his second, related conclusion is pathbreaking. He concluded that during the course of the eighteenth century planters became more threatened with the rise of American independence and liberty. To maintain their elite positions, planters tightened their control over society. This control was expressed in the so-called "Georgian

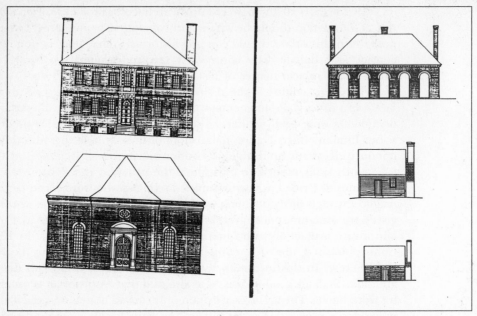

Figure 2.5 *Hierarchy of buildings in eighteenth-century Virginia, ranging from mansion to slave cabin.*

Order." The Georgian Order was uniquely expressed in material culture. House styles became more symmetrical and neat; dining and dance became more structured and orderly (see Chapter 9). To see these changes, Isaac, a historian, had to look toward the material expressions of daily life. He had to examine them as would an anthropologist who has just gained admission to a foreign culture.

However, in 1986, Ian Hodder, a British prehistorian, wrote that "archaeology should recapture its traditional links with history." As a prehistorian, Hodder had not thought too much about "history" until the writings of eccentric Australian-born archaeologist V. Gordon Childe again became popular in archaeological circles in the early 1980s. Childe considered prehistoric archaeology to be a form of history. In the 1930s and 1940s he wrote tremendously popular books about Europe's remote past, using potsherds and metal ornaments and weapons to fashion archaeological "cultures." To Childe, archaeologists were historians; Hodder wanted to reemphasize this perspective.

Historical archaeologists have explored the connections between history and anthropology in numerous ways. The history-or-anthropology debate has forced historical archaeologists to acknowledge and to appreciate the multidisciplinary foundations of their field. In 1982, Kathleen Deagan, well known for her research on Spanish Florida, noted that the "debate over the proper orientation of historical archaeology has not altogether been resolved." In her many important projects in what was once colonial New Spain, Deagan has repeatedly demonstrated the power of using historical records in archaeological research to study such topics as domestic architecture in early St. Augustine. In many of her researches, she has teamed up with professional historians in a further attempt to link anthropology and history, as in her recent excavations at Fort Mose, the earliest free African-American settlement in North America. As recently as 1987, the history-or-anthropology debate was still being formally discussed at the annual meeting of the Society for Historical Archaeology.

Stanley South's *Method and Theory in Historical Archaeology,* with its strong arguments for anthropological perspectives, appeared in 1977, the most influential work on the subject in the late 1970s and early 1980s. South had been a graduate student with Lewis Binford at the University of North Carolina in the 1950s. He was a confirmed believer in the theories of cultural evolutionism pioneered by anthropologist Leslie White. Following White, South believed that cultural progress could be measured in the amount of energy that a culture could control. This captured energy could be measured in terms of any human technological achievement, extending from the controlled use of fire to atomic power.

South also agreed with Binford's ideas about archaeological reasoning, and argued that historical archaeology could be a science, with historical archaeologists making regular use of hypotheses, laws, and scientific testing procedures. As part of this idea, South proposed that historical archaeology could be quantifiable, meaning that the artifacts found at different sites could be counted, grouped into categories, and then compared in a scientific manner with the artifact groups at other sites. The comparisons would reveal cultural information about the people who once lived at the different sites. Although archaeologists have been conducting comparative analysis for years, South's "pattern" concept was unique because of its strong anthropological and scientific basis (Chapter 5).

People Without History

Historical archaeology truly came of age in the late 1960s and 1970s, when both archaeologists and historians realized the potential of the humblest of artifacts for studying people whose daily lives are not well documented in historical sources. These "undocumented" people came from generally diverse ethnic groups: African-American slaves, Chinese railroad laborers, Métis fur trappers, immigrant miners, farmers, and others.

The realization that historical archaeology provides a unique way in which to study the peoples of history who seldom left detailed, written commentaries on their lives probably stemmed from two different yet related directions. First, by the late 1960s and early 1970s, it had become clear that it would be anthropologically trained archaeologists who would conduct most historical archaeology. Although most of these archaeologists also had some formal training in, or at least experience with, archival research methods, they also had considerable knowledge of the ethnography of nonliterate peoples around the globe. For example, historical documents, for all of the information they present about the construction of railroads through the American West, tell us virtually nothing of the daily lives of the Chinese people who actually did the construction: What kind of housing was supplied to the workers? What ceramic dishes and other objects did they use? Did they retain certain elements of Chinese culture in North America? Which elements did they retain; which did they surrender? It rapidly became apparent that historical archaeology was the only academic discipline that could address such basic questions in minute and exacting detail.

Second, the general revival of ethnic pride in North America in the 1960s and 1970s convinced many historical archaeologists that their discipline was relevant to society at large, and that their specialized knowledge was meaningful well beyond the sometimes narrow confines of professional archaeology. As a result, historical archaeologists have provided abundant detail about the daily lives of many peoples whose contributions might otherwise be forgotten in the broader panorama of history. Let us briefly examine two examples.

Yaughan and Curriboo Plantations, South Carolina

Yaughan and Curriboo were two eighteenth-century slave plantations in coastal South Carolina, a part of the southern United States that was home to thousands of African slaves.

Historical records make it possible to reconstruct the basic histories of ownership and family association within Yaughan and Curriboo. These records, however, focus on the "official" or legal history of the plantations and provide no information about the slave community, the people who actually performed the manual labor that helped to amass the riches of the slave-owning families. Thomas Wheaton, Amy Friedlander, and Patrick Garrow excavated the dwellings of the plantation workers and added an entirely new dimension to the history of the region.

Thomas Wheaton and Patrick Garrow excavated 29 buildings at Yaughan and Curriboo. They showed that between the 1740s and 1770s, the slaves lived in rectangular, mud-walled buildings that may have resembled buildings in Africa or the Caribbean. From the 1780s to the 1820s they lived in smaller, square buildings placed on brick piers. Wheaton and Garrow believe the change resulted from slave "acculturation." With contact and interaction, African slaves slowly learned to mimic the daily lives of people who lived in square houses on brick piers. Their interpretation is hotly contested, for it can just as easily be argued that slaves who once resided in African-like houses lived in European-style houses because they were forced to do so.

Artist's reconstruction of slave cabins at Curriboo Plantation, South Carolina.

Yaughan and Curriboo yielded a wealth of information on slave diet. The workers lived on a diet of corn, rice, beef, and pork, supplemented with minor quantities of wild plants and game. We know they used firearms to kill local game, for musket parts came from several dwellings. In addition to using a wide variety of European objects in their daily lives, the slaves also made their own pottery and probably also used some wares made by local Native Americans. These latter ceramics, some made to resemble European-made vessels, were not imported from abroad, and so must have been produced by African-American slaves, Native American potters, or perhaps both.

Historical archaeology thus adds a richness to our knowledge of slave life, and gives these "undocumented" people a chance to be heard. We can learn about the wealthy slave owners by a combined use of archaeological and written sources, but only with archaeology (and sometimes oral accounts) can we document the daily lives of slave men and women.

Gold Bar Camp, Nevada

Gold Bar Camp in Nevada was a classic western mining settlement between 1905 and 1909. Only about 100 gold and silver miners and their families lived there. Because the camp was settled after the 1900 federal census and abandoned before the 1910 count, it is largely invisible in official documents. Only a few newspaper articles refer to the camp. These limited historical accounts mention the presence of boarding houses, bunk houses, and a superintendent's bungalow. There were 18 school-aged children at the camp in 1908, a hint that there were individual family houses, too. A number of photographs of the camp show general views of the settlement while it was occupied, but, like contemporary writings, they reveal little about daily life.

The Gold Bar Camp, Nevada, as it looked in 1908.

Archaeologist Donald Hardesty used excavation and survey to add an entirely new dimension to the historical accounts. He showed that the Gold Bar miners lived in houses from 400 to over 1,000 square feet (37.1 to 92.9 sq m) in size, that many of these residences seemed to have special functions, and that the people at the camp used a wide variety of artifacts. Then there are the tin cans. They tell us the Gold Bar community imported fruits and vegetables, meats, coffee, and milk for their meals. Glass bottles and lamp glasses document whiskey, wine, and beer drinking and the lighting of homes with kerosene lamps. The Gold Bar people maintained regular contacts with the outside world—they wrote and received letters and were visited by traveling merchants and salespeople—and lived much like people in the United States do today. The difference, of course, is that these folk were hardrock miners who have been forgotten in written history.

TODAY'S HISTORICAL ARCHAEOLOGY

Historical archaeologists' interest in the rich and famous, as well as in the poor and undocumented, helps define the history of the discipline. The change in interest reflects the growing awareness among historical archaeologists of both anthropology and the increasing cultural diversity of late nineteenth-century society. The changing attitude is easy to identify in the literature because it is so obvious: whereas before the early 1960s the focus was on a slave owner's opulent mansion, by the late 1960s the emphasis had shifted to the slaves' humble cabins. This shift in orientation, although not absolute, is nonetheless striking.

As the number of historical archaeologists continues to grow, historical archaeology has become a truly international discipline. Once confined largely to North America, today historical archaeology flourishes on all continents, from South America to the South Pacific, from Cape Town to the Arctic Circle (see Chapter 11).

Theoretical Foundations

Historical archaeology continues to mature. A number of archaeologists, sensing this intellectual growth, are experimenting with different ideas and theoretical points of view at a wide variety of sites. For this reason it is impossible to provide a single theoretical theme to describe the field after the mid-1980s (see Chapter 10). Today's historical archaeologists use ideas and concepts from numerous disciplines, including anthropology, sociology, philosophy, material culture studies, and political economics. No longer content with simply describing collections of artifacts or preparing archaeological reports that document the undocumented, many scholars are beginning to examine the deeper meanings of artifacts and the complex relationship that exist between people and the things around them, including buildings and landscapes. These new concerns are taking the field in fascinating new directions.

Annapolis: the Paca Mansion

Annapolis, Maryland, has a rich history and has been the subject of intense archaeological investigations for more than a decade. Mark Leone is one of those who have investigated eighteenth-century residences in what was then a prosperous city, including a large mansion built by William Paca, a wealthy lawyer and signer of the Declaration of Independence. Some of this research has focused on Paca's magnificent garden. Leone demonstrates how the garden was used to reinforce the existing social order of early America. Paca commissioned a large and rigidly structured formal yard that stretched out behind his mansion in four different terraces (Figure 2.6). The first three were symmetrically designed with trees and shrubs to give the garden a neat, manicured appearance. At the back of the property, however, was a "wilderness" that was not planted in such an ordered manner. Instead, the plants here seemed to grow wildly and without attention. Leone interpreted the difference between the garden and the wilderness as representing increased chaos as one moved further away from the order and symmetry of the garden and the mansion. In addition to the trees and shrubs, the designer of the garden incorporated a number of optical illusions in the design that altered the visitor's perspective of space and distance. Leone believes these illusions were intended to hide, in a symbolic sense, both the contradictions in Paca's own life—as a passionate defender of liberty and an owner of slaves—and the same contradictions in American society at large, contradictions that could assign inalienable rights to some people and condone lifelong bondage for others.

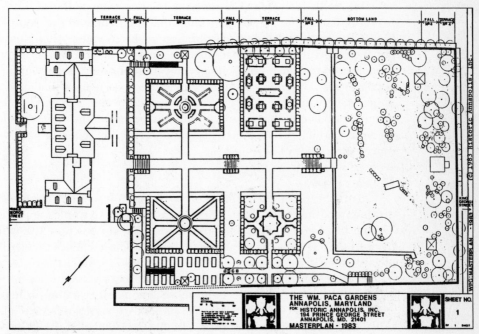

Figure 2.6 *Plan of William Paca's Garden, Annapolis, Maryland.*

Leone could easily have used his archaeological research simply to define the limits of the garden and to document the exact locations of trees and shrubs. Paca was an important historical personage, and architectural information about his mansion and its garden would interest many people. Leone chose, however, to attempt an innovative interpretation by using the archaeological information in a new way. The importance of Leone's article, whether or not one accepts his interpretation—and it has been much discussed—is that it demonstrates that historical archaeologists are entering into important anthropological and historical debates about the past.

Boott Mill, Lowell, Massachusetts

Mary Beaudry, Lauren Cook, and Stephen Mrozowski, in a study of the Boott Mill in Lowell, Massachusetts, write about the need to see artifacts in the same way as language—as a complex discourse that incorporates a wide number of subtle meanings. Beaudry and her colleagues propose that "undocumented" people such as mill workers, although they may be uncounted in many historical records, did communicate through the artifacts they used. These people are only undocumented if historical archaeologists fail to study the ways in which they documented themselves. The object of such analysis is not to study the "undocumented" from the "top down" (from the viewpoint of their social "betters") or from the "bottom up" (from the peoples' own viewpoint), but rather from the "inside out," meaning from the place in society in which they document themselves. The way to learn to document the "undocumented" is to learn how they created their own world in their own terms.

When the archaeologists unearthed liquor, wine, and beer bottles, along with beer mugs and wine glasses, they knew that the people of the Boott Mill boarding houses flagrantly violated the corporation's sobriety rules. When they found flowerpot fragments it became clear that the workers made every attempt to brighten their lives, to reclaim a small bit of beauty in their otherwise monotonous and regulated routine. The presence of marbles and doll parts show that children were able to breathe life into the daily grind experienced by the men and women who toiled in the mills. These objects, and all the others located in the excavations, point to the ways in which ordinary men and women took the things around them and documented themselves.

The Chesapeake

Some historical archaeologists are using information from individual sites to provide new insights about whole regions. For example, archaeologist Anne Yentsch has used ceramics and animal bones, in conjunction with written records, from 16 sites in the Chesapeake in the eastern United States to identify small-scale social change in the period from about 1680 to 1740. Since the eighteenth century, people have considered "the Chesapeake" to be the region around Chesapeake Bay, one of the world's largest and most famous estuarine environments. For her study, Yentsch selected archaeological sites in Annapolis, in a small Maryland town called St. Mary's City, and in rural Virginia. Yentsch used the information she assembled to probe into the changing use of food and to seek to understand how

Excavating at Boott Hill, Massachusetts.

such a mundane topic can shed new light on the past. By adopting a regional and long-term perspective, Yentsch was able to perceive changes in her information. She observed, for instance, a shift from wooden and pewter plates to ceramic dishes, an increase in the number of plates and a greater variation in plate sizes in households, and a trend away from communal servings to individualized portions. The cultural issues involving changes in food preferences, of course, are complicated. However, Yentsch's focus on them allows her to think like an anthropologist interested in cultural continuity and social change, instead of like an antiquarian concerned only with artifacts. In essence, Yentsch has provided one avenue for historical archaeologists to examine the transition from a premodern to modern way of life.

Studies from the inside out—in effect, allowing us to examine cultural complexity with mundane objects—requires the careful construction of the people's context, or the cultural, social, and natural environments within which people lived. As a result of projects like those mentioned, most historical archaeologists now view artifacts as active objects that helped to create, structure, and maintain life rather than merely as passive, inanimate objects that yield information only about the date at which were made (see Chapter 4). Before we can move to a consideration of how historical archaeologists study artifacts, we must first explore the realm of culture. The idea of culture forms the core of most archaeological research.

CHAPTER
3

Historical Culture and Historical Sites

"Not a having and a resting, but a growing and a becoming is the character of perfection as culture conceives it"

Matthew Arnold, 1869

Most people have an interest in what archaeologists do. When they encounter them in the field, perhaps at a place they have driven by without noticing day after day, they usually have a number of questions to ask: How do you know where to dig? What is so special about this place? How do you know what to look for? How deep do you dig, and how do you know when to stop? Archaeology seems so exacting, so meticulous, that it holds a mystique all its own. Even the casual onlooker is fascinated by how an archaeologist carefully strips away the layers of centuries-old dirt to reveal the objects made and used in a far distant time.

One question frequently asked of historical archaeologists is seldom posed to prehistorians: Why excavate history? Why should historical archaeologists spend scarce grant funds, endure long, tiring days in the hot sun, often in unsafe or even dangerous environments, and teach students to excavate a period that is usually well known in historical records? Wouldn't it be less expensive and safer to go to an archive to learn about this more recent past? People can readily understand why archaeologists may be drawn to the study of the ancient Egyptians or the pyramid-building Mayas of Central America, but they find it more difficult to understand why archaeologists would wish to excavate the home of an early twentieth-century coal miner. Surely historical records provide us with enough information about coal mining to make this archaeology unnecessary?

We could provide many deeply philosophical reasons why all archaeology is important in helping us to construct knowledge about the past, and we have presented some ideas about this subject in Chapter 1. The value of excavating history was neatly summarized, however, by prominent historian and the Librarian of the United States Congress, Daniel Boorstin, when he wrote that "We know more about some aspects of daily life in the ancient Babylon of 3,000 B.C. than we do about daily life in parts of Europe or America a hundred years ago." Boorstin's comment is perceptive. In Chapter 2 we touched on some of the values of excavating history in our brief history of our specialty. In this chapter we explain more fully that it is an interest in "culture" that makes the excavation of history important. The information about historical culture collected by archaeologists helps us to explain why today's world is the way it is.

ANTHROPOLOGY

Anthropology is the science that studies human culture. The roots of anthropology—defined broadly as the study of humanity—go back to the Greek historian and traveler Herodotus, who was born in 484 B.C. Herodotus wrote extensively about many aspects of the ancient Greek world, exploring in his writings trade and market customs, differences in peoples' dress, and the division of labor between men and women in different cultures. He also wrote about more unusual cultural practices, such as how Ancient Egyptians mourned the death of a house pet: "If a cat dies in a private house by a natural death, all the inmates of the house shave their eyebrows; on the death of a dog they shave the head and the whole of the body."

Anthropology only acquired its scientific credentials in the late nineteenth century. Since then, the field has been made famous by such luminaries as Franz Boas, Margaret Mead, Bronislaw Malinowski, and Ruth Benedict. These pioneer anthropologists were engaging writers who put their discipline on the map. As a result, many people believe an anthropologist is a person who goes to remote South America, Africa, or New Guinea to live with "primitive" peoples to learn about how they live. Such research is known as *participant observation*. Some of today's anthropologists do indeed spend long periods among such non-Western cultures, but anthropology itself has become an incredibly diverse discipline that studies all aspects of humanity.

Anthropology is generally taught in the United States as a four-field discipline. The four fields are cultural or social anthropology (sometimes called "sociocultural" anthropology), physical anthropology, anthropological linguistics, and archaeology. If we define anthropology as the study of humankind, past and present, then we can well imagine the breadth of modern anthropology. American anthropologists view each subdiscipline as an integral part of the larger study of humanity. Cultural or social anthropologists study the ways in which current people live: how and what they eat, what stories they tell one another, how they practice religion, how they decide to whom they are related, and every other aspect of daily life that

Herodotus, the great traveler.

can be imagined. Simply put, cultural anthropology is the study of custom. A cultural anthropologist may study the customs of the Karaja in Central Brazil as they appeared while he or she lived with them. The anthropologist also may write about how the Karaja are adapting to or resisting the cultural changes caused by the construction of the Belém-to-Brasília Highway. Physical anthropologists study humans both as biologic and as social animals. Physical anthropologists study everything from the very earliest appearance of humans in the world—by examining the fossils of our earliest ancestors such as the famed "Lucy" found in Ethiopia by Donald Johanson—to the genetic compositions of living peoples. The study of physical characteristics, primate behavior, and the development of human social organization all fall within the realm of physical anthropology. Anthropological linguists study human speech, how language is used by people, language history, and nonverbal communication. Anthropological linguists may study what it means socially to cross one's arms while talking, or what English speakers mean when they say "blue" and "green." Archaeologists contribute to this larger study of humanity by conducting research that differs from that of their anthropological colleagues only in their interest in the past and the remains past peoples left behind.

The common thread that binds together the four subfields of anthropology is the idea of "culture." The concept of culture is no less important for historical archaeologists than it is for cultural anthropologists.

CULTURE

We all use the word *culture,* but we employ it in many ways. For example, we may describe someone who goes to the opera as "cultured," and someone who makes loud noises while eating soup in a restaurant as "uncultured." When used in this popular way, the word *culture* often says more about the individual using the term than about the person or group being referred to. In a popular sense, the term *culture* only means what one person (or perhaps one group of people) thinks is appropriate behavior in a certain setting. Some behavior reflects "culture," some reflects a lack of it. This popular use of the term may be widespread, but it is not anthropological.

Another popular sense of the word *culture* is closer to the anthropological meaning. We all know that other cultures exist, we often see their—to us—strange dress and odd customs in television documentaries. We can gaze at a museum display to examine the unusual objects they made and used. We can even directly experience something of another culture by eating their native dishes in restaurants and by meeting people from different cultures in large, multicultural cities. We know that these people, called "foreigners" to indicate that they come from someplace else, may speak odd-sounding languages, may prefer unusual foods, and may even worship a deity other than our own. These differences allow us to sense that "foreign" people are indeed different from us—but how do we really know it? What are we really sensing when we meet "foreign" peoples? Surely we are not observing any real biologic difference in the people themselves, because physical anthropology teaches us that we are all one species. What we are encountering is a difference in culture.

The concept of culture is at the very core of anthropology, and all anthropologists seek to contribute something to its understanding. The diversity of the world's cultures and the multitude of ways that culture can be studied has meant, however, that anthropologists have formulated numerous definitions for this one important concept. One might reasonably expect all anthropologists to agree on a definition of a concept so central to their field, but this is not the case. In 1952 when two American anthropologists, Alfred Kroeber and Clyde Kluckhohn, collected all of the definitions of culture that had been used by anthropologists, they found more than 160 of them!

In the face of such overwhelming disagreement, the best definition is perhaps the first one ever proposed. In his book *Primitive Culture,* published in 1871, Edward Tylor defined culture as "the complex whole which includes knowledge, belief, art, morals, law, custom, and any other capabilities and habits acquired by man [humans] as a member of society." Tylor's definition captures three important elements of culture: first, that culture is composed of many diverse elements—from pot shapes to belief systems—that are brought together in unity; second, that culture is not instinctual, but must be learned; and third, that people learn culture in societies, groups of people who are bound together by a shared way of life and who engage in social interaction. From the members of our culture we learn how to sit at a table to eat, how to arrange the place setting in the "correct" way, what is acceptable to serve at a meal, how to perceive what is served, and how to eat. Much of our culture is internalized during our enculturation process, an often unconscious way of learning what is "right" and what is "wrong" in a culture, but sometimes we learn the rules of our culture purposefully. Formal schooling provides a good example. In class we learn, in a formally structured way, many of the rules of our culture. On the playground during recess we also learn the rules of our culture, but in a nonstructured, informal way. Both ways of learning are equally important for teaching individuals in a culture what is expected of them and how to behave toward others, and as members of a group.

Humans use their cultures to help them adapt to their environments. In this sense, human culture is unique. People use their intelligence, traditions, and experience to feed themselves, to shelter themselves from the heat and cold, and to protect themselves from predatory animals. All of these ways of surviving in the environment are determined by culture.

Culture is not the same as behavior because not everyone in a culture acts exactly alike. Ants, for example, have societies—they engage in interaction and have a shared way of life—but they do not have culture. Culture structures the rules and standards that are deemed acceptable, but it provides for variability within the limits of acceptability. If culture were not variable, then everyone would act exactly the same, just as ants do.

HUMAN BEHAVIOR IN THE PAST: ANALOGIES AND DIRECT HISTORICAL APPROACHES

The concept of culture helps archaeologists to explain what they find at archaeological sites. The material objects and the other remains archaeologists find, however, do not represent culture as such, but rather the results of behaviors of people acting within a culture. Archaeologists cannot directly observe past behavior, and so they must infer behavior and even ideas from what they find during excavation. For prehistorians, this process of inferring the past can be assisted by ethnographic analogy and by the direct historical approach.

Ethnographic analogy refers to the archaeological use of a cultural anthropologist's ethnography about a living people as added support for an inference about past behavior. In a famous example, when Lewis Binford found shallow, basin-shaped pits filled with charred corncobs at the prehistoric Toothsome Site in Illinois, he used ethnographies of Native Americans to infer that these pits were used during the process of tanning hides. The tanners placed the hides over the pits, and the smoke from the smoldering corncobs made the hides pliable and more easily worked. Binford was willing to make the connection between what he read in the ethnographies about the use of shallow pits and the pits he discovered at the site. Without the ethnographic analogy, Binford was unable to interpret the function of the pits. Archaeologist Patrick Munson later questioned Binford's conclusion, stating that the shallow pits may have been used to give a blackened surface to pottery. Munson also used ethnographic analogy to make his claim.

The direct historical approach is similar to ethnographic analogy, except that in the direct historical approach there is a direct link between the "ethnographic" and the archaeological cultures. In the direct historical approach, an archaeologist uses a culture that still inhabits the region in which the archaeological site is found to show connections between the two cultures. The direct historical approach is as old as the European invasion of the New World. Spanish explorers in Middle America and Peru used it to connect the stone monuments they saw with the native cultures around them. In modern archaeology, a classic example is A. V. Kidder's use of the approach in the 1910s and 1920s. Excavating at Pecos Pueblo in northern New Mexico, Kidder correlated his stratified layers of prehistoric occupation and their painted potsherds with artifacts used by modern Pueblo Indians in the region (Figure 3.1). Kidder's methodology was a blueprint for all subsequent research in the Southwest and much farther afield.

Direct historical research is based on the establishment of a cultural and technological link between past and present. Once this link is made, archaeologists can use information from the current culture to infer the past with greater confidence than is possible in ethnographic analogy. If a Southwestern archaeologist finds smooth, flat stones at an archaeological site and native people 60 miles (96 km) away grind corn using flat stones, then, using the direct historical approach, one may reasonably conclude that the ancient flat stones were also used for grinding corn. From this material evidence, the archaeologist can infer the behaviors of growing, grinding, and eating corn in the past.

Both ethnographic analogy and direct historical approach are used by historical archaeologists, but they are seldom required. The analogies used in historical archaeology are often taken from historical documents or from other materials that date to the exact time that a site was inhabited. For example, historical archaeologists know from their own archival research and from studies by historians that certain behaviors were expected of slaves by slave owners—deference, ignorance, a willingness to work—and that slaves, for their part, cherished other images—bravery in the face of bondage and cruelty, the ability to trick the master, the skill to leave the plantation surreptitiously by night, and even the power to harm the planter's family in secret. For example, in the 1760s, the *Charleston (South Carolina) Gazette* complained that "The negroes have again begun the hellish practice of poisoning."

Where records or historical studies exist, historical archaeologists need not rely on ethnographic analogies or the direct historical approach to help them de-

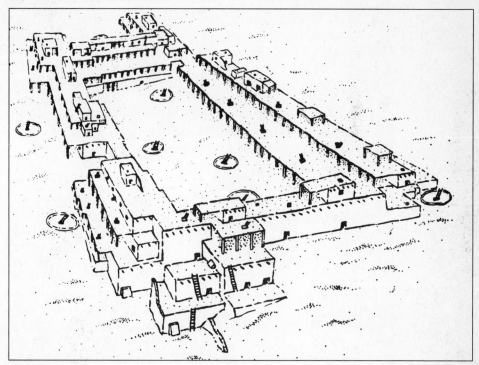

Figure 3.1 *Artist's view of how Pecos Pueblo, New Mexico, looked when the Spanish colony was established in 1598.*

vise interpretations. Rather than referring to these kinds of analogies as ethnographic, we may think of them as direct analogies, because exact agreement in time exists between the archaeological site and the nonarchaeological material that can be used to help interpret life at the site. Historical archaeologists are often able to make direct analogies because the people being written about and the people who lived at the archaeological site being excavated are often one and the same. Prehistorians by definition cannot make direct analogies because the people they study did not write about themselves or the times in which they lived.

CULTURAL SYSTEMS

Tylor's idea that culture is a "complex whole" makes the point that culture is composed of many elements. These elements are both tangible (erasers, chairs, and blackboards) and intangible (religious beliefs, economic attitudes, and folklore). These tangible and intangible elements all work together as a system, or interconnected network, in which the various spheres of life are related. This cultural system allows individuals to adapt to another system, the natural environment, or ecosystem.

One important feature of any system is the idea that when one of its elements changes, other elements change as well. This sort of change is easy to understand

Prince Henry of Portugal, The Navigator.

in an ecosystem. Deforestation, for example, allows rain to strike the ground directly, thereby causing erosion and increased sedimentation in nearby rivers and streams. The change in one part of the ecosystem—in this case, the trees—has brought about changes in another—the soil and the nearby watercourses.

This notion that change in one part of the system causes change in another is also easy to envision in small, relatively simple cultures, where little social stratification exists. It may be relatively easy to imagine how a change in the leadership structure of a small culture that sustains itself by hunting game and collecting wild plants may change the way trade is conducted. Systemic change is more difficult to envision in highly complex, hierarchical cultures, such as those studied by historical archaeologists. Neat one-to-one correlations between changes in one sphere and changes in another are often extremely difficult to make clearly and unambiguously in large, complex cultures. Too many interacting factors make simple interpretations impossible.

Consider the case of Henry the Navigator, Prince of Portugal. Henry, born in 1394, was a studious young man who had a strong interest in mathematics and astronomy. He and his two older brothers, to prove themselves worthy of knighthood, raised an army in 1415 and captured Ceuta, an Islamic commercial town across the Straits of Gibraltar in Morocco. Ceuta was a major center of the Saharan gold trade. Once he had a foothold in North Africa, Henry aimed to control the gold trade and to obtain more African wealth. Systematically, he sponsored ship-borne expeditions southward along the African coast, with the long-term objective of outflanking the Saharan trade routes controlled by his Islamic enemies. In 1441, one of his captains, Antão Gonçalves, returned to Portugal with two black African captives, one male, the other female. These individuals were the first African slaves taken to Europe. As Portuguese ships coasted southward, they discovered Madeira and the Cape Verde Islands. On these tiny islands, they developed labor-intensive sugar plantations worked by slaves. As a bonus, these plantation outposts were rela-tively close to a seemingly unlimited supply of African captives. The Portuguese soon became obsessed with the economic potential of the African slave trade, not only for human cargoes to work fields at home, but, eventually, for export to sugar plantations in Brazil and elsewhere.

We know that the African men and women taken to Portugal caused Por-tuguese citizens to think about their world differently. This world was shaped by a wider view of the world's cultural systems. Instead of seeing the world composed simply of "Christians" and "non-Christians," as before, Portuguese men and women began to envision the world as being divided between "slaves" and "nonslaves," "black" and "white," "our culture" and "their culture." We know about these changes in perspective from historical sources.

The presence of Africans on the cobbled streets of Lisbon forced the Por-tuguese to think about new categories of people, to contemplate the men and women among them who were from wholly different, non-Portuguese cultural sys-tems. What is much harder for us to say, however, is that the influx of Africans af-fected *every* part of Portuguese life. For example, can it be said that the presence of Africans in Portugal changed the Portuguese system of government? Portuguese strategies and plans for their empire changed over time, but to say that these changes were the direct result of African slavery tends to deny the complexity of Portuguese culture. The Portuguese were undoubtedly changed forever because of their involvement with African slavery. The true extent of this change, however, will be studied for years.

All cultural systems are complex, no matter how large the population. At first glance, the Tiwi hunter-gatherers of northern Australia appear to be a "simple" cul-ture. They live on two islands off the northern coast of Australia and maintained minimal contacts with the outside world before 1890. Early European visitors to the islands found them living in small bands, armed only with boomerangs and stone-pointed spears. By our standards, the Tiwi are a "simple" people. This "simplicity" is highly misleading. The complexity of their culture is amply demonstrated by some-thing we take for granted: our names. Personal names among the Tiwi are be-stowed on a child by its father or the man currently married to its mother. When-ever a husband dies and the widow remarries, however, the child receives a new name. In fact, all names given by the dead man are taboo and are not to be spoken again. Because women could marry several times in their lives, their children could have several different names! Logically, a person would not receive a permanent name until their mother was dead and could no longer remarry! The Tiwi, how-ever, got around this problem by only exercising the name taboo for a short time.

Adult Tiwi man in Australia, dressed for ceremony.

After what was judged a decent period, most people slip back into calling the person by their most familiar name. For men, this generally means the one they received in their twenties and thirties, for women it is usually that from early adolescence. Cultural complexity cannot be measured in artifacts and food remains alone, for many societies, like the Tiwi, enjoy elaborate and highly sophisticated belief systems and ceremonial lives.

The archaeologist's task is especially difficult because most information about cultural complexity comes from material remains—artifacts, food remains, structures, and so on. Even with exceptional preservation conditions, the intangible aspects of human culture such as language and religious beliefs have vanished with their users. Historical archaeologists are often at an advantage in being able to understand past cultural systems because of the presence of written texts and other nonarchaeological materials, such as photographs and maps. Very often, the sheer complexity of historical cultures makes their interpretation an intricate task.

CULTURAL PROCESS

All cultures change constantly, regardless of size and complexity. Changes occur in all spheres of culture because people are active beings who invent new ways of doing things, who find new ideas more acceptable than old ones, and who come into contact with other peoples and learn from them. Change can be endogenous, originating within a culture, or exogenous, originating outside a culture.

Archaeologists view change primarily through the material remains people left behind. One of the advantages of archaeology is that it allows anthropologists to study change over long periods. At sites spanning two centuries, a prehistorian may observe changes in pottery from red painted to black and white painted. His or her task is to find a plausible explanation for this process of change: was it caused by a switch from male to female potters? Was a religious ban on red-painted pottery enforced by powerful priests? Or did red pigment sources become depleted? Did, perhaps, the foreign makers of black and white pottery acquire more influence in society, through peaceful means or military conquest? Or did a combination of several factors account for the changeover? This search for solutions to the processes of cultural change makes archaeology an exciting but challenging discipline.

Historical archaeologists face similar problems in understanding cultural processes. In many cases, however, cultural changes in historical times may be truly exogenous, and far beyond the control of most historical peoples. For example, as we discuss in more detail in Chapter 4, changes in ceramic usage may be mandated by a factory owner. For example, in the early 1760s, famous English potter Josiah Wedgwood introduced a ceramic he called "cream-colored ware." This ware has a creamy appearance and enjoyed widespread popularity after its introduction. It is much sought by modern antique collectors. Of course, by no means did every consumer necessarily like cream-colored ware, but many of them had to buy it anyhow in an era when choices were far more limited and fine pottery was often in short supply. Even then, however, smart factory owners listened to the marketplace, a lesson that Ford learned the hard way with the failure of its Edsel automobile in the 1950s. Many changes can originate thousands of miles from an archaeological site. For instance, the changing fashions in beaver fur hats in seventeenth and eighteenth century Europe had profound effects on the native fur trade of the St. Lawrence River valley in northeastern Canada.

A family's preference for blue-banded or red-banded plates would, of course, have little effect on culture change outside the narrow confines of a single household. But many changes are of lasting significance. For instance, a shift from communal planting of crops using horse-drawn plows to the use of diesel-powered planting machines by individuals would ripple right through even a complex culture and affect everything from threshing technology to crop yields. One of the strengths of historical archaeology, however, is its ability to assess the impact of what may appear at first to be minor cultural changes. It may be that Wedgwood's cream-colored plates were rejected by some people, who chose instead to build their own kilns to continue the production of earlier styles. This kind of replacement is difficult to document. However, the continuation of traditional pottery styles has been demonstrated by historical archaeologists. For example, in New Hampshire, archaeologists David Starbuck and Mary Dupré have used archaeological specimens to show that the potters of Millville, an area on the western edge of Concord, produced traditional redwares from 1790 until about 1900. This pottery tradition was virtually unchanged during the 110-year period.

Whereas the change in technology from horse-drawn to engine-powered planters may be noted in historical records, the change in plate color may not be. Starbuck and Dupré point out that even though there were 250 potters in New England before 1800, and more than 500 after 1850, they were seldom mentioned in written records. Historical archaeology, by its use of archaeological and nonarchaeological sources of information, makes it possible to study both large and small cultural processes.

GOALS OF HISTORICAL ARCHAEOLOGY

In Chapter 2, we showed that the development of historical archaeology unfolded in three broad stages. These same phases reflect not only the increasing sophistication of historical archaeology, but also the development of its three major goals:

- to provide information useful for historic preservation and site interpretation
- to document the lifeways of past peoples
- to study the complex process of modernization

These goals can be met at a single site or at different sites, depending on how the research is planned and what issues an archaeologist seeks to address.

Preservation and Site Interpretation

Historical archaeology has a large role to play in documenting how buildings looked in the past. Archaeology can provide information about building size, when room additions were added or removed, and where fence lines and outbuildings were located in yards. Homeowners of the past often made reference in their letters and diaries to room additions or the construction of new buildings on their property and, in many cases, may have even kept sketches or plans. Many people may have made the effort to document the buildings in which they lived, but most homeowners did not. In addition, people often wrote about what they hoped to do to their property, not necessarily what they could afford to do. Almost nobody left a record of where they located their privy or how often they moved it, thinking perhaps that the subject was too indelicate or perhaps too unimportant to be mentioned in writing. As Benjamin Franklin wrote his wife, Deborah, from London in 1765: "I cannot but complain in my mind of Mr. Smith that the house is so long unfit for you to get into, the fences not put up, nor the other necessary articles got ready." We cannot know precisely what these "necessary articles" were, but it is possible that Franklin was referring to the privy behind the house. Archaeologist Paul Schumacher found one of these "necessaries" near the back of this very house in 1953.

Living history museums—old houses and settlements where history is actively interpreted for the public—and historical organizations that try to preserve or restore old buildings are usually interested in knowing "where things were" and "what they looked like." This detailed information enriches the stories interpreters can tell about the past. Historical archaeology, even where abundant historical records do exist, is often the only way to document the full history of a building, from the day it was built to the day it was abandoned, to when it was torn down. Archaeological excavation can provide exacting details that permit the better interpretation and understanding of sites by visitors, thereby helping history to come alive. In addition to providing information about when buildings were built, how they were built, how large they were, and the location of outbuildings, historical archaeologists also have been able to provide unique information about the furnishings inside homes and other buildings. When these kinds of archaeological findings are compared with probate inventories—lists of a person's possessions at the time of death—a full picture of a property can emerge (see Chapter 4).

Undocumented Lifeways

We indicated in Chapter 2 that in the 1960s historical archaeologists developed a strong interest in providing information about people not well represented in historical records. Many historical archaeologists have since provided important information about past lifeways, how people in the past actually lived. Research into the lifeways of people from the recent past is generally thought to be most effective in shedding light on the disenfranchised or forgotten of history—slaves, miners, farmers, and so forth. This search for information about past lifeways can be expanded to include people generally well known in history. For example, historians have told us a great deal about the large industrialists and financiers who built America into a powerful capitalist country, who took their products throughout the world, and who in the course of time amassed sizable fortunes. Almost every public library has more than one biography of men like Henry Ford and J. P. Morgan. Although we may know where such people went to school, where they lived, or on what boards of directors they served, what do we really know about their day-to-day existence?

Henry Ford's assembly line production methods and his vision of providing affordable automobiles to the American public changed our lives and our landscapes forever. Concerned about preserving the nineteenth-century world he was altering, Ford built a living monument to America called Greenfield Village, in Dearborn, Michigan, in the 1920s. His plan was to identify and purchase buildings where important "American" events had occurred or where famous Americans had lived. Once acquired, Ford had the buildings disassembled and removed to Michigan, where they were carefully and accurately reconstructed. As Ford proudly said of his village, "We have no Egyptian mummies here, nor any relics of the Battle of

The reconstruction of Thomas Edison's laboratory complex at Greenfield Village, Michigan, in January 1929.

Waterloo nor do we have any curios from Pompeii, for everything we have is strictly American," Although the research was neither systematic nor up to today's professional standards, Ford used archaeological methods to compile architectural histories of the buildings he removed and rebuilt. He was interested in only the bricks, the clapboards, and the floorboards of Edison's Menlo Park laboratory, the Armington and Sims Machine Shop, the Logan County Courthouse where Abraham Lincoln practiced law, and the other two dozen buildings he reconstructed. Ford was definitely not interested in documenting anyone's lifeways. An archaeologist *could* have excavated around Ford's birthplace (the first home Ford restored, but the last he had moved to Greenfield Village) and collected valuable information about the daily life of the Ford family during Henry's formative years, but this was not done. If historical archaeology had been conducted at Ford's birthplace, it would have underscored the discipline's ability to answer questions about all past peoples, regardless of social position, sex, or ethnic affiliation.

The Process of Globalization

The greatest challenge faced by historical archaeologists is in the area of studying globalization, the worldwide spread of material objects, people, cultures, and ideas. Globalization includes such complex topics as the spread of urbanization, industrialization, and capitalism, and the expansion of Western nations and their institutions to all parts of the world. The archaeologist studies these processes from the archaeological record, from artifacts, architecture, and food remains, to mention but a few sources of information.

The Age of Discovery brought Europeans in contact with non-Western societies throughout the globe. These were complex interactions, which involved far more than the mere imposition of Western culture on indigenous peoples. Both sides borrowed from the other in their creation of the modern "world system." One only has to mention the American potato, which became a staple of European peasants, or tobacco, to get the point. At the same time, the European nations built forts, missions, and small colonies in distant lands, settlements that were transplanted versions of communities at home. Portugal became a world superpower in the sixteenth and seventeenth centuries by virtue of its international trade in gold, spices, sugar, and human beings. She planted colonies along the coasts of Africa, in India, throughout the Far East, and across the Atlantic in Brazil. In each place, the colonists erected buildings that were slavish copies of prototypes back home. For example, their late fifteenth-century fort at Elmina, on the Ghanian coast in West Africa, was built according to the latest European ideas on fortification, with no concession to local conditions (see Chapter 11). Even entire town plans were imported to foreign lands. The eighteenth-century town of Ouro Prêto in Brazil looks as if it were mail-ordered from Portugal. The streets are narrow and cobblestoned, the houses are small and have red-tiled roofs, and the language heard in the shops is Portuguese. Often, minute details of architecture and material culture disclose telling differences between colonial towns and their prototypes back home, details that are never mentioned in documents of the day.

HISTORICAL ARCHAEOLOGICAL SITES

Historical archaeology, like all archaeology, is based on the recovery of information from sites. A *site* is any place that contains traces of past human activity. The site is where archaeologists get a glimpse of past culture and behavior. Many different kinds of sites exist, ranging from sites occupied for a few hours to those inhabited for hundreds of years. Archaeologists often classify sites in terms of their past function.

Domestic Sites

Domestic sites are places where people lived. These sites can range from the smallest, simplest structures to the grandest mansions. Historical archaeologists are interested in domestic structures because they provide the clearest information about how people lived. Domestic sites tell archaeologists about the kinds of objects people used, the varieties of foods they ate, and how they chose to discard their broken and unwanted articles.

Domestic sites can be studied alone or in groups. Archaeologists have studied many towns and cities, and their excavations have disclosed little-known information about the people who lived there. For example, when archaeologists from Archeo-Tec, a private consulting firm, excavated a small Chinese immigrant village at Rincon Point, California, they learned a great deal about Chinese life in one part of the American West in the mid-nineteenth century. The village was inhabited from about 1850 until only about 1865. Today, the village site lies beneath the western approach to the San Francisco Bay Bridge. Archaeology in the village filled in many blank spots in our knowledge about Chinese domestic life in America. During their work, the research team found bones and shells to prove that these industrious immigrants had become California's first commercial fishermen, and that they were the first to recognize the commercial potential of abalone. The immigrants used the sea as a way of adapting to American life. For example, they ate the meat from the abalone and sold the colorful shells to craftsmen, who were soon making popular jewelry for northern California's shoppers. The archaeologists also discovered that the Chinese who lived at the Rincon Point village used equal proportions of American and Chinese objects, ranging from brown stoneware jars used to store traditional Chinese foods to American beer bottles and tooth powder. Rising real estate prices and increased selective taxes (imposed only on the Chinese) soon drove the Chinese away from their town, and by 1870, the area had become part of the booming San Francisco waterfront. Only careful archaeology has been able to provide details of the Rincon Point domestic sites.

Long before the creation of the public landfill, many historic peoples threw their trash into their yards, tossed things under their houses, or swept their refuse against the back fence. Many people also used their privy as a place to discard objects they did not want others to know about, such as alcohol bottles.

A privy excavated by Kenneth Lewis of the University of South Carolina provided a unique look at the consumption habits of the planters who lived on a late seventeenth- and early eighteenth-century sugar plantation near Charleston. Middleton Place Plantation was founded upstream of the city around 1675. Its founder, Henry Middleton, owned no less than 800 slaves and 20 individual plantations. Middleton Place prospered for nearly two centuries. It had two beautifully landscaped formal gardens, a spring house, and a long drive leading to the mansion. Then General Sherman cut his scorched path through the South in 1865 and destroyed all the buildings at the plantation except one, the privy. By the 1920s, the abandoned shaft was practically filled to the top with broken and unusable household articles. Layer by layer, the archaeologists dissected the accumulation of rubbish in the privy, recovering priceless information about its users. They learned, for example, that the plantation residents used blue and white porcelain imported from China; dishes with a pattern of delicate flowers, called French Bourbon Sprig, popular before the French Revolution; and finely cut glass decanters and stemware. The mass of medicine bottles in the privy told the archaeologists that the

Ruins of the main house at Middleton Place Plantation, South Carolina.

people of the plantation had a wide variety of ailments, ranging from upset stomachs to nervous conditions to night sweats associated with consumption.

The Middleton Place privy, like all such facilities, provides an imperfect picture of past life because it encapsulated only the things that people meant to throw down the hole. Nonetheless, long-sealed privies can be a revealing source of information about the daily lives of every level of society.

Historical archaeologists often use their techniques to reconstruct the architectural history of standing buildings, in a more scientific way than did Henry Ford. When archaeologist Theodore Reinhart took a crew of students from the College of William and Mary to Shirley Plantation, Virginia, in 1980, one of his objectives was to reconstruct the mansion's history. Many historians thought that this stately brick mansion, overlooking the James River about 35 miles (56 km) west of Williamsburg, was built in the sixteenth century, probably after 1660. Because no one knew for certain, Reinhart decided to dig next to the mansion's wall to look for a builders' trench. Construction workers of the day excavated linear trenches to allow them to construct the lower courses of the walls. As work proceeded, the laborers would sometimes lose coins or drop broken vessels and other objects under

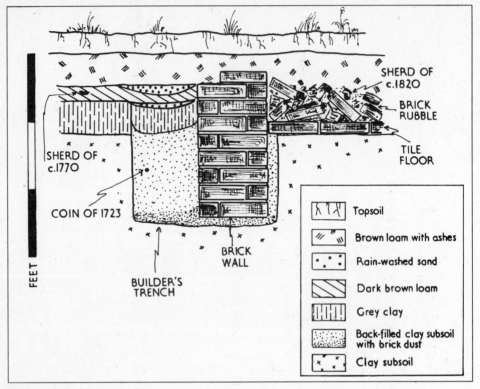

Figure 3.2 *Builder's trench.*

foot. Then the trenches were filled in and the rubbish buried next to the wall. Such objects can be used to date the trench filling, and thereby the building's construction (Figure 3.2). The common English ceramics found by Reinhart's team in the trench—creamware, pearlware, shiny jet-black Jackfield ware—convinced him that the mansion was not erected in the sixteenth century, but that the mansion "was built by John Carter, sometime before his death in 1742 and possibly in the years 1738 and 1739." In the case of the Shirley mansion, archaeology was the only way to answer a seemingly straightforward, historical question.

Industrial Sites

Places once used for manufacturing or production are known as industrial sites. The study of industrial sites is actually a subfield of historical archaeology, known, logically, as Industrial Archaeology. Industrial archaeologists typically study a wide array of manufacturing sites—mills, factories, kilns, mines—that date from the European Industrial Revolution. Industrial sites are often complex and require complete documentation using photographs and accurate architectural renderings. This kind of archaeology may not involve actual excavation, but rather only documentation. At large, standing industrial sites—such as the Silver King Ore-Loading Station in Park City, Utah, or the Sloss Blast Furnaces in Birmingham, Alabama—archaeologists may be called in to assess what might remain buried at such

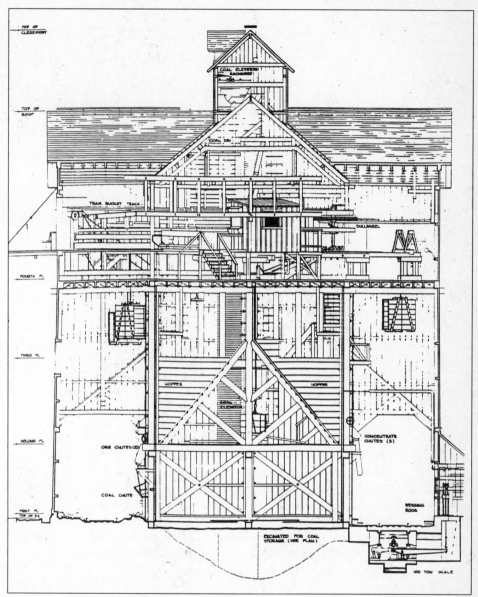

Figure 3.3 *Measured drawing of the Silver King Ore-Loading Station, Park City, Utah, built in 1901.*

sites (Figure 3.3). They may be asked to excavate one or two small areas to search for details about construction techniques or even dates. Such research typically involves not only industrial architects, but also the collaboration of historians of technology, who are experts on such arcane subjects as iron bridges or nineteenth-century railroad stations.

In some cases, archaeological research provides one important way to learn about a past technology that may have been small in scale. A prime example is the

Three tin cans produced at the Lebanon cannery, Delaware.

arrastra found in the western United States. Arrastras were circular, stone-lined depressions ranging in size from 8 to 20 feet (2.4–6.1 m) in diameter. In their thirsty search for gold and silver, prospectors used arrastras to crush stones. They performed the actual crushing with heavy grinding stones that would turn about ten revolutions per minute. Contemporary photographs show that miners used horses, steam engines, and water wheels to turn the huge grinding stones. Archaeologists Roger Kelly and Marsha Kelly studied an arrastra site in northwest Arizona. Built sometime in the early twentieth century, this arrastra consisted of the arrastra itself, a long, narrow outlet trough made of flat stones reaching out from the arrastra, a stone wall, an ore pile, and a possible camp area. The workers at the site had scratched dates of between 1910 and 1916 on the stones, and someone had written "Hello Bill" on one of them. In the large sweep of world history, this one arrastra will not change the way we think. But, as the Kellys correctly point out, arrastras challenge archaeologists to think about industrial sites, regardless of size, as storehouses of information about technological development and the people who made industry possible.

Sometimes archaeologists research industrial sites to learn about the production of artifacts. As one important example, Edward Heite studied the Collins, Geddes Cannery Site, in Lebanon, Delaware, in 1988 and 1989. Although the site of the cannery was by then largely forgotten by the local residents, this was not always the case. More than one hundred years before, in 1873, a local reporter wrote that "The large fruit canning establishment of Collins & Co. at Lebanon, near Camden, is now running day and night in manufacturing sixty thousand gallons of catsup for parties in Philadelphia and New York, at one dollar per gallon." Cans, such as those that contained catsup, are common finds at late nineteenth-century archaeological sites. As an archaeologist, Heite was concerned, not with catsup production as such, but with the manufacture of the tin cans themselves.

Heite was called in to study the cannery because the site was slated to be destroyed by construction. The site, by then overgrown with trees and brush, stood in the path of a much-needed new bridge over the Tidbury Branch of the St. Jones

River in central Delaware. Heite examined the site using a combination of surface survey and small test pits (see Chapters 6 and 8). He also used a backhoe to help him expose the cannery's brick foundations. During the course of the fieldwork he found many of the wall foundations (discovering in places that someone had robbed much of the brick for use elsewhere), the brick foundations for two boilers, the building's cellar, and a dump.

Many of the most interesting artifacts from the site were small scraps of tin. These pieces, fragments that many people would consider to be "junk," told the story of tin can production at the Lebanon cannery. For example, Heite learned by examining the scraps that two ways existed to make the ends of cans. In one process, the circular top was cut from a sheet of tin by a stamping die. At the same time, the die also cut the "fill hole," the spot through which the can's contents were later added. At the cannery in Lebanon, however, Heite discovered that the producers used a second method. Their die first cut the can top and then the fill hole was added in a separate process. He made this discovery by observing that the fill holes were off-centered and not systematically placed on the can lids he found at the site. Heite also learned that the tin can producers in the Lebanon factory cut their cans from sheets of tin that averaged about 16 inches (40.6 cm) square, although they sometimes used sheets half this size. The size of the sheets seems irrelevant, but it is not. Tin can producers made cans based on the size of the sheets. The ideal was to be able to cut four can bodies from one sheet. Interestingly, tin can producers still make cans in the same sizes, even though the tin is now on rolls instead of sheets.

Heite's research may strike some as trivial. After all, he only studied a few tin cans made at a single cannery in Delaware. However, it is by such detailed research that historical archaeologists expand our knowledge about all aspects of history, even the lowly tin can. Heite was correct when he wrote that his research provided "a laboratory in which to study the changes in canneries over the past century." Industrial sites of all kinds provide these important laboratories.

Military Sites

Military sites are places associated with armed conflict or with military occupation. Forts, blockhouses, earthworks, and locations where battles were fought are all classified as military sites. Fort Michilimackinac, Michigan, the place where Lewis Binford first became familiar with historical archaeology, provides a good example. The fort, at the tip of lower Michigan, has been the site of a continuous archaeological campaign since 1959. Much of the fort's interior, including several buildings, has been excavated, and almost one million artifacts have been unearthed, among them glass bottles, religious medals, brass kettle fragments, and trade beads. Such excavations can provide important information about how fortifications were built, what modifications in ideal fortification design were required in certain environments, and how forts were enlarged and rebuilt to adapt to changing circumstances.

Adaptation has figured prominently in many military situations, and historical archaeologists can show how individual companies of soldiers lived. In many cases, the soldiers may be well known, though their actual everyday lives may be something of a mystery. In North America, the Royal Canadian Mounted Police—the redoubtable Mounties—are among the most famous. The Canadian government created this force in 1874, as the North-West Mounted Police, to protect Canada's sovereignty over its most western territories, and to keep the peace among European settlers and Native Americans. The Mounties built several outposts along the frontier, one of which they called Fort Walsh. The Mounties erected Fort Walsh in 1875 in today's southwestern Saskatchewan, not far from the United States border. They dismantled the post in 1883, selling its logs to the ranchers who were just moving into the region.

Beginning in 1973, Canadian archaeologists excavated the hospital at Fort Walsh. The fort and the town that grew up around it became the centerpiece of a 1,600-acre (648-ha) national historical park. The excavations showed that the Mounties built their hospital to be 16.4 feet by 44.5 feet (5 × 13.6 m) in size, with an attached wing measuring 12.5 by 13.5 feet (3.8 × 4.1 m). They divided the hospital into three equal rooms, with those on the ends being used as sick wards. The post's doctors apparently used the central room as an office and examination room. The excavations yielded 150,000 artifacts, including numerous bottles that once held medicines. Historical records indicate that the Mounties were often beset with sickness, including a malady they called "mountain fever." Today we know this illness as Rocky Mountain spotted fever.

Many of the townspeople who lived near the fort died of the fever, but during its eight years of operation, only one Mountie died at Fort Walsh. The excavated medicine bottles hold the key to the difference in the death rates. The presence of 2.5-gallon (9.5-l) bottle fragments in the hospital deposits show that the fort's doctors had bulk medicines shipped to the post. Specimens of smaller medicine bottles suggest that the doctors dispersed their own prepared remedies to the Mounties. Surprisingly, the archaeologists found no patent medicine bottles inside the hospital. Their absence is noteworthy because patent medicines were the wonder drugs of the nineteenth century. The archaeologists, however, did find numerous patent medicine bottles outside the hospital. The location of these bottles imply that the fort's residents actually did consume great quantities of self-prescribed miracle drugs, but only out of sight of the post's doctors. The doctors, for their part, may have refused to use patent medicines, recognizing them for what they were: long on advertising fluff and short on restorative power.

Archaeological researches can even document how battles were fought. By recording and examining patterns of bullets and matériel found in the ground, archaeologists can provide important information about military tactics and can even document what weapons were used in a battle.

A dramatic example comes from just south of Fort Walsh, in the fields of Montana where George Custer fought his famous battle with the Sioux and Cheyenne in 1876. By examining the distribution of cavalry equipment and Native American artifacts at the battlefield, Douglas Scott was able to reconstruct the sequence of the battle. The distribution of spent cartridge cases showed that Custer, or someone in command, deployed a line of men facing south from Custer Ridge to meet the onrush of the Cheyenne from the west and of the Sioux from the south. At the same time, another group of Sioux attacked from the east against the end of the soldier's line. Scott's team of archaeologists found at least 15 Springfield carbines and two Colt pistols in this part of the field. In the course of the battle, the solders formed themselves into a broad V, with Last Stand Hill to the north. When the soldiers' position on the east caved in, the Sioux on the east began a two-pronged attack toward the main body of soldiers, who, as the cartridges show, were already under intense attack from the west and south. The physical evidence also shows that several Native Americans used captured arms to shoot back at the soldiers. At the end, the remaining soldiers were on the west end of the ridge and were completely surrounded by the hostile force.

In a related study, archaeologist Richard Fox used artifact finds and Native American testimony to shatter the Custer myth. Fox shows that the Seventh Cavalry entered the battle in a disciplined manner, in full accordance with their training. However, when they met stiff resistance and overwhelming enemy numbers, the soldiers' order suddenly broke down. The famed "Last Stand," far from being a heroic battle-to-the-death, was characterized by chaos and panic. The soldiers, in complete disarray, engaged in little determined fighting.

The research by Fox and Scott at the famous Little Big Horn battle, and by numerous archaeologists working at other less controversial battlefields, does more than just fill in the gaps in our knowledge about specific military encounters. These archaeologists challenge us to think about how archaeology can be used to study warfare, tactics, and strategy.

Burial Sites

Individual graves as well as cemeteries provide a mine of information about ancient societies. In studying cemeteries, historical archaeologists usually work closely with physical anthropologists. They can provide information about diets, growth rates of children and adults, the prevalence of dental cavities, and the effects of lead poisoning from water pipes and other sources on numerous historic populations.

In the mid-1980s, Jerome Handler used a collection of excavated African skeletons from a slave plantation in Barbados (dating from about 1660 to 1820) to study the effects of lead poisoning. Handler discovered that the ailment, dry belly-ache, of which the slaves constantly complained, was actually the effects of lead poisoning. When teetotalers said that "there was a demon in the rum," they did not know how right they were. As it turns out, the apparatus used in making rum was constructed with lead seams. Lead would leach into the rum during the fermentation process and drinkers would unknowingly ingest it. As a result, the rate of lead poisoning was probably fairly high in Caribbean populations that relied heavily relied on rum for entertainment and refreshment.

Non-African skeletons are not available from Barbados to compare with those of slaves. However, another dramatic example demonstrates that no one in the historic period was immune to lead poisoning. When Sir John Franklin left England with 129 crewmen and officers to find the elusive Northwest Passage through the Canadian Arctic in 1845, people widely considered his expedition one of the most exciting of the day. When Franklin and "his gallant crew" (as they were immortalized in song) vanished without a trace, England was stunned. What had happened?

When the bodies of several crewmen were discovered, in an almost perfect state of preservation, in far northern Canada and examined by Owen Beattie in the 1980s, the answer was clear: the expedition's massive supply of canned foods had killed them. High-tech atomic absorption analysis of tissues from the buried crewmen showed that the men suffered from acute lead intoxication. The heavy solder seams on their food cans leached into the food, causing lead poisoning. Because each man on the expedition had 248 pounds (111.6 kg) of canned meats, stews, soups, and vegetables allocated to him, their chance of being poisoned was quite high. Before this discovery, Arctic explorers and archaeologists had been puzzled by the apparent aimless wanderings of the Franklin crew shown by the rock cairns they built and by irregular scatters of abandoned supplies. Lead intoxication may have been the culprit.

Studies such as these provide a richness to the past that is seldom matched. Instead of working with the artifacts and food remains, biologic anthropologists work with the remains of the people themselves.

The excavation of cemeteries is a sensitive matter, especially if there is reason to believe that direct relatives of the deceased are still alive. For this reason, the investigation of historic burials is often expressly forbidden or highly regulated by law. Not that these regulations have been universally applied, for it is only in recent years that laws have been enacted to control the investigation of ancient Native American burials.

One recent controversy surrounded an eighteenth-century "Negro Burial Ground" in Lower Manhattan. The historic cemetery came to light during the construction of a 34-story office tower intended for the General Services Administration. The remains of more than 400 individuals were discovered from 16 to 28 feet (4.9–8.5 m) below the current street level. When the burial ground was first found, an outcry came from the African-American community. Some people favored academic study of the remains, some thought that any study was irreverent and unnecessary. Some activists believed that more African-American participation was needed in the excavation. In September 1993, an African religious ceremony was held to commemorate the transfer of the remains from Lehman College in New York City to Howard University in Washington, DC. In October, a second ceremony marked the final "homecoming" of the remains, as the last skeletons were transferred to Howard University. At Howard, the remains will be the subject of a five-year scientific study by African-American physical anthropologist Michael Blakey. His research will provide important new information about the daily lives of hundreds of eighteenth-century men and women of African descent who resided in New York as slaves and servants.

Special-Purpose Sites

Places where people once performed tasks that were not related to industrial production, military activities, or domestic life are termed special-purpose sites. Churches, stores, mental hospitals, and other special-purpose sites give archaeologists the chance to interpret chapters of the past that are often overlooked.

Historical archaeologists have excavated many special-purpose sites. One of the most intriguing is William C. Hoff's store in San Francisco, California. William

Hoff, from New York, was one of thousands of "forty-niners" who traveled west during the great California Gold Rush. Hoff's dreams of wealth lay not in the gold fields but in merchandizing, and less than a year after his arrival in the West he had established a general store and ship supply house on the bustling San Francisco waterfront. Unfortunately for Hoff, however, about a year later, on May 3–4, 1851, the "Fifth Great Fire" completely engulfed his store, destroying it along with hundreds of homes, hotels, and other businesses.

In early 1986, archaeologist Allen Pastron led a group of investigators to the site of Hoff's Store. After almost a full year of excavation, the research team had pulled thousands of artifacts from the old store remains, encapsulated 15 feet (4.6 m) beneath the streets of San Francisco. These artifacts give us the rare opportunity to put our noses up against the glass of a mid-nineteenth-century store and peer at the merchandise purchased by hopeful forty-niners. The archaeologists found leather shoes, brass military buttons, books of matches, whole crocks, patent medicine bottles, copper pennies, silver forks, brass spoons, ceramic crucibles used for melting gold, and even a charred wooden bowling pin. They also found numerous foodstuffs in the store deposits, including cut pork bones, perfectly preserved olives still in their tightly closed jars, coffee beans, walnuts, peach pits, and even cakes, breads, and crackers.

Multipurpose Sites

Multipurpose sites are complex sites where the occupants carried out several often equally important tasks. Multipurpose sites cannot be classified simply as domestic, industrial, or special purpose because their former inhabitants performed all of those tasks there. Historical archaeologists often encounter several kinds of multipurpose sites. Richard Beavers of the University of New Orleans found that Destrehan Plantation, Louisiana, was the perfect example of a multipurpose site. Destrehan was built in 1787 as an indigo plantation. Three-quarters of a century later, its owners converted it into a more profitable sugar-producing estate. An inventory made in 1792 listed the following buildings on the plantation's grounds: the mansion, a detached kitchen, a storehouse, two hospitals for sick slaves, a pigeon house, a coach house, three cabins, a "Negro camp" of 19 cabins, a blacksmith shop, a drying house for indigo, a hay shed, a pump house, a series of sheds needed for churning indigo during fermentation, and an engine house for the indigo grinder. With the conversion to sugar cultivation, the plantation's owners built a sugar boiling house and mill. At this one site, Beavers and his research team investigated different domestic buildings, several special-use structures, and many buildings associated with production.

Underwater Sites

Underwater archaeology is actually a highly specialized kind of archaeology that is not restricted to historic sites. Underwater archaeologists have been particularly successful in documenting ship design, trade routes, and certain aspects of technology among Phoenicians, Romans, and other seagoing cultures. Historical archaeologists, however, do regularly conduct excavations underwater.

In the mid-sixteenth century, Basque whalers from northern Spain pursued their prey in the Strait of Belle Isle off southern Labrador. They hunted and processed whales with great efficiency from a shore base in a sheltered anchorage at Red Bay. This was whaling on a near-industrial scale, studied by meticulous land excavations by James Tuck of Memorial University in Newfoundland. Meanwhile, Robert Grenier of Environment Canada searched the floor of the bay for the wreck of the whaling ship *San Juan,* known from Basque archives to have sunk off the whaling station in late fall 1565, just as she was about to leave for home with a full cargo. After eight years' work, Grenier's team located the wrecks of three whaling ships, one of them almost certainly the *San Juan,* a mid-sized sailing vessel, and several small boats. All were well preserved by the cold water and fine silt. After months of diving on the *San Juan,* the divers recovered more than 200 whale oil barrels, parts of the ship's rigging, some navigational instruments, and most important of all, details of the 250-ton (227 mt) ship herself. Every timber, every joint, tool mark, and hole were drawn and photographed before the wood was returned to the favorable preservation conditions on the sea bed. The result: a detailed reconstruction of a sixteenth-century whaling vessel.

Whether on land or underwater, historical archaeologists study past human behavior in all its many ramifications. To do so they must rely heavily on artifacts, the topic we discuss in Chapter 4.

CHAPTER
4

Historical Artifacts

"For life and joy, and for objects and knowledge curious"

Walt Whitman, 1855

In the "Adventure of the Blue Carbuncle" Dr. Watson arrives at 221B Baker Street, London, to find Sherlock Holmes contemplating "a very seedy and disreputable hard-felt hat, much worse for wear, and cracked in several places." From this hat, judged by Watson to be rather ordinary, Holmes deduces brilliantly a wealth of information, as only he can do. The great detective concludes that the owner of the hat was an intellectual man, that he was once prosperous, that he is middle-aged, and that he recently has had his hair cut. Holmes also figures that the owner's wife has ceased to love him and that the man has no gaslight in his house.

Almost everyone in the Western world is familiar with the exploits of the illustrious, fictional Sherlock Holmes. His deductive methods will live forever. It may surprise some readers, however, to find his name in a serious book about historical archaeology. After all, Sherlock Holmes is only the literary creation of an English physician. Although Holmes is fictitious, he has much in common with modern archaeologists. When Holmes says in "The Boscombe Valley Mystery" that his method is "founded upon on the observation of trifles" he could have been speaking as an archaeologist. Archaeologists, no matter what time or culture they study, focus on what James Deetz calls the "small things forgotten." These "small things" are the many objects ordinary people used in their daily lives, things sometimes so trivial that their users may never have thought about them consciously. In historical archaeology, these "trifles" bear a striking resemblance to the things the average North American uses every day: glass bottles, ceramic dishes, mirrors, buttons, thimbles, and a hundred and one other things.

ARTIFACTS AND MATERIAL CULTURE

Archaeologists sometimes use the terms *artifact* and *material culture* interchangeably. They often talk about the "material culture" of a particular site when they refer to collections of artifacts, and sometimes say "artifact" when they mean "material culture."

In its simplest sense, an *artifact* is anything that is made or modified by conscious human action. A stone arrow point, a soft drink bottle, a carved wooden mask, and a table are all artifacts. Humans are constantly surrounded by artifacts: we cook with them, eat with and from them, drive in them, sleep on them, and get buried in them. The artifacts we use help to define who we are. The term *material culture* includes artifacts, but is generally conceived of more broadly. According to material culture specialist Thomas Schlereth, material culture includes "the entire natural and man-made environment with which researchers can interpret the past."

The stone circle known as The Big Horn Medicine Wheel lies in the mountains of that name in northern Wyoming. Most Americans know of the Big Horn Mountains because of their association with "Custer's Last Stand," but they were home to Native American cultures for thousands of years before Custer was born. These Native Americans built the Big Horn Medicine Wheel some time in the prehistoric past. The wheel looks like a wagon wheel with a central "hub" of stones out of which radiate a series of "spokes." A stone "rim" connects the ends of the spokes. The exact reason Native Americans built the wheel is hotly contested today. Archaeologists have put forward a number of explanations: that Native Americans used the wheel as an ancient observatory; as a monument to deceased, revered leaders; as a location for the vision quests of adolescents who fasted and prayed in the hope that the Great Spirit would lead them to adulthood; or as a symbolic representation of the universe on a grand scale. Many Crow people on the northern Plains today regard the wheel as a sacred site, and say that no one needs to "explain" it to them; they know its meaning the way any believer understands what is sacred within their belief system.

The Big Horn Medicine Wheel is a fascinating object, but is it an artifact? The stones that constitute the wheel cannot be considered artifacts in the strictest sense of the term because they were not actually modified by human action. The only difference between the stones of the wheel and others nearby is that the former are arranged in such as way as to resemble a wheel. If any one of these stones were found someplace else by itself, an archaeologist would probably not consider it to be an artifact. Arranged as a medicine wheel, though, these stones can be considered to be an example of Native American material culture. The medicine wheel makes a cultural statement about past ideas even though these ideas are not currently understood. Material culture thus includes objects that may have been shaped by humanity but not necessarily physically altered in any way. A gravel road is an example of material culture, but the thousands of pebbles in the road are not technically artifacts.

A house presents more of a challenge for an historical archaeologist to classify neatly as either an artifact or as an example of material culture. A house is clearly

Big Horn Medicine Wheel, Wyoming.

something that was made by conscious human activity, but is it an artifact? Houses are composed of hundreds of things that clearly *are* artifacts: nails, roofing tiles, floor boards, and plaster walls—but should we consider a house an artifact in the same way that we might consider a bottle an artifact? To make matters more complex, James Deetz has even argued that the "complex and often bizarre configurations performed on football fields during halftime such as a band forming the word 'OHIO' is, as far as I'm concerned, just as much material culture as an arrowhead."

In the final analysis, the difference between an "artifact" and "material culture" is perhaps not all that significant. For our purposes, we consider an artifact to be any readily *portable* object, and material culture to be all the physical expressions created by the people of a culture.

What is important about artifacts and material culture is that both require interpretation. Artifacts need interpretation because they are not simply passive creations. People do not simply make tools, use them, and then forget about them. In fact, artifacts impose structure on people's lives in the very same way that people impose structure on an artifact in the process of fashioning it. The relationship between humans and things may best be considered by thinking about a small farmhouse. Farmhouses, like all buildings, are built in ways that make cultural sense to their builders. When War of 1812 veteran Charles Ames moved from New England to Indiana in the early nineteenth century, he built a house that was true to his memories of New England. Let us suppose that Ames was used to looking at his fields out of his back door in New England but that in Indiana the topography made it impossible for him to see his pastures from this vantage point. We can readily see how the house in Indiana would "structure" Ames' life. For him to be able to survey his fields in the manner in which he was accustomed, he could make changes in his house, alter the landscape, or change his way of looking at his fields. In any case, part of Ames' material culture—his house—has affected his behavior.

Material culture can structure human reactions in powerful ways. In an innovative study, archaeologist Gregory Monks argues that the architecture used by the Hudson's Bay Company at Upper Fort Garry in today's Manitoba, Canada, served as a form of nonverbal communication. The mighty Hudson's Bay Company built the fur trading and commercial post in 1836 and used it as their administrative center for their activities in the Red River/Assiniboine River region. Monks does not accept the conventional idea that the fort was built simply to be used by traders and governmental officials in their daily affairs. Instead, he proposes that Upper Fort Garry was an active participant in promoting the quasi-military and economic goals of the Hudson's Bay Company. The placement of the flagpole, with its British Red Ensign proudly emblazoned with "HBC," directly opposite the entrance; the construction of an interior wall to segregate living quarters from storehouses; and the expansion of economic areas at the expense of living and administrative parts of the post were not simply done for convenience. These changes were meant to symbolize that the Hudson's Bay Company gave its economic motives greatest importance. The movement of the outer wall to make the once-interior sales store accessible from outside the fort was perhaps the clearest nonverbal message the Company could send. They were saying, in effect, that they wanted local trade, but only on their terms. The quality of material culture to embody one or more meanings make them a centrally important, though frustratingly complex, subject for historical archaeologists.

INTERPRETING ARTIFACTS

In his book *Reading Matter: Multidisciplinary Perspectives on Material Culture,* Arthur Asa Berger creates a hypothetical situation in which the offices of six scholars look down on and surround a small courtyard. On a picnic table in the center of the courtyard the scholars see a McDonald's hamburger, some French fries, and a milkshake. The scholars are a semiotician (someone who studies signs or symbols), a psychoanalytic psychologist, an anthropologist, a historian, a sociologist, and a Marxist political scientist. On looking at the objects, each scholar perceives something quite different. The semiotician views McDonald's as a symbol of America, its standardization, and its efficiency; the psychologist sees the success of McDonald's as an example of the need for gratification of individuals and an element of depersonalization. The anthropologist sees the hamburger and fries in a ritualistic sense and envisions how the McDonald's experience has become part of American folklore. The historian considers the same food as an example of the history of a successful corporation and as a visible reminder of the growing importance of corporations in American history. The sociologist sees in the hamburger an example of the youth culture or the way in which immigrant groups work their way into the American workforce through low-paying jobs. Finally, the Marxist political scientist sees in the objects examples of how different classes of people are exploited by multinational corporations and how McDonald's hides the class-based aspect of capitalist society by providing inexpensive products to all members of society.

Berger's hypothetical situation shows vividly how scholars from diverse disciplinary backgrounds and with disparate perspectives can interpret the same objects differently. This already intricate situation can be made even more complex by adding, for example, a number of historians, each of whom have a slightly distinct slant on history, or a group of anthropologists who see culture in different ways. No matter how many scholars are added, what is missing from Berger's mix is a historical archaeologist. How would an historical archaeologist see Berger's hamburger, fries, and milkshake?

The easy answer is that historical archaeologists can see the objects in all the same ways as Berger's scholars. We showed in Chapter 1 that historical archaeology is a field that reaches across disciplinary boundaries, so its practitioners are perfectly free to borrow ideas from diverse fields, and from the numerous perspectives that exist within them. American studies expert Thomas Schlereth outlines nine of the diverse perspectives—what he terms "conceptual positions"—that current students of material culture adopt: art history, symbolist, cultural history, environmentalist, functionalist, structuralist, behavioralistic, national character, and social history. Although he places historical archaeology in the "cultural history" category, it is obviously a much broader field. In fact, historical archaeologists have conducted research in all of Schlereth's categories, choosing to examine artifacts from various perspectives.

For the sake of brevity, we discuss the interpretation of artifacts from only three broad perspectives: as historical documents (Schlereth's art history, cultural history, national character, and social history), as commodities (Schlereth's functionalist, behavioralistic), and as ideas (Schlereth's symbolist and structuralist). These three categories of interpretation are not mutually exclusive. Instead, each builds on the other, starting with the use of physical things as historical documents.

ARTIFACTS AS HISTORICAL DOCUMENTS

All archaeology is based on the fundamental assumption that artifacts provide information about the past. For more than a century, archaeologists have considered them as the equivalent of historical documents. John L. Stephens, the nineteenth-century American explorer of Copán, the majestic city of the Maya, understood this usage. On beholding a finely carved stela, or upright stone slab, at the site, Stephens remarked that it proved "as a newly discovered historical text might have done, that the peoples who once occupied the American continent were no savages." He likened the stelae of the Maya to historical documents in that they provide important information about life in ancient Mexico. Recently, historical archaeologist Ivor Noël Hume has given Stephens' comment a more modern twist by proclaiming artifacts to be "signposts of the past."

The idea that artifacts can be read as historical texts has much to do with the technology of artifact production. People who made artifacts in prehistoric times probably relied almost exclusively on cultural conventions when fashioning an object. They developed the technology, the decoration, and the form of objects over many years. Prehistorians can chart changes in artifact design or decoration, but only broadly. For instance, when Donald Lehmer complied the cultural chronology of a region archaeologists call the "Middle Missouri," the Missouri River valley in North and South Dakota, he knew that pottery with surfaces roughened with cord-wrapped sticks characterized the Initial Coalescent Variant of the Central Plains Tradition. He also knew that the people who lived during the more recent Extended Coalescent Variant did not cord-roughen their pottery. "Cord roughening is so rare," says Lehmer about the Extended Coalescent Variant, "that it cannot be considered an integral part of the ceramic tradition." Archaeologists of the American Plains generally agree that the Initial Coalescent Variant dates from about A.D. 1400 to 1550 (150 years) and that the Extended Coalescent Variant dates from about A.D. 1550 to 1675 (125 years). In South Dakota, therefore, a cord-roughened sherd found along the Missouri River could be dated to sometime within a 150-year period. The precise placement of this sherd within this period, however, will forever remain a mystery without other compelling information.

Historical archaeologists often have a distinct advantage over their prehistorian colleagues when it comes to using artifacts as historical documents. In many cases, historical archaeologists can recognize changes in artifacts, not over centuries, but in individual years, or sometimes even days. This fine-grained understanding of artifacts as historical documents exists because most historical artifacts were manufactured by factories or corporations. These corporations, because they were economic concerns, usually kept careful, detailed records as part of their responsibilities to their shareholders. In many cases, these archives provide abundant information about changes in artifact design, style, and decoration.

Josiah Wedgwood, the famous eighteenth-century English ceramic designer, celebrated for his beautifully crafted light blue wares decorated with white appliqués, is known to have kept detailed records of his ceramic patterns, shapes, and decorations. Wedgwood's decorated plates called "Old Feather Edge," "New Feather Edge," "Queen Pattern," and "Royal Pattern," are well known today because of his factory records. Archaeologists throughout North America have found ceramic sherds bearing these patterns at numerous colonial sites, Colonial Williamsburg being the best known.

Historical archaeologists use artifacts as historical documents in many ways. Most often, they use them to date specific occupation layers. The common Coca-Cola bottle provides an excellent case in point.

The Coca-Cola Bottle

Coca-Cola, or more accurately, "Coca-Cola Syrup and Elixir," was invented in Atlanta, Georgia, by pharmacist John S. Pemberton in 1886. Pemberton originally designed Coca-Cola as a headache and hangover remedy, but it became such a popular beverage that in 1892 his business became "The Coca-Cola Company." The following year, with the prospect of Coca-Cola becoming a major sensation, Pem-

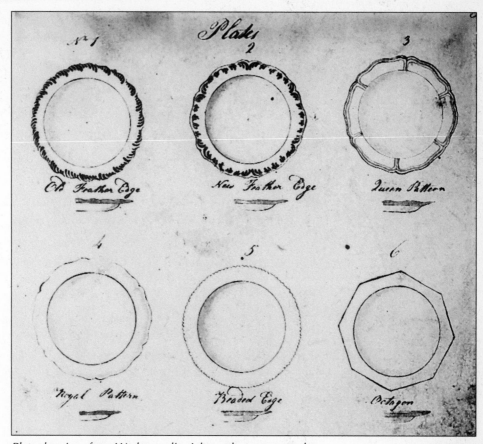

Plate drawings from Wedgwood's eighteenth-century catalog.

berton registered his now-classic signature "Coca-Cola" with the United States Patent Office. Between 1894 and 1915, Pemberton paid little attention to the bottles in which Coca-Cola was sold, using straight-sided bottles of every color. In 1916, however, the company decided to adopt a standardized, patented bottle design to protect its popular product from the countless imitators who sought to cash in on Pemberton's soft drink gold mine.

Many early twentieth-century manufacturers of liquid foodstuffs chose to patent their bottle designs rather than what was inside the bottle. To patent a bottle's contents required announcing the product's formula, something that few manufacturers of highly sought-after products wished to do. Having patented the bottle, all of Pemberton's Coca-Cola sold between 1916 and 1923 came in bottles reading "Bottle Pat'd Nov. 1915" on the base. The company patented a new design on Christmas Day, 1923, so all Coca-Cola bottles sold between 1924 and 1937 came in bottles reading "Bottle Pat'd Dec. 25, 1923." Other design innovations followed in 1937. Consequently, all Coke bottles sold between 1937 and 1951 read "Bottle Pat. D-105529." The company had the word "Coke" first painted on their bottles in 1958, and between 1963 and 1965 they also included "6 $1/2$ oz." on one side panel.

1915 prototype of the classic Coca-Cola bottle. Its shape led people to call it the "Mae West bottle," after a buxom actress popular at the time.

The constant changes in the common Coca-Cola bottle form the official patent history of one of the world's most widely known products. Thus, in archaeological sites, Coca-Cola bottles can function as documents in a way that few prehistoric artifacts ever could. For example, when David Gradwohl and Nancy Osborn found a bottle with the "Coca-Cola" script painted on it at Buxton, Iowa, a coal mining town with a large African-American population, they immediately knew that the bottle dated to after 1893.

Many mass-produced ceramic vessels and glass bottles carry manufacturers' marks on them that serve as valuable chronological markers. Manufacturers did not place such symbols on their products for the benefit of future archaeologists. They served as company icons, or as a factory's identifying signature.

Ceramic Makers' Marks

Makers' marks on the bottom of ceramic dishes go back centuries. For example, a Roman potter named M. Perennius lived sometime between 100 B.C. and A.D. 100. Perennius was renowned for his skill at copying Greek designs and was widely considered a great ceramic artist. He stamped his pottery "M. PERINNI," "M. PEREN," or "M. PERE." This has proved a wonderful time marker, for his wares have come from digs in Rome, northern France, and Spain. Perennius is said to have employed 17 slaves in his pottery, the most famous of them Tigranes. He was also proud of his work, so he stamped his pieces "TIGRAN," "TIGRA," or just plain "TIGR." Following a tradition that dates from classical times, potters have etched their wares with a variety of initials, shapes, and symbols that served as their personal, unique marks ever since.

During the Industrial Revolution of the late eighteenth century, large pottery houses adopted the same procedure to mark their products. The most well-developed set of makers' marks appear on post–Industrial Revolution British ceramics, but American potters quickly followed suit by marking their wares as well. Potters on both sides of the Atlantic soon compiled a massive array of unique and distinguishing marks. As may be expected, the numbers of icons expanded rapidly with the growth of the ceramics industry and the increase in competition between potteries. Before 1770, English potters seldom marked their wares; after this date, they almost always did. Ceramic scholars have spent years compiling catalogs of pottery marks.

Historical archaeologists use these catalogs to identify and to date the marked ceramics sherds they find. To be identified, a recognizable portion of a mark must remain visible on the sherd. Maker's marks are also termed *bottom marks* because they were placed on the outside bottom of vessels. For example, a sherd that is marked with a globe with the word *MINTON* written across was a product of the Minton pottery of Staffordshire, England. Established in 1793, the Minton pottery used the globe from about 1863 to 1872. In 1873, the Mintons added a crown to the top of the globe and an *S* to the word *MINTON*. (Figure 4.1). Thus, individual marked sherds can be dated within broad limits. In addition to such individualized

Figure 4.1 *Marks from the bottle of Minton ceramics. Without crown: about 1863–72; with crown: about 1873. The word England was added below the crown in 1891. The symbol on the right was used from about 1912 to 1950.*

marks, many English potters incorporated the British Royal Arms in their marks. These marks are characterized by a lion (on the left) and a unicorn (on the right) flanking an oblong shield with a crown on top of it. The marks included a quartered shield with a smaller shield in the middle before 1837, but after this date the small shield disappeared.

Ceramics from Victorian England, made from 1842 to 1883, carry one of the most diagnostic bottom marks a historical archaeologist can ever find. Such diamond-shaped marks show that the pottery factory had registered the design or shape of the vessel with the Patent Office in London. Because the purpose of the symbol was to protect the pottery from piracy for at least three years, the bottom mark contains an exact date of registry. The Patent Office assigned codes to ceramic manufacturers and required that they place them in the corners of the diamond. Thus, a piece of English pottery marked in this manner and reading "E" in the left corner of the diamond, "IV" in the right corner, and "C" in the top corner, can be identified as having been registered at the British Patent Office on May (E) 4 (IV), 1844 (C). (Figure 4.2). This date has little to do with when the ceramic vessel may have been used, except that it serves as a *terminus post quem,* or "date after which" it was made. We know, because of the 1844 date on the vessel itself, that this piece could not have been used *before* 1844. However, only more detailed knowledge of the site itself will provide a *terminus ante quem,* or "date before which." If we knew for certain, from other sources, that the site was completely abandoned in 1864, then we can date the ceramic sherd with the diamond-shaped mark from 1844 to 1864.

Bottle Makers' Marks

Glass bottles also carry makers' marks. The first known marked glass reads in Greek "Ennion made it." Since the first century A.D., when Ennion put his mark on his glass products, most factories have done likewise. Historical archaeologists use catalogs complied by glass specialists in the same way they use books of ceramic makers' marks.

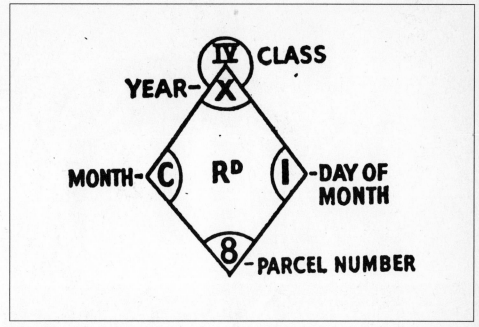

Figure 4.2 *British registry mark, used from 1842 to 1867. Class "IV" refers to pottery and porcelain.*

Glass manufacturers, like potters, used distinctive marks to identify their wares. For example, a "C" with a square around it on the bottom of a bottle indicates that this bottle was made between 1921 and 1928 by the Crystal Glass Company of Los Angeles. The words *KEARNS & CO.* identify a bottle as being made by the Kearns, Gorsuch Bottle Company of Zanesville, Ohio, between 1864 and 1876; and the letters *ABGMCo.* show that the bottle was manufactured by the Adolphus Busch Glass Manufacturing Company of Belleville, Illinois, sometime between 1886 and 1928. Many other equally distinctive marks identify other glass manufacturers.

Technological Attributes

The prevalence of artifacts like bottles and glass that have clearly identifiable marks increases with time, so that late nineteenth- and early twentieth-century sites are more likely to contain marked and readily datable objects. As a result, historical archaeologists who study sites that date before the late nineteenth century seldom have the advantage of discovering marked ceramics and glass. In such cases, historical archaeologists have learned how to date many artifacts by their *attributes,* or physical characteristics.

Prehistoric Mimbres bowl from New Mexico.

The physical attributes found on prehistoric objects are largely the result of culturally recognized and understood conventions. The beautifully decorated Mimbres black-on-white pottery from southwestern New Mexico (A.D. 1000–1130) is emblazoned with bold geometric designs and delicately drawn animal figures that would be widely and immediately recognized by every member of that culture. The physical attributes of these ceremonial bowls are culturally expressive, in that they depict legends of the creation and other aspects of long-forgotten Mimbres ideology.

In contrast, the physical attributes of historical objects seem to relate more to a manufacturer's efforts to produce an object that consumers find pleasing and appealing, or to simplify and streamline a costly manufacturing process. As a result, physical attributes on historical objects have much to do with technological change and innovation.

Glass bottles provide an excellent example of how technological change can be documented through time. Since antiquity, makers of glass objects have made bottles by using a blowing process. The glassblower places a ball of molten glass on the end of a hollow rod, then blows a bottle from the ball of glass. The stretched air bubbles remain, caught for all time, in the glass of such a blown bottle. So does the distinctive rough mark on the bottom, called the *pontil scar,* where the glassblower broke the glass rod free from the bottle. Glass blowing was a slow, laborious process. The uniformity of the bottles rested largely on the skill of the glassblower.

To standardize the size and shape of bottles, producers began to make them in molds. Anonymous bottle makers invented the two-piece mold sometime around 1750. Now the glass blowers blew bottles inside a hinged mold. The ridges on the bottle necks were made by hand using a shaping tool run around the outside of the glass before it cooled. When the vessel had cooled and hardened sufficiently, the completed bottle was removed from the mold and the process repeated with a new lump of molten glass. Such molded bottles bear a seam line from the mold that runs from the top to bottom of the bottle, and diagonally across the base. Glass factories used the innovative two-piece mold until about 1880. English bottle maker Henry Ricketts patented a three-piece (or "Ricketts mold") in 1821. Manufacturers used this mold type, characterized by a seam running around the bottle's shoulder, until about the 1920s. Michael Owens, then general manager of the Toledo Glass Company, invented the first fully automatic bottle-making machine in 1903, and today, after a series of improvements, we have the modern bottle. The attributes of bottles—seam lines, pontil marks, and glass bubbles—all are valuable chronological markers.

Even inconspicuous attributes are chronologically significant. For example, bottle makers used threads on bottle necks only after about the mid-1850s. William Painter patented the "crown cap" in 1892, on which he attached the familiar bottle cap. Painter was especially proud of his invention and called it the "crown cork" because it "gives a crowning and beautiful effect to the bottle." As may be expected, perhaps, Painter's official patent for the "Bottle-Sealing Device" gave a less poetic description of his achievement, calling it "a metallic flanged sealing-cap adapted to receive the head of a bottle and containing a concavo-convex sealing disk"! (Figure 4.3).

Even the common, everyday nail has a well-documented manufacturing history. The round-headed, fully machine-made wire nail we know today only dates to the 1850s. Before then, nail producers used a variety of other methods to make their products. One can recognize completely handmade nails, produced before machine-made nails, by their hammered heads, flattened points, and irregular shapes. Nails made between the 1790s and the 1820s, for example, were cut with a die from a flat, solid "nail plate." These nails are recognizable by their rectangular, rather than round, cross sections and their hand-hammered heads. By the 1880s, wire nails were much less expensive to manufacture than their machine-cut cousins, and so they were cheaper to sell. Most builders shifted to using the less expensive nails at about that time.

The list of potentially datable objects is enormous. Technological innovations in the manufacture of lighting devices, locks, horseshoes, smoking pipes, necklace beads, tin cans, and hair combs, among other familiar day-to-day artifacts, can be dated with remarkable precision. Thus, even the most prosaic of artifacts and tiny attributes become important historical documents.

ARTIFACTS AS COMMODITIES

Most historical artifacts were mass-produced, for sale on a large scale. This means that most historical artifacts were *commodities,* objects created specifically for exchange.

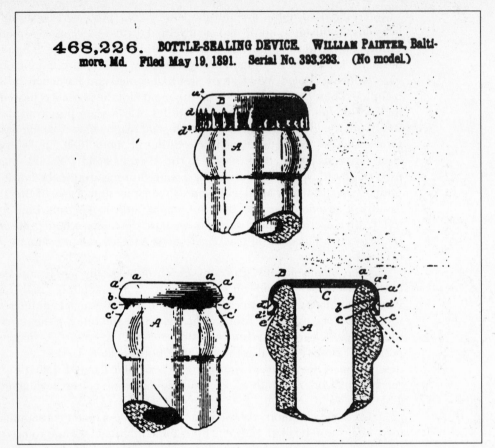

468,226. BOTTLE-SEALING DEVICE. WILLIAM PAINTER, Baltimore, Md. Filed May 19, 1891. Serial No. 393,293. (No model.)

Figure 4.3 *Patent information for common bottle cap, 1891.*

The manufacture and sale of commodities extends back thousands of years. British prehistorian V. Gordon Childe remarked how the presence of cylinder seals throughout ancient Mesopotamia and the Indus Valley provided the "earliest recorded instance of the transmission of manufactures over such vast distances." Many archaeologists think the Kulli "merchant venturers," early traveling salesmen, of the third millennium connected the Mesopotamians with the Harappans in the Indus Valley. The Kulli lived in Baluchistan, a region that now straddles western Pakistan and southeastern Iran.

Every community, however small, however self-sufficient, was connected to its neighbors, to entire regions, and to a much wider world, not only through kin ties, but by its need for both day-to-day commodities and more exotic, often valuable luxuries. Archaeologists study the material remains of human behavior, and use surviving artifacts as a way of studying such long-distance connections, whether commercial, political, or social. Historical sites offer an unusual potential for such research, because we can learn much about artifacts as commodities from both historical and archaeological sources.

Using Historical Records in Commodity Research

Historical records provide abundant information not only about the kinds of commodities that were available, but about the ways in which people selected them. Probate records, advertisements, catalogs, even storekeepers' inventory books are a mine of information about consumer preferences.

Probate records were often filed on someone's death. Typically, assessors went through the deceased person's home carefully inventorying and recording each object they saw. This provided an accurate list of objects to pass on to heirs or to prepare for an estate sale. Probate inventories can be extremely informative because they can help to identify objects found at archaeological sites. They also describe perishable household effects (such as books), which leave no durable archaeological signature. They can even provide information about objects that were never on-site at all, like, for example, cattle herds, farm implements, or carriages. In short, probate inventories tell us what objects surrounded a person immediately before his or her death. The probate list of James Edward Calhoun, of rural Abbeville County, South Carolina, makes the point.

James Edward Calhoun was the cousin of John C. Calhoun, the "Great Nullifier" and ardent defender of the South's slaveocracy. James Edward—world traveler, speaker of 17 languages, and young scholar—served as the astronomer with the Stephen A. Long expedition of 1823 as it traveled along the old fur trade routes of the Upper Midwest. Settling down on two cotton plantations in northwestern South Carolina—Midway and Millwood—Calhoun promised to become a full-fledged member of the South's antebellum slave-owning elite. However, when his young wife died in the epidemic of 1844 that ravaged the South Carolina backcountry, Calhoun gave up the life of the high-born southern gentleman. Calhoun soon became known as the "Hermit of Millwood," a gentleman widely known for his harmless eccentricities. On his death in 1889, assessors carefully inventoried Calhoun's personal property. Although Millwood Plantation, Calhoun's final home, was located in the South Carolina backwoods, Calhoun's probate list includes numerous objects that belie his seclusion: a pair of dueling pistols, three gold watches, a telescope, two surveying compasses, a Chinese clothes basket, a silver dog whistle, a silver tea service, $100 worth of Confederate war bonds, and the usual assortment of buttons, dishes, tools, rifles, and agricultural implements that one might expect to find in a Southern planter's home.

As an added bonus for historical archaeologists, an estate sale was held after the inventory. This additional list can be used to assess the relative value of the items Calhoun owned. The Chinese clothes basket sold for $1.55, the dog whistle for $5.00, and the gold watches for $22, $40, and $41. All told, Calhoun's estate sold for $1,644.27, not a paltry sum in rural South Carolina in 1890.

Because all of the fancy items that belonged to Calhoun were obviously cared for by him when he was alive (otherwise they could not be sold after his death), archaeologists excavating his homesite found little of extraordinary value. The archaeologists did learn, however, that Calhoun ate from dishes decorated with a blue pattern called "Italian Flower Garden," that he used a variety of patent medicines, and that he smoked a small pipe that had a face etched into it. All these items had obviously been discarded by Calhoun, did not appear in the probate inventory, and thus were unavailable for sale.

Our fast-moving twentieth-century world runs off advertising, off aggressive marketing. Inventive merchants devised the now-classic methods of modern advertising in the nineteenth century. A classic example is the Sears Roebuck Catalog. Back in the 1890s, Sears executives reasoned that if most American consumers could not make it to their store in Chicago, then they would take their store to their customers "through the agency of Uncle Sam's Mail." More than 700 crammed pages listed everything from clothing to cast iron pots, beds to broughams. "Nearly all our customers send cash in full. It's the best way," Sears said in an early catalog. "If you send too much money we will always refund the balance with the bill." And so they did, ushering in a revolution in American retailing. An excavator can use contemporary advertisements to develop some idea of what goods were available in different regions at various times and how advertisers attempted to interest consumers in their products. They tell us much about consumer attitudes, because, obviously, marketers wish to capitalize on widely held perceptions to sell their products. The selling of St. Jakob's Oel, a popular late-nineteenth-century patent medicine, provides an excellent example of nineteenth-century advertising techniques (Figure 4.4).

St. Jakob's Oel was first marketed in the 1880s by Charles A. Voegeler of Baltimore, Maryland, under the name of "Keller's Roman Liniment." Voegeler used a picture of Caesar to imply that his product had been used by the ancient Romans. He hoped that people would assume that what was good for the world-conquering Romans would be good for them as well. However, when the Roman motif did not sell, Voegeler changed the name of the product first to "St. Jacob's Oil" and then to "St. Jakob's Oel." He now marketed the oil as if it were made by German monks living in the Black Forest.

Advertisements in *The Chicago Tribune* show the way in which Voegeler shifted his medical ground. An advertisement dated January 1, 1880, states that St. Jakob's Oel cures "rheumatism, neuralgia, pains, soreness, stiffness, cuts, [and] sores." Three days later, advertisements claimed that the medicine cured "backache, toothache, headache, swellings, sprains, bruises, burns, [and] scalds." Two days subsequently, Voegeler added "chilblains, wounds, [and] corns" to the maladies cured by his remarkable elixir. We can only guess whether careful readers of the newspaper realized that St. Jakob's Oel was getting better by the day. Archaeology shows that Voegeler certainly sold his oil; witness the Illinois State University excavations at the Drake Farmstead in northern Illinois. The Drake family lived at the homestead from about 1838 to 1896. Over the years, they bought at least 51 bottles

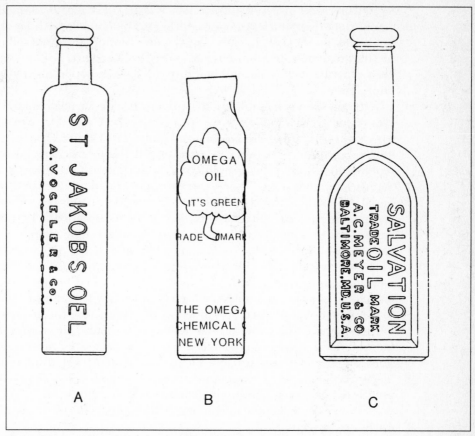

Figure 4.4 *Patent medicine bottles (B, C) found at the nineteenth-century Drake site in northern Illinois. A St. Jakob's Oel (A) bottle is on the left.*

of this "German" remedy. At the historically documented price of 50 cents a bottle, the Drake family spent over $25 on this one medicine, a not inconsiderable sum at the time!

Using Artifacts in Commodity Research

Apart from historical records, the artifacts themselves tell us much about their roles as commodities, not only from their labels or attributes, but also from their distributions within sites and over entire regions. Archaeologists have a unique ability to obtain an often clear picture of the kinds of material objects that were purchased by consumers over wide areas. Perhaps even more revealing, they can often discover things that were intended to be hidden from public view. John Cotter was surprised to find the left half of a male pelvis and the bones of the left leg and foot in a seventeenth-century well at colonial Jamestown. Was this evidence for an unsolved, or even undetected, murder of a person dismembered after death? Cotter was at a loss to explain why part of a human body lay in the well, for there were no signs of violence. These bones cannot be considered commodities, but they demonstrate how wells and other archaeological features can be used to hide elements of daily life, and how they can provide important, and often unique, information.

It may be possible to hide some things from your neighbors, but the prying eyes of the archaeologist can see into every corner of a site. When David Hurst Thomas excavated Spanish colonial and Native American sites on St. Catherine's Island, off the coast of Georgia, he discovered that the Franciscan missionaries there required their Indian charges to accept all the outward trappings of devout Christianity. They encouraged the Native Americans to adopt the Christian manner of burial—unmarked graves beneath the church floor, hands crossed over the chest, feet pointing toward the altar—yet they also compromised, letting them deposit grave goods with the deceased. Many of these artifacts were aboriginal—a shell gorget, several stone projectile points, and a "chunky" stone, perhaps used in a game. There were commodities like entire ceramic vessels, mirrors, and bronze religious medallions as well. The Church frowned on this practice, but the Native Americans had placed objects with their dead friends and family for centuries and they sought to continue doing so. A compromise was reached, so the Indians were able to follow their traditional custom, while following Christian burial rites. Interestingly, they did not do this at every mission site, for many graves, notably at Florida missions, are devoid of any artifacts. The precise reason for this difference eludes us, but it does point to an important reality of Spanish colonialism—the friars' approach to converting native populations was far from inflexible. Local priests apparently had some latitude in enforcing Church regulations, or else turned a blind eye to what was going on.

Archaeologists have traditionally studied the flow of commodities through large trade networks by calculating the distance that artifacts had to be transported to reach the site of their use and final deposition. Prehistorians sometimes use a "fall-off" model to study the transportation costs of prehistoric commodities. A fall-off model rests on the simple idea that the abundance of an object at an archaeological site decreases the farther away one gets from its source. In studying the distribution of imported obsidian among the prehistoric Mayas, archaeologist Raymond Sidrys found that during the Classic Period (A.D. 250–900) obsidian was transported in greater amounts to ceremonial centers than to smaller settlements, regardless of the distance to the natural sources. In the Postclassic Period (A.D. 1000–1450), however, obsidian was more widely distributed as the Mayas developed sea canoe routes of trade and built ports of call.

Historical archaeologists, by using company records, patent information, and other sources of information—in addition to direct information from artifacts themselves—are often able to establish exact manufacturing locales of artifacts found at archaeological sites and need not rely on fall-off models. From this information, they can develop ideas about the long-distance connections maintained by people who lived at today's archaeological sites.

Arkansas archaeologist Leslie Stewart-Abernathy discovered that people in the remote Ozarks maintained many connections with the outside world. He excavated the isolated Moser farm, occupied from about 1875 to 1919 and located in extreme northwestern Arkansas. But the cultural boundaries of this remote homestead extended "well beyond the fences of the farm." Moser yielded artifacts from all over the world. The farmers who once lived there ate from dishes made in Ohio and England, administered to their ailments with "Dr. King's New Discovery for Consumption" from Chicago and "Dr. Jayne's Expectorant" from Philadelphia, and canned the vegetables from their gardens in fruit jars that had zinc lids with white glass lid liners made in West Virginia and New York. Stewart-Abernathy's excavations show that the Ozarks, a region often assumed to be well out of the American mainstream, was as much a participant in the world's marketplace as anywhere else.

The presence of such exotic commodities at archaeological sites of recent date is easy to understand because the roots of our own economic lives were forged in the late nineteenth and early twentieth centuries. In fact, similar exotics come from historical sites all over the world, including many dating to the earliest period of European expansion after the fifteenth century. For example, in her long-term studies of historic St. Augustine, Florida, Kathleen Deagan has documented the wide range of goods available to colonial settlers. Spanish agents founded St. Augustine in 1565, and the town served as the headquarters for Spanish economic, military, and religious activities in eastern North America, "La Florida," until 1821. The main cultural ties of the citizens of St. Augustine were with Spain itself, but Deagan showed that the residents received goods from elsewhere as well. She found several kinds of Native American pottery from around Florida, red-painted wares from Mexican potters, redware ceramics possibly from Italian workshops, and porcelain from the Orient. Even at this early stage in the colonization of the Americas, even remote settlements on the very fringes of the Spanish empire used imported artifacts from several European nations and from Asia, as well as local wares.

ARTIFACTS AS IDEAS

One of the most interesting, yet difficult, aspects of understanding artifacts of any date is determining what they actually meant to the people who made and used them. It may be relatively easy for us today to envision how artifacts serve as historical documents—objects that tell us about the past—or as commodities—things bought and sold in the marketplaces of the past. But it is harder to understand that the meaning of artifacts may not be so obvious or straightforward. Many archaeologists now think of artifacts as "signs." A sign, as defined by the Italian semiotician Umberto Eco, is anything that "can be taken as significantly substituting for something else." Eco has become famous outside the narrow field of semiotics for his novels, especially *The Name of the Rose* and *Foucault's Pendulum*. Although Eco's books can be read simply as good stories, semioticians pore over them in search of much deeper symbolism reflected in the deeds and dialog of the main characters.

Signs are strongly associated with physical things, especially when objects are defined as bits of information that are intended to invoke an image. The Coca-Cola Company's famous red and white sign is an excellent example. On one level it simply advertises the soft drink product. On another, it has become synonymous with the United States in distant lands. In this sense, all artifacts can be seen, in the words of folklorist Henry Glassie, as "meaningful things."

Ideas underlay all physical things and give them meaning. Even our early human ancestors who lived at Olduvai Gorge, East Africa, put ideas into their simple stone choppers and flakes. Such artifacts were multipurpose tools, made to accomplish tasks related to survival, such as breaking bones during food preparation. Such functional interpretations are relatively straightforward to achieve, by replicating tool manufacture and studying telltale edgewear through microscopes. But what about such minor attributes as the decorative motifs on clay pots? Here you are moving from the functional to the stylistic, to the intangible. The first farmers along the Danube River etched spirals and meandering designs into their pottery during the Neolithic Period, but no one knows precisely what these designs are meant to represent. We have no documents to inform us.

The meaning of artifacts from the historic past can be somewhat easier to comprehend because of the role of most historical objects as commodities. Thus, we can assume that artifact designers produced artifacts that would become "objects of desire," things people wanted but did not necessarily need. The question that archaeologists, as well as modern advertisers and product manufacturers ask, however, is: What makes an artifact desired? Does an object's appearance, often meant to represent something else, make an object more desired? Another way to ask these questions is: Are there ideas behind artifacts that allow them to become expressions of something else?

Artifacts and Structuralism

Many archaeologists who study artifacts as ideas use a theory called "structuralism." Structuralism, a complex and hotly debated theory, has as one of its main interpretive goals the understanding of the basic, universal patterns that structure human ideas and, thereby, actions. The most fundamental universal pattern is binary opposition, an idea often postulated as basic to the production of meaning. Some of the opposites that material culture specialists have used in studying objects are bright/dull, modern/classical, expensive/cheap, handcrafted/mass-produced, and stylish/common. In exploring the role of binary opposites in structuring common Anglo-American material culture during the colonial period, James Deetz uses such categories as private/public, artificial/natural, and complex/simple (see Chapter 9). In terms of ceramics, Deetz proposes that a difference between individual and shared utensils represents the private/public opposite; blue and white pieces and brown, green, and yellow pieces represent the artificial/natural opposite; and multicolored and blue and white dishes represent the complex/simple binary opposite.

Deetz uses these binary opposites to shed light on the "oppositional structures that underlay American world view over three decades." Deetz's plan is not to perceive ceramics, or any other class of artifact, as historical documents—found in the ground instead of in an archive—or as a commodity, but rather as a way to delve into the mentality of people in the past. His foundation for such an approach stems from his belief that "Material culture is certainly more democratic than documents, and it is less sensitive to the subjectivity that every person brought, however unconsciously, to his or her accounting of peoples and events."

Another intriguing but different way of exploring artifacts as ideas was presented by material culture specialist Ann Smart Martin, in her study of pewter in colonial America. Archaeologists excavating eighteenth-century sites in the eastern United States typically find abundant evidence for the use of ceramic dishes, but usually find no pewter objects. However, pewter artifacts are commonly mentioned in probate inventories and other historical documents. Undoubtedly, the scarcity of pewter relative to ceramics in archaeological deposits may simply relate to physics: ceramics break and are discarded, pewter dents but does not break and is kept. Although this simple reality is no doubt true, Martin seeks a deeper understanding of the relationship between pewter and ceramic dishes at colonial sites. She argues that the meaning of the different proportions of ceramics and pewter may relate to simple consumer preference for ceramics over pewter or to a deeper meaning in which pewter was "of conservative stability and wealth" in a rapidly changing society. Martin proposes, then, that the difference between the presence of pewter (traditional objects) and ceramics (modern objects) was not based on physical differences alone, but on a subtle idea of social standing. Pewter and ceramics were chosen by people because of the ideas behind each.

In another study, archaeologist Paul Shackel describes how many of the mundane objects of daily life provide unique insights both about artifact meaning and how artifacts present and encapsulate ideas. Shackel uses a combination of historical and archaeological information to show how one common object, the toothbrush, can be immensely important in helping archaeologists to understand past ideas. Archaeologists typically give toothbrushes little thought, and quickly assign a functional meaning to them when found: People used toothbrushes for dental hygiene. Using historical records, however, Shackel shows how the placement of toothbrush bristles was related to larger concerns of social order and discipline in society (Figure 4.5).

Toothbrushes were invented by the Chinese, but travelers did not bring them to the West until 1498. Before synthetics, European toothbrush makers used boar hair bristles from Poland, Russia, China, Japan, and Tibet. Shackel proposes that the change in bristle placement on the toothbrush—from widely haphazard to neatly structured in rows—reflects a deeper idea of increased order, both in society at large and in the workplace. He believes that the increased regularity of bristle placement reflects more than a simple technological breakthrough. He believes that an *idea* of orderliness began to permeate society to such an extent that people *expected* orderliness in all elements of society, even in their toothbrushes. Shackel sees in the neat rows of bristle holes in the common everyday toothbrush a sign of the increased importance of personal discipline in Western society. In short, the toothbrush symbolizes the idea of discipline and order.

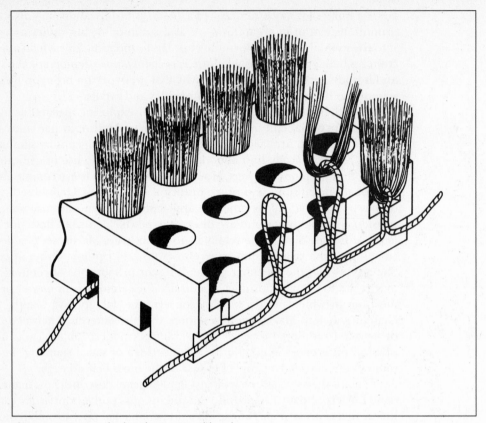

Figure 4.5 *Putting the bristles in a toothbrush.*

Critical Archaeology

By no means do all archaeologists agree that accurate meanings reflecting past ideas can be discerned from artifacts. One school of thought believes that all of our perceptions and perspectives about both the past and present are filtered through our own life experiences and education. They argue that because no one can ever really "know" the past, most of what we say about it actually derives from our own times. We construct a past that is meaningful to us.

"Critical archaeologists" of this school argue that no matter how much we may wish to understand the past, we can never truly know it. This point was made as long ago as 1926 by American historian Carl Becker in a paper before the American Historical Association when he said that "the historical fact is in someone's mind or it is nowhere." Critical archaeologists seem to have a particularly strong case when it comes to providing meaning to artifacts from prehistoric times. How can anyone alive today know the ideas that a prehistoric potter along the banks of the Danube River in southeastern Europe put into her pots? Clearly, ideas about the meaning of the designs on the pots come from someplace, and that place is typically the "here and now" of the archaeologist. In contrast, historical archaeologists can rely on numerous pieces of well-documented information to study the meaning of artifacts in the past. Contemporary writings do much to help us "get inside people's heads" and to see the world somewhat as the writers saw it in their time.

Having introduced some of the ways that historical archaeologists think about their data, we must now turn to the critical issue of archaeological context, which anchors all artifacts and other archaeological finds in dimensions of time and space.

CHAPTER
5

Time and Space

"Time is central to archaeology"

Michael Shanks and Christopher Tilley, 1987

"It has slowly emerged that there is archaeological information in the spatial relationships between things as well as in things themselves"

David L. Clarke, 1977

In Chapter 4 we explored ways in which historical archaeologists use artifacts as documents. In doing so, we touched on the dimension of time in archaeology. We must now explore archaeological context—the contexts of time and space—more closely.

TIME

We are obsessed with time—with its passage, with using it productively, with the evils of "wasting" time, to mention only a few concerns. Not that this passion with measuring and using time is particularly ancient. For thousands of years people measured the passage of time by the rising and setting of the sun and organized their lives accordingly. The first public clock is said to have been built in Milan, Italy, in 1335, but it was not until about 1500 that Peter Henlein, a German locksmith, made the first spring-wound, portable clock. His invention ultimately made it possible for us to carry time around with us on our wrists and in our pockets. We take time zones for granted, but they were not invented until 1883 to satisfy railroad companies in the United States, who were concerned about standardizing their schedules. To this day, Amtrak trains remain stationary for an hour at 2:00 A.M., wherever they are, when we change to Summer Time and back, so that they arrive at their next station on time.

Unlike many societies, we Westerners have always thought of time in linear terms, extended back far into the past, these days back over more than 2.5 million years of human existence. In contrast, many Native American groups and African societies conceive of time in cyclical terms, as an endlessly repeating passage of seasons, years, and longer periods of time. The Aztecs of central Mexico measured time in great 52-year cycles, and Pueblo Indians in the Southwest used the movements of heavenly bodies to mark the passing of seasons of planting and harvest. Our linear view of time lies behind all archaeological research.

Archaeology is like history, a chronicle of the passage of time through centuries and millennia. The celebrated Roman orator Marcus Cicero put it well when he wrote that "History is the witness that testifies to the passing of time; it illuminates reality, vitalizes memory, provides guidance in daily life, and brings us tidings of antiquity." We people the landscape of history with cultural developments and events that act as signposts to the passage of time. Excavations in East Africa tell us that ancestral humans roamed the tropical savanna more than two million years ago. A combination of archaeological and historical sources set the unification of Egypt and the beginnings of ancient Egyptian civilization at about 2,900 B.C. More recent events are accurate to the day. Columbus landed on the island of San Salvador on October 12, 1492. On April 9, 1865, General Robert E. Lee walked up the steps of the stately Appomattox Courthouse in Virginia and surrendered, to end the deadliest war ever fought on United States soil.

The more recent the event, the more accurate its recorded date. For instance, the exact time of every space shuttle launch in Florida is chronicled to the second. Columbus' movements in the Indies are known to within the day, sometimes to the time of day. Roman history is accurate, for the most part to within a year or a decade, and the reigns of the ancient Egyptian pharaohs are accurate within a quarter century or so. At least rudimentary documents go back some 5,000 years in the Near East, not nearly so far in the Americas. Earlier than that, prehistoric archaeology measures cultural developments in centuries, more often millennia. For generations, prehistoric archaeologists have been obsessed with dating ancient sites and societies in calendar years. Their historical colleagues have the same passion, but their time scales are much shorter, and illuminated by documents and artifacts of known age that can sometimes fix even unimportant events remarkably accurately. Historical archaeologists satisfy their obsession with time by using four dating techniques—relative dating, objects of known age, formula dating, and dendrochronology.

Relative Dating

All objects in the world have a different time relationship with every other object. Even today's rapidly mass-produced objects—bottles being filled with catsup on a mechanized assembly line, for instance—individually can be said to have a different "date." These dates may only differ by seconds, but they are different nonetheless. We may not be aware of the difference in time between the individual bottles, but we would certainly notice it once the bottles were filled, capped, and boxed for shipment. The boxes of bottles would be stacked up in the warehouse, awaiting shipment. Simple common sense would tell you that the bottom boxes were placed in position earlier than the ones on the top of the pile. Presumably, they came off the assembly line earlier, too.

Suppose you are walking down a street in such bad condition that pothole after pothole gapes through the tarmac, exposing all four layers of the long-established highway. The top layer is a new, brilliantly black, smooth surface. Beneath this lies the gray surface of the old, worn blacktop, below that a layer of red paving bricks. A layer of grayish-white gravel forms the base. Obviously, the current surface is more recent in date than the paving bricks, but you cannot date either layer in years. You can only say that the uppermost surface is *relatively more recent* than the brick paving.

These kinds of relative time differences are what archaeologists call "relative chronology," relationships between stratified layers. Relative chronology is based on a classic geological principle, known as the *Law of Superposition.* This law holds that, under normal circumstances, deeper layers of soil, sediment, or rock are older than those above them. Thus, relative chronology comes from *stratigraphy,* the sequences of layered, or stratified, deposits. Like geological exposures, archaeological sites usually contain stratified layers, some of them the result of human activity, like house building, others from natural phenomena like rain and wind.

The archaeological record comes down to us in many forms, but almost invariably, it is buried below later strata, layers that have accumulated, usually through natural geological processes over centuries or millennia, but often from human activity. Archaeologist Michael Schiffer refers to these as "formation processes" because they work together to "make" archaeological sites—and relative chronology.

Nature exercises a powerful effect on every archaeological site. Each time you walk through a suburban neighborhood, take a close look at a neglected backyard, where nature is slowly taking over. After a few months, unkempt grass slowly creeps over the edges of the sidewalk and front path in an effort to reclaim them. Eventually the grass, and a thin layer of soil, will cover the concrete, causing them to disappear entirely from view. This is exactly what happens to archaeological sites of all kinds. Strong winds blow fine sand over collapsed mudbrick dwellings. A torrential thunderstorm overflows a nearby creek; soft mud flows over nearby houses and buries them in minutes. One famous example: on August 25, A.D. 79, an erupting Mount Vesuvius deposited several feet of fine ash over the nearby Roman towns of Herculaneum and Pompeii in Italy. Dramatic excavations have chronicled the last moments of Herculaneum. The sudden eruption trapped hundreds of people as they fled the clogging ash. Families jostled their neighbors to reach the harbor and the safety of the boats moored there. Dozens of sprawling skeletons wear their finest jewelry—rings with precious stones, golden bracelets, and multicolored glass beads. In this case, a natural disaster left a priceless historical legacy behind it.

Human activity can be a powerful and destructive agent. Twentieth-century cities like London, York, Bremen, and Annapolis have undergone massive development in recent years. Such large-scale construction projects slice deep into underlying strata, creating havoc with the remains of earlier structures on the same site. Gaping foundation trenches often reveal layer on layer of earlier occupation, shoveled away in the haste of urban renewal.

The Elizabethan Rose Theatre came to light in the foundations of a new high-rise office building on the south bank of the Thames River in central London in 1989. Here William Shakespeare's *Henry VI* received its first public performance, in a modest, circular theater known only from distant views. Public outcry greeted the news that the remaining wooden foundations were to be bulldozed away. Teams of archaeologists worked day and night to record details of the theater before the remains were covered over, to be reexcavated for display once the building was completed. If ever they are displayed in the basement of the modern office complex, they will offer a dramatic example of superposition and relative chronology.

Relative chronologies in archaeology derive from the close study of human occupation layers. The famous Koster prehistoric site in south-central Illinois reflects more than 9,000 years of human activity. Koster contains no less than 12 separate layers of past occupation, dating from modern times to about 7,000 B.C. and extending to a depth of 34 feet (10.4 m). The Koster Site provides a perfect example of how the Law of Superposition works in archaeology. Simply because of the superposition of the various occupation layers, the Koster archaeologists knew that the sixth living floor, located about 7 feet (2.1 m) below ground, was more recent than the eleventh living surface, located almost 30 feet (9.1 m) down—even before they found any artifacts.

Although Koster is dwarfed by some Near Eastern city mounds like Jericho or Ur, its stratified layers cover a much longer period, and extend to a greater depth, than most historic sites. When Colonial Williamsburg archaeologist Ivor Noël Hume excavated Martin's Hundred, the lost seventeenth-century settlement associated with Jamestown, he found the remains of the town almost directly beneath the present ground surface. Only three and a half centuries have passed since Martin's Hundred was abandoned, time for little more than a few inches of soil to accumulate over the remains of the settlement. Koster's stratigraphy was well defined, the occupation layers separated by natural levels accumulated during periods of abandonment that sometimes lasted many centuries. In contrast, Martin's Hundred has minute stratigraphy, requiring meticulous recording and observation of a relative chronology that concerns not only the date of the site as a whole, but also of the individual buildings within it. Such thin layers require very meticulous observation, so much so that people call the process *microstratigraphy*.

The Martin's Hundred archaeologists found microstratigraphy inside the remains of a subterranean, "cellar" dwelling. This house had a steeply pitched, A-frame style roof supported by large, upright, interior posts. During the life of the dwelling, its inhabitants deposited a thin layer of gray clay on the floor. Subsequent to its abandonment, clay and earth washed into the building, creating about 4 feet (1.2 m) of fingering soil layers. Isolating the artifacts in each of these inconspicuous lenses took many months, but they contained artifacts of known age that provided a chronology for the dwelling.

Dating with Objects of Known Age

Historical archaeologists are lucky, for they excavate sites where objects of known age can provide accurate calendar dates for buildings, graves, stratified layers, and other features. As we saw in Chapter 4, such items include humble artifacts like dated coins, domestic table wares, even lead seals bearing telltale manufacturers' marks.

Ivor Noël Hume's Martin's Hundred excavation provides a superb example of such dating, using not the objects themselves, but depictions of them, as chronological markers. After carefully digging through the silted clay that had washed into the foundation of the abandoned A-frame house, the excavators reached the building's original floor. It appeared as a thin, even layer of gray clay (Figure 5.1). The artifacts within it included tiny pieces of blue and white fireplace or wall tile, probably imported from the Netherlands, known to date after the 1630s. Similar examples are depicted in a painting by Pieter de Hooch of 1660. Another painting,

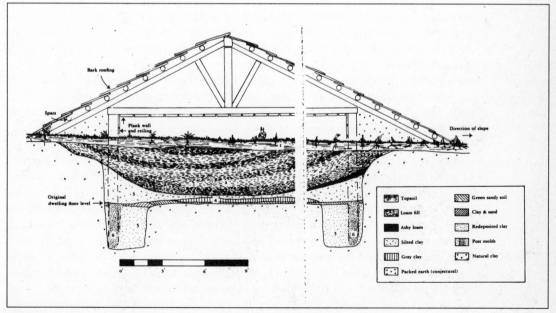

Figure 5.1 *Seventeenth-century A-frame house at Martin's Hundred, Virginia.*

made by Dutch artist Jan Olis in 1644, shows a pair of fireplace tongs exactly like those also found on the floor of the A-frame house. Other objects—such as a green-and-yellow-glazed pot intended for kitchen use—can be seen in paintings from the mid-1660s. Noël Hume used these finds to assign the occupation to the early part of the seventeenth century.

Another dating problem resolved with objects of known age arose at Millwood Plantation, a nineteenth- and early-twentieth-century cotton plantation in the South Carolina upcountry. Twenty-one stone building foundations could still be seen among the trees and underbrush that had grown up at the site since its abandonment in the 1920s. Census rolls, court records, and personal papers written by the historic plantation's owner established the occupation dates for all these buildings from 1832 until about 1925. Charles Orser excavated the foundations in an attempt to date them more closely with artifacts.

One foundation was a roughly rectangular pile of red bricks and granite stones set in the middle of a larger depression. The latter appeared to represent the former wall line of a building, with the rubble pile being what was left of a central chimney. When the crew excavated the rubble, they discovered that it was indeed a stone chimney support that had been faced with brick. Because the floor of the cabin was probably raised off the ground, the brick facing must have been visible under the house. Orser decided to excavate inside the brick-lined support in an attempt to establish the construction date. The building could have dated to the plantation's slave period (1832–1865) or to its postwar era (1865–1925). The archaeologists found three layers of stones inside the chimney support used to reinforce and strengthen the foundation. A layer of loose, small cobbles appeared first, followed by a slightly thinner layer of small pebbles mixed with red clay. On the bottom was a layer of large, tightly packed stones. But when did the builders construct the support? A Seated Liberty quarter dollar, dated 1876, was found lodged in a space in the deepest stone layer (Figure 5.2). Because the two stone layers above it were tightly sealed, it was impossible for this coin to have fallen into the support after it was constructed. The coin was either lost or purposely placed among the stones sometime after 1876, during the construction of the chimney support. Orser could not tell exactly when the support—and the building—were built, but it was clear that it was constructed sometime between 1876 (the date of the coin) and 1925 (the date of the site's abandonment).

The use of artifacts to date sites, features, and soil layers at Martin's Hundred and Millwood Plantation involved only one or two key artifacts. More often, the use of artifacts to refine relative chronologies embraces several soil layers and possibly hundreds of artifacts, making the dating problem far more complex.

When they excavated part of a city block in Sacramento, California, archaeologists Mary and Adrian Praetzellis used the artifacts they found to construct a chronology for the block. As is true of most urban settings, a mix of people had lived and worked on the excavated lots. The Praetzellises could identify four individual households from historical records: the Reeber family of German bakers; an unknown Gold Rush–era trader; James Meeker, a carriage lumber merchant; and the Goepel family from Germany. The Praetzellises assumed that each family contributed to the artifacts they discovered in the block, creating a complex stratigraphic puzzle.

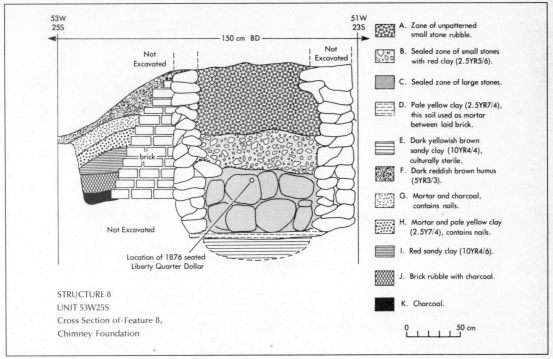

Figure 5.2 *Position of 1876 quarter at building support, Millwood Plantation, South Carolina.*

In an excavation 18 feet long and 3 feet wide (5.5 by 0.9 m) called Trench 3 West, the Praetzellises found at least 11 different soil layers (Figure 5.3). They were able to date many of them by using the associated artifacts. They dated the deepest layer (038) at about 1852, based on the 18 coins they found there. Some of the coins were earlier—a tenpence, Irish coin, dated 1806; a five lire, Italian coin dated 1811; an Indian rupee, dated 1840—but, for obvious reasons, they dated the layer on the basis of the *latest* coin—an 1852 ten-dollar gold piece issued in San Francisco. They dated the next highest soil layer (032) to the late 1850s, based on a bottle of "Mrs. Winslow's Soothing Syrup." This elixir, intended to calm the patient, was bottled in New York City, beginning in 1849. The Praetzellises dated a small soil lens (027) above layer 032 to about 1862, based on the "Davenport" registry mark (see Chapter 4) of November 14, 1856 they found on the bottom of a white saucer. In the case of both layers 027 and 032, the Praetzellises made the assumption that it would take a few years for the artifacts to reach Sacramento. The next soil layer (024) they assigned to 1861–1863. They made this interpretation based on the dates of the glass and ceramics within it. However, the presence of a wine or whiskey bottle marked "ELLENVILLE GLASS WORKS," only made between 1866 and the 1880s, indicated that people continued to toss broken or unwanted objects here until the late 1860s. A thin transition zone (023) and the soil layer above it (016) they dated to the 1863–1868 period, using the embossed "Corn and Oats" pattern that they found on pieces of white ceramics. This pattern was produced by the famous Wedgwood factory in England in the mid-1860s. In addition, these

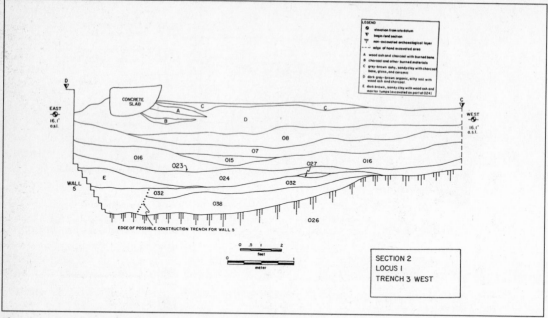

Figure 5.3 *Soil layers in Trench 3, Sacramento, California.*

pieces carried a registry mark of October 31, 1863. They dated the soil lens directly above the last layer (015) to 1868, using the same "Corn and Oats" ceramics. The next soil layer (07) they dated to about 1875, based on a small piece of a brown bottle marked "Dickey Chemist." This bottle originated in San Francisco and dates to the 1873–1920 period. The soil layers above layer 07 consisted of urban debris and artifacts dating from the mid-1870s to the present.

Formula Dating

Many historical archaeologist have turned to formula dating to help them date artifact collections. Formula dating works on the notion that historic artifacts change over time and that these changes, no matter how imperceptible they may be, are sometimes amenable to measurement in years, and can be represented in a mathematical formula. The case of the common white clay smoking pipe shows how formula dating came about, and illustrates how it is used.

The clay smoking pipe was in the past what the disposable razor is today— used for a few days or weeks, then thrown away. They date roughly from the mid-sixteenth century to the early twentieth century. Historical archaeologists excavating colonial sites usually find hundreds of pieces of white clay smoking pipes on their sites. For example, excavations at Fort Michilimackinac, Michigan, yielded no fewer than 5,328 pipe fragments from between 1959 and 1966 alone.

A clay smoking pipe consists of two parts: a bowl and a stem (Figure 5.4). Fortunately for historical archaeologists, the bowls of these white, long-stemmed pipes were altered over the decades, beginning with the late 1500s. Pipe experts have charted these changes, showing the years in which each style was popular. In the

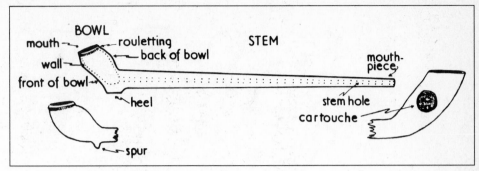

Figure 5.4 *Parts of a clay smoking pipe.*

sixteenth century, the bowls were usually undecorated and simple. They were made with a sharp angle to the pipe stem. With time, the sides of the bowls were straightened and the angle with the stem made smoother. By the early eighteenth century, the bowls were very straight and smooth. Also in the early eighteenth century, pipe makers began to put intricate symbols and decorations on the bowls. By the late eighteenth century, even the short-stemmed pipe was becoming popular. These pipes were smoked by inserting a reed or stem into the bowl, which was short and stubby (Figure 5.5).

Fortunately for the archaeologist, the fine, white clay pipe was fragile and easily smashed into small fragments when tapped to remove the old tobacco plug. Typically, the bowl may break into two or three pieces, but the stems generally fracture into several sections measuring about 1 inch (2.5 cm) long. A broken pipe usually produced more pieces of stem than of bowl. For example, of the pipes found at Fort Michilimackinac between 1959 and 1966, fully 4,347, or almost 82 percent, were pipe stems. An enormous literature surrounds clay pipe bowls, which can be dated with considerable precision. But what about the more common stems?

On the face of it, pipe stems are hardly promising dating material. Back in the 1950s, pioneer historical archaeologist J. C. Harrington, in a monumental display of patience, examined more than 50,000 pipe stems he had excavated at Jamestown, Virginia. He noticed that the size of the hole, or bore, appeared to get smaller through time. Harrington concluded that "if this represented a definite and consistent trend, then it might possibly be useful as a dating criterion." Then he measured 330 stems from colonial sites in Virginia. Between 1620 and 1650, most of the bores measured $8/_{64}$ ths of an inch (31.7 mm) across, whereas between 1750 and 1800, they were only $4/_{64}$ ths of an inch (15.9 mm) (Figure 5.6). Here, then, was potential for dating clay pipe fragments on a much larger scale.

Seven years later, in 1961, Lewis Binford made the first strides in what is now called formula dating. He believed that Harrington's observations could be converted into what mathematicians call a regression formula. A regression formula is a mathematical way of representing the relationship between two variables, in this case, bore diameter and date. With bore diameter plotted on the Y axis of a graph and date on the X axis, the regression formula will show the precise relationship

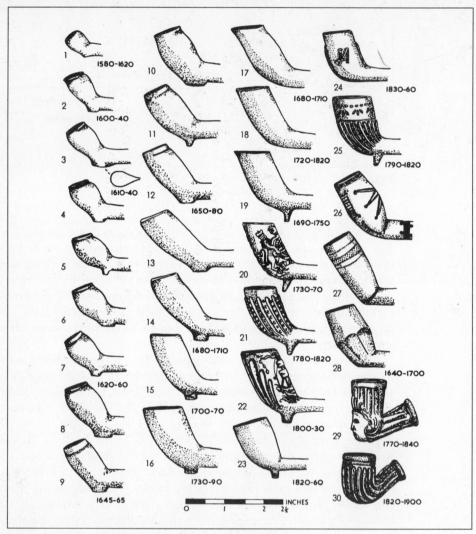

Figure 5.5 *The evolution of the pipe bowl 1580–1900.*

between the two. According to Binford, the formula $Y = 1931.85 - 38.26X$ could be used to date collections of broken pipe stems, with Y being the mean date to be calculated, 1931.85 being the statistical date that pipe stem bores would theoretically disappear (!), and 38.26 being the number of years that it took for a pipe stem bore to be reduced by $1/64$ of an inch (1.6 mm). Using this formula, an archaeologist could determine the date of any pipe stem by the diameter of its bore. Binford used 64ths of an inch as his measurement because Harrington had originally measured the pipe stem bores with the only tools he could think of that were available in various, accurate sizes: a set of drill bits. These drill bits happened to be made in com-

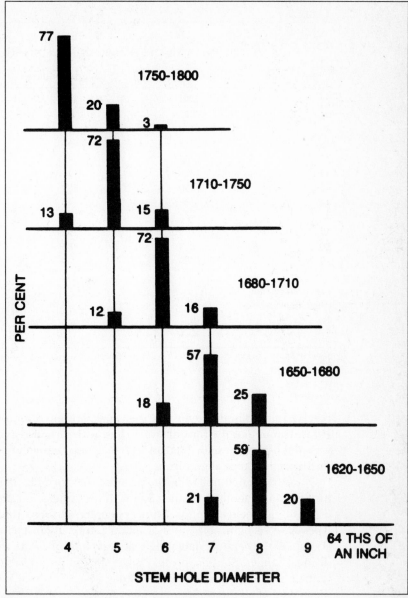

Figure 5.6 *Harrington's pipe stem measurements.*

mon 64th of an inch sizes. The "X" is calculated by multiplying the number of pipe stems by the number of 64ths of an inch in their measurement (7 stems measuring $^6/_{64}$ = 42; 35 stems measuring $^7/_{64}$ = 245), and then adding the products together and dividing by the total number of pipe stems.

Many archaeologists were enthusiastic about Binford's idea, so they began to experiment with his formula. Robert Heighton and Kathleen Deagan discovered that the regression line was not straight, but curved. They reasoned that bores

TABLE 5.1

CALCULATING A MEAN CERAMIC DATE USING SOUTH'S METHOD

Ceramic type	Type median (X_i)	Sherd count (f_i)	Product
22	1791	483	865,053
33	1767	25	44,175
34	1760	32	56,320
36	1755	55	96,525
37	1733	40	69,320
43	1758	327	574,866
49	(1750)	583	1,020,250
44	1738	40	69,520
47	1748	28	48,944
53, 54	1733	52	90,116
56	1733	286	495,638
29	1760	9	15,840
		1960	3,446,567 ÷ 1960 = 1758.4

The mean ceramic date formula

$$Y = \frac{\sum_{i=1}^{n} x_i \cdot f_i}{\sum_{i=1}^{n} f_i} \qquad Y = \frac{3,446.567}{1960} = 1758.4$$

Source: Stanley South, Method and Theory in Historical Archaeology *(New York: Academic Press, 1977), p. 220.*

reach a minimum diameter and then stay constant after about A.D. 1800. Ivor Noël Hume found that the formula works best with samples of more than 900 stems that were deposited between 1680 and 1760. These refinements have strengthened Binford's original pipe stem formula.

Perhaps encouraged by the promise that formula dating appeared to hold for historical archaeology, Stanley South devised mean ceramic dating, a formula for use with eighteenth-century British ceramics. He reasoned that if English ceramic types have recognizable dates of manufacture, then it should be relatively easy to add up all the ceramic date ranges at a site and calculate the midpoint of all the individual ranges. South's formula is easy to compute (Table 5.1), and it has the advantage of yielding an actual calendar year. The year calculated represents the mean date of all the ceramics in the sample.

South's mean ceramic dating formula has found a far wider audience than the pipe stem dating formula, but only because potsherds of all kinds are more common finds. Where its results have been tested against historically documented occupations, the mean ceramic dates have been generally consistent. It should work just as well at historic sites of unknown date.

All formula dates should be checked against other dates—preferably documentary ones. Obviously, if we are excavating a site with a historically documented date range of 1690 to 1740 and the ceramic formula yields a date of 1770, something is amiss. Either you have misidentified the ceramics, or the historical sources are wrong or incomplete. Sometimes the mean ceramic date can provide unexpected information. Archaeologists from the University of Delaware who studied the Williams Site in Glasgow, Delaware, found that their ceramic collection yielded a mean date much earlier than they expected. Legal records dated the mean historic date of the site to 1887. Its occupant was an African-American farm laborer named Sidney Stump. However, the mean ceramic date they obtained from South's formula was 40 years earlier, 1844. How can one explain such a discrepancy? One possible answer is that Stump used second-hand or hand-me-down ceramics. Since he was a farm laborer for the entire time he lived at the Williams Site, this interpretation is not unreasonable.

Formula dating methods provide one more line of evidence that can be evaluated against others when attempting to date historic sites.

Dendrochronology

Dendrochronology, or tree-ring dating, was invented in 1904 in the American Southwest by astronomer A. E. Douglass, who was interested in ancient sun spot activity. He soon extended it to the ancient beams preserved in prehistoric pueblos, providing his archaeological colleagues with an elegant and extremely accurate dating method.

Trees grow seasonally, especially in environments with well-defined wet and dry seasons. Their seasonal growth varies from year to year, largely as result of differing rainfall patterns and number of frost-free days, leaving distinctive, concentric growth rings in the trunk. Dendrochronologists take sequences of growth rings from ancient logs and match them by computer with a master tree-ring sequence for a major region like the Southwest. Such master sequences are based on ring counts from living trees, providing an extremely accurate chronology that extends back more than 8,000 years in the Southwest. Even a small log from an ancient pueblo can be matched with the master curve.

Tree-rings are used both to calibrate radiocarbon dates, and also to date isolated wood fragments, such as roof beams in archaeological sites. In Europe, experts have linked living trees to church beams and farmhouse timbers, to ancient logs found in bogs, providing an oak-based archaeological tree-ring chronology that goes back to before 5,200 B.C. in Ireland, and almost as far in Germany.

Unlike radiocarbon dating, dendrochronology is of great potential in historical archaeology. For example, it was recently used to date the historic Pueblo de Acoma, the famous "Sky City," in New Mexico. The Spanish first visited the pueblo in 1540 during the Coronado expedition to the Southwest, which sought the legendary, gold-laden Seven Lost Cities of Cibola. In 1599, they destroyed Acoma as part of their effort to control the pueblo peoples in the region, but the residents soon rebuilt it. Modern Acoma is a tapestry of building and rebuilding going back many centuries. In 1987, the people of Acoma invited the Laboratory of Tree-Ring Dating at the University of Arizona to date the oldest part of the village. They planned to restore the rooms of the old pueblo, and wanted to be certain of their construction dates. The Laboratory took core samples from well-preserved beams that enabled them to date 50 rooms to the year. They found that the seventeenth-century pueblo was begun in 1646, and had achieved its current form by 1652. In 1934, the Historic American Buildings Survey (see Chapter 7) had completed an accurate architectural drawing of the pueblo. When the archaeologists compared the buildings on this detailed map with their tree-ring dates, they were surprised to learn that the pueblo had changed little between 1652 and 1934, a span of 282 years.

Dendrochronology cannot be applied everywhere, but in cases where master tree-ring sequences exist and wood is well preserved, it has few rivals as an accurate historical dating method.

SPACE

Space in archaeological terms refers to the precise location of any find, site, or structure in latitude, longitude, and depth measurement. Taken together, these measures locate any point in space absolutely and uniquely.

Another way to think about archaeological space is to think of the word "position." Position can be a key element in understanding how things were related in the past. For instance, Sherlock Holmes solved many of his most challenging mysteries by his careful understanding of where things were located in relation to one another. In "The Adventure of the Priory School," he confronts the disappearance of Lord Saltire, the 10-year-old son and heir of the Duke of Holdernesse. The young lord had disappeared one night, along with Heidegger, the German master. To solve this baffling mystery—which the police had characteristically abandoned with their despairing hands in the air—Holmes draws a sketch of the landscape. Using this map, he is able to reconstruct the route taken by the abductors, is led to the body of Heidegger, and deduces—from the bicycle tracks, also on the map—that young Saltire is being held at the Fighting Cock Inn, on the top of the map near Holdernesse Hall!

Archaeologists are not scientific versions of the fictional Sherlock Holmes, but his methods are instructive. Like the historical archaeologist, he had an intense interest in where things were located. Holmes could have been an archaeologist when he said to Watson, "I want you to realize those geographical features which may have a good deal to do with our investigation." Archaeologists refer to the analysis of location—from the placement of artifacts at a site to the placement of the features on a landscape—as *spatial analysis.*

Spatial analysis proceeds on many levels. Information about the past can be collected from the spatial associations of artifacts found at a site. The relationships of the sites themselves can yield valuable cultural and historical information. Also, the placement of sites in relation to natural resources—fertile soils, stands of good timber for house construction, streams and rivers that run cold and clear the year around—provide abundant information about what natural features people

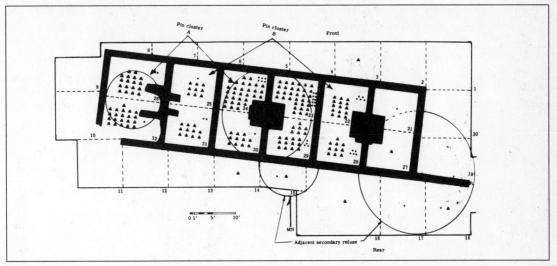

Figure 5.7 *Plan of the Public House and Taylor Shop show the location of pins and beads.*

sought. Then there is the placement of sites in relation to objects of human construction—mills, bridges, roads. In the flat, fertile prairies and plains of North America, the railroads were an important, and indeed central, determinant of settlement. For example, on the plains of Saskatchewan, the Canadian Pacific Railroad gobbled up the best land and then convinced immigrants to settle on it. Author James Minifie recalls the irresistible pull this land had on his father in 1909: "The last, best West was filling up fast; my father determined to get in while he could. He closed down his business and decided to go as far west as his money would take him. . . ." Historical maps of Saskatchewan show the network of railroads in the southern half of this province with the settlements appearing as beads on a necklace, strung out along the rail lines.

The scale, or level, of a spatial analysis is determined by the research questions being studied. The transportation of commodities from one place to another is essentially a problem in spatial analysis, with a varied scale that can even extend to entire continents. When British archaeologist Peter Danks studied the distribution of late eighteenth-century ceramics made by the Lowestoft factory on the east England coast, his region of interest was all the British Isles. He had no written records and no surviving pattern books, so he had to rely strictly on artifacts to establish the spatial distribution of the Lowestoft wares. In contrast, most settlement analysis is on a far smaller scale. When Stanley South became interested in the spatial placement of pins and beads at the eighteenth-century Public House and Tailor Shop in Brunswick Town, North Carolina, he focused only on this one 3,600 square feet (324 sq m) building. He found almost all the beads and pins in five of the six rooms (Figure 5.7). Apparently, they had fallen through the cracks in the floorboards during the building's use. The unequal distribution of beads and pins led

Artist's reconstruction of the Public House and Taylor Shop, Brunswick Town, North Carolina, as it may have looked in the early eighteenth century.

South to conclude that "Room 6 must have been used for merchandising the objects sewn together in the five other rooms."

Whether an entire world system within which commodities move, which takes into its sweep whole continents and great distances, or an individual site, the concepts of spatial analysis are the same, beginning with the site and ending with an entire settlement system.

Space at Archaeological Sites

The study of space is based on another fundamental principle of archaeology, the *Law of Association*. This is the principle that an artifact or other find is contemporary with the other objects found in the same soil layer in which it is found.

We mentioned above how Mary and Adrian Praetzellis dated the different soil layers in one city block in Sacramento, California, using one or two datable artifacts. Using the Law of Association, we would say that all of the finds within the layers were contemporaneous with the datable artifacts. Burials and their associated grave goods are an excellent example of the Law of Association, for an interment is a single event, which took place at a particular moment in time. We can be certain that all the artifacts deposited with the deceased were used in the society at the time of death.

In the early 1970s, cultural anthropologist Jerome Handler and archaeologist Frederick Lange excavated the remains of several seventeenth-century slaves from Newton Plantation, Barbados. They discovered that some of the individuals had been interred in the same pit. Thus, they could rightly conclude that all of the artifacts found with these burials—glass bottles, clay smoking pipes, buttons, red ceramics—were all used together when these individuals were alive.

Beyond such simple contexts as burials and individual soil layers, the Law of Association permits archaeologists to perceive the sites they routinely study (see Chapter 1) as being situated within a spatial hierarchy. The hierarchy extends from small spaces to very large ones. The idea behind these levels of analysis is that people use space in patterned, regular ways, because the use of space is culturally determined. We can discern something of the patterns of spatial use in a culture by the careful analysis of artifacts, features, and whole sites.

The hierarchy of spatial analysis in archaeology extends from the activity area to entire communities.

Activity Areas

The smallest spatial unit studied by archaeologists is the activity area. These areas are places within a site where people conducted a specific activity. They usually can be identified by the clusters of artifacts they contain. Typically, these artifacts indicate the range of past activities carried out there. For example, at an aboriginal site, the presence of a pile of stone debris may indicate the place where stone tools were manufactured.

As part of her investigation into the archaeology of activity areas, prehistorian Susan Kent decided to examine a number of site locations in the American Southwest. During her fieldwork, she identified five archaeological sites associated with the Navajo. One site she examined had an occupation date of from about 1890 to around 1930. She found coffee can lids, pieces of a porcelain doll, glass bottle fragments, sheep and cow bones, and a 1927 New Mexico automobile license plate scattered across the site. She could identify several activity areas (Figure 5.8). Some were related to chipping wood, others were ash areas where people had once built fires. The presence of at least three traditional Navajo dwellings, or hogans, suggested to Kent that three related families, perhaps members of the same extended family, had created the activity areas at the site through their daily actions.

Historical archaeologists often shy away from the term "activity area," in favor of more descriptive labels. For example, while excavating at Jamestown, Virginia, in the 1950s, John Cotter found a cluster of three kilns used by the settlers to make pottery, perhaps once housed in a building. Cotter's crew unearthed two other archaeological features nearby: the foundation of a seventeenth-century workshop or brewhouse and a shallow pit, probably dug for clay during the construction of the kilns and later used for refuse. A workshop/brewhouse was located only 20 feet (6.1 m) to the east of the kilns; the pit was only 10 feet (3.1 m) to the south. In addition, three other features were located within 160 feet (48.8 m) of the three kilns—a large dwelling, a small outbuilding, and a smaller house. At this one spot

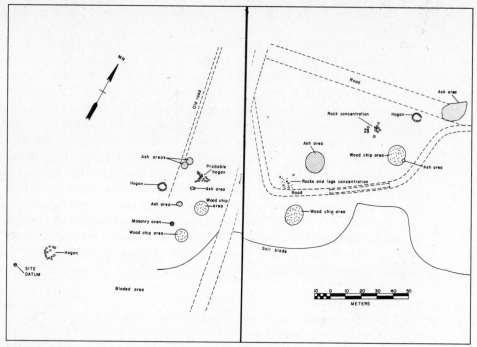

Figure 5.8 *Activity areas at a Navajo site, 1890–1930.*

in colonial Jamestown, Cotter found what may be described as eight separate activity areas: a large house, a small building associated with it, a small house, a workshop or brewhouse, three kilns, and one pit. Each one represents the remains of activities that produced archaeological evidence.

The finding of the three Navajo hogan remains in the American Southwest by Kent and the two house sites at Jamestown by Cotter illustrates an important point: in historical archaeology, the word "site" often equates with "household."

Households

The United States Bureau of the Census defines a household as "all the persons who occupy a housing unit." Houses, apartments, groups of rooms, and even a single room all qualify as housing units. Many of us may think of a household as being composed of people who are related by kinship. We sometimes equate "household" with "family." Within the past several years, Westerners have seen the composition of the traditional male-centered family change dramatically. Today, so-called "nontraditional" families are becoming ever more commonplace. As early as 1900, however, the U.S. Census Bureau defined the "family" in broad terms, as "a group of individuals who occupy jointly a dwelling place or part of a dwelling place." They even said that "All the occupants and employees of a hotel, if they regularly sleep there, make up a single family." Given this historical definition, coupled with the changes that family structure is undergoing, perhaps the best way to think about households is simply as a group of people who live together.

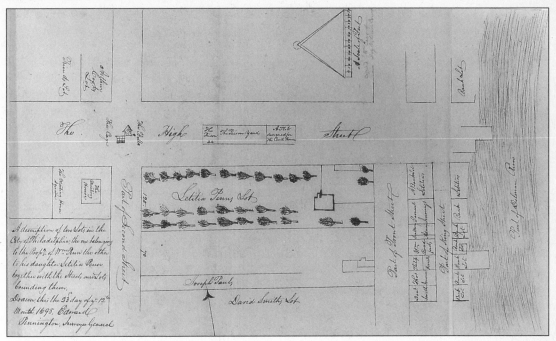

Section of a 1698 survey map of Philadelphia showing the location of Letitia Penn's lot and those of her neighbors.

Households are particularly interesting because their members were the consumers who bought, used, and discarded the artifacts and food remains that chronicle society at the time. The distributions of these finds tell us much about household activities. In their archaeological history of Philadelphia, John Cotter, Daniel Roberts, and Michael Parrington describe excavations at 8 South Front Street. Located about one and one-half blocks from the Delaware River and not too far from Independence Hall, this address was home to three different households from 1683 to 1833. Historic land plats show that Letitia Penn, of the prominent Penn family, lived there from 1683 to 1713. From 1713 to 1736, a bricklayer named Joseph Yard lived on the property with his family, but in 1736, Joseph's son, John, sold the property to Andrew Bradford. Bradford's son, Thomas, would later become a lieutenant colonel in the American militia fighting for independence. Thomas lived much of his later life in the house. In 1833, the Bradfords sold the property to John Moss, a prominent shipping merchant, who never lived there.

The analysis of the archaeological remains from 8 South Front Street is not yet complete. Still, even the preliminary information sheds light on the activities of the three households who lived there. For example, the occupants of the house dug three deep pits on the property. Near the end of their stay on the lot, the Yards built a privy pit near the back of the house. However, because they dug it only eight feet (2.4 m) deep, it quickly filled with trash. They found it a convenient place to dump unwanted or broken things. It contained one datable artifact, a gray stoneware chamber pot bearing the mark "A.D." This came from the kiln of Philadelphia potter, Anthony Duché, between about 1720 and 1730.

When the Bradfords purchased the residence, they did not bother to have this privy cleaned, but built a second one, 15 feet (4.6 m) deep directly adjacent to it. This yielded a 1734 British coin. Sometime between 1736 and 1756, the Bradfords added a kitchen to their house. Space considerations forced them to build this addition over their existing privy, so they began to use an old brick-lined 26-foot (7.9 m) well in the backyard as an alternative. As Cotter, Roberts, and Parrington said, "With its greater depth, it would have served the needs of the site's occupants better than either of the previous privy pits. The health of anyone using water from wells in the vicinity of this deep privy would, however, have been ill-served." We know nothing about the health of the members of these households, or of their neighbors. But the research at 8 South Front Street has shed light on some of the household activities of the three families who inhabited the site. Much more remains to be learned, but the archaeology has opened up some interesting avenues for future research.

Households formed the basic economic unit for Letitia Penn, the Yards, and the Bradfords at 8 South Front Street, just as they have for many people around the world for centuries. But no matter how tightly knit the household, it did not exist in a vacuum. It was part of a larger unit, called a neighborhood.

Neighborhoods

Neighborhoods are collections of households. In the terms of the U.S. Bureau of the Census, neighborhoods are composed of several "housing units": single-household dwellings, apartment buildings, and hotels. In urban settings neighborhoods can be tightly compacted spaces, with people virtually living on top of one another in apartments and tenements. In the country, neighborhoods may cover much larger areas, with dwellings widely separated.

The families who once called 8 South Front Street home were members of a larger area, the local neighborhood. When Thomas Holme, William Penn's general surveyor, drew the lots on Front Street, he listed not only Letitia, but also Daniel Smith, Charles Pickering, Thomas Harriet, and other landowners who were Letitia Penn's neighbors. All of these people, members of households, were also members of the neighborhood. They probably nodded to one another on the street, perhaps took tea in the others' houses, and perhaps even knew some of the others' personal business.

The archaeological record for neighborhoods can often be amplified from other sources. In large cities, invaluable neighborhood maps were once published by the D. A. Sanborn National Insurance Diagram Bureau, later called the Sanborn Map and Publishing Company. The Aetna Insurance Company hired Sanborn in 1867 to make maps of several cities in Tennessee, as they appeared just after the devastation of the Civil War. He soon created a company to specialize in producing these so-called "fire insurance maps." By the time the company stopped making them 100 years later, they had published 700,000 maps of 12,000 cities and towns in the United States. In Great Britain, similar maps were produced by Chas. E. Goad, Ltd. Memories of the highly devastating Chicago fire in 1871, and knowledge of historic fires, such as that in London in 1666, convinced people of the wisdom of knowing where buildings were located, what they were made of, and what fire precautions their owners had taken. Sanborn maps show how close together urban buildings stood, whether they were constructed of brick, stone, or wood. They distinguish between dwellings, stores, stables, and special-use buildings, such as glasshouses. In an era of coal and wood fires, the maps inventoried chimney designs for firefighters combatting the many chimney fires of the day. The maps also show porches, outbuildings, and lot lines. In short, where they are available, the Sanborn maps are priceless archives of the spatial relationships of late nineteenth- and early twentieth-century urban neighborhoods.

The aptly named "bird's-eye views" of some American cities and towns are equally valuable. Such views are really "artistic maps" because they provide a three-dimensional perspective on many of the same places portrayed in the Sanborn maps. This time, though, the buildings appear as actual structures with windows, doors, and roofs. They also show trees and landscaping, boats sailing on rivers, horse-drawn buggies on busy thoroughfares, and horses side by side on racetracks. Superficially, they are more realistic, but they display far more artistic license than the sober diagrams of the Sanborn maps. Bird's-eye view artists often made the drawings look better than the towns they portrayed. Taken together, however, the two images provide compelling documentation of long-forgotten urban neighborhoods in their heyday. Unlike the Egyptologist laboring in an ancient Egyptian town, the historical archaeologist can reconstruct a neighborhood not only with the spade, but through the eyes of those who once walked its streets—even before excavation begins.

When Mary and Adrian Praetzellis investigated their Sacramento city block, they excavated the household of Mary Collins at 808 I Street. The first family to live at this address was the Leonard Kellogg family, who were there by 1858. Mary Collins, a widowed Irish woman, followed them. Her household resided there until sometime before 1910. The 1900 census shows that Mary had three children, who also lived with her. To develop the site history of the neighborhood, the Praetzellises used both the 1869 bird's-eye view and the 1895 Sanborn map of the block. These sources helped them to reconstruct the neighborhood in which the Collins family lived. An examination of the images allows us to reconstruct the buildings of their neighborhood. For example, a small dwelling was adjacent to their yard on the right at 810 I Street, and a narrow alleyway was on the left. Next to the alley were two small buildings, behind which was a large house situated on the corner, at 901 8th Street, on a large lot. A large "Wood & Coal Yard" was directly behind the Collins home. Next to the coal yard was the "A. Meister & Sons Carriage Mfg." company. Further behind the house, fronting J Street, were one or two other dwellings. All of these properties—the dwellings, the coal yard, the manufacturing company—were part of the Collins' neighborhood in 1895.

This one block in Sacramento, California, shows the many different kinds of buildings that exist in a neighborhood. Historical archaeologists can study all of them: domestic, commercial, and manufacturing sites. It is not difficult to see from the 1869 bird's-eye view of Sacramento that the Collins neighborhood did not exist by itself. It was part of a community.

Communities

In Chapter 1 we mentioned the research of William Adams at Silcott, Washington, a late nineteenth- and early twentieth-century town in eastern Washington,

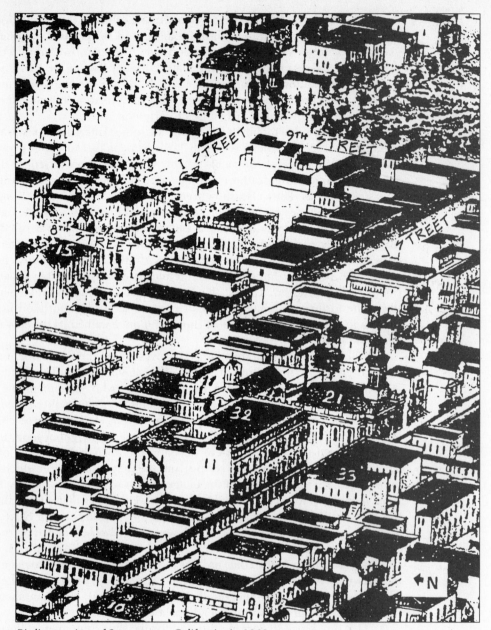

Bird's-eye view of Sacramento, California, in 1869.

not far from the Idaho border. Adams' study focuses on Silcott strictly as a community, as a collection of households and neighborhoods. In his words, "We sought information from which inferences could be made on the basis of the community as a whole, rather than on individual sites within it." His plan called for the excavation of several sites to get some sense of the community.

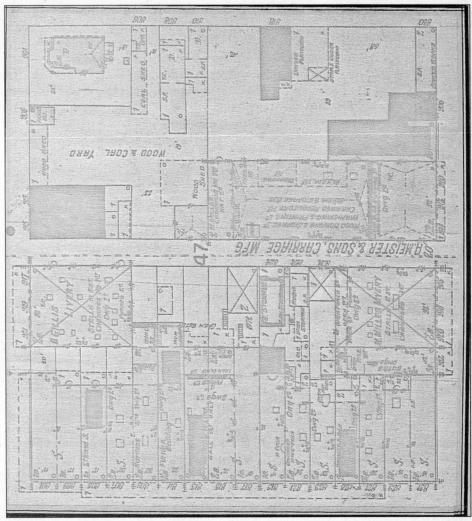

Sanborn map, 1895, showing the location of Mary Collins' home at 808 I Street (top of map),
Sacramento, California.

His research team began with Bill Wilson's Store, because they viewed it as a microcosm of community life. All of the manufactured things the people of Silcott bought in town would have come through Wilson's Store. Adams' team also excavated three households. Many of the artifacts they found during excavation—cups and saucers, pitchers, crocks, marbles, tin cans, medicine bottles—appeared at all four sites. Using these artifacts in conjunction with oral histories and pictorial images, Adams constructed historical vignettes of the community as it may have appeared in 1917. For example, for the Ireland Place, one of the dwellings he excavated, Adams begins, "Strange the way names stick to a place. The first house you come to from the ferry is known as the Ireland Place, even though Richard Ireland only lived here about a year or so and that was over fifteen years ago, in 1902. But somehow his name stuck to it. Right now Jim Stanfill and family live here." Adams' accounts describe households that are firmly rooted to the community of Silcott. They exist as households within the larger community.

The households of the Yards in Philadelphia, Collinses in Sacramento, and the Stanfills in Silcott, were members of neighborhoods and even whole communities. When looked at regionally, we can say that the communities therein represent an entire settlement pattern.

Settlement Patterns

The study of *settlement patterns* is the analysis of ways in which archaeological sites are distributed across the ancient landscape. This specialty is known as *settlement archaeology*.

Settlement archaeology is based on the assumption that people with free choice made informed decisions about where they chose to live, and that they lived in specific locales because they sought to satisfy some want or need. In the case of the ancient Egyptians, for instance, village farming communities were founded on high ground on or just outside the river floodplain, so that they became islands in years when unusually high Nile floods inundated the surrounding farm lands. Some people lived on the edge of the desert because farming land was so important that none was wasted on village sites.

More recent historic sites were located with careful regard for such factors as water supplies, protection against Indian raids, and so on. For example, Richard Ireland located his homestead on the banks of the Snake River in Silcott in the late 1890s to take advantage of the ferry. As Adams said, "The front door opens onto the road leading down to the ferry."

Settlement decisions can be complex, involving many different but interrelated buildings. When the Civil War ended, most of the slaves of James Calhoun—the "Hermit of Millwood" introduced in Chapter 4—decided to remain on his 15,000-acre (6,073 ha) cotton plantation as semi-autonomous tenant farmers. This South Carolina plantation had been their home for decades, and most of them wanted to stay there. When Charles Orser excavated Calhoun's plantation in the early 1980s, he realized that the site presented a rare opportunity to study the settlement pattern of the former slaves. These tenant farmers did not want to live in their old slave cabins, for they were free to establish their homes anywhere on the estate. Knowing this, the question that became important was, "What criteria did the tenant farmers use when deciding where on the plantation they should live?" Using old maps, the archaeological team identified 66 tenant sites within the plantation. Next, they assessed these sites in terms of a number of factors, including agricultural potential, feet above mean sea level, degree and direction of land slope, and the distances to nearest stream, road, railroad, neighbor, and town, named "Calhoun Falls."

The Millwood researchers soon learned that most of the tenant farmers located their homes 475 feet (148 m) above sea level, and situated them to the southwest, west, or southeast, $3/10$ of a mile (0.5 km) from the nearest stream, and 1 $1/2$

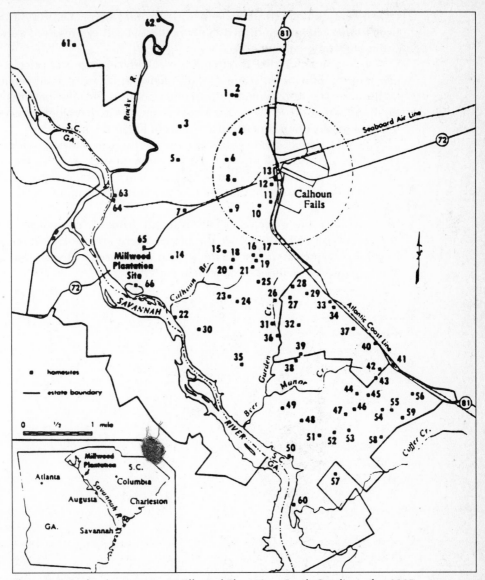

Figure 5.9 *Settlement pattern at Millwood Plantation, South Carolina, after 1865.*

miles (2.4 km) from the Savannah River, which bordered the plantation. This typical farmer was less than $1/2$ mile (0.8 km) from his closest neighbor, less than $1^1/_2$ miles (2.4 km) from both the nearest road and the nearest railroad, and more than $1^1/_2$ miles (2.4 km) from the town (Figure 5.9). Thus, the Millwood farmers established their homes on high ground close to a neighbor and to a road, but not too near town. The Millwood tenants, by the placement of their farms, appear to have been saying that their community was defined to look inward, toward one another, rather than outward, to the wider world around them. Oral traditions collected from former tenants confirmed this hypothesis, for they preserved a strong sense of community on the plantation.

It is in situations like this that historical archaeology is of priceless value. Tell-tale house foundations, scatters of distinctive artifacts, of food remains, provide highly accurate, dispassionate information about settlement patterns and the cultural values that drove them. Again and again, the archaeological record amplifies impressionistic, often superficial accounts of life in the past.

People actively create space, and once it is created they give it meaning. People create networks of physical things—sites, houses, towns—with a logic that makes sense to them, that is consistent with their cultural beliefs and attitudes. We saw this process at work in the case of William Paca's Annapolis garden (see Chapter 4).

We must now move on to the meat and drink of archaeology, to the finding and excavation of historic sites, the places where archaeological context is established. In Chapter 6, we discuss the ways in which archaeologists find the sites that make up the raw material of settlement patterns.

CHAPTER
6

Historical Site Survey and Location

"Simply walking around the countryside in the hopes of stumbling on an archaeological site is good exercise, but the rewards are likely to be small unless the searcher knows what to look for and approximately where to find it"

Ivor Noël Hume, 1969

How do archaeologists know where to look for historic sites, especially when so many of them are invisible, even to the expert eye? This chapter discusses some of the ways in which archaeologists find archaeological sites of all kinds.

The Pyramids of Giza in Egypt, the city of Teotihuacán in Mexico, the Mission St. Xavier del Bac near Tucson, Arizona—all of these are conspicuous archaeological sites with large standing structures that have survived into modern times. Most historical sites are much more inconspicuous, often invisible, even to the trained eye. Egyptologist Howard Carter spent seven years clearing the Valley of Kings before he found Tutankhamun's tomb in 1922. It took years for archaeologists to locate L'Anse-aux-Meadows, a Norse settlement of about A.D. 1000 in northern Newfoundland. In both cases, even a trained eye faced formidable difficulties in locating a once-famous place. Many archaeological sites come to light by accident, like, for example, the Elizabethan Rose Theatre, mentioned in Chapter 5. But most are found by archaeologists using a combination of common sense, a well-designed research plan, and sophisticated techniques and equipment.

Rose Theatre, London, on the last day of excavation, May 14, 1989. The large objects in the open area are modern building foundations.

KNOWN SITES

Historical sites, unlike prehistoric ones, are often conspicuous features of the landscape. Many locations—California missions, southern plantation mansions, industrial sites in New England—have been continuously inhabited or otherwise maintained since their construction. These kinds of sites have been studied by historical archaeologists for years. Indeed, the study of such well-known sites characterized the field's earliest years (see Chapter 2). Archaeology at well-known historical sites is often directed at providing architectural details that can be used by preservationists to restore or reconstruct famous properties. Colonial Williamsburg, Virginia, provides a perfect example.

Henry Wetherburn built his tavern in 1743 on Duke of Gloucester Street just about midway between the Capitol of Virginia on the east and the colonial courthouse on the west. About ten years later, with a thriving and expanding business, Wetherburn enlarged his tavern. Over the next two centuries, this eighteenth-century building served as a tavern, store, dwelling, boarding house, and girls' school. In its prime, it was even the site of numerous public meetings and scientific lectures. Wetherburn's tavern was a landmark in Williamsburg. When the Colonial

Archaeology in progress behind Wetherburn's Tavern, Williamsburg, Virginia, in the mid-1960s. A dairy foundation appears on the left; that of a kitchen on the right.

Williamsburg Foundation decided to renovate the tavern in the 1960s, they called on a team of architects, historians—and historical archaeologists. Their chief archaeologist, Ivor Noël Hume, dug along one wall of the tavern to answer specific questions about the design of the entrance porches. He also excavated in the tavern's backyard in the attempt to find outbuildings, discovering the foundations of two kitchens, a dairy, and two buildings of unknown use, as well as evidence of several old porches. Noël Hume's field crew collected more than 200,000 artifacts, like, for example, tiny pieces of brass from the bases of small chafing dishes and sherds of the "white flowered China" listed in Henry Wetherburn's inventory of 1760. These objects now adorn the building once again and help bring it to life for the twentieth-century visitor. So do delicate stems from elaborate wine glasses and white plates with "SUCCESS TO THE KING OF PRUSSIA AND HIS FORCES" around their edges in raised letters. These commemorative plates were popular from 1757 to 1763. They commemorated King Frederick the Great's victory in 1757 against the combined armies of Austria, France, and Russia at Rossbach. These artifacts, like many others found with them, have been duplicated by today's skilled craftpersons and are displayed to recreate the atmosphere of the once-popular tavern.

Known sites can yield very detailed information indeed. The Battle of the Little Bighorn matched George Custer's Seventh Regiment of U.S. Cavalry against the combined forces of the Dakota (Sioux) and the Northern Cheyenne in 1876. The engagement lasted but an hour or so, but is notorious in the history of the American West. An enormous historical literature surrounds Little Bighorn, a literature drawn from contemporary records, eyewitness accounts, and from minute-by-minute reconstructions of the battle. "Custer's Last Stand" has been immortalized in many highly imaginative paintings, and has been the subject of many fanciful motion pictures. Until recently, it never occurred to anyone to use archaeological methods to amplify eyewitness and textual accounts. For example, some historians have long argued that cartridge extraction failure on the part of the cavalry's carbines may have been one cause of Custer's defeat. In other words, the soldiers were unable to defend themselves properly because their rifles malfunctioned. To address this, and other, questions, a National Park Service team led by Douglas Scott made a detailed study of the battlefield site (also see Chapter 3). First, they conducted full-scale excavations around several of the marble markers that commemorate fallen soldiers, and also on Calhoun Hill, south of the place where the famous "last stand" occurred. They also surveyed the entire battlefield with metal detectors to locate spent bullets and other significant artifacts. With meticulous care, they plotted the position of every artifact, even individual spent cartridges. Back in the laboratory, Scott and his team members examined the excavated cartridges for telltale signs of jamming. They found that, in fact, *both* sides had problems with jamming carbines, to the point that jamming weapons were not a significant factor in the battle's outcome.

Many Americans have a mental picture of Custer's final moments. In one famous image, we find him bravely standing amid his fallen comrades, pistols in both hands, golden hair flowing. We imagine from such paintings that Custer, the brave leader, was the last to fall and that he withstood the onslaught for a relatively long time. On the contrary, the archaeological research shows that the battle was merely a brief firefight and that most of the cavalry dead were wounded—by either bullets or metal-tipped arrows—and then were killed at close range by a deadly blow to the head. Thus, the archaeological record at a site as well known as Little Big Horn has yielded vital, and dispassionate, information about a famous historical event that amplifies, and in some cases, corrects, surviving historical information.

ACCIDENTAL DISCOVERIES

Historical archaeology at places such as Colonial Williamsburg and at the Little Big Horn Battlefield National Monument demonstrates the field's interpretive power even at well-known sites that require no discovery. Accidental discoveries represent a significant proportion of major archaeological finds, especially in urban settings, where construction, demolition, and rebuilding goes on all the time.

One of the most spectacular, accidental discoveries made in recent years occurred in New York City in 1991. The General Services Administration planned to build a 34-story office building to house a number of federal offices in lower Manhattan. When the archaeologists retained to examine the building site examined city maps of the day, they found that a "Negro Burial Ground" had existed at this location in the mid-eighteenth century. As many as 20,000 African-Americans and poor whites could have been buried in this five-to-six-acre (2 to 2.4 ha) lot. But the experts assumed that the digging of several deep nineteenth-century basements had destroyed most, if not all, the burials in the then-abandoned cemetery. Their report could not have been more explicit: "The construction of deep sub-basements would have obliterated any remains within the lots that fall within the historic bounds of the cemetery." Six weeks before construction was scheduled to begin, the cautious General Services Administration hired a group of archaeologists to check the lot just in case one or two odd burials still remained. Dozens of undisturbed graves came to light in the next two months. The General Services Administration was stunned. They had spent $104 million on the property, and the offices they planned to build were slated to cost another $276 million. Had they known the cemetery was undisturbed, they would never have purchased the property. By law, the GSA had to clear the burials, arrange for their scientific study, and make arrangements either for their reburial or permanent safe storage. In the end, 420 skeletons were removed from the cemetery, the largest sample of historic African-American remains ever discovered. African-American physical anthropologist Michael Blakey of Howard University is now engaged in a five-year study of the skeletal remains, which will yield priceless scientific information about eighteenth-century New Yorkers.

Even well-known historic sites can yield unexpected discoveries. The Spanish Presidio in Santa Barbara, California, was founded in 1782 and remained in use for 17 years. Over the next two centuries, the fort and its buildings fell into disrepair, much of it vanishing under a nineteenth-century Chinatown. In 1967, archaeologists and local volunteers under the direction of Richard Humphrey excavated the foundations of the Presidio Chapel to provide architectural and historical information for future reconstruction. During their otherwise routine excavation to trace the building's foundations, the excavators found three burials under the church floor. When archaeologist Julia Costello and physical anthropologist Phillip Walker studied the bones and graves, they discovered that Humphrey had actually found the remains of four people. They compared the physical remains with Presidio records and tried to associate the graves with actual individuals. They did not know the exact individual each skeleton represented, but they could suggest one or two candidates. In archaeology, this close a match is remarkable. Burial 1 was a middle-aged adult of unknown sex whose teeth suggested either Native American or Asiatic ancestry. The chapel's registry showed that Domingo Carrillo died in 1845 at the age of 45, and that José Antonio Ortega also died that year, but at an unknown age. Records show that Ortega was called "El Chino," or "The Chinaman," and so he is the best candidate for Burial 1. A newborn baby and a young child were interred in Burial 2. Four infants, between the ages of 3 and 25 days, were buried in the chapel after 1797, and Costello and Walker could not identify the newborn child. However, the older child was probably María Dominga Carrillo, who died in 1840 at age 2 years 6 months. Burial 3 was that of a woman between the ages of 16 and 20. Using Presidio records, Costello and Walker argue that the remains could be those of one or two unmarried young women: Soledad Carrillo (who died in 1837, at age 17) or María Antonia Carrillo (who died in 1844 at age 16 years 9 months). The woman in Burial 3—Soledad Carrillo or María Carrillo—had been placed in her redwood coffin wearing a long cape ornamented with sequins, glass beads, and flower bundles. Remains of her cape remained partly preserved with the bones.

FINDING HISTORICAL SITES

Historical archaeologists use three techniques for locating sites—historical maps, formal archaeological survey methods, and, mainly on-site, sophisticated subsurface surveying techniques.

Using Maps to Find Historical Sites

In Chapter 5 we made reference to the use of Sanborn maps for developing ideas about past urban neighborhoods. They are but the tip of a rewarding historical iceberg, for maps of all kinds are a mine of information on potential archaeological sites of all kinds. The problem is locating them. As we shall see in Chapter 7, there are various reference works or repositories that can help in the search, but in many cases maps come from the most obscure or unsuspected sources, such as City Hall files or military records. Anyone serious about using historical maps has a great deal of patient detective work in front of them. Nevertheless, they are among the most useful sources at an archaeologist's disposal.

The Minute Man National Historical Park in Massachusetts was created in 1959 to commemorate "the significant events, structures, and sites of the opening day of the War of the American Revolution" in 1775. This park protects the famous sites of Lexington and Concord, where "the shot heard round the world" rang out, but it also includes a number of other, less well-known sites, such as the Brooks "tanyard," or tannery. Members of the Brooks family operated their tanning business on the Concord road west of Lexington from about 1700 to 1829. Although this tanyard was important locally, it had no regional significance. After its demise, the buildings fell into disrepair and the century-and-a-quarter-old tannery vanished without trace. In 1984, the National Park Service decided to conduct a full archaeological survey of the sites within the boundaries of the Minute Man park, under the direction of archaeologist Alan Synenki.

When historian Martha Holland combed through old newspaper accounts, notes and maps of boundary surveys, tax rolls, and census lists, she found two maps that showed the location of the Brooks business. One, drawn in 1749, provides a sketch of the Brooks property and shows the "Tan House" located next to the "High way." The map simply shows the tanyard as a small square with a cross in the middle, a symbol that resembles a window with four panes. A document of 1745 notes that the tannery included "a Tann House and Tann pits." These are undoubtedly the structures the cartographer meant to show four years later. A map

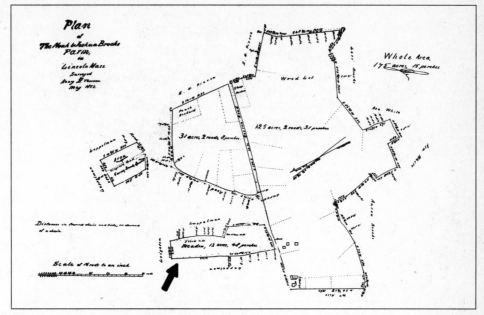

Figure 6.1 *Thoreau map, 1852, of the Brooks Tannery.*

made nearly a century later, in 1830, shows no sign of the tannery. Twelve years later, and two years before he published his immortal *Walden,* nearby resident Henry David Thoreau drew another map of the town. He showed but an empty "Meadow" where the tannery once lay (Figure 6.1). Unfortunately, the archaeologists were unable to match precisely the old maps with the current landscape. Their very limited excavations did not produce clear evidence of the tannery. Instead, they found the remains of a house, probably demolished in the nineteenth century, before 1875. The archaeologists' failure to locate the tannery does not negate the importance of the historical maps. Rather, it simply illustrates the need for further archaeology.

Not all maps are useful. Most early colonial maps, for example, often simply include a large dot to show where a site—fort, mission, trading post, Native American village—was located. By tracking maps as they change over the generations, one can use them to establish the dates when major buildings were built, abandoned, or destroyed, but they tell us little else.

Fort de Chartres was a colonial French outpost near the tiny town of Prairie du Rocher in southern Illinois. During the eighteenth century, the French established a number of towns along the Mississippi River in today's Illinois and Missouri as a means of connecting their Canadian settlements with those around New Orleans. They named one of their strongholds Fort de Chartres. The first fort was a simple wooden stockade, replaced by a more elaborate structure, then, in the mid-1750s, by an impressive stone-walled fortress. The first map to show Fort de Chartres was drawn by Francois-Benjamin Dumont de Montigny in the 1720s. It shows the location of the first fort, adorning it with four bastions. Even though this

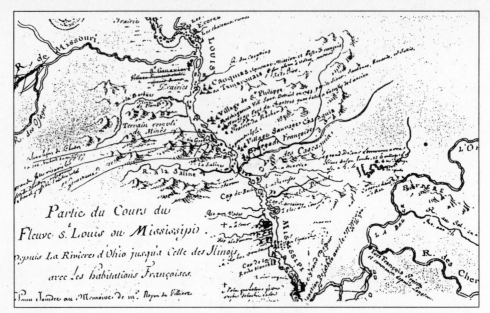

Section of a map drawn in 1755 by Jacques Nicolas Bellin. It shows the area around Fort de Chartres.

map shows only one small section of the Mississippi Valley, it is not accurate enough to permit an archaeologist to locate the first fort. A later map, drawn in 1755 by Jacques Nicolas Bellin, is even worse, depicting the stone-built "Nouveau Fort de Chartres" sandwiched between the town of Prairie du Rocher and a Native American village. Were it not for the physical presence of this stone fort today, an archaeologist would have an extremely difficult time locating it simply using the map as a guide. Eventually, the site of the first fort came to light fortuitously in an old air photograph.

Archaeological Survey

However informative their documents, historical archaeologists rely heavily on formal archaeological survey techniques—exactly the same as those used by prehistorians. There is nothing glamorous about such methods, for they involve a systematic search for historic sites within a circumscribed area, whether it be a small urban lot, a neighborhood, a plantation, or even an entire geographical region.

The survey begins in the library and laboratory—researching archival sources, maps, and background climatic and geological information, anything that provides a background to the fieldwork that follows. For example, a survey of a lot destined for a warehouse might involve a title search, to establish the ownership and uses of the land before it was purchased by its current owner. Such preliminary investigations are vital, for they provide clues as to the nature of the archaeological record. Did previous owners erect houses on the property, or did they sink wells? Were cattle corralled there, or did a store once stand on the land? The more background information that is on hand, the more effective one's time in the field.

Pedestrian Survey

The most effective archaeological surveys are those carried out on foot, moving slowly over the ground looking for telltale signs of human occupation. Such traces of human activity come in many forms—surface scatters of potsherds, telltale gray midden soil spilling from a gopher hole, piles of bricks or stones, relict walls and fences, cellar depressions, and capped wells. In northern Michigan and Wisconsin, for example, one or two small mounds of earth, a small depression here and there, and a scatter of broken whiskey bottles, and bent, corroded enameled tin plates and cups is all that may indicate the location of a once-active logging camp (Figure 6.2). In the American West, the same evidence may reveal an abandoned nineteenth-century mining community.

In a great many cases, the presence of large, stately shade trees and domestic flowers, still blooming after years of neglect, may reveal the past location of a former house. For example, as part of a recent survey for the expansion of a small airport in central Illinois, historical archaeologist David Babson located two nineteenth-century farmhouses by carefully observing the surrounding landscape. Babson knew that farmers on the flat, windswept prairies of the Midwest usually surrounded their homes with windbreaks of stately elms and maples. Walking among the trees of these two sites, Babson found broken bottles, small fragments of ceramic dishes, and iron nails; in short, everything that we would expect to have been used at a nineteenth-century farmstead.

Sampling

Surveying a small city lot is one thing, a matter of combing a few thousand square feet of level terrain. Locating archaeological sites over an entire region is

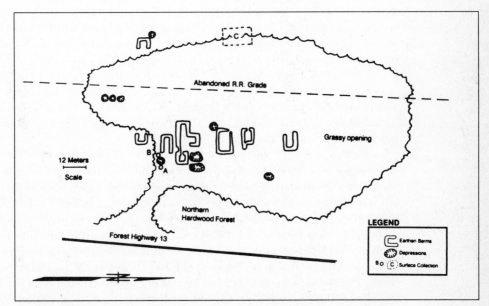

Figure 6.2 *Archaeologist's map of Hardwood era logging camp in Michigan.*

another matter, for it is simply impossible for any fieldworker to record every trace of human settlement over such a large area. One hundred percent field survey coverage is a rarity in anything but the smallest areas, and sometimes even that does not reveal everything. There are many instances of people returning to well-trodden areas and promptly finding more sites. Almost invariably, a field survey of anything but a small plot of land involves the use of formal sampling methods. The realities of fieldwork, such as time limits and financial constraints, make complete survey coverage a rarity.

An enormous body of literature surrounds sampling methods in archaeology, for they remain both controversial and difficult to apply. In all cases, effective sampling depends on formal sampling strategies, intended to provide statistically valid, and hopefully representative, samples of sites within the survey units selected for detailed examination. Common strategies involve the use of transects, or straight corridors, and quadrats, or square units. For instance, the planning for a mid-1970s survey to locate prehistoric sites in the Chaco Canyon National Monument in northern New Mexico shows that the sampling units can be selected in one of two ways. They can either be chosen at random, or they can be assigned systematically, according to some criterion, such as landform, elevation, or tree cover (Figure 6.3). No matter how complex or how simple, sampling strategies are employed simply to permit archaeologists to examine as much territory as possible with a maximum of efficiency.

In late 1986 and early 1987, a crew from Southwest Missouri State University, under the direction of archaeologist David Benn, conducted a systematic survey in the Big Sioux River valley in northwestern Iowa. Their goal was to locate previously unknown prehistoric and historical sites. They wanted to investigate at least 8,000 acres (3,239 ha), and they knew they would have to devise a careful sampling strategy to do so. Benn decided to survey eight different sections of the valley, using systematic criteria that focused on the topographic features in the region. His survey sections thus included floodplains, river terraces, and uplands. By the end of the survey, the crew had walked over 10,732 acres (4,345 ha). Within this area, they found 109 prehistoric sites and 20 historic sites that contained evidence of buildings. The prehistoric sites ranged from small, temporary camp sites to larger settlements with mounds, and dated from about 500 B.C. to A.D. 1500. The historic sites included not only individual log cabins, but the town of Beloit, whose first European-American settlers arrived in 1868.

Benn's survey in northwestern Iowa illustrates an important point: sampling designs are especially useful under circumstances where one is dealing with large numbers of inconspicuous sites, such as stone-walled cattle enclosures on the grasslands of southeast Africa, or Anglo-Saxon field systems in Britain. For the most part, however, a historical landscape consists of large, humanly made features that can dictate the distribution of all kinds of sites large and small. Builders of roads, bridges, and mills knew exactly why they built such structures where they did. For example, when J. A. Carpenter built the Beloit Mill in 1871—within one of Benn's survey units—he knew exactly what he was doing. He erected it on the banks of the Big Sioux River because he needed to harness the energy of the water to grind flour. As was a common practice, he even constructed a dam to permit him to con-

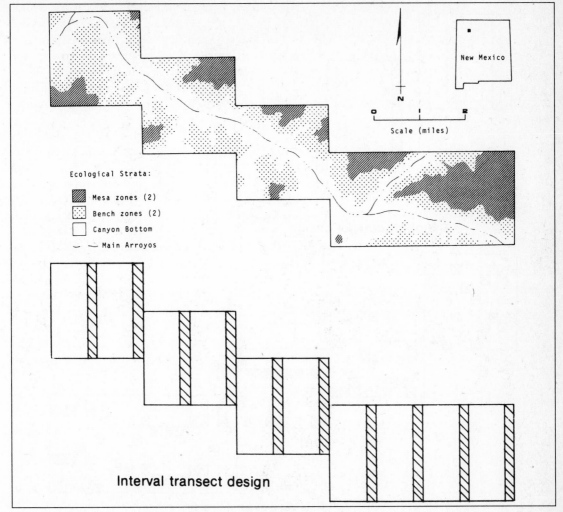

Ecological Strata:

▨ Mesa zones (2)

▦ Bench zones (2)

▢ Canyon Bottom

⌐⌐ Main Arroyos

New Mexico

N

0   1   2

Scale (miles)

Interval transect design

Figure 6.3 *Possible survey strategies at Chaco Canyon National Monument, New Mexico.*

trol the river's flow past the mill. Carpenter was obviously successful because the 1880 industrial census reveals that his mill had three water wheels with a daily grinding capacity of 250 bushels of grain. He would have been shortsighted indeed to have located his mill in the Iowa uplands, 20 miles from the Big Sioux River! With very little effort and a sense of landscape, a twentieth-century archaeologist can soon work out why the location was chosen, for it is easy for us to slip into their mindset, since we built and used similar structures until very recently.

Thus, in historical archaeology, locating sites requires not only knowledge of a region's history, but also good science to construct sampling designs that make sense and that have the greatest potential for locating previously unknown sites.

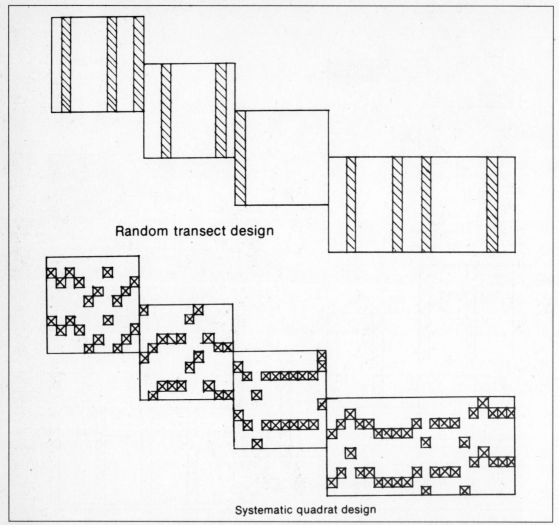

Random transect design

Systematic quadrat design

Figure 6.3 (Continued) *Possible survey strategies at Chaco Canyon National Monument, New Mexico.*

Subsurface Surveying, Remote Sensing

Archaeology has taken to the air and to space in its search for long-forgotten human settlements. Such remote sensing techniques are highly effective for examining entire landscapes, or major cultural features such as Roman roads or ancient field systems that cover many acres of ground.

Aerial photography has been part of the archaeologist's tool kit since World War I, when excavators turned military observers realized that the overhead view was an unrivalled way of identifying inconspicuous earthworks, Roman forts, and other such locations. Aerial photography was helpful in locating the site of the first Fort de Chartres in southern Illinois. In 1981, U.S. Army Corps of Engineers' archaeologist Terry Norris found an air photograph of the fort's general area taken

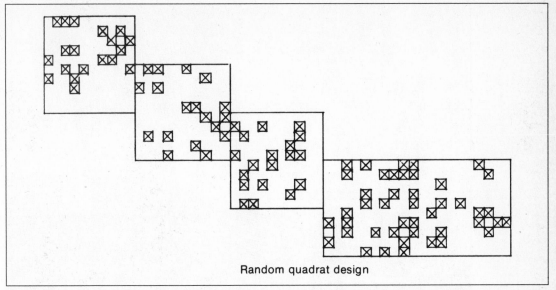

Random quadrat design

Figure 6.3 (Continued) *Possible survey strategies at Chaco Canyon National Monument, New Mexico.*

in 1928 that just happened to show a rectangular stain, the foundations of the first fort. This piece of information became central to the eventual discovery of the early eighteenth-century outpost.

Subsurface detection methods are of critical importance on site, however, because they allow an investigator to acquire information about what lies underground before excavation begins. Such techniques are noninvasive (or nondestructive) methods of site assessment, employing geophysical and geochemical techniques. Geophysical techniques include magnetic and electrical resistivity surveying, ground-penetrating radar, and sonar methods.

Metal Detectors

Metal detectors are electromagnetic instruments that can be used to locate metal objects beneath the earth's surface, originally developed, of course, as mine detectors. These instruments can be quite sophisticated and expensive. The more costly models can be set to distinguish between different kinds of metal, and can penetrate further into the ground than their less expensive counterparts. They also can be used to find buried kilns, walls, and ditches. Typically, these machines issue a "beep" or electronic hum when they pass over a disturbance in the earth's magnetic field. Many detectors come equipped with a highly sensitive meter and headphones. Today, metal detecting is a popular hobby, and many metal detecting enthusiasts are skilled operators. Most hobbyists use their detectors to locate missing coins and rings. Beer can collectors sometimes use them to find early specimens to add to their collections. Historical archaeologists occasionally will call on a skilled operator to provide assistance because they offer an inexpensive and quick way to learn about a site's subsurface features. As we said above, the team that investigated the Little Bighorn battlefield successfully used metal detectors in their field survey.

Aerial photograph, taken in 1928, showing the rectangular stain of the first Fort de Chartres, Illinois.

Many historical archaeologists, however, prefer to use the more exacting proton magnetometer.

Proton Magnetometers

Like its cousin the metal detector, the more sophisticated proton magnetometer locates "anomalies," or disturbances in the earth's natural magnetic field. They give readings as quickly as a metal detector, but usually with more accuracy.

A proton magnetometer survey begins by laying out a grid of equal-sized squares over the site area. Next, the magnetometer operator measures the normal magnetization of the site in a number of places. With this magnetic background known, the surveyors take one reading from each point where the grid squares intersect. The resulting data are then used to create a "map" of the magnetic readings. The various anomalies present appear as obvious "hot spots," or high magnetic readings, on the map. These kinds of magnetic surveys have proven effective at archaeological sites that could be expected to contain large numbers of ferrous artifacts. For example, at the eighteenth-century French Fort Ouiatenon in Indiana, the map of magnetic anomalies helped guide archaeologists to a number of subsurface features, including a cache of iron trade objects deposited outside one of the fort's buildings. The magnetic survey also helped locate four eighteenth-century burials at the fort.

Proton magnetometer surveys also can be conducted underwater, to locate anchors, chains, ship spikes, and other ferrous objects associated with shipwrecks.

Marine archaeologist J. Barto Arnold successfully used a proton magnetometer in a survey off the coast of Galveston, Texas. Historic records and maps revealed 327 known shipwrecks in Galveston Bay, many dating to the Civil War. The most interesting was that of the ill-fated USS *Selma,* built of reinforced concrete by the United States Government during World War I. She sank on her maiden voyage after ramming jetties off the coast of Mexico. The government abandoned her a couple of years later in Galveston Bay. The wreck's general location had been known for years, but Arnold's magnetometer survey confirmed its precise placement on the Gulf floor.

Electrical, or Soil, Resistivity Surveys

All rocks and soils are porous, so they absorb different amounts of moisture. This means that all porous objects and features under the ground conduct varying degrees of electricity. A soil resistivity meter measures the amount of resistance encountered by an electrical current passed through these objects. For instance, a trash pit with many open spaces holds more moisture than the dense clay surrounding it, and a brick wall absorbs less water than the surrounding soil. The electrical current encounters greater resistance when trying to pass through the wall than through the soil.

Like magnetometer work, resistivity surveys involve placing metal probes, or electrodes, within a grid. An electrical current is passed to the ground by the electrodes and the resistance encountered by the current measured with the resistivity meter. The readings are plotted as profiles of differing resistance across the site. Any anomalies that appear may represent buried archaeological features.

Soil resistivity is very useful under circumstances where excavation is impracticable. For example, University of Texas archaeologists used an electrical resistivity survey to locate a series of lost graves in a small, early Anglo-Texan cemetery in south Dallas that dated to before the Civil War. The investigators established a grid over the site, and conducted their resistivity survey. They were able to distinguish eight anomalies that probably were grave sites. They knew that early Anglo Texans buried their dead with an east-to-west orientation; thus, any anomaly pointing north-south was probably not a burial. In this particular case, the archaeologists were allowed to check their findings by excavating the anomalies, because the skeletons were to be reinterred in a more secure location. Excavations revealed the bones of four children in three anomalies (one contained two skeletons). The burials were about 6 feet (2 m) beneath the current ground surface, the last 1.5 feet (0.5 m) of the graves chipped into the natural limestone underlying the cemetery.

Soil resistivity surveying, like all nonintrusive survey methods, is particularly useful at cemeteries, locales that people usually do not want disturbed by full-scale excavation.

Ground-Penetrating Radar (GPR)

Ground-penetrating radar works by transmitting a low-frequency electromagnetic signal into the ground by way of a radar system pulled along the ground. The path of the radar is a series of transecting lines established by the archaeologists. When the signal encounters an anomaly it sends a signal back to the receiver that indicates that it has struck something that is unlike the surrounding soil. Specialists can interpret the signal "profiles" to determine the locations of buried features.

Ground-penetrating radar was used effectively by a survey team led by geoar-chaeologist Bruce Bevan in Virginia. Working in association with the National Park Service, Bevan and his researchers were attempting to find "Spring Garden," the home of a Mr. William Taylor in Petersburg. Taylor was a person of no particular historical note; he was simply a victim of circumstance, for his house was destroyed by the Union Army in their unsuccessful attempt to capture Petersburg in 1864. In 1978, the National Park Service wanted to find the precise location of the home so that they could include it in their interpretive program. Test excavations made in 1978 came up empty-handed. The archaeologists found one or two outbuildings, but failed to find the Taylor home. At that point, Bevan's team was called in.

Bevan ran the radar along the ground in a series of parallel rows across the suspected location of the home, where the outbuildings had come to light. The radar beam used could detect anomalies 3 feet (1 m) to the right and to the left of the path at a depth of 3 feet (1 m). He surveyed an area of about 2.2 acres (slightly less than 1 ha) in four days. Using the radar, he was able to delineate a buried feature that seemed to measure about 20 to 25 feet by 50 to 55 feet (6 to 8 by 15 to 17 m). The anomaly was rectangular and was exactly parallel to a standing outbuilding.

Two years later, in 1981, the National Park Service sponsored test excavations over Bevan's anomaly, which located the northeast and southwest corners of a brick-lined cellar. Remarkably, the cellar measured 19 by 55 feet (6 by17 m), exactly the dimensions the radar showed. The archaeologists could date the ceramics they found in the cellar to the last years of the eighteenth century and to the first half of the nineteenth. Without question, this was the foundations of Taylor's house.

Sonar

Marine archaeologists use a related technique, sonar, to locate lost ship-wrecks. Sonar, whose name is derived from Sound Navigation And Ranging, is a complex detection device. It emits a sharp pulse of sound that produces an echo when the sound waves strike an object such as a submerged submarine.

Sonar was invaluable for studying the wreck of the *USS Monitor*. The *Monitor*, once referred to as a "tin can on a shingle," is famous for her battle with her Con-federate counterpart, the *Merrimack*, on March 9, 1862, off the coast of Maryland. The *Merrimack* was actually a rebuilt Union frigate. Union forces had scuttled her at the Navy yard at Portsmouth, Virginia, when they evacuated the town in 1861. The Confederacy raised the vessel, encased her in iron plates, and renamed her *Virginia*, even though many people today still use her original name. The inconclusive engagement between the two ships became the stuff of legend, even though it did no serious harm to either. The guns of the *Merrimack* could not stop the *Monitor*, but nature could. Her ignominious end came as the ship filled with water during a violent storm, as she was being towed to safety by a more buoyant vessel. The *Monitor* lay on the floor of the Atlantic Ocean until 1973, when divers found the wreck site off the coast of Cape Hatteras, North Carolina. It was promptly declared a Na-tional Marine Sanctuary and a National Historic Landmark under the administration of the National Oceanic and Atmospheric Administration. The NOAA conducted extensive remote sensing at the wreck site in 1985 and 1987. The 1987 project used state-of-the-art surveying equipment, including high-resolution sector-scanning sonar imaging that produced a computer-generated, three-dimensional view of the entire wreck.

Historical archaeologists use ground-penetrating radar, soil resistivity, and magnetometer surveys whenever and wherever possible. These methods can be expensive and usually require the collaboration of a highly skilled operator who fully understands how to interpret the readings.

Soil Phosphate Analysis

Soil-phosphate analysis is a geochemical subsurface surveying technique used to locate ancient habitation sites. Chemical changes occur in the soil of past settlements simply because of human occupation. Chemicals such as calcium, nitrogen, carbon, and phosphorus are added to soils through human activity, but only phosphorus is stable over time. Phosphorus plays a role in the composition of fluids in the digestive tract, is fixed with calcium in bones and teeth, and occurs in significant amounts in animal and human excreta. The presence of humans and even domesticated animals at a locale can increase the amount of phosphorus in the soil. Because phosphorus moves so little once it has been deposited, archaeologists can even use phosphate testing to identify stratified habitation levels.

A soil phosphate analysis begins with laying out a site grid. Then a soil coring tool or auger is used to collect samples below the topsoil. A rigorous quantitative laboratory analysis can reveal precisely how much phosphorus is contained in a soil sample, but a less accurate spot test is generally adequate for most archaeological research. In the spot test method, a small amount of soil from each stratum is tested for the presence of phosphorus, using first, a solution of distilled water, ammonium molybdate, and dilute hydrochloric acid, and second, a solution of distilled water and ascorbic acid (vitamin C). After applying the two solutions to the soil sample, the analyst checks for a blue color produced by the reaction of the phosphorous and the chemicals. Depending on the intensity of the color and the length of the blue rays emanating outward from the sample, the analyst assigns a number from 1 to 6 to the test. When all of the soil samples are similarly tested, the values are placed on a map at the proper coordinates, making a contour map of phosphorus amounts at the site. This map is used to determine areas of high phosphorus concentrations at the site. These "hot spots" are likely to be the locations of past houses, yard areas, animal pens, fence lines, privies, and other areas that would be the focus of past human activity.

Soil phosphate expert William Woods used a quantitative test to help locate the first Fort de Chartres in southern Illinois. While the reconstructed stone fort is a familiar landmark, the two earlier fortresses were buried under featureless topography. Their locations were unknown until the 1928 air photograph revealed a large soil discoloration near the stone fort. The precise location of the first fort, however, was not known until Wood's phosphate testing program located the high phosphorus values associated with human occupation within the fortifications. Excavations later confirmed the reliability of the tests by discovering the ditches that once held the palisade walls of the fort.

Dowsing

We should mention a distinctly low-tech detection method—dowsing. Some people can find underground water using a forked stick. In a similar procedure, others use two bent, metal coat hangers, which they prefer to call "angle rods," to locate buried metal objects and substantial underground features, such as stone walls. Ivor Noël Hume introduced dowsing to historical archaeology in the 1950s, and wrote about it in his well-known book *Historical Archaeology*. He mentions having success with the method at Colonial Williamsburg, but does not elaborate. But

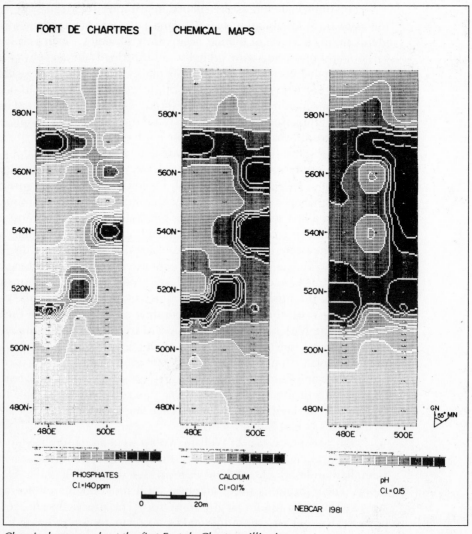

Chemical map made at the first Fort de Chartres, Illinois.

he tells us he felt "a little idiotic walking across a field intently watching two pieces of coat hanger." Perhaps his most curious discovery was that 80 percent of men can make dowsing rods work, but that only 30 percent of women can use them successfully. Perhaps this says more about who is willing to walk around archaeological sites looking idiotic, than about anything else!

Dowsing is more widely used in Britain. Noël Hume, a British national, mentions the existence of a British Society of Dowsers. A recent book, *Dowsing and Church Archaeology*, describes the successes dowsers have had on medieval sites. St. Mary's Church at Woodhorn in northern England dates to at least the Norman period (post-A.D. 1066), and perhaps even earlier. It also exhibits clear thirteenth-century and early nineteenth-century design elements. In 1973, the building was no longer needed as a house of worship and was converted into a museum and cultural center. In 1982, two dowsers, Eric Cambridge and Richard Bailey, were given the opportunity to conduct a survey of the church. They found what they took to be possible foundation walls beneath the existing chancel. The location of these walls suggested that the chancel had once been smaller, probably being enlarged in the nineteenth century. Given the opportunity to test their findings, Cambridge and Bailey set about excavating in the spot their "angle rods" showed the presence of a foundation wall. They quickly discovered a mortared-stone wall precisely where they said it would be! The wall was 8 inches (20 cm) below the paved surface of the chancel, and was approximately 39 inches (100 cm) wide. They were not able to provide an exact date for the wall, finding both medieval floor tiles and a white clay pipe bowl dating to the 1650–1680 period in association with it. The remarkable thing is that the wall was there at all!

The authors of *Dowsing and Church Archaeology* complain that professional archaeologists have "bitterly attacked" them as occultists because their technique has "no underpinning theoretical explanation." These British dowsers swear that their method of subsurface surveying works, and they provide a serious argument for it. We present dowsing here, not because we have ever tried it or, for that matter, even believe that it works, but because it is an unusual method that some historical archaeologist have used with apparent success. Perhaps some day all archaeologists will include "angle rods" in their tool boxes!

Finding archaeological sites is, of course, only the beginning of archaeological research. In the next chapter, we discuss the processes of archaeological excavation.

CHAPTER

7

Pre-excavation Fieldwork: Documents, Interviews, Buildings

"The past is everywhere. All around us lie features which, like ourselves and our thoughts, have more or less recognizable antecedents"

David Lowenthal, 1985

Archaeology is a multidisciplinary enterprise. Whether studying the earliest humans, great pueblos in the American Southwest, or Inca road systems high in the Andes, prehistoric archaeologists rely on not only on artifacts, structures, and food remains, but on information from many sciences, among them biology and climatology. Historical archaeology also relies on the sciences, but it is unique because of its strong reliance on sources of information not usually associated with excavation: historical documents, interviews with informants, and standing buildings. In this chapter we explain how archaeologists use these "nonarchaeological" sources in the study of the recent past.

HISTORICAL FIELDWORK AND DOCUMENTS

Historians James Davidson and Mark Lytle state that "The writing of history is one of the most familiar ways of organizing human knowledge. And yet, if familiarity has not always bred contempt, it has at least encouraged a good bit of misunderstanding." This misunderstanding stems from the common assumption that "history" consists of a series of dry "facts." Many people believe the job of the historian is simply to find the "facts," like an archaeologist unearthing potsherds, and then to compile them into a "history," just as the archaeologist reconstructs a pot from its many broken fragments. Unfortunately, many of us encounter history this way in our early years, as a stultifyingly dull, almost relentless recitation of dates and sterile facts.

Modern historians have worked hard to dispel this stereotype. In their fascinating book, *After the Fact: The Art of Historical Detection,* Davidson and Lytle demonstrate how historians actually work. Rather than simply looking for new facts about an old topic or rehashing old ones, historians engage in a great deal of evaluation and interpretation. Davidson and Lytle use several case studies, ranging from Colonial times to Watergate, to show that "what happened in the past" is not necessarily the same as "history." For example, in their essay on early photography, they show how the photographers of the past can affect our vision of past reality. We often imagine the camera to be an impartial observer, or what Davidson and Lytle call a "mirror with a memory." We point it at something and it simply records the image on film. In truth, though, the photographer behind the camera has the ability to insert his or her own biases into any picture. Images of lodgers in overcrowded tenements or children playing in dirty alleyways may not truly represent "how things used to be." However, because these are the photographs we have available today, they become our visual reality of the past. The great French historian, Marc Bloch—a member of the French Resistance during World War II who was captured and executed by the Nazis on June 16, 1944, only ten days after D-Day—wrote that the "faculty of understanding the living is, in very truth, the master quality of the historian." The writing of history, technically termed "historiography," thus involves an interplay between the past (what actually happened) and the present (what the historian can document and is interested in studying). Thus, the past is not a file of dead facts, but a living body of knowledge from which we draw our interpretations using various changing perspectives and attitudes.

Nowhere does the interpretive task of the historian come across better than in T.H. Breen's brilliant study of East Hampton, New York, on the east end of Long Island. Breen, a historian of early America, writes a history of this seventeenth-century town that is actually an "interpretive journey." During this journey, he holds firm to the idea "that people like ourselves have ultimately decided what will or will not be treated as a historical 'fact'." Breen realizes that the histories of East Hampton that have already been written are "products of an interpretive process that at the very best can generate only partial truths." Thus, when John Lyon Gardiner wrote the first history of the town in 1798, we see East Hampton as a pastoral, idyllic place that stood tall and proud for American Independence and staunch in its support of democracy. The only sore spot for Gardiner was the Montauk Indians. Gardiner perceived them as being in a self-inflicted degenerate condition. He regarded their extreme poverty as the result of their own "idle disposition and savage manners." Without them, East Hampton would have been a perfect place.

Today, Gardiner's eighteenth-century history seems ill informed at best and racist at worst. Gardiner was an educated member of the elite. All he was doing was putting the "facts" down on paper for posterity. Other educated, literate members of his society assumed that the Montauk—and all other Native Americans still in the East, for that matter—were degenerates and that they only had themselves to blame for their debased condition. We know today that what Gardiner recounted to his readers were not the "facts," but only his interpretation of certain elements of the past. Carl Becker, a leading American historian, told the assembled members of the prestigious American Historical Association in 1926 that "the simple historical fact turns out to be not a hard, cold something with clear outline, and measurable pressure, like a brick." Historical facts have a much more nebulous character; they change and mutate with our attitudes.

Breen grew to understand this curious mutation. He became adept at writing several East Hampton histories at once, of seeing the past from different angles. He traveled easily between the past and the present, learning that history is written by looking back at the past with different lenses. For instance, he learned about a man named Samuel Mulford, perhaps East Hampton's most prominent citizen in the 1680s. Mulford owned a whaling company employing 24 men. He was also a Puritan, widely known for his dogmatic and rigid views on Calvinism. Some people, including the colonial governor of New York, characterized Mulford, in Breen's terms, as "a long-winded, self-righteous bore." Breen began to develop an impression of what Mulford must have been like. As Breen said, the written accounts "allow us to imagine a person who was extraordinarily ambitious. They suggest other adjectives as well: tough, clever, articulate, blunt, and obstinate." Breen also discovered that Mulford had the curious nickname of "Fishhook." The story told in East Hampton is that early in the eighteenth century, Mulford traveled to London in the hopes of obtaining a personal audience with the king. However, while waiting outside the palace, Mulford had most of his money stolen by a pickpocket. So distressed was the pennywise Mulford that he promptly sewed a series of fishhooks inside his coat to secure his remaining cash. The storytellers say that all of London, and even the king himself, was impressed by Mulford's ingenuity.

Breen doubted that the fishhook incident ever happened. He argued that its truth was less important than the story itself. He believed the story to be about the entire East Hampton community. A small town in the process of being overwhelmed by the world around it, East Hampton used ingenious methods—like Samuel Mulford and the fishhooks—to protect and preserve itself. That the story uses Mulford as its focus merely shows how important he was, and still is, viewed in the town's history.

Breen could not shake the image of Samuel Mulford. So he visited with a direct descendant, the Presbyterian Reverend David Mulford, to learn more about him. David Mulford lives in the house the Mulfords have owned for more than three centuries. Mulford is the family genealogist, and Breen hoped that he could "add something to what I had found in the colonial town records." Breen also hoped that his visit might remind Mulford "of half-forgotten letters or documents from the seventeenth century now stored in some corner of the attic." During their discussion, Breen told Mulford what he knew about Samuel Mulford and the seventeenth century; Mulford in turn told him about East Hampton's three-hundredth-year celebration in 1948, and of his father's "outspoken belief that the automobile had ruined the village." It was in these conversations that Breen traveled, sometimes even unwittingly, between the past and the present. Breen had to admit to himself that "months after this conversation took place, I still wonder how much of Samuel I saw in David." He also had to admit that he "had somehow constructed a mental image of Samuel Mulford."

The Historian's Craft

Breen's detailed and interesting account of how he learned the many histories of East Hampton, New York, illustrates that the act of writing history, really the art of interpreting the past, is an expert field of research in its own right. Few archaeologists have extensive formal training in its intricacies, or in the subtle nuances of historical research (we cite one or two standard works on the subject in the Guide to Further Reading). Still, all historical archaeologists must know the basics of historiography because at some point in their careers they will be called on to conduct some original research of this kind, simply because no one else is available to do the work. In many respects, an historical archaeologist's abilities will show from the quality of his or her documentary research. Breen's East Hampton research shows that the best historians may not be men and women who know everything, but rather people who simply know where to find the pertinent information when they need it. Their real skills as historians, however, show in how they interpret what they find. In this sense, being a historian is just like being an archaeologist. Glass bottles, ceramic cups and bowls—like legal papers, personal diaries, and correspondences—do not speak; they must be interpreted.

Historians study both primary and secondary sources. *Primary sources* are contemporary records, generally written by eyewitnesses or people who may have a direct understanding or a personal insight into the events or attitudes of the day. Breen used many primary documents in his East Hampton research. One of these is intriguing. In the late 1600s, the economy of East Hampton was dependant on whaling. Many of the town's most prominent citizens—Samuel Mulford, included—were involved in the "whale design," the economy of whaling. The local residents knew, however, that to hunt for whales they would require the assistance of several common laborers. In late seventeenth-century New England, the majority of able-bodied workers were Native Americans. Realizing the need for laborers, the whalers of East Hampton entered into binding contracts with them for the whaling season. However, there were not always enough Natives Americans to meet the demand, so the competition for them was fierce. In April 1678, the Reverend Thomas James—an ambitious whaler—wrote the following primary document, apparently because he did not trust his parishioners:

> I, Thomas James of East Hampton, having together with my copartners for the whale design made several contracts and agreements with the Indians . . . I do by these presents both in my own name and name of my copartners enter a solemn protest against any person or persons who have or shall contrary to all law of God or man, justice or equity, go about to violate or infringe the above mentioned contracts or agreements without our consent.

This primary document gives a clear picture of what Thomas James thought about people who would try to steal his Native American laborers from him.

Secondary sources are interpretations of primary sources, written long after the events they describe unfolded. Breen's history is now a secondary source. He himself also read a number of other secondary sources, including Gardiner's, to learn about earlier interpretations of the town's history.

The historian's craft involves knowing precisely where to look for primary sources, a task that often requires tact and ingenuity. Primary sources come from government archives, from courthouse basements, from dusty trunks in Victorian attics, even from auction room lots. The search for them never ends, long after research is well under way. Even letters of Abraham Lincoln—possibly the most well-researched historical figure in American history—occasionally turn up unexpectedly. Recently, 34 previously unknown papers of Lincoln were discovered by the Circuit Clerk of Tazewell County Courthouse in Pekin, Illinois, who simply pulled a file marked "Re: Lincoln." These documents were written by Lincoln when he was a circuit-riding lawyer in central Illinois, and include instructions to juries, bills of indictments, affidavits, and pleas. Lincoln rode a 15-county circuit twice a year and worked day and night when he visited local courthouses. William Beard, the assistant editor of the Lincoln Legal Papers project, said that the 34 new documents represent a "King Solomon's mine in Pekin." The discovery of these new papers, along with 75 others recently found unexpectedly at Illinois State University and at other Illinois courthouses, have sparked great excitement among Lincoln scholars around the world. Documents from even the great figures of history, like important archaeological sites, still await discovery.

The archaeologist may not be as unrelenting in the search for primary sources, for his or her concerns are usually less specialized than those of historians. Here are some common places where they may be found:

- Federal repositories (official, governmental correspondence; government maps and charts; photographic collections; statistical reports; acts and statutes; business charters; newspapers; military records; census rolls; immigration lists);
- State and provincial archives (official correspondence; local statutes; personal letters and diaries; militia records; photographic collections; newspapers);
- Private and university archives (special collections of correspondence and records of prominent individuals and important places; rare manuscripts and books; maps and charts);
- Local repositories and governmental offices (personal correspondence; land ownership records and plat maps; local tax rolls; birth and death records).

This is but an incomplete list, but fortunately for the researcher, most large archives and special collections facilities publish up-to-date catalogues and summaries of their holdings.

A project at the Adobe Walls trading post site in the Texas panhandle demonstrates the value of primary sources in historical archaeology. This remote trading post came into being in 1874, when enterprising merchants followed buffalo hunters flooding onto the American Plains. The merchants only occupied their sod-and-picket post for six months. Local Native American groups harassed the tiny post, threatening the traders with death. They retreated hastily to Kansas. When archaeologist Billy Harrison began to study the post in 1975, he teamed up with historian T. Lindsay Baker. Baker sifted through nineteenth-century newspapers, including those with the romantic names of the *Dodge City Times* and the *Leavenworth Times,* personal papers, letters, reports, and books and articles housed in no less than 55 separate repositories. These archives ranged from the National Archives in Washington, to a personal library in South Croydon, England. Thus, the historical documentation for even this one site, inhabited for only one-half year, kept Baker busy for months as he located, read, evaluated, and interpreted the abundant historical record.

Harrison's excavations at Adobe Walls benefited tremendously from Baker's historical research. For example, in a sworn deposition made on October 11, 1892, Charles Rath, partner of the Rath and Company store at the post, described his building. As he remembered it, the store was built of sod, was 25 by 50 feet (7.6 by 15.3 m) in size, and had two "block houses" on opposite corners. He said these block houses measured 12 or 15 feet (3.7 or 4.6 m) square. Andrew Johnson, "Andy the Swede," was also at the post during its occupation. In his deposition, made the same day as Rath's, he recalled the Rath and Company store as being 24 or 25 feet (7.3 or 7.6 m) wide and about 50 or 60 feet (15.3 or 18.3 m) long. He said it was made of sod with a log roof. He also mentioned the two "block houses" as being about 12 by 12 feet (3.7 by 3.7 m). Baker found these depositions in files at the United States National Archives in Washington, during the course of his primary document research. When Harrison began his excavation at the store, he had some idea of what he would find, based on these important eyewitness accounts. He knew he was looking for a sod building that measured somewhere around 25 by 50 feet (7.6 by 15.3 m) in size. That the excavators found the actual building to measure 16.5 feet (5.0 m) by almost 53 feet (16.2 m) is not surprising. We should expect some error in the informants' memories. After all, how many people actually know how big the rooms in their house are? Also, because the Adobe Walls trading post was only occupied for six months, we cannot expect its brief occupants to recall every minute detail about the buildings. What is more surprising, however, is that Harrison found archaeological evidence for only one "block house," on the southeast corner. The building never had two block houses. The discrepancy between the accounts and the physical evidence cannot be explained.

The Adobe Walls research highlights some of the difficulties inherent in using primary documents in archaeological science. The problems become even more complicated when international relations or trade are involved. Quite apart from an expertise in, say, sixteenth-century Spanish language and script, access to even official archives may be difficult to arrange, even with the cooperation of local scholars. For example, the study of colonial sites in North America and elsewhere usually means acquiring a familiarity with the colonial archives of Spain, Portugal, Great Britain, France, or the Netherlands, depending on the history of the site involved. This was the case when archaeologist Kathleen Deagan teamed up with historian Jane Landers in the study of Fort Mose, outside the historic city of St. Augustine, Florida, the first permanent European city in the United States. Fort Mose, more properly called "Gracia Real de Santa Teresa de Mose," was the creation of

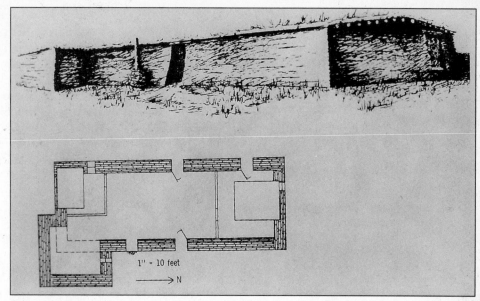

Excavated floor plan and artist's reconstruction of the Rath and Company Store, Adobe Walls trading post, Texas.

African-American escapees from British plantations to the north. The Spanish welcomed these new inhabitants. Fort Mose was founded in 1738 and became the first legally approved free black community in what would become the United States. The residents of Fort Mose helped the Spanish to defeat their former masters when the British attacked St. Augustine in the early 1740s. To learn something of the history of this important site, Deagan and Landers spent the first six months of their archaeological project becoming familiar with Spanish parish records held in Florida and official governmental dispatches taken from Spanish archives. These Spanish records tell the "official" story of Fort Mose, or what the British derisively called simply a "Negroe Fort."

Deagan's archaeological research is just beginning to expose the history of Fort Mose. The site of the fort was first identified in 1971 by a crew working under the direction of Charles Fairbanks, a pioneer in American historical archaeology at the University of Florida. Deagan was a student on this crew. She returned to the site in 1976 as a professor to conduct a more detailed examination of the fort. She confirmed the fort's location, but it was not until 1985 that she could obtain enough funding for a large-scale excavation. Her research is still ongoing, and the results are still being interpreted. However, Deagan's team has learned several unique things about the fort, including details of its construction. For instance, they have learned that the fort's walls were about 5 feet (1.5 m) tall, faced on the outside with marsh clay and planted along the top with prickly pear cactus. They found evidence of the moat in three places. It was almost 7 feet (2 m) wide and about 2.5 feet (0.8 m) deep. The researchers also found posts from a watchtower or large building, and evidence of a smaller, circular wood and thatch building that may have been a dwelling. The many artifacts include round lead shot, carefully

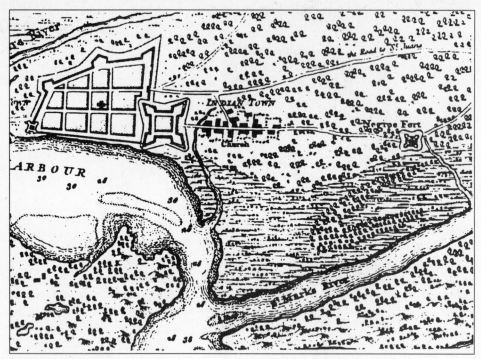

Detail of 1792 map of St. Augustine, Florida, showing "Negroe Fort."

chipped gunflints, white clay smoking pipes, brass buckles, bone buttons, and glass bottles. Surprisingly, 62 percent of the finds comprise non-European pottery. Deagan associated these wares with the local Native American Timucua. It seems surprising that most of the European ceramics in the collection are English, not Spanish, in origin. However, the English dominated the world ceramic market at this time, and also, smugglers were adept at bringing British goods into Spanish America. Deagan's archaeological program at Fort Mose, supported as it is by Landers' extensive, thoughtful research in the relevant Spanish-language documents, promises to provide exciting new information about early African-American history.

ORAL INTERVIEWING

Oral sources can be as valuable as written documentation. Anthropologists discovered early on that they would have to talk to people to learn about their kinship system, genealogical terms, religious beliefs, attitudes about infanticide, and birth control methods—to mention only a few topics. These, and many other elements of daily life, could not be observed, were seldom talked about, and were not recorded by missionaries and early explorers. As a result, the only way to learn a good deal about oral cultures—those without writing—is to ask. This is "participant observation," a fundamental anthropological tool.

Anthropologist Frances Densmore getting an interpretation of a Blackfoot song.

Polish-born Bronislaw Malinowski was one of the first professional anthropologists to spend a long period living among, and studying, the people of one culture. His work among the Trobriand Islanders, near New Guinea, produced many important works that now stand as classics in the history of anthropology. His *The Sexual Life of Savages in North-Western Melanesia* created a public sensation when it appeared in 1929 for its frank discussions of Trobriand sexuality. Malinowski is best known in anthropological circles for developing techniques of participant observation. His fieldwork involved a great deal of oral interviewing and face-to-face interaction. For instance, his diary entry for January 18, 1915, shows that he was well aware of the difficulty of obtaining oral information: "Yesterday before noon, Pikana came. With great effort—for he was sleepy, kept yawning, and I had a headache and felt poorly—I wormed out of him material relating to kinship." This information, "wormed" from Pikana with the greatest of difficulty, forms the core of what many anthropology students learn about kinship today.

Historical archaeologists often sympathize with Malinowski. They search for what Carl Becker calls the kind of history people "carry around in their heads." Everyone, no matter what their station in life, knows some history that is unique, and sometimes private to them. The layout and use of the rooms in our house, when we graduated from high school or started college, and what our first job was like are all part of our "history." We remember what we thought about important national or international crises, and how these events affected us, our families, and our friends. These things we know; they are part of who we are. This often transitory history, though personal and unique, can be central to learning about the recent past. Today, oral histories are central to modern history. There are oral anthologies of the Woodstock Festival and of Pearl Harbor, both based on nonwritten sources of information. Studs Terkel's bestselling *Hard Times: An Oral History of the Great Depression* is just one demonstration of how compelling oral histories can be. Even though Terkel modestly describes his book as "simply an attempt to get the story of the holocaust known as The Great Depression from an improvised battalion of survivors," his informants tell stories that have no equal. Most importantly, perhaps, these stories cannot be culled from articles, books, or newspaper accounts; they exist only in the peoples' memories. The oral historian, like the anthropologist among traditional peoples, commits these personal tales to the written page and gives them a permanence for later generations.

The very fact that these remembrances exist only in memory means that they are a nonrenewable resource. The people who remember Pearl Harbor, Woodstock, the Great Depression, or for that matter, the Boston Tea Party, have died, or will eventually die. When a generation dies, it is like burning down an archive full of unique and nonretrievable information. In this sense, the conduct of oral interviewing, for whatever reason, is just like archaeology. The only difference is that when interviewing you can learn about the past directly from the people who lived it. You can ask them questions, elicit further information, clarify obscurities or ambiguous statements as you go along. Oral history is living history. Archaeologists study a static archaeological record of artifacts, soil layers, pollen samples, and so forth—the surviving results of ancient human behavior. For this reason, oral histories are of vital importance to students of the recent past.

The lines between oral history, anthropology, and historical research are often fuzzy. When Baker and Harrison studied Adobe Walls, they used a number of interviews with still-living veterans of the post set down in the 1920s and 1930s. The transcripts were invaluable sources of colorful information that could come from no one but a participant. Many of the informants—for example, J. Wright Mooar, a Chicago streetcar conductor turned professional buffalo hunter—remembered Adobe Walls and spoke about it in an insightful and personal way. "We had 11 outlaws hired," he remembered. "I remember some of them. They were good fellows. They stayed with us. We never had any preachers with us. . . ."

In 1922, during a visit to the old site, Andrew "Andy the Swede" Johnson and Orlando A. "Brick" Bond, two former residents of the post, drew a sketch map of the post's store as they remembered it. Billy Dixon was a hunter of rare ability and a holder of the Congressional Medal of Honor for his bravery at the Battle of Buffalo Wallow, in which six soldiers and scouts held off an overwhelming number of attacking Native Americans. He recalled the area of the post as "a vast wilderness, inhabited by game—truly a hunter's paradise." Describing a fellow hunter, Dixon said that he was a man "who had lots of nerve and knew all the ins and outs of frontier life." These priceless accounts seem to be from the fictional pens of Zane Grey or Louis L'Amour, but they are real. They proved invaluable as Baker and Harrison excavated the post.

Orlando Bond and Andrew Johnson at the Adobe Walls Site in 1922.

Billy Dixon in 1876.

We have mentioned above how some of the eyewitnesses' comments about the construction of the Rath and Company store were confirmed by the archaeological research. Often, the combination of oral information with archaeological findings serves to flesh out the small details of daily life. For instance, many of the men interviewed in the 1920s remembered the popularity of wild plums and coffee at the trading post. Sixteen plum pits came from the excavations, also 25 coffee beans from the mess hall to confirm their recollections of life on a remote post in 1874.

Archaeologist Peter Schmidt used oral history in a somewhat broader way when investigating farming villages among the Buhaya, who live on the shores of Lake Victoria in Tanzania, East Africa (also see Chapter 1). Schmidt calls his research "historical archaeology," when in fact some of his sites date to the time óf Christ or even earlier, far earlier than colonial sites in Florida or Massachusetts. He uses the term *historical* to refer to the use of written and oral sources in conjunction with archaeological information in a way that is common to much historical archaeology. Using local informants, Schmidt learned a great deal about the political history of the Buhaya, their religious traditions, and the present-day land tenure system. Schmidt conducted two- to four-hour interviews in Swahili and then used what he heard to guide his excavations. Collecting such histories required persistence and patience. He visited some informants several times before he could make them comfortable enough to talk freely. Even then, most informants would agree to but one interview, because "They reasoned that we had covered the subject already and that another discussion was an obvious waste of time."

Much of what Schmidt learned was not the kind of eyewitness information used by Baker and Harrison at Adobe Walls. Instead, his Buhaya informants spoke of the past by using mnemonic devices, mental images meant as memory aids. They used these mental tricks because they could not possibly have witnessed key events that unfolded centuries ago. They recited what they learned from their parents, and what their parents had learned from their parents, and so on, back several generations. After some experience with the informants and their way of thinking about the past, Schmidt came to understand how the people of this one part of Tanzania perceived their physical environment. He came to see the landscape as "a collage of mythology, folklore, and local legends of untold permutations."

The significance of Schmidt's study to historical archaeology lies in his understanding that people have many different ways of remembering the past. Some are direct memories, resting on actual events seen and recalled, on reminiscences of individuals known and respected. At times the informants talk of events shrouded in folklore and tradition, accounts of a mythic, long-vanished past that were passed from father to son, mother to daughter over the generations.

Sometimes, oral information can contain a subtle mix of an eyewitness account and the retelling of a tradition. Such is the case with Black Elk, holy man of the Oglala Sioux (Dakota), who at age 13 witnessed the Battle of the Little Big Horn. His autobiography stands today as one of the most beautifully told accounts in American history. In beginning his life story, Black Elk said that it was a story "of us two-leggeds sharing in it with the four-leggeds and the wings of the air and all green things; for these are children of one mother and their father is one Spirit." Black Elk recounts the events of his life with a mixture of eyewitness remembrance and Oglala oral tradition. Speaking of the famous battle with Custer, he recalled that "it seemed that my people were all thunder-beings and that the soldiers would be rubbed out." His account is both spiritual and factual, personal and cultural at the same time.

Oral accounts, when added to written records, provide a greater depth and add a strong personal touch to the past.

ARCHITECTURAL FIELDWORK

Not all sites studied by historical archaeologists are empty fields. In many cases, the places where the most exciting excavating can be done contain standing buildings, pieces of complex machinery, or bridges. Historical archaeologists cannot ignore these "large artifacts." In fact, they are frequently called on to conduct surveys of standing buildings and other extant structures.

Large-scale architectural surveys are often required when areas to be affected by whole-scale land modification projects are to change the landscape and everything on its surface, including existing buildings. The buildings, like the oral interviews, represent a nonrenewable resource. If preservation, or moving the structure, is an impossibility, then archaeologists or architects may be called in to document them before destruction. When the U.S. Army Corps of Engineers constructed a huge dam to provide increased power to the City of Atlanta on the Savannah River, between Georgia and South Carolina, they created a gigantic artificial lake, about 25 miles (40 km) long, which rose roughly 60 feet (18.2 m) above the former river banks. Thousands of archaeological and historic sites were threatened by the Richard B. Russell Reservoir.

The Corps of Engineers hired teams of archaeologists to excavate both historic and prehistoric sites within the dam area. They also contracted with a group of historical architects to document the standing buildings that would be destroyed by the dam and lake. The inundated area had once been home to slaves and freedmen, to small farms and plantations. Architect Linda Worthy, the editor of the project's final report, states that "The dwelling house is the most important component of the cultural landscape." Folklorist Henry Glassie, in his monumental *Folk Housing in Middle Virginia,* shows us how an old house can be "read" like an old book to reveal "a more human history." Windows boarded up, new rooms added, and altered roof lines—all tell part of a story that can be interpreted if one wishes to look for it.

In compiling what they called the "more human history" of the Russell Dam area, architectural surveyors found and photographed 93 abandoned houses, including wood-framed farmhouses of freed slave farmers, two-story plantation mansions of slave owners, and hewn-log cabins of the region's earliest settlers (Figures 7.1, 7.2). Traveling an intertwined network of dusty backroads, they also discovered log barns and sheds, a blacksmith shop, and iron bridges. Collectively dating from well before the Civil War to the mid-1950s, the buildings tell the recent history of the region: its initial European-American settlement, its growth into a rich plantation belt based on the labor of African-American slaves, and its transition into a region of small tenant farms clinging precariously to the near-exhausted red soil of the Upland South.

HABS/HAER Surveys

The conduct of architectural surveys tends to be highly specialized work, requiring not only highly detailed and exacting mapping, but precise interpretation of the buildings' physical characteristics. The ultimate standards for architectural surveys have been established in the United States by the Historic American Buildings Survey (HABS), founded in 1933, and the Historic American Engineering Record

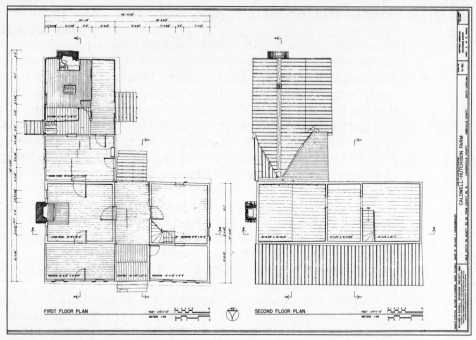

Figure 7.1 *First- and second-floor plans of late eighteenth–nineteenth-century Caldwell-Hutchinson Farm, South Carolina.*

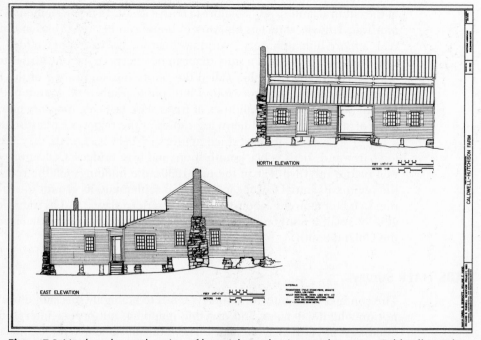

Figure 7.2 *North and east elevation of late eighteenth–nineteenth-century Caldwell-Hutchinson Farm, South Carolina.*

(HAER), founded in 1969. Congress formally combined HABS and HAER in 1983 as HABS/HAER. The measured drawings executed by HABS/HAER are completed to extremely precise specifications and are intended as a permanent, archival record of structures of historic significance. Precise measured drawings have been completed for the Statue of Liberty in New York, for the original Smithsonian Institution building in Washington, the steam-powered hoist at the Quincy copper mine in northern Michigan, and many other important buildings, bridges, mechanical systems, historic ships, and landscapes. The staff of HABS/HAER also helped to document the buildings within the Richard B. Russell Reservoir.

HABS/HAER staff members were involved in documenting the architectural majesty of the White House in Washington, D.C. The removal of several layers of old paint laid bare walls that had not been exposed since 1798, and revealed the scorch marks that are the silent testimony to the British attempt to burn the mansion in 1814. With the paint removed, architects from HABS/HAER made exacting measured drawings of the windows, doors, and building facades. Their drawing of the main entrance reveals an ornate design of oak leaves and roses that harkens back to an age when formally trained architects ornamented their masterpieces with such ostentatious adornments.

HABS/HAER recorders also create a photographic record to amplify their drawings. Photographs are often preferred to measured drawings because they are quicker and easier to produce and are less expensive. These photographs are not simple snapshots, but highly professional images intended to convey a building's three-dimensional qualities, its spatial relationships with other buildings, its condition or state of preservation at the time of the photograph, and the texture of the building's many surfaces. Even though many of these photographs are quite artistic and beautiful, they are actually documents that constitute a formal photographic record. Along with their architectural drawings, HABS/HAER architects also made an extensive photographic record of the White House. These photographs, along with the measured drawings, are now part of the documentary history of the President's home.

Other Architectural Surveys

Obviously, historical archaeologists cannot prepare high-standard HABS/HAER drawings and photographs without considerable, specialized training. However, many universities with schools of architecture and some governmental agencies provide summer internships for architecture students. As interns, students can participate in HABS/HAER surveys and documentation projects throughout the country. Linda Worthy, who prepared the final report on the architectural survey of the Richard Russell Reservoir, served as just such an intern with the National Park Service when she compiled the report.

Unfortunately, time does not always permit the creation of perfectly accurate measured drawings, and budgets sometimes cannot allow architectural specialists to be hired for archaeological projects. In practice, archaeologists are often called on to make measured drawings and photographs of a building's elevations (sides), and floorplan. These drawings may not meet the stringent standards of HABS/

HAER, but they nonetheless help to provide the "more human history" mentioned by Glassie.

Archaeologists from Southern Methodist University in Dallas performed an architectural survey in north central Texas as part of a larger study of the Richland/Chambers Reservoir project, an engineering feat similar to the Richard B. Russell Reservoir. Their work resulted in the documentation of 26 dwellings, four bridges, and 12 "special purpose structures," like storage sheds, various kinds of outbuildings, and even a store. The settlers in this part of Texas built these still-standing buildings between 1848 and 1945. The documentation provided by the Southern Methodist team offers a clear look at the kinds of houses in which the people of this region lived, the sheds in which they stored their farming implements, the stores in which they shopped for the necessities of daily life, and the bridges they crossed as they traveled around the region.

Historical records, oral interviews, and architectural information provide a rich element to historical archaeology, and they truly do add a "more human" touch to our understanding of the past. When "nonarchaeological" information is added to archaeological findings, a powerful interpretation results. In the next chapter, we turn to the actual excavation of historic sites and the processing of the artifacts in the laboratory.

CHAPTER
8

Archaeological Fieldwork: Field and Laboratory

"The excavator without an intelligent policy may be described as an archaeological food-gatherer, master of a skill, perhaps, but not creative in the wider terms of constructive science"

Mortimer Wheeler, 1954

Archaeological excavation: the very words conjure up images of Indiana Jones–like heroes hacking their way through dense forest in search of stone pyramids, golden idols, and lost civilizations. Today, such Indiana Jones–like stereotypes are the stuff of Hollywood escapist fantasies, reflecting not what archaeologists really do, but only what somebody thinks they do. The pages of *National Geographic Magazine* and Public Television programs paint a far more realistic portrait of archaeology today. Here, scientific excavation is the rule—instead of armies of workmen, archaeologists use toothbrushes and dental picks and high technology in pursuit of the past. The adventurer of yesterday is the time detective of today, spending as much time in the laboratory as the trench, tracking down ancient mysteries with all the scientific fervor of a latter-day Sherlock Holmes. Today's excavations may be less spectacular than the well-funded, overpublicized treasure hunts of the past, but they are just as fascinating and exciting. The fascination comes not from buried gold, but from uncovering knowledge.

Stereotypes of archaeology stress digging and discovery and the use of spectacular high-tech equipment for the simple reason that these things engage the enthusiasm of a wide audience. However dazzling the finds, however significant the site, the most important and time-consuming task of archaeologists is not the actual excavation. It is detailed record keeping and processes of conservation that go along with it. Today, the computer keyboard and the notepad are in some ways more apt symbols of excavation than the spade or the trowel.

In this chapter we explore some of the basic field procedures used by historical archaeologists. We also discuss the role of laboratory work in historical archaeology.

ARCHAEOLOGICAL PROCEDURES

"All excavation is destruction." These words of Sir Leonard Woolley, the British excavator of Ur—the great Sumerian city in today's Iraq—succinctly describe archaeological excavation. Simply put, when archaeologists excavate a site, they destroy it. They generally destroy it carefully, taking it apart piece by piece, but nonetheless, they do demolish it. As archaeologist Kent Flannery once said, "Archaeology is the only branch of anthropology where we kill off our subjects!" This conscious destruction may be somewhat difficult to imagine. We generally do not think of archaeologists as men and women who destroy the very thing they love. Instead, we often envision archaeologists standing boldly in the face of a raging bulldozer, willing to risk life and limb as the last line of defense against the wanton destruction of archaeological sites. We see archaeologists as front-line warriors in the battle for historic preservation. In reality, even though archaeologists are usually strong advocates of historic preservation, they must destroy archaeological sites to excavate them. Destruction is a sad but inescapable feature of all archaeological excavation.

Here is an apt analogy to explain archaeological excavation. Take an old library card catalog file, the kind used before the introduction of today's familiar computerized data bases. Imagine that the catalog has 40 card drawers arranged in four rows and ten columns. Each row represents one layer of earth. Each card within the drawers represents one piece of information. This information can be an artifact, a post hole, a stone foundation wall, a trench, a soil color, or any other element of the archaeological record. If the archaeologist has planned a 10 percent sample (see Chapter 6), then he or she will be able to look into only four of the drawers. Within these four drawers, our archaeologist will remove and keep the ones marked "artifact," but will only be able to record the information from the other cards before destroying them. Because all of the nonartifact cards must be destroyed, future investigators will only have 36 drawers left to examine. They also will have the "artifact" cards and the notes the original archaeologist took from the other cards: soil colors, thicknesses of soil layers, width and height of stone walls. Our researcher knows that once his or her study is finished, the destroyed cards will be lost forever. His or her research notes will be the only record of the destroyed cards.

This example is, of course, fictional; archaeological sites are not card files. Still, the exact process is repeated in archaeological excavation. Some of the archaeological record vanishes forever (soil layers, pit outlines), while some of it (artifacts, soil samples) ends up in a museum or storage facility. In many cases, the archaeological features themselves are destroyed by the realities of excavation. When Kenneth Kidd excavated Sainte Marie I in 1941, the seventeenth-century Jesuit mission in Ontario we mentioned in Chapter 2, he was only able to measure, record, and photograph the small post holes that the mission's builders placed beneath the still-visible wooden sill of the chapel's original wall. Kidd could not actually save the post holes themselves because they were simply dark stains in the soil. As a result, all we know today about these post holes derives from Kidd's records and from his archaeological report; the holes themselves no longer exist. Thus, when Kidd states that the posts had an average diameter of "4 inches" (10 cm) and an average depth of "about 20 inches," (51 cm) we must believe him because we can never see the post holes ourselves. Kidd destroyed them during his excavation, but he left us a thorough record of how they looked and precisely where they were located.

In general, the same excavation procedures apply in historical archaeology as in prehistoric archaeology. Archaeologists would excavate a colonial tavern in Massachusetts using the same basic methods they would use to excavate an eleventh-century Anasazi pueblo in Arizona. Excavation is an unfolding process of carefully applied scientific procedures, procedures that have been developed and refined by decades of archaeological research.

The Process of Archaeological Excavation

Excavation, like other research procedures, is a slowly unfolding, ever flexible process. We can identify six stages:

Research Design

All archaeological fieldwork begins with a carefully developed research design. This is a carefully organized plan for carrying out the project, an explicit statement of the way in which the researcher seeks to answer questions posed before the excavation begins. The number of sites to be investigated, the size of the sample needed (see Chapter 6), and the kinds of specialists to be involved are all specified in the research design.

In an ideal world, we might imagine that an archaeologist constructs a research design based solely on the needs and requirements of the research. It would be comforting to think that archaeologists can always conduct the sort of research that interests them in the best and most scientific ways. In reality, however, excavators must always balance what they want to do with what they can realistically accomplish given the many constraints placed on them. Constraints can be funding limits, the availability of students and other field workers, the difficulty of obtaining permits and licenses, the development of volatile, dangerous political situations, or the occurrence of environmental catastrophes, like floods, volcanic eruptions, or droughts. Almost anything can happen to change the course of an archaeological field project. Even the most carefully and well-planned research design must be flexible to adapt to the changing conditions of fieldwork.

When historical archaeologist William Lees devised the research design for his study of Limerick Plantation, South Carolina, in the late 1970s, he did so with

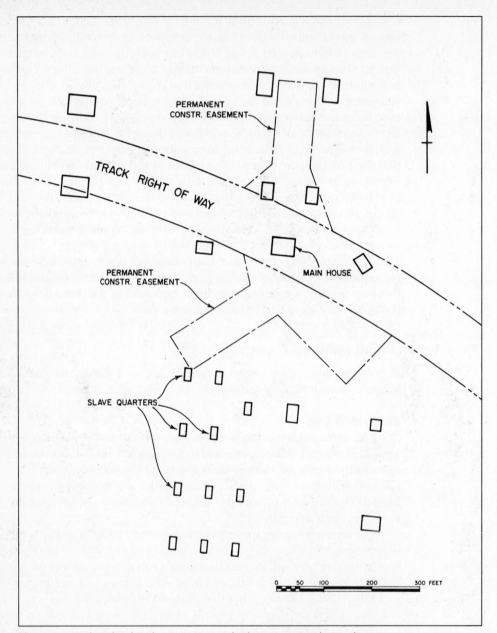

Figure 8.1 *Railroad right-of-way at Limerick Plantation, South Carolina.*

the knowledge that he had to match his desire to learn about plantation life with
the needs of the project's sponsor. The sponsor, the South Carolina Public Rail-
ways Commission, was overseeing the construction of a railway line right through
the center of the late eighteenth- and nineteenth-century plantation. The right-of-
way was to destroy the wooden, main house, but would leave the slave quarters un-
touched (Figure 8.1). Lees knew that his research design had to be guided by the

right-of-way boundaries established by the railroad. The railroad did not wish to pay for research on the slave quarters, but only on the portion of the plantation that they would affect by construction. Lees may have been interested in the slaves who lived at Limerick, but the research design he devised had to be structured so as to exclude them from serious consideration.

As a result, Lees tailored much of his project around the architecture of the main house and its support structures, focusing specifically on "the origin and evolution of these buildings." The house remained largely unaltered between 1709 and 1945, when it burnt down. When Lees first saw the mansion it was in ruins. As part of the research design, Lees presented a thorough historical picture of the Limerick Plantation, using photographs from the 1940s and even Historic American Buildings Survey (see Chapter 7) elevation drawings and floor plans to flesh it out. The carefully planned field research confirmed the presence of seven buildings within the railroad right-of-way. At the main house, ceramics of known age told Lees that a porch had been added sometime between 1775 and 1795. He found a detached kitchen building, complete with its own interior well and flagstone walkway, southwest of the main house, constructed sometime between 1797 (because it does not appear on a plat map of this date) and 1904 (because a deed of this date mentions an outbuilding near the house). Lees also uncovered a small building of unknown function about 12 feet (3.7 m) due south of the kitchen. Clusters of artifacts also led him to two carriage houses, an eighteenth-century kitchen, and a barn.

Lees' research design was successful because he planned it well. The project's sponsors limited him to the boundaries of the new railroad track. Within these limits he presented a realistic and wholly workable research design. His findings about the plantation's main complex—the design of its buildings and the spatial relationships between them—did not lead to their reconstruction. The rail line made this impossible. But the research design enabled him to collect architectural details that can be compared with plantation complexes at other sites.

Implementation

Grant writing, fund raising, and the acquisition of all required permits—every archaeologist spends months on these mundane, frustrating tasks.

The process of implementation involves not only fund raising, but it can also include the refinement of the research plan to accommodate the realities of available funding. For example, at Limerick, Lees knew that he had only enough funding for 14 weeks of fieldwork and 38 weeks of laboratory analysis and report preparation. Given this reality, it would have made no sense for him to plan 25 weeks of fieldwork and 45 weeks of laboratory analysis. He would have run out of funds long before the project was completed.

These are weeks and months when the investigators complete their background research and reading, not only of the archaeological literature, but of readily accessible historical sources. They also attempt to track down as many primary sources as possible, to save time in the field. Very often, oral interviewing, archival investigation, and architectural analysis (see Chapter 7) will have begun or even be completed before any excavation starts. For instance, Lees studied historic maps of the region around Limerick, read extensively about the history of early South Carolina, and examined the papers of the family who lived at the plantation as part of the background research necessary for the archaeological excavation.

Fieldwork

The time spent in the field varies infinitely with the research design and funding available. For example, a total excavation of a large colonial building might require a large crew and weeks of careful investigation of foundation trenches, post holes, even standing stone walls, to say nothing of garden layouts. In contrast, at Limerick, Lees used a combination of 94 auger holes, 88 five-foot (1.5 m) square excavation units, seven backhoe trenches, and 409 eight-inch (20.3 cm) diameter post hole–sized units. His plan was to excavate as much of the site as possible within the time available. Other archaeologists may have chosen other strategies, not because Lees was wrong, but simply because several, equally valid ways exist to excavate an archaeological site.

Every excavation, however modest, requires meticulous records and a place to work on them. Many fieldworkers construct on-site artifact processing facilities, sometimes a shelter as simple as a tarpaulin strung between some trees. It is here that artifacts are washed, bagged, and inventoried, where emergency conservation work takes place, where computer entries and inventories are logged. This in-field processing is preliminary to the longer-term, more thorough laboratory analysis that follows any archaeological excavation. It has the advantage, however, of allowing the archaeologists to see the objects they are finding while they are still in the field, enabling them to adjust their research design while the excavation is in progress.

Analysis

Most excavators say that one month in the field requires three months in the laboratory. This estimate may be conservative because special circumstances may prolong the analysis for many months, and often even years. These are the months when the researchers process all the information they collected during the fieldwork. A laboratory usually has large, long tables for cleaning, marking, and analyzing artifacts. The laboratory workers have access to measuring calipers, scales, and microscopes, while they enter their data directly onto laptop or desktop computers. Many excavators use bar codes (like those on groceries and books) to mark bags of artifacts. Most field laboratories also have comparative artifact collections for comparison with excavated pieces, and small reference libraries. All artifacts must be processed and accessioned in a consistent format for future identification and for long-term curation. Oral interviews are typed up from audio cassettes, architectural plans and sketches cleaned and redrafted, photographs developed, printed, and cataloged, and archaeological plans and maps redrawn and made ready for publication.

Once all of the finds are properly accessioned, the research team examines each one, describes it, and prepares inventories and tables showing the kinds and quantities of artifacts found at the site. For example, Lees and his research team found 63,672 artifacts—ceramics, glass, metal, and other materials—at Limerick Plantation. They included 36 different kinds of European ceramics and 1,026 smoking pipe fragments. Of the 12,486 ceramic pieces, fully 4,818 or almost 39 percent, were unglazed, low-fired wares made by African-American slaves and Native American potters. The presence of these non-European ceramic pieces in the planter's main house raised several questions that have yet to be satisfactorily answered. Were these pottery vessels used by slave cooks? Did the planter's family accept and use these wares? Do they reflect cultural borrowing by European slave owners from Africans? Did African-American potters learn this pottery tradition from local Native Americans? Preliminary artifact processing is just the first stage of the analysis, one that sometimes reveals fascinating general trends like the high frequencies of low-fired wares at Limerick.

Food remains such as animal bones and plants require not only preliminary sorting on site, but careful analysis by specialist experts. Such finds are of vital importance, because they enable the excavator to reconstruct the dietary habits of past households, neighborhoods, and communities.

Zooarchaeologists specialize in the study of animal bones of all kinds. Most are trained in both archaeology and biology, for their research goes far beyond the mere identification of animals once consumed for food. They separate domestic animals like cattle and sheep from game like deer and rabbits. They calculate the minimum number of individuals in the collection, as a way of establishing the amount of meat represented by the bones. Many bones bear revealing evidence of ancient butchering techniques—knife cut marks, saw marks, and other kinds of trauma resulting from human activities. These small telltale signs can sometimes provide fascinating information on the distinct ways in which a variety of ethnic or social groups used animals for food.

Zooarchaeologist Diana Crader had great success studying the faunal remains from one of the slave buildings at Jefferson's Monticello (Figure 8.2). She discovered that the bones told a different story than historical documents, which stated that pork was a staple of the slaves' diet. Pig bones did indeed outnumber cow bones in the archaeological deposits, but as Crader said, "beef seems to play a very large role in the diet based on estimates of pounds (kg) of available meat." Overall, she expected the quality of the meat at the slave building to be low, but she learned from the bones that Jefferson's slaves ate both high-quality limbs and low-quality heads and feet. At another slave dwelling at Monticello, however, Crader found that the slaves did not eat high-quality meats. She believes Jefferson's slaves may have been arranged in a social hierarchy, in which some had a better diet than others. This surprising evidence for a perhaps unspoken social hierarchy among Monticello's slave community can only be detected in the archaeological record.

Ethnobotanists, sometimes called "archaeobotanists," are specialists in plant remains and have both archaeological and botanical training. They study both direct evidence for the human use of plants—seeds, nutshells, corn cobs—and indirect evidence—leaves, bulbs, rinds, pollen. Like zooarchaeologists, their researches go far beyond mere identification of domesticated and wild plants, but they generally have more difficulty than zooarchaeologists in presenting exact counts because larger seeds like peach pits may be underrepresented as opposed to smaller ones, such as grape pips. In their research on the subsistence patterns of the colonial Spanish in Florida, Georgia, and South Carolina, ethnobotanist Margaret Scarry,

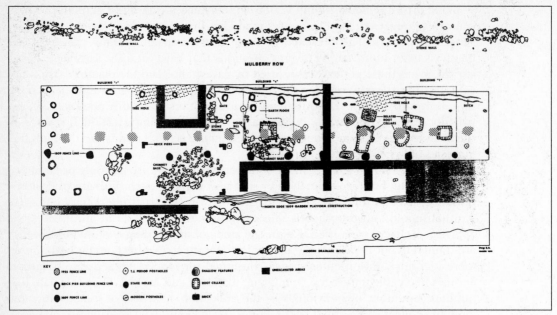

Figure 8.2 *Mulberry Row slave quarters, Monticello, Virginia, as excavated in 1983–1984.*

working closely with zooarchaeologist Elizabeth Reitz, found evidence for a wide variety of plants at Spanish forts and town sites. These included Old World cultigens (watermelon, cantaloupe, peach, grape, olive), indigenous, New World species (squash/pumpkin, bean, maize), and exotic, New World plants (lima bean, chili pepper). Thus, Spanish settlers introduced their own plants into the New World, accepted many that the natives grew locally, and imported still others from their other colonial outposts in the Caribbean, Mesoamerica, and South America. Although the Spanish colonists accepted many plant foods from the local native peoples, Reitz and Scarry remark: "It is important to note that although much of the new subsistence system had an aboriginal flavor, it remained distinctly Spanish in many ways."

Careful attention to food remains of all kinds provides unexpected insights into even recent history.

Interpretation

Interpretation tests an archaeologist's skills, insights, and understanding to the maximum; it is the process of making sense of all the accumulated data, of testing it against theoretical formulations. Historical archaeologists use not only anthropological theory, but historiography and historical data for this purpose. These skills are amply demonstrated by Reitz and Scarry's analysis of colonial Spanish subsistence strategies in the eastern United States. They not only conducted a thorough analysis of the plant and animal remains found at several sites, they also understood the natural world the Spanish encountered, in what was for them a New World. They explored the Spanish response to their new environment in the light of such anthropological issues as adaptation—how the Spanish learned to live in the new environment—and acculturation—how the Spanish and the coastal Native Americans learned from one another, and adopted elements of one another's culture.

To help guide their interpretations, some historical archaeologists have adopted a broad framework introduced by the French historian, Fernand Braudel. According to Braudel, the past can be viewed as consisting of three scales: individual time, social time, and geographical time, or long-term history. Individual time is the history of people "in reference to the environment within which they are encompassed." Social time is the history of "groups and groupings," and long-term history is "traditional history," the history of "oscillations" and trends. In archaeology, the individual scale consists of studies of artifact styles and particular sites. These are elements of the past that are influenced by specific events and by the actions of individuals. The social scale involves the study of social groups and the larger circumstances that affect families, kin networks, classes, and other groupings of people. In prehistoric archaeology, the long-term scale considers the large archaeological picture of entire continents or huge geographical regions. In historical archaeology, this scale is more likely to involve the large trends that exist across national and even international boundaries. Long-term history concerns the unfolding of history over several generations.

Lees did not use Braudel's terminology at Limerick, but the scales can be easily adapted to his interpretations. The specific information he provides about the artifacts and the building remains he found relate to the individual scale. His effort to place the history of Limerick into a wider historical context by identifying several key "transformations" in South Carolina from 1707 to about 1890 relate both to the social and to the geographical scales. These "transformations" involve an increased regional reliance on African slave labor in the mid-eighteenth century, and the death of the slave system in 1865.

The interpretations that historical archaeologists offer about the sites they study are varied and sometimes even controversial. No formula can be presented to show precisely how archaeologists frame their interpretations. Ultimately, ideas about the past spring partly from each individual's attitudes, perceptions, and educational experiences. In addition, interpretations tend to be like clothing: they come into style and after a while they go out of vogue and are discarded. Like clothing, it is sometimes difficult to imagine that archaeologist once held certain interpretations to be true. Attempts to disprove the myth of the Mound Builders (see Chapter 1) helped to transform North American archaeology from a hobby of the idle rich into a serious scientific pursuit. Today, we shudder to think that many nineteenth-century archaeologists once thought that the Lost Tribes of Israel, Vikings, or some other Indo-European peoples built many of the mounds that dot the North American landscape. Still, such ideas did hold sway in parts of the scientific community of the day. Like an old suit, however, the Mound Builder myth has been confined to the closet of old ideas.

Publication

No archaeological project is truly complete until the results are published. Without some dissemination of their findings and interpretations, the excavators have done nothing more than to wrest artifacts from the ground. The very act of recovery can be meaningful when a site is threatened with imminent destruction, but unless the results of an excavation are widely available, then the archaeological information is effectively lost, the site destroyed.

In most cases, specialist archaeological site reports are highly technical and are published in sources not readily accessible to nonarchaeologists. For example, the South Carolina Institute of Archaeology and Anthropology published Lees' study of Limerick Plantation in their "Anthropological Studies" series. This report is well known to professional historical archaeologists, but it is effectively inaccessible to a wider audience. For this reason, many historical archaeologists write popular accounts of their research in addition to their highly technical site reports. Ivor Noël Hume is well known for his ability to make dense, complex archaeological information accessible to the public. *Martin's Hundred: The Discovery of a Lost Colonial Virginia Settlement,* his book about the excavations at Wolstenholme Towne, Virginia, stands as one of the great popular accounts of historical archaeology.

EXCAVATION

The thrill of archaeological discovery is very real, but extreme caution is the watchword. British excavator Sir Mortimer Wheeler, one of the finest excavators in archaeological history, said that "It is essential to check any sort of excitement instantly, and to insist firmly on quiet routine." Modern excavation is as much science as is a carefully controlled experiment in a chemistry laboratory. When Noël Hume excavated at Martin's Hundred in the 1980s, his excavators found an early seventeenth-century close helmet, the first ever found in North America. A close helmet has a heavy visor that can be closed to cover and protect the entire head and face. The much corroded find took many hours to remove in one piece from the ground (see below), but the entire removal took place under controlled conditions. Everyone knew that undue haste could break the helmet into tiny pieces.

Context of Space

All excavation is based on the contexts of time and space. Thus, the excavator has to record data in two dimensions—horizontal and vertical. The horizontal dimension is maintained by the use of a site grid, a checkerboard of standard-sized squares placed across the entire site. There is nothing magical about any particular size square. Archaeologists typically use a size that meets their needs at the site being excavated. Also, historical archaeologists may be evenly split as to the use of meters/centimeters or feet/inches. Regardless of size and measurement scale, each square receives a unique designation based on its distance from a datum point, or main point of reference, keyed into a local map. Using this reference, all the material from each excavation unit can be distinguished from all other finds, structures, or features from the site.

The use of this reference point allows the archaeologist to keep accurate records on horizontal location year after year, and even permits someone to excavate the same site and to use the identical grid years later. When Samuel Smith excavated Fort Southwest Point, a late eighteenth- and early nineteenth-century American military post in eastern Tennessee, he used a grid of ten-foot (3.1 m) squares (Figure 8.3). In 1984, he thought the grid covered the entire site. When he revisited the site two years later, he found that he had to expand it to conduct further excavations on one end of the site. Because he used a uniform grid in 1984, it was no problem at all to expand it in 1986. Also, because of the grid's regularity, he was easily able to correlate the information from the new part of the grid with the material found in 1984. The horizontal grid made it possible for Smith to keep track of the horizontal location of the 34,666 artifacts he found at the fort.

Context of Time

Space is horizontal; time is usually vertical. As we saw in Chapter 5, the context of time is based on the Law of Superposition, on stratified layers identified during the excavation. Smith divided the history of Fort Southwest Point into five stages, based on historical documents: 1779–1796, 1797–1800, 1801–1807, 1808–1811, and 1812–present. Ideally, he would have preferred to isolate each historical stage in distinct, easily diggable soil layers. Unfortunately, the correlation between historical phases and soil layers was not so clear-cut. When he excavated a 40-foot (12.2 m) long trench through a depression in the soil, he not only discovered two parallel stone walls from a barracks building; he found no less than 11 separate soil layers.

Because soil and artifacts are deposited in layers, archaeologists like to excavate each layer separately. Historic sites are particularly challenging in this regard, not only because they were occupied for only a few generations, or, at most for a few centuries, but also because the occupation layers can be much compressed. In Manhattan, for example, generation after generation rebuilt on the same spot, clearing away earlier buildings and foundations oblivious to their historical importance. All that is left for the archaeologist are small lenses of soil and datable artifacts that can take weeks to dissect and analyze. Most sites, like military forts or rural farm houses, were occupied for much shorter periods. At Fort Southwest Point, for example, most of the soil layers Smith encountered were only inches thick.

Excavation Methods

Like all archaeologists, historical archaeologists conduct both vertical and horizontal excavations, depending on their research design.

Vertical excavation is used at small sites or in situations where the archaeological team has limited funds. This kind of trenching is intended to provide as much information as possible about soil layers and past occupations without excavating the entire site. In vertical excavation, only small parts of a site are excavated with trenches and small excavation units usually measuring less than 10 feet (3.1 m) square.

Archaeologists at Fort Southwest Point, Tennessee, used this approach as a quick and easy way to locate building foundations when they first started working there. In 1973, they cut two long, perpendicular trenches through the center of the site, using a mechanical backhoe. One trench, running southeast to northwest, was 185 feet (56.4 m) long; the other, running southwest to northeast, extended for

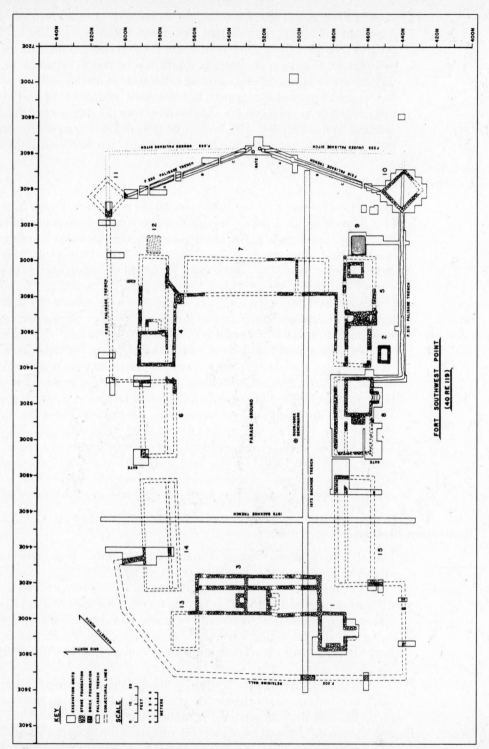

Figure 8.3 *Vertical and horizontal excavations at Fort Southwest Point, Tennessee, 1973–1986.*

Vertical trench excavation in the west wall of Southwest Point, Tennessee.

300 feet (91.5 m). The second trench crossed the walls of six different buildings inside the fort. In a second season in 1974, the diggers excavated a number of 10-foot-square (3.1 59 m) excavation units, which gave them more control than mechanical excavation, but at the cost of much slower progress. This approach was used to locate more features, working several areas simultaneously. Once found, these could be excavated more carefully when more funds became available.

Ten years passed before the State of Tennessee developed plans to reconstruct the fort. At this point, the archaeological research design had to be changed from merely locating foundations to large-scale investigation of their architecture as a preliminary to reconstruction. Samuel Smith, a historical archaeologist with the State of Tennessee's Division of Archaeology, used limited vertical excavation both to relocate the buried walls found by the student excavators in 1973–1974, and to find more foundations. However, because Smith was most interested in exposing entire buildings, he used horizontal excavation in several places throughout the fort.

Horizontal excavation, or area or block excavation, is used to expose entire building foundations and large areas of sites. By exposing entire buildings, the excavator can study not only architecture, but relationships between wells, outbuildings, houses, dumps, and other features, to say nothing of the internal alterations made to a building over long periods.

This approach worked well at Fort Southwest Point, where Samuel Smith wanted to expose the entire foundations, not just one or two corners. For example, before he began the horizontal excavation of a building called Structure 8, it appeared only as a large depression in the ground on the northeast side of the fort.

His excavation over this depression was roughly 30 by 46 feet (9.2 by 14.0 m) in size (Figure 8.4). Because the foundation of Structure 8 was 22 feet wide and 43 feet (6.7 by 13.1 m) long, Smith's excavation was perfectly planned. The building was positioned directly in front of the fort's front wall so that anyone approaching the fort would have encountered Structure 8 rather than the exterior wall itself (Figure 8.5). Smith's careful excavation of Structure 8 allowed him to envision how it was built: "This 43 by 22 ft. building was almost certainly constructed of logs (but with plank floors) with a central chimney and a full-length front porch. . . . it would have been two stories in height . . . Windows were probably present on the side of the building facing the fort's interior but not on the exterior side. On the first floor, the central chimney no doubt had fireboxes on its east and west sides."

During the excavation Smith found three clay stairs leading down into the building's cellar. He wondered if the building was used for storing valuable goods while the fort served as the Cherokee Indian Agency during the early nineteenth century. Local Native Americans were able to receive ploughs, spinning wheels, and other items from the United States government at Fort Southwest Point during this period. The steps into the cellar may have been designed so that "goods could have been distributed to the Indians without allowing them actual entry into the fort."

Tools

Excavation is destruction, and excavation itself is a deliberate, slow-moving process requiring infinite patience. The spade is the symbol of archaeological excavation, but the diamond-shaped, "pointing trowel" is a more appropriate one. Today's archaeologists use everything from bulldozers and skiploaders to remove sterile overburden, to picks and shovels for rough work, to the finest of brushes and dental picks for burial excavation. In the hands of an expert, any of these digging tools, even the bulldozer, is a craftsperson's artifact. One British archaeologist is famous for his artistry with a bulldozer, which he uses to clear overburden to within an inch of archaeological layers. He even has a heavy equipment operator's license. On the side of caution, however, bulldozers and heavy equipment cannot be used at all sites. On sites with soft or sandy soil, the weight of the machine can crush artifacts directly beneath the surface.

The archaeologist's trowel is a remarkable implement, used not only for straightening edges and smoothing stratigraphic profiles, but for fine-grained digging of house foundations or hearths. It is at its best when its long edges scrape delicately across damp soil, delineating the boundary between a dark, inconspicuous posthole and the surrounding lighter soil. No fieldworker ever walks without a trowel, for it is the Swiss Army knife of the archaeologist. Many times, however, the trowel is simply too coarse a tool for the job at hand. Clearing burials, exposing waterlogged plant remains, cleaning the decaying plaster surface of an early Spanish adobe—these tasks are the "watchmaker's tasks" of archaeology, as Mortimer Wheeler once called them. Dust pans, whisk brooms, paint brushes, dental picks, even sharpened nails come into play at critical moments. Dental picks are especially useful when cleaning bones, for their varied working edges allow you to scoop or scrape, lever, or dig tiny holes, just as your friendly neighborhood dentist does on your teeth. Many archaeologists make friends with their dentists and acquire their worn-out tools for the field—not that this is necessarily a good reason to go to

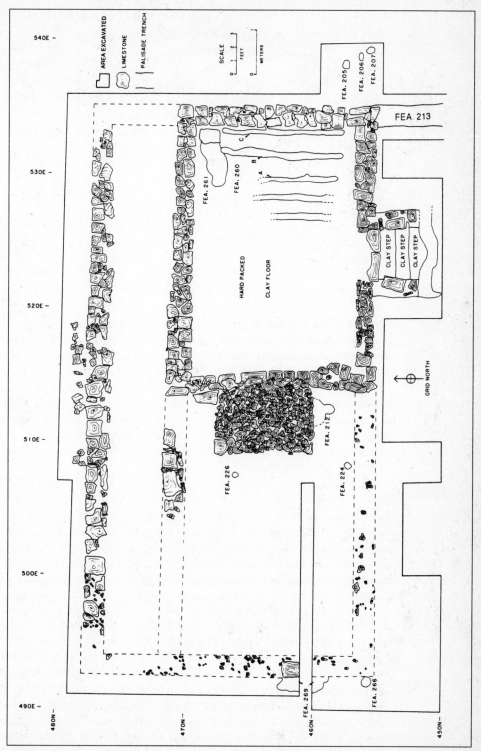

Figure 8.4 *Map of horizontal excavation of Structure 8, Fort Southwest Point, Tennessee.*

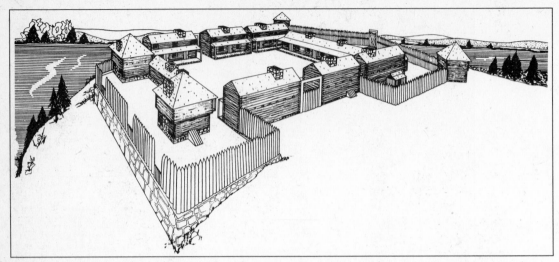

Figure 8.5 *Artist's reconstruction of Fort Southwest Point, Tennessee, based on archaeological findings. Structure 8 is to the right of the main gate. The entrance to the cellar appears in front.*

the dentist! The archaeologist hunched over an excavation carefully using a dental pick and dust pan to remove tiny pieces of soil does bear a striking similarity to the watchmaker bent over the tiniest screws, springs, and gears of a timepiece. Both jobs require patience and skill.

Archaeologists also screen all, or in some cases a sizable portion, of the soil they excavate. This procedure is used so that even the smallest artifacts—straight pins, glass beads, buttons—are found during excavation. Meshes vary with the problem at hand, but quarter-inch or even eighth-inch is commonly used when such finds as glass beads are likely to be encountered.

Field Recording

"Excavation, no matter how skillfully conducted, is sheer wasted effort unless the results are properly recorded." These words of Ivor Noël Hume's emphasize the need for careful record keeping in archaeological research. Without accurate records even the best of excavations is an exercise in destruction. In the final analysis, every archaeological dig is only as good as the records that survive from it. Here are some of the day-to-day records kept on a well-organized excavation:

- Field Notes. These are a diary of the excavation, and a meticulously thorough description of the trenches and daily activity kept by the site director and his or her assistants. Field notes are the synthesis of the excavation, the place where stratigraphy is analyzed, unfolding interpretations of the site jotted down, the locations of structures and major finds laid out. Field notes are a formal, yet informal record of an excavation, compiled not only for the excavator, but also as a permanent record for posterity. Ideally, they should err on the side of overcoverage. Nothing is

Structure 8, Fort Southwest Point, Tennessee, before and after horizonital excavation.

worse than inadequate notes that omit, for example, critical stratigraphic information or architectural data. The great Mesopotamian archaeologist Leonard Woolley used to inspect his assistants' field notes at the Sumerian city of Ur every evening. He was right, for these notes constitute our only insights into this most important of excavations half a century later.

- Site Maps and Plans. A detailed, scale map of the entire site, drawings of each excavation with stratigraphic profiles, a complete stratigraphic sequence, structural and feature plans, and architectural drawings if appropriate.
- Artifact and Finds Inventory. Complete inventories of all finds, whether bagged in units or cataloged individually. This is often kept on computer software, the catalog being keyed to a bar code system.
- Complete Photographic Record. A set of photographs taken in color and black and white. This provides a visual record of the unfolding excavation.
- Administrative Records and Accounts; payroll, etc. Such records are invaluable for keeping track of per-day costs of an excavation. Collectively, these records constitute an irreplaceable archive of the past, of a destroyed, or partially destroyed archaeological site. Even after publication, they are a vital part of the archaeological record and should be treated, and preserved as, archival records.

CONSERVATION

The soil is the archaeologist's worst enemy, for the vagaries of preservation play havoc on the archaeological record. Sometimes, miracles of survival come to light, like the marvelous wooden artifacts and jewelry from Egyptian pharaoh Tutankhamun's tomb, or the Bronze Age wooden planks a foot wide and up to 8 feet long (0.3 to 2.4 m) from the waterlogged Bronze Age village at Flag Fen, England. Most often, however, natural soil chemicals cause both perishable wood and other organic artifacts and food remains to deteriorate and often to disappear completely. For example, when Kenneth Kidd found the post holes at Sainte Marie I, all that remained were dark soil stains where the posts had been. The wood itself had long since disappeared because of the natural action of the chemicals in the soil.

Luckily, not all objects disappear completely, even in the harshest of soil conditions. Ceramics, glass, and stone objects typically survive, even under the harshest of conditions. Objects of iron, lead, pewter, copper, gold, and silver can endure with the proper soil and climatic conditions, but will probably vanish in time. Leather, wood, and even paper sometimes last over short periods or under waterlogged or very dry conditions. For example, when excavating Fort Bowie, a nineteenth-century U.S. Army post at Apache Pass, Arizona, archaeologists from the University of Arizona found soda pop bottles that still had remnants of the labels adhering to them. These bottles show that the soldiers at the fort drank strawberry soda, sarsaparilla with iron, and orange cider. At the Hoff's Store, a nineteenth-century California gold-rush store in San Francisco, excavators working for Archaeo-Tech, a private research firm, discovered a wooden ammunition case that was still stenciled "Buck and Ball Cartrid/1845 120 G." This box once held 120 packages of .64 caliber buck and ball cartridges.

Conservator Per Guldbeck accurately describes artifact conservation as "sometimes likened to the dramatic stories of surgeons saving people from the consequences of disease or accident." Like a surgeon, the artifact conservator must be highly and intensively trained, a training that includes equal doses of common sense, knowledge of chemistry, and patience. Laboratory conservation is rarely dramatic. It is typically a slow-moving process that involves weeks, even months, of delicate renovation, soaking organic materials in chemicals, and devising ingenious restoration techniques. The procedures are largely routine and well established, the hardest part being to judge when the expense of permanent conservation is justified. In most cases, this is reserved for artifacts destined for museum display or for unusually important and unique finds.

The most dramatic conservation efforts come in the field, as when Ivor Noël Hume discovered an early seventeenth-century close helmet at Wolstenholme Towne. The excavators faced a challenging problem: how to remove it so that conservators could stabilize it for study and museum display. When found, the helmet was no longer iron; it had been reduced to a rusty ferrous shell encased in clay. The conservators devised a simple scheme. They built a steel box frame around the helmet, then poured a silicone molding compound into the box. The 200-pound (91 kg) load was then winched out of the ground and taken to the laboratory for further conservation. The removal of the boxed helmet from the field took two full days. By the time the excavators found a second helmet close by, the conservators had devised a new system of recovery. The steel box and molding compound was replaced with strips of fiberglass screen softened with glue. These strips were carefully placed over the shell of the helmet. Wet paper and plaster-of-paris were applied to the screen, and the conservators removed the entire compound in an old tire. The second helmet was much lighter and therefore easier to transport.

The second part of the conservation process took place in the laboratory. Using small tools, Colonial Williamsburg conservator Gary McQuillen carefully removed the dirt from the inside of the helmet. He pried off the plaster and dissolved the screen and the glue. Next he used a tiny air-blasting tool to remove the surface of the rust to the thinnest, firm surface, often leaving the helmet in places only a millimeter thick. This delicate work of conservation brought the helmet back to life. It is now a triumphant centerpiece in The Winthrop Rockefeller Archaeology Museum at the Wolstenholme Towne site in Williamsburg.

Most conservation is undertaken either for display or to acquire additional information about a poorly preserved artifact. For instance, a skilled conservator can provide information about hidden, corroded design features, discover identifying makers' marks, and make otherwise deteriorated artifacts ready for museum display.

Conservation has been highly successful at Fort Michilimackinac, Michigan. More than 20 years of excavation have yielded hundreds of metal objects, among them knives, eating utensils, gun parts, and tools. Most of them required conservation treatment before study. For example, the treated military buttons from the fort have helped to identify individual regiments that served in the fort. Records say that the British Tenth Regiment served at Michilimackinac between 1772 and 1774. Many pewter buttons, emblazoned with a large "10," confirm official documents. Some other buttons marked with a raised "RI 18" belong to the British Eighteenth Regiment, or Royal Irish. This regiment is known to have served in the American Revolution in 1777, but there is no record of some of its members having garrisoned Fort Michilimackinac. The dispassionate eye of archaeology documents their presence in northern Michigan.

BACK TO THE LABORATORY

For all the glamour of excavation, most research time is spent back in the laboratory, working on artifacts and other finds in far more detail than is possible in the field. It is here, in much greater comfort, that the long process of classifying artifacts unfolds.

Classifying Historical Artifacts

Everyone classifies objects as part of day-to-day living. We classify eating utensils: knives, forks, and spoons—each type has a different use and is kept in a separate compartment in the drawer. We classify roads according to their surface finishes, distinguish station wagons from minivans. We classify lifestyles, artifacts, even cultures, and make choices between them. By the same token the archaeologist classifies artifacts, not in the same way we do in everyday life, but as a means of ordering data.

Artifact classification in archaeology of any kind has four main objectives:

- Organizing data into manageable units. This means separating potsherds from metal objects, bone tools from leather garments—preliminary data processing.
- Describing types. By identifying the individual features (attributes) of hundreds of artifacts, or clusters of artifacts, the archaeologist can group them by common attributes, into relatively few types. Such types are economical ways of describing large numbers of artifacts.
- Describing artifact types provides a hierarchy, which orders the relationships between artifacts. These stem, in part, from the use of a variety of raw materials, manufacturing techniques, and functions.
- Studying artifact variability. Classification provides a way of comparing different artifact assemblages in the archaeological record, and of studying the differences between them.

Archaeological classifications are artificial formulations based on criteria set up by archaeologists. These classificatory systems do not necessarily coincide with those developed by the people who made the original artifacts. Archaeological classification is a way of giving artifacts meaning. It is a process that creates types that can have meaning based on function (knives, forks, spoons), shape (round pots, tall narrow pots), style (red pots, black pots, black and red pots), and material of manufacture (copper beads, wooden beads, glass beads). Whole systems of classification are called *typologies*.

When prehistoric archaeologists classify artifacts made and used in the remote past, they hope that the types they have created had at least some reality in the past. For example, Mary Leakey studied the extremely simple artifacts and stone technology used by the inhabitants of Olduvai Gorge in East Africa 1.75 million years ago. She described sharp-edged flakes, also jagged choppers made from lava pebbles, using simple descriptive classifications. Leakey argued that these "Oldowan" people used choppers to hunt and dismember game, and assumed that her interpretation of their use coincided with that of the original makers. Some years later, archaeologist Nicholas Toth approached Oldowan technology from an entirely different perspective. He spent months learning the simple stoneworking methods of 1.75-million-year-old humans, then replicated their artifacts, comparing his copies to the originals. So precise were his experiments that he managed to show that some of the makers were left-handed! He also demonstrated that the so-called choppers were not artifacts at all, but convenient lumps from which simple artifacts—sharp-edged flakes—were removed. The choppers were byproducts rather than artifacts.

Toth's innovative research shows just how hard it is to link arbitrary archaeological classifications with real-life uses of artifacts. This is an acute problem with prehistoric societies, for whom we lack written records or other independent forms of documentation, which tell us how people used their artifacts. Even comparisons between, say, San hunters' bows and arrows from the Kalahari and those found in 3,000-year-old waterlogged site a few hundred miles away are risky analogies, simply because of the passing of time and local environmental conditions.

Historical archaeologists often have an easier time because of their use of folk taxonomies, classification systems created by the people who actually made and used the artifacts. Using the original taxonomy employed by the artifact makers themselves makes the task of classification immeasurably easier, because the arbitrary types formulated by archaeologists now coincide with those used by their subjects. Ceramics form the most common body of artifacts from historic sites, many of them widely used, mass-produced forms, whose evolution and intended uses are well documented in contemporary records.

Between 1640 and 1680, English artist Randle Holme tried to record and draw the objects, including ceramics, with which he was familiar. Holme was researching the symbols of English heraldry for a book first published in 1688. As he showed, the terms used could be confusing. He said, for instance, that the following could all describe a "dish": platter, dish, midleing dish, broth dish, bason, sallet dish, trencher plate or plate, and saucer. In 1770, the anonymous author of *The Complete Appraiser* was more precise than Holme had been, using measurements to distinguish between different kinds of ceramic vessels. He said that "plates" were between 7 $\frac{3}{4}$ inches (19.7 cm) and 9 $\frac{3}{4}$ inches (24.8 cm) in diameter, whereas "dishes" ranged from 10 $\frac{3}{4}$ inches (27.3 cm) to 28 inches (71.1 cm) across.

The classifications presented by Randle Holme and by the author of *The Complete Appraiser* are folk taxonomies. Each is an attempt to define material culture—in this case, ceramic dishes—in ways that make sense to the people who use them.

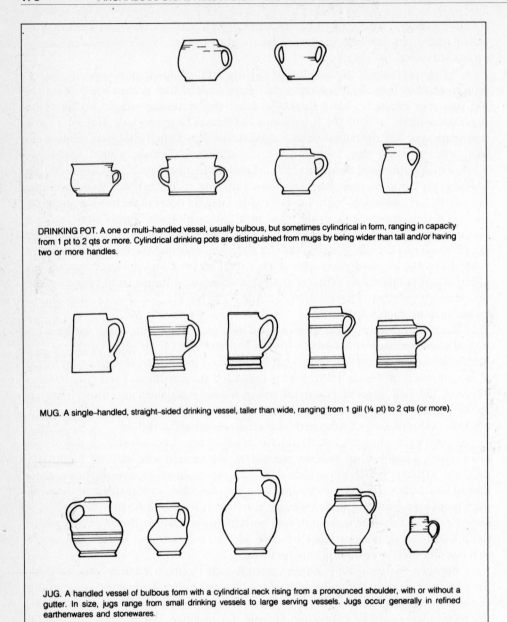

DRINKING POT. A one or multi–handled vessel, usually bulbous, but sometimes cylindrical in form, ranging in capacity from 1 pt to 2 qts or more. Cylindrical drinking pots are distinguished from mugs by being wider than tall and/or having two or more handles.

MUG. A single–handled, straight–sided drinking vessel, taller than wide, ranging from 1 gill (¼ pt) to 2 qts (or more).

JUG. A handled vessel of bulbous form with a cylindrical neck rising from a pronounced shoulder, with or without a gutter. In size, jugs range from small drinking vessels to large serving vessels. Jugs occur generally in refined earthenwares and stonewares.

Figure 8.6 *Seventeenth-century ceramic vessel forms in the Chesapeake.*

These kinds of classification systems are important to historical archaeologists, because they can be used to provide a foundation for understanding how people in the past used and thought about their material culture.

Mary Beaudry of Boston University and five colleagues used folk taxonomies to develop a classification system for ceramics from colonial period, domestic sites in the Chesapeake region of Maryland and Virginia. Their Potomac Typological System, or POTS for short, was based on the work of Randle Holme, the author of *The Complete Appraiser,* and several probate inventories. They used the probate lists to acquire an idea of the range of vessels present in the colonial Chesapeake, and to give them insight into the terms used to describe them. For example, the inventory of Francis Lewis, who died in 1677, lists "2 pewter dishes, 3 plates, 2 porringers"; the inventory of Robert Slye's slave quarters, for the year 1671, includes "1 iron bottle, 1 iron pot, 1 frying pan."

POTS is an elaborate, widely used typology with a basis in solid historical fact. Beaudry and her colleagues have defined 28 separate types of ceramics used in the seventeenth century (Figure 8.6). Their system includes vessel forms commonly recognizable today: cups, saucers, jugs, and candlesticks. Many of the forms are no longer used today, and may strike us as curious. For example, a "costrel" is a jug or bottle with two handles. Travelers and field workers used these vessels as drink containers, much like canteens today. A "sillabub pot" was a short, squat pot with two handles and a spout like a tea kettle. It was used for serving sillabub (wine or liquor mixed with sweetened milk or cream), posset (hot, sweetened milk curdled with wine or ale), and wassail (ale or wine spiced with roasted apples and sugar).

POTS is a good example of how historical documents and archaeological finds can be melded together into an analytical typology, a way in which archaeologists can classify collections, while still retaining the historical integrity of the folk typology used by the original makers.

All archaeological research, whether into the earliest humans, Southwestern pueblo communities, or historic sites, is based not only on sound research design, but on theory. The process of interpretation of the past depends on such archaeological theory, which we discuss in Chapter 9.

CHAPTER
9

Explaining the Historical Past

"Look not mournfully into the past"

Henry Wadsworth Longfellow, 1839

Of all the many subfields of archaeology, none is more multidisciplinary in its perspective than historical archaeology, not only in its research methodology, but in its attempts to explain the recent past. We draw on ideas from many disciplines, from anthropology, history, geography, sociology, and landscape architecture—to mention but a few sources called on in these pages. In this chapter, we discuss some of the theoretical approaches that form the basis for interpretation of the archaeological record from historic sites, for these are the foundations of all scientific research in historical archaeology.

Three broad categories of approach illuminate historical archaeology: humanistic, scientific, and humanistic science. We consider each in turn.

HUMANISTIC HISTORICAL ARCHAEOLOGY

As a philosophy, humanism focuses on the inherent dignity of humanity, on the potential, sensibilities, and actions of real men and women. The humanistic approach is expressed well by historical reconstructions which attempt to put today's visitors in touch with their historical counterparts by showing how people in the past lived. Historical reconstructions that place the modern visitor "inside" the past at historic homes are humanistic. As we have seen at Colonial Williamsburg, Virginia, and Greenfield Village, Michigan (see Chapter 3), the act of taking visitors back to the past usually involves not only documents, but such archaeological data as artifacts and building foundations. The material remains of the past—fine furniture, glass-ware, humble domestic utensils—can create a powerful impression in the mind of the onlooker. They are a vivid way of bringing the past alive, by the simple expedi-ent of using commonplace, and more exotic, artifacts to recreate the human di-mension of a once-busy building or community.

Humanistic historical archaeology is often associated with the physical recon-struction of buildings, but not invariably. In a classic study of the late 1960s, Robert Ascher and Charles Fairbanks provided a compelling picture of slavery by adopting a humanistic approach. They excavated the ruins of a slave cabin on Rayfield Plan-tation on Cumberland Island, directly off the coast of Georgia. This part of the South was long associated with slavery. Some of the largest and richest estates in the hemisphere were located here. Ascher and Fairbanks estimated that slaves had lived in the cabin from about 1834, when Robert Stafford bought Rayfield, until the end of the Civil War in 1865. All that remained of the cabin a century later was a brick chimney. In digging the cabin, Ascher and Fairbanks said their goal was "to discover and convey a sense of daily life as it might have been experienced by the people who lived in the cabin." To bring slavery to life, Ascher and Fairbanks adopted a unique approach. They interspersed their archaeological report—with its stratigraphic drawings and excavation photographs—with a literary "sound-track" taken from primary accounts. They quoted the great African-American ora-tor Frederick Douglass speaking about what it was like to be considered property: "I had now a new conception of my degraded condition. Prior to this, I had become, if not insensible to my lot, at least partly so."

At another point, they took a list of slaves from the archives, people sold to Stafford as part of the plantation in April, 1834. "We think that some of the people just named lived in the excavated cabin," they comment with vivid understatement. Discussing their archaeological findings, they reported that "Life inside the cabin produced an ash layer that eventually spilled out of the fireplace and onto the floor where the sand turned a darker color through time and use." Through this master-ful combination of historical and archaeological sources, Ascher and Fairbanks linked the differences they observed in the layers at the cabin site with the lives of once-living, real slaves. They succeeded in creating a picture of slave life; they have placed us in the slave cabin without actually building it. When they illustrate a small, blue-glass bead found in the cabin, we have no doubt that it was worn by someone who lived the slave experience. Slavery is not an abstraction to Ascher and Fairbanks.

The roots of humanism in historical archaeology go back to the field's earliest days, to the time when historical archaeology was associated almost totally with the discipline of history. When John Cotter excavated Jamestown in the 1950s, one of his primary goals was to summarize the archaeological findings "so as to indicate the way of life which was developing in Virginia during the 17th century." When Kenneth Kidd studied the mission of Sainte Marie I in Ontario in the 1940s, his in-tent was to provide information about "the activities of the Jesuit Fathers in the decade of their residence among the Huron Indians." These archaeological projects were viewed as part of the study of history as a humanistic discipline. In 1964 Noël Hume described the fledgling field of historical archaeology as the "handmaiden to history." By this he meant that its research was intended to complement the humanistic side of historical study. The humanistic approach remains a pervasive and fruitful thread through historical archaeology to this day, witness William Kelso's research at Kingsmill, Virginia.

Humanistic Archaeology at Kingsmill

A model example of humanistic historical archaeology is William Kelso's 1984 study of seven plantations at Kingsmill, near Williamsburg, Virginia. Kelso, the senior archaeologist for the Thomas Jefferson Memorial Foundation in Charlottesville, Virginia, is a social historian, who has considerable experience and expertise using historical archaeology as a tool for understanding colonial Virginia.

The subtitle of his book *Kingsmill Plantations, 1619–1800: Archaeology of Country Life in Colonial Virginia,* aptly summarizes Kelso's perspective, for he is interested in presenting a complete picture of past seventeenth- and eighteenth-century life in Virginia. To do this, Kelso focuses on three central elements of the past: history, things, and people. He constructs the historical context of colonial Virginia from primary documents. He tells the history of the rise of the tobacco economy, briefly recounts the incidents of Bacon's Rebellion in 1676, then charts the development of the Virginian frontier as it marched from coast to hinterland. As a social historian, Kelso realizes that historical events are situated within a physical environment partly composed of things. With time, "colonial Virginians surrounded themselves with an evolving material culture that from documents alone is difficult to reconstruct." Undoubtedly, an important element of this material culture was housing. One of Kelso's goals is to explain the changes in housing forms. In Virginia, this change means moving from a time when most people lived in small "earthfast" homes—with dirt floors and upright support posts buried in the ground—to the monumental brick mansions of the big plantation economy. At the same time, the contents of even great houses varied enormously. Kelso's research in estate records shows that "what people furnished their houses with varied considerably, so much so that it is difficult to generalize for any one period or class." The dishes from which families ate, the bottles from which they poured their wine, and the hardware on their furniture must all be reconstructed from archaeological finds. In most cases, it is from the archaeology that all evidence related to slavery derives. In any case, none of the historical events of the Kingsmill area, and not one material object, could exist without people.

To bring the historical actors in, Kelso focused on the area's elites, because they were the people who wrote about themselves and in turn were written about. He introduces us to individuals such as Humphrey Higginson, who "arrived in Virginia in 1635, soon married into the 700-acre [283 ha] Tuttey's Neck land and, with the rank of captain, soon added the 320-acre [130 ha] Harrop tract to his growing Kingsmill estate." We learn as well of George Percy, Jamestown's "lieutenant governor," who described the Kingsmill area in 1607 as a paradise: "The soil was good

Horizontal excavation of Burwell mansion and kitchen, Kingsmill, Virginia, 1975.

and fruitful, with excellent good timber. There are also great stores of vines in big-
ness of a man's thigh, running up to the tops of tress in great abundance. We also
did see many squirrels, conies, blackbirds. . . ."

Kelso's archaeological research at the seven sites encompassed the full range
of colonial society, including the excavation of planter's mansions and slave quarters. Because many of Kelso's excavations were horizontal, they provided maximum
information about housing condition and site layout. It is easy to see the social dis-
tinctions between slaves and owners at his sites. As Kelso said, "Certain reasonably
clear patterns emerge from the comparison of the Kingsmill archaeological remains. The reasons for the similarities and their cultural meaning are not so easy to
grasp. There are definite settlement patterns, certain architectural traditions, an
evolving landscape architecture, and consistency in certain aspects of slave life."
Large-scale, eighteenth-century planters chose prominent locations for their mansions and built dramatic gardens. Slaves constructed root cellars in their homes,
maybe without their masters' knowledge, and made do. These images come
through Kelso's humanistic perspective. From him we learn to "reconstruct the setting within which landlords and laborers went about their lives within Virginia's tobacco empire."

Excavated root cellar of a slave cabin, Kingsmill, Virginia.

SCIENTIFIC HISTORICAL ARCHAEOLOGY

When, in the 1960s, American archaeologists "discovered" anthropology (see Chapter 2), they also embraced the scientific method. In their attempts to make anthropological archaeology more rigorous, a number of excavators urged their colleagues to conduct research that was explicitly scientific. Archaeologists should be able to meet the highest scientific standards in their research, they argued. They should devise intricate models of past societies that could be tested with carefully designed hypotheses, they should contribute to knowledge of human life by discovering general laws of behavior. The final goal for scientific archaeologists should be to explain cultural process, the processes of culture change in the past.

Interest in scientific archaeology exploded in both historical and prehistoric archaeology in the late 1960s and 1970s. The leading proponent of an explicitly scientific perspective in historical archaeology was Stanley South at the University of South Carolina. His book *Method and Theory in Historical Archaeology* published in 1977, was a clarion call for historical archaeologists to be overtly scientific in their research. For several years, South's book was probably the most important book in the field.

South believed that the route toward a scientific historical archaeology started with archaeologists being able to recognize patterns among the artifacts they excavated. He argued that men and women living in the same cultural tradition should leave the same kinds of artifacts, in roughly similar percentages, in the soils of their past residences. The way to pick out these patterns was through quantifying the artifacts into categories. He called the ones he used: Kitchen, Bone, Architectural, Furniture, Arms, Clothing, Personal, Tobacco Pipe, and Activities. He devised these general classes of artifacts during his study of several colonial sites—from dwellings to forts—in the Carolinas. To South, the percentages of the artifacts in each of the nine groups constitute the pattern at that site. Some sites are characterized by large numbers of architectural artifacts and almost no tobacco pipes; others have high percentages of kitchen and architectural artifacts and almost no furniture objects. Regardless of the actual percentages that form the pattern, similar sites should produce patterns that resemble one another. Grossly different sites should have different artifact patterns. All this is revealed by the quantification of the artifacts in the nine groups.

The identification of South's patterns represented only one of the first steps in the scientific process in historical archaeology. The patterns could be used to construct theories of behavior that themselves could be tested at new sites, he argued. This continuing process of site excavation, pattern recognition, and testing would lead to a scientific archaeology that is as rigorous as chemistry or physics (Figure 9.1). For South and other scholars of this persuasion, archaeology can only receive the attention and respect it deserves by using such a rigorous methodology.

Many archaeologists found South's idea very appealing. After all, it presented an easy way to analyze the mass of archaeological finds from even a small site. Simple comparison was all that was required to determine whether the newly excavated site was just like any of the others for which patterns already had been calculated.

Scientific Historical Archaeology at Camden

One of the most explicit studies to follow the scientific methodology outlined by South was conducted by Kenneth Lewis in the mid-1970s at Camden, in north-central South Carolina. At the time, Lewis, now at Michigan State University, was a colleague of South's at the Institute of Archaeology and Anthropology at the University of South Carolina.

During the height of the American Revolution in 1780, British soldiers built Camden in the South Carolina backcountry. They originally intended it as one of a chain of posts across the state that would secure the region for the British. However, Camden's geographical position made it a perfect communication hub for the frontier. The British soon used it as a main redistribution point for war munitions com-

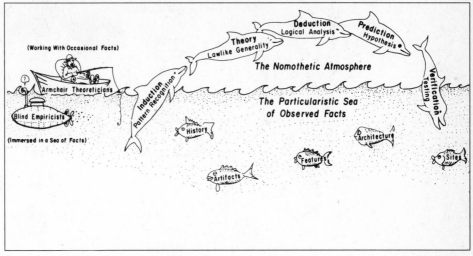

Figure 9.1 *South's flowchart showing the scientific method. The archaeologist should follow the path of the dolphin.*

ing inland from Charleston. The British fortified the town, and two battles were fought nearby. After the war, Camden continued to operate as a frontier center, rapidly growing in regional importance. As the town prospered, new residents moved to the town's north side. By 1812, much of the old town was abandoned.

In late 1974 and early 1975, Lewis was given the opportunity to excavate part of the old town. The Camden Historical Commission wished to develop the site, and they needed specific architectural information that only archaeology could supply. Lewis excavated along the southwest palisade of the town and on a tiny part of its interior. Rather than to offer a humanistic portrait of daily life in Camden, Lewis chose an overtly scientific research plan that focused on the town's place in the South Carolina frontier.

Lewis began by constructing a model of frontiers that emphasized "primarily cultural change among intrusive cultures faced with adaptation to a frontier situation." The model was composed of a number of generalizations that Lewis drew from relevant anthropological and historical studies. For example, his first generalization was that "complexly organized intrusive societies react or adapt in a patterned way to the conditions imposed by a frontier situation." What this means is that English settlers, for instance, will react to a frontier situation in a nonrandom, or patterned, way. This patterned reaction will be a cultural one. Another generalization was that "as the colony moves through time it also travels through space, expanding with the influx of new settlers." Lewis devised 11 hypotheses from these generalizations "around which new data may be organized and analyzed." One such hypothesis was that "the colonial settlement tended to lie adjacent to the significant routes of transportation and communication connecting Camden with the outside world."

Lewis used vertical excavations, small trenches and excavation units, to test the hypotheses. For example, the spatial distribution of architectural artifacts—nails and bricks—convinced him that 17 buildings had indeed been built next to

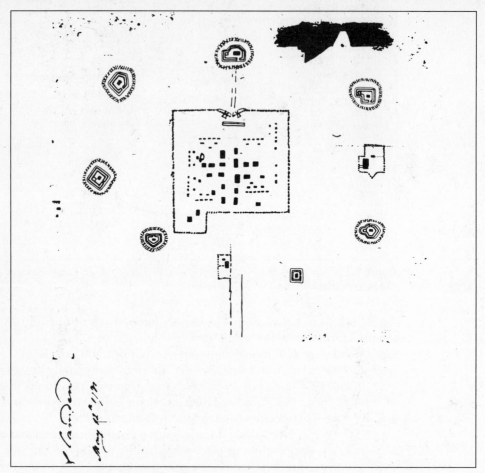

1781 map of Camden, South Carolina.

the roads that ran through old Camden. This finding lead him to conclude that his hypothesis about the settlement pattern was original confirmed: "the general form of the colonial occupation at Camden is basically that of an English two-row settlement, with a single main street and 2 cross-streets."

Lewis' study of Camden, South Carolina, is very scientific. He includes no artifact photographs or drawings in his report. He does not focus on important individuals or interpret how significant historical events affected the people of the town. Instead, his focus is on the process of frontier settlement: how the settlement pattern of the town changed over time, how Camden fitted into the frontier economy as a communication center, how Native American villages were not a barrier to the frontier process. From him, we obtain a picture of how Camden, as a frontier town, was part of a larger process of settlement and life in the New World.

Row of bricks in excavation unit at Camden, South Carolina, 1975.

The Camden study brings science to the core of historical archaeology, opting for scientific precision as a way of examining changes in a historic community over time, an approach that is commonplace in prehistoric archaeology.

HUMANISTIC SCIENCE IN HISTORICAL ARCHAEOLOGY

Since interest in scientific historical archaeology peaked in the 1970s, most historical archaeologists have pursued a perspective that is not easily characterized simply as either humanistic or scientific. Perhaps the best term for this varied perspective is "humanistic science," because most practitioners have adopted something from both humanism and science. Many historical archaeologists want to contribute something meaningful to knowledge about past daily life, as would the humanist, but as anthropologists, most also would not wish to leave social science behind. As a result, most historical archaeologists now blend the humanistic and the scientific perspective.

This happy blending has bred many innovative perspectives, giving a dynamism and excitement to the field that is sometimes lacking elsewhere. Historical archaeologists are actively pushing the frontiers of knowledge by presenting and exploring innovative approaches and interpretations. Here we focus on the work of two major theorists, James Deetz and Mark Leone.

Historical Structuralism

The approach used by James Deetz may best be described as *historical structuralism.* Deetz, now a professor of anthropology at the University of Virginia, began by studying the late prehistoric and early historic Arikara Indians who lived along the Missouri River in today's South Dakota. His doctoral dissertation, published in 1965, was part of the movement to test the waters of process-oriented, scientific archaeology. With the Arikara, Deetz sought to determine whether he could observe a correlation between the pottery they made and the social transformations they were undergoing after contact with Europeans. During the eighteenth century, the Arikara underwent a series of dramatic changes. Their numbers dropped precipitously as they suffered from European diseases, they steadily moved their villages further and further up the Missouri River, and they changed their ideas about where newly married couples should live. Traditionally, the Arikara had a residence pattern that included a rule that newly married couples should live in the villages of the bride's family. As epidemics spread through their villages and hostile neighbors encroached on their lands, the people moved north. They now abandoned this pattern for a more liberal one that was not so strict about postmarriage residence. Deetz wondered whether this change had an impact on pottery, because, among the Arikara, the women were the potters. Girls learned the craft of pottery manufacture from their mothers or grandmothers. Deetz wanted to know whether the movement of girls away from their maternal kin had any affect on their pottery. When he studied the pottery excavated from a number of village sites along the Missouri River, he observed that over time the pottery did indeed show an increased irregularity of design elements. The maximum stress among the people, as revealed in the pottery, occurred between 1720 and 1750. This seemed to be the greatest time of variability as young women experimented with new designs and incorporated design elements from the pottery traditions of other native peoples.

Deetz's study, while much criticized, quickly became a classic because his method was scientific and his perspective was anthropological. However, over the next several years Deetz turned away from the study of historic Native Americans to that of America's earliest colonial English settlers. It was then that he developed his structuralist approach to the recent past.

Structuralism is a perspective that aims to discover the hidden themes and relations in a culture rather than to explain how a culture works. It has a complex history as a major theoretical approach in anthropology, beginning with the work of a number of French scholars, most notably sociologist, Emile Durkheim, and cultural anthropologist, Claude Levi-Strauss. They and their followers developed structuralism partly in reaction to another pervasive theoretical perspective, that of *functionalism.* Functionalists are interested in the ways cultural institutions fit together and function together to keep culture going. Under this rubric, cultures are composed of several individual institutions that, like the pieces of a jigsaw puzzle, can be assembled and understood in their totality. The job of the functionalist anthropologist is to study cultural institutions—marriage, kinship, cosmology—and to determine how they fit together. Structuralists found the functional view lacking because it never explained the deeper structures of the culture. How did the social institutions actually work? Instead of being interested in the pieces of the puzzle, structuralists are interested in the driveshaft that caused the machine to cut the pieces into their individual shapes. Their interest is in the deep structure of culture.

Deetz was strongly drawn to structuralism, but only when combined "with a strong dose of old fashioned historiography." He drew much of his intellectual inspiration from the research of American folklorist, Henry Glassie. In his classic *Folk Housing in Middle Virginia,* published in 1975, Glassie presented a structuralist interpretation of vernacular architecture as revealed in about one hundred standing houses in two counties in Virginia, between Williamsburg and Charlottesville. His goal was to write a "grammar" of vernacular architecture that would show the choices individual builders had available to them when they built a new house. For example, when it came to deciding the location of various features of the house— fireplace, stairway, hall, porch—builders faced many options. They could locate a stairway in a public or a private space, enclose a porch to make an artificial climate or do without, cluster their outbuildings at one location or scatter them across the lot. That vernacular builders consistently choose certain options meant that they were following some deep structure, some patterned logic of the culture that was like the grammar of a language.

Glassie focused specifically on standing buildings. Deetz, however, chose several kinds of material culture to study the deep structure of the colonial human mind. He argued that material culture is "the track of our collective existence." In looking across the American landscape, at tombstones, house designs, ceramic colors, customs of eating, and music, Deetz observed significant changes over time. For example, eighteenth-century tombstones underwent a dramatic change. In the early years of the century, craftsmen put images of skulls on gravestones, but in the later years they carved angelic cherubs on them. During the same time period, cuts of meat went from being hacked from the carcass with chopping tools to being carefully removed with a saw. Ceramics also underwent a transformation. By the late eighteenth century, bone white had replaced the once-fashionable browns, greens, and yellows.

Deetz saw these dramatic changes in material culture as purposeful and interconnected. Tombstone carvers simply did not grow tired of using the same old death-head patterns and, for a change, decided to start using cherubs; ceramic makers did not stop making earth-tone vessels on a whim. Instead, Deetz said that all of the changes in material culture—from houses to cuts of meat—represented the Georgian mind set. This way of thinking was the way Englishmen and women saw the world during the reigns of the English kings George I, II, and III (1714–1820). A series of structural rules—the grammar—operated behind this mind set to arrange culture, to order things in a sensible way. According to Deetz, each culture has these rules and, even though their members may not be aware of them, they can be ob-

Death's Head and Cherub on colonial gravestones in New England.

served in their material culture. On tombstones, the death's head is a powerful emotional device connoting Puritan orthodoxy, whereas the angel suggests a liberalization of Puritanism and the rise of an intellectual belief system. The use of a saw to remove meat from a carcass denotes a change to individualism through the use of "portion control." The hacked cuts were imprecise and impersonal; the sawn portions are neat and individualized. The popularity of white dishes symbolizes a movement away from nature and toward artificiality. It is not enough to say that the change in dish color is a merely a technological innovation. There is a deeper meaning, a hidden structure that all of a culture's material objects represent.

Many of Deetz's colleagues and students have followed his theoretical lead. For the most part, these scholars have not been content simply to mimic him, but use his ideas and approach as a starting point for their own research. One is Martin Hall, a professor of historical archaeology at the University of Cape Town, South Africa. In a paper published in 1992, Hall builds on Deetz's historical structuralism by adding the idea of "discourse." For him, a "discourse" is created by the interaction, the "conversation," among material objects, written texts, and spoken words. This "conversation" of things takes place within specific historical contexts. There are no formal laws of the human mind in these settings, only discourses that make their own rules as they are developed. The rules make sense within the cultural tradition. Much of the discourse is symbolic. As an example, Hall briefly considers Westover Plantation, the baronial estate of the powerful Byrds of colonial Virginia. A purely structural analysis of the plantation would tend to push the Byrds, as historical actors, into the background. The way they built their mansion, the position of their slave quarters, the very dishes from which they ate, would all be structured by the Enlightenment Mind. This Mind also includes "the Georgian mansions of England, Mozart's music, Jane Austen's novels, and formal gardens." In Hall's discursive analysis, the Byrds are pushed to center stage as members of the ruling elite. Their architecture and their displays of public wealth were symbolic reminders of their supreme social power. When considered in its totality, "the material world of Westover and the actions of patriarch, family, and slave would be statements in a discourse."

Hall sees the world of artifacts as a uniquely powerful one, in which individual men and women use material things to resist the influence of domination, to redefine themselves within the social order as conditions change. Hall shows how colonial ceramics at the Cape of Good Hope in South Africa were used in this way. The Dutch East India Company adopted a three-tiered hierarchy of ceramics. On the lowest level were common, cheaply made red wares decorated with bright green and yellow glazes. Above them were coarse porcelains brought to the Cape from Indonesia. At the top were the rare fine porcelains imported from the royal kilns of China. The finest Chinese porcelains were far more than elegant domestic ware; they also formed part of an elaborate ceremony of display that included tea drinking and formal dinners. Fine porcelains were widely displayed as symbolic reminders of power and status. Not surprisingly, sherds of such delicate wares occur frequently in archaeological sites once inhabited by members of the Dutch colonial elite, a straightforward association of power with fine porcelain. But Hall also found such fragments in slave dwellings, together with coarse red wares used by the lower classes of society. Interestingly, coarse porcelains are absent, the domestic wares most common in the deposits left by Dutch soldiers. Conceivably, slaves were not issued the same ceramics commonly used by Dutch soldiers. But can we explain the fine porcelain in the slave quarters?

Hall believes the slaves stole fine dishware, as a gesture of symbolic defiance. On a deeper level, these same fine porcelains symbolically "turned the world upside down, allowing the repressed victims of a patriarchal world to reconstitute

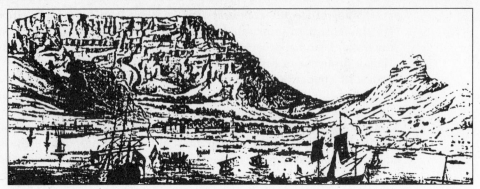

Cape Town, South Africa, as it looked in 1762.

daily a 'space' for themselves." The fine porcelains meant something quite different to the slaves as opposed to their Dutch masters.

Hall expands the boundaries of historical structuralism, and his approach is innovative and interesting. Nonetheless, he and Deetz are not the only historical archaeologists who have combined science and humanism in the effort to understand the historical past. Another approach espouses what can be called "critical materialism."

Critical Materialism

Critical materialism is our term for an approach that combines "critical theory" with "materialism." Materialism is an ancient perspective in which the reality of physical matter generally takes precedence over ideas and thought processes. Critical theory is a twentieth-century refinement of the nineteenth-century ideas of Karl Marx. It was proposed by scholars of the Frankfort School of sociology in the 1920s, among them Theodor Adorno, Max Horkheimer, and Herbert Marcuse. They argued that knowledge is never neutral, but is affected by the scholar's class interests. The affect can be intended, but usually it is unconscious. Rather than to pretend that research is unbiased and free of judgment, critical theorists argue that we should recognize the prejudices inherent in our research. In other words, our research is "reflexive"; it reflects back on itself. Critical theories argue that their research is never passionless, never atheoretical.

Mark Leone of the University of Maryland has developed an approach that links materialism with "critical theory." His focus is on the close relationship between the class structure in a society and its technology.

Like Deetz, Leone began his career in process-oriented archaeology. In a study of Mormon fences published in 1973, Leone emphasized a perspective that considered archaeology as a science of technology. The anthropologist in Leone was interested in "how technology affects culture and how technology is manipulated by culture." As a historical archaeologist, he was equally concerned with the

Early eighteenth-century fine Chinese porcelain dinner plate from Cape Town, South Africa.

historical aspects of technology. Mormons built fences, walls, and partitions in the nineteenth century, and they continue to build them today. A traditional historical explanation for the Mormon use of fences held that this technology was merely a throwback to their days in New England. When the Mormons traveled west through Illinois and the Great Plains, finally settling in Utah, they brought the idea of fences with them. Thus, fences simply represented something the Mormons knew in New England. But Leone was dissatisfied with this simplistic explanation. So he asked a perceptive question: why did the same settlers not bring other elements of New England material culture with them? Why just fences, and why do Mormon farmers continue to build similar fences today? Leone believed that the Mormons used fences to divide their space in ways that made sense within the context of their religious beliefs. Technology, as represented by fences, was embedded in Mormon life at every level. The use of space, subsistence strategies, and their ways of social interaction were all tied to technology in some way. As Leone said, "It is not just that Mormons and their religion created settlements and spatial subdivisions and made life work: Mormonism could not exist without the spatial representations and technological devices that allowed its population to exist." In other words, the fences and the religion tended to reinforce one another.

A strong thread of mental process ran through Leone's Mormon study, the notion that there was a relationship between technology and the kind of ideas that allowed Mormons to build fences. He also argued that while archaeology is about the past, it is conducted in the present. As he wrote in his Mormon study, "Archaeology is a product of the present; it is used by the present."

Leone brings class relations to the forefront of his analyses. He uses "critical theory" to emphasize the importance of class analysis and to demonstrate the modern uses of archaeology.

Critical theory has a wide following not only in archaeology, but in legal scholarship, history, geography, and other disciplines. Archaeologists espousing this approach argue that the scientific objectivity sought by process-oriented archaeologists like South is not possible. Artifacts do not "speak" for themselves; archaeologist are not mere translators. Even when quantified, artifacts are not value-free. Archaeologists create artificial categories for sorting artifacts, and the very act of creating them is a biased process. For example, why did South have a separate category "Smoking pipes" rather than just including them under "Activities"? Why was "Kitchen" a category instead of "Food Preparation"? Archaeologists give artifacts meaning; they are interpreters. That these meanings sometimes may have importance outside archaeology should be celebrated as a way for archaeology to develop a greater sense of relevance to modern society. As Leone said, "an exploration of the political function of archaeology may produce both a consciousness of the social function of archaeology as well as a set of questions for archaeology to address that may be of greater social benefit." To give only one example, the complex relationship between politics and archaeology has surfaced in the recent controversies over the reburial of Native American skeletal remains and grave goods.

Leone himself has focused on a major historical phenomenon of recent centuries—the growth of capitalism. He uses capitalism as a way of organizing life, as a way of setting up categories, in Annapolis, Maryland. For Leone, capitalism was not just an economic system, something that could be removed from social analysis. Capitalism was part and parcel of each and every segment of life, a culture in and of itself. Thus, all activity in historic Annapolis had an umbrella of capitalism spread over it. But saying this is not enough, the important question is, as Leone said, "How did capitalism actually operate on the ground—that is, in people's daily lives?" Or: "How can historical archaeologists study capitalism?"

At Annapolis, Leone began with probate inventories. From these lists of property he constructed four wealth-holding groups for the years from 1690 to 1775. These categories do not include African-American slaves, poor whites, most women, and free African-Americans, but they do subsume a major segment of the

TABLE 9.1

CERAMIC INDEX FOR ANNAPOLIS, MARYLAND

	Plate Diameter (Inches)					
Ceramic Type	4	5	6	7	8	9
Porcelain	—	—	—	—	x	—
Pearlware	—	—	—	x	—	x
Whiteware	x	—	—	—	—	x

Source: Mark P. Leone, Parker B. Potter, Jr., and Paul A. Shackel, "Toward a Critical Archaeology," Current Anthropology, vol. 28, no. 3 (1987), p. 288.

historical population. Historians have shown that capitalism had an increasing influence on life in Annapolis throughout the eighteenth century. When the early years of the century were compared with later decades, more people worked for wages, merchants made more money, and more consumer goods came into the city in the later part of the century. Leone took this fact as a starting point and combined it with his ideas about the importance of class.

Working closely with colleagues Parker Potter and Paul Shackel, Leone showed how people's lives became more standardized over time and how there existed an "increasing interchangeability of things, acts, and persons." In the early seventeenth century, men and women often acted communally. They slept in the same rooms, they ate their meals from one or two bowls, they did not use silverware. With the rising influence of capitalism, however, people's life became more regulated, more interchangeable with everyone else. Men and women now paid attention to clocks, they had a certain time for lunch, they each had their own dishes and forks during dinner. It was at this time that the various kinds of ceramics vessels in the POTS program mentioned in Chapter 8 were developed.

To study these important changes, Leone and his colleagues excavated three domestic household sites in Annapolis. One represented the upper-wealth group; one was a middle-wealth group. The third site represented a household that had climbed from the lowest wealth group in the 1740s to the highest group over the next several years. To provide a way to measure social change using artifacts, Leone, Potter, and Shackel devised a clever formula to measure ceramic variability. Their idea was that an increase in ceramic variation would signal the increasing impact of capitalism on the daily lives of ordinary men and women. They took the number of types of ceramics in a sample, combined with the number of plate sizes—the "type-sizes"—and divided it by the number of types present. They then multiplied the quotient by the number of plate sizes to produce an index number. The index value of a soil layer that had five type-sizes, three different ceramic types (porcelain, pearlware, whiteware), and four different sizes of plates, would be calculated as: $(5/3)(4) = 6.67$ (Table 9.1). The higher the value, the greater the variation. When they computed this index value for the three sites at Annapolis, they saw that the values indeed increased over time.

For example, at the Hammond-Harwood House, belonging to the upper-wealth household, the value increased from 2.0 in the mid-to-late eighteenth century to 27.0 in the late 18th-to-early 19th century. At the Thomas Hyde House site—where the household went from the lowest wealth group to the highest—the index values started at 1.0 in the early eighteenth century. By the mid-to-late eighteenth century the index value was 2.0, and for the late 18th to early 19th century, it was 24.5. For the mid-19th century the value was 73.1. To Leone and his colleagues the message from these values was inescapable: "The greater variety of dish sizes and wares in the archaeological record reflects a new etiquette, and increasing segmentation at the table that served both as a training ground for the new order and as reinforcement for it." Thus, the changes in material culture that archaeologists can see between the seventeenth and the nineteenth centuries along the Atlantic Coast do not simply reflect transformations of a deep mental construct. They represent wholesale social changes brought about because of, and through, human experiences within capitalism.

Perhaps the best analogy for thinking about theory in historical archaeology is to envision a music store. The CDs are arranged by categories in neat rows. Some people will find the jazz section appealing, others will be drawn to rock and roll, others to alternative. Many people will make their way to several categories, finding something they like about each one of them. Like trends in music, archaeological theories come and go. The music store of 1980 did not look like the music store of 1990, that of 1991 did not resemble that of 1990. Scholars pick and choose theories as well, perhaps not with the rapidity of music styles, but change is inherent in scholarship. Some archaeologists are drawn to class analysis, some to the mental constructs that underlie the creation of bottles, dishes, and houses. Still others continue to find something worthwhile in scientific perspectives developed in the 1960s. Individual archaeologists tend to defend their own way of looking at the past as the only, correct way to do so, but in the final analysis most experts are willing to accept that several equally valid ways can be used to interpret the past.

Whatever their theoretical perspective, archaeologists are engaged in the study not of individuals, but of groups. Even on historic sites, the archaeological record only rarely allows one to associate artifacts or structures with actual known individuals. For the most part, we usually study the actions of people organized into social groups, many of them without significant historical voices. It is to the study of such groups that we must now turn.

CHAPTER
10

The Archaeology of Groups

"The adequate treatment of the disenfranchised groups in America's past, excluded from historical sources because of race, religion, isolation, or poverty, is an important function of contemporary historical archaeology and one that cannot be ignored"

Kathleen Deagan, 1982

In the late 1980s, archaeologist Mary Beaudry and her colleagues at the Center for Archaeological Studies at Boston University set about studying the nineteenth-century Boott Cotton Mills in Lowell, Massachusetts. They learned from historical documents that wealthy entrepreneurs from Boston incorporated the mill on March 22, 1835; that they named it after Kirk Boott, their agent; that two other agents were named Benjamin French and Linus Child. The documents said much about the prominent men of Boott Mills, but what about the others? More than 1,000 mill workers, 950 women and 120 men, produced about nine million yards of cloth annually. These were the working men and women, who made money for the well-documented Boston entrepreneurs. For the most part, the mill workers are an anonymous labor force, mentioned only rarely in factory records. We know some of their names. In 1860, 32-year-old James Stoddard was a mill hand; 34-year-old Mary Hanscom was a seamstress, and 24-year-old Charles E. Dodge a beltmaker. Beyond this, the mill records are silent, but archaeology was not. This chapter discusses ways in which historical archaeology can throw light on anonymous social groups within ever more complex industrial societies.

Beaudry's Boott Cotton Mill excavations shed new light on the mill workers' diet. Account books provided the official version of what men and women mill hands ate. A list published in 1886 reported on the food provided for 66 men and 11 women for one month. It included 400 lbs (149.2 kg) of roast beef, 272 lbs (101.5 kg) of beef steak, 160 lbs (59.7 kg) of ham, and 70 lbs (26.1 kg) of salt pork. The workers also consumed mackerel, cod, and other fish, as well as an assortment of beans, rice, squash, and cheese, but meat constituted an important part of their daily diet.

The account books appear thorough and complete, but the animal bones and plant remains excavated from the boarding house site provide a closer look at the average mill worker's diet. The lists provide for "the demands for nutrients to 75 laboring men at moderate work for 30 days, or 1 man for 2,250 days." The faunal remains suggest, however, that the people in the mill found it desirable, and perhaps even necessary, to supplement their diet with other foodstuffs. Zooarchaeologist David Landon's analysis reveals that the families at Boott Mill also ate turkey, chicken, and mutton, even though these foods are not mentioned in the records. The sheep bones in the collection show that the workers ate the least expensive shank cuts and the forequarters. The workers probably purchased these foods on their own. This would explain the absence of these foods in the records. Ethnobotanist Gerald Kelso found that, in addition to undocumented cuts of meat, they also ate grains, grapes, and blackberries or raspberries. The archaeologists cannot tell which employees ate the grapes, grains, and mutton, but their physical evidence does provide a complete picture of the diet of the workers as a group.

One great strength of historical archaeology is that it can sometimes flesh out the more commonplace details of the lives of society's anonymous working people, men and women like Stoddard, Hanscom, Dodge, and the hundreds of others who toiled alongside them every day. More often, however, individuals are blurred in the archaeological record. Their names are lost to history. So they come down to us through their artifacts and food remains, as members of once well-defined social and economic classes, as males and females, as ethnic groups. How, then, does the archaeologist study such groups?

CULTURAL COMPLEXITY AND SOCIAL STRATIFICATION

Almost invariably, the historical archaeologist works with complex, socially stratified societies, with people living in literate, pre-industrial, or industrial civilizations. *Social stratification* simply means that a society is divided into two or more groups of people that are ranked relative to one another in terms of economic, social, or other criteria. Many years ago, anthropologist Elman Service divided human societies into pre-state and state-organized societies, the former mainly hunting bands and farming societies, the latter pre-industrial civilizations. State-organized societies such as those of the Sumerians, ancient Egyptians, or the Aztecs, were marked

Kinds.	Prices per lb.	Quanti- ties.	Costs.	Protein.	Fats.	Carbohy- drates.
	cents.	lbs.		lbs.	lbs.	lbs.
Beef, roast, . . .	10	400	$40 00	60.4	79.9	–
Beef steak, . . .	14	272	38 08	39.4	42.4	–
Beef, corned, . . .	7	350	24 50	40.3	99.8	–
Beef tongue, . . .	10	62	6 20	9.2	9.5	–
Beef stew, . . .	5	167	8 35	23.4	52.3	–
Beef, tripe, . . .	6	20	1 20	4.2	0.2	–
Pork, roast, . . .	10	150	15 00	17.1	54.3	–
Ham, . . .	11	160	17 60	23.4	54.9	–
Salt pork, . . .	10	70	7 00	2.0	53.6	–
Lard, . . .	8	260	20 80	–	257.4	–
Haddock, . . .	7	168	11 76	13.9	0.2	–
Halibut, . . .	12	50	6 00	7.6	2.1	–
Mackerel, . . .	3	40	1 20	4.0	1.6	–
Salt fish (cod), . . .	4½	50	2 25	8.0	0.2	–
Total meats, fish, etc., . . .	. . .	2,219	$199 94	252.9	708.4	–
Milk, . . .	2	3,024	$60 48	102.8	111.9	145.2
Cheese, . . .	11	63.5	6 98	17.2	22.5	1.5
Butter, . . .	22 and 10	291	54 54	2.9	254.6	1.5
Eggs, . . .	14	107	14 82	12.4	10.9	0.6
Total dairy products and eggs, . . .	. . .	3,485.5	$136 82	135.3	399.9	148.8
Flour, . . .	3	1,568	$47 04	174.0	17.2	1,182.3
Sugar, . . .	7½	600	45 00	–	–	580.2
Molasses, . . .	4½	99	4 50	–	–	70.3
Beans, . . .	3	124	3 74	28.8	2.6	66.6
Rice, . . .	8	25	2 00	1.9	0.1	19.9
Oatmeal, . . .	4	25	1 00	3.8	1.8	16.8
Potatoes, . . .	1	2,520	25 20	47.9	5.0	463.7
Squash, . . .	1½	250	3 75	1.3	0.3	13.3
Onions, . . .	2	26	50	0.3	–	2.0
Beets, . . .	5-9	90	50	1.6	0.1	9.0
Turnips, . . .	3-6	120	1 00	1.1	0.2	6.1
Tomatoes, . . .	5-6	120	1 00	1.6	0.4	5.4
Apples, . . .	1½	300	5 00	0.9	–	32.7
Raisins, . . .	12½	24	3 00	0.6	0.1	15.1
Currants, . . .	10	15	1 50	0.3	–	9.5
Corn starch, . . .	9	12	1 08	–	–	11.0
Crackers, . . .	5	48	2 40	5.1	4.8	34.0
Total vegetable food, . . .	. . .	5,266	$143 21	269.2	32.6	2,537.9
Total animal food, . . .	. . .	5,704.5	336 76	388.2	1,108.3	148.8
Total food, . . .	. . .	11,670.5	$484 97	657.4	1,140.9	2,686.7
Meats, fish, etc., per man per day, . . .	. . .	.99	$0 09	.11	.31	–
Dairy products and eggs, per man per day, . . .	. . .	1.55	06	.06	.18	.07
Animal food, per man per day, . . .	. . .	2.54	$0 15	.17	.49	.8
Vegetable food, " " . . .	. . .	2.65	07	.12	.01	1.13
Total food, " " . . .	. . .	5.19	$0 22	.29	.50	1.20

Account book of food for millworker, Lowell, Massachusetts, published in 1886.

by a highly stratified social organization, headed by a small class of rulers and no-bles. Aztec society, for example, was made up of nobles, commoners and slaves, but within these broad social groupings were numerous important economic classes, like merchants, priest, and warriors. Early pre-industrial civilizations depended not on fossil fuels, but on simple technologies and the labor of human hands, as well as highly centralized government. Many of their institutions persisted for long periods, right through Roman times into the European Renaissance, and to the Age of Discovery. Each of these societies comprised numerous, often competing social groups.

These cultures, even though stratified, did not have capitalistic—or profit-motivated—economies that were intended to be global. The Europeans who went to other lands planned to find great sources of wealth. When Prince Henry the Navigator of Portugal sent his ships southward round the western bulge of Africa in the 1420s, his captains sailed in the service of the Crown. So did Christopher Columbus on his famous voyages to the Indies, while Hernán Cortes was supposed, at least in theory, to remit a fifth of the Aztec gold he discovered to the Spanish monarch when he sacked the Aztec capital, Tenochtitlán, in 1521. The conquistadors were members of complex, highly stratified societies, where individuals were members of distinct social classes, and everyone had a well-defined place in society. Some were soldiers, some priests, others blacksmiths. We know from contemporary documents that many Spanish immigrants to New Spain (now Mexico) after the Conquest were poor, land-hungry men from rural farming villages. They came without wives and often married into Indian families, creating the mestizo class of today.

The archaeological problem is simply stated: historical records tell us the names of monarchs, captains, and generals, even of some priests and merchants. They also refer to humbler folk in general terms. How, then, do we identify such groups in the archaeological record—from their artifacts, food remains, structures, or through their burials? Often, the available historical records will indicate that certain groups of people—such as African slaves, Native American women, European immigrant laborers—once lived at a particular site. In such cases, the archaeological problem is not simply to identify these groups from the remains they left behind, but to try to understand how the people used their material culture to indicate and to symbolize their identity. Clearly, this is a much more difficult task, but it is one that makes historical archaeology an important social science. However, because historical archaeology is a relatively new field of study, a body of sophisticated works on the deeper issues involving archaeological groups is just now being developed. Many historical archaeologists have had to be content with first being certain that they can actually identify past groups in the archaeological remains.

Associating collections of artifacts with, say, blacksmiths is difficult at the best of times, especially in domestic situations, where people live in families, away from their place of work. Only very rarely does the excavator find an artifact that belongs to a historically identifiable individual. For example, while excavating the overseer's cabin at Cannon's Point Plantation, an early nineteenth-century cotton-growing estate on St. Simons Island, Georgia, archaeologist John Otto found a glass disk engraved "Hugh F. Grant" and the date "1829." This disk, possibly a lens of some sort, was undoubtedly owned by Hugh Fraser Grant, the son of a wealthy planter who lived in the area. Records show that Grant was 18 years old in 1829. At this time, he may have served as the Cannon's Point overseer before his marriage in 1831. Wealthy planters' sons often worked as overseers so that they could learn the business of running a large plantation before they acquired their own. The etched inscription allows us to state with confidence that the lens was once the property of Hugh Grant.

Any study of social groups requires meticulous historical research ahead of time, for they provide the context for the specific questions that may be answered underground. For instance, in 1085, William the Conqueror dispatched census takers throughout England to take stock of all that he had conquered 19 years earlier. He was in search of statistical information to keep at his fingertips, which came to him in the celebrated Domesday Book. When recorders compiled the Book the following year, they crammed it with names and numbers—of those who paid taxes and tithes. In Staffordshire, for instance, the elites are frequently mentioned: "The King has 18 burgesses. . . . The Bishop of Chester has 14 dwellings. . . . Earl Roger has 3 dwellings. . . . Robert of Stafford has 3 dwellings." Despite this careful recording, the Domesday Book "does not enable us to arrive at a really close estimate of the total population of 11th-century England," says expert R. Welldon Finn. Why? Because commoners, lesser folk, are mentioned, not by name, but only in reference to some larger group. For instance, Totmonslow Hundred contains "1 free man and 10 villagers who have 5 ploughs"; at Pirehill Hundred are "4 villagers, 8 smallholders and 4 slaves who have 2 ploughs."

Cemeteries, although controversial to excavate, often provide important clues about stratification. Archaeologists generally assume that in death men and women reflect the social standing they held in life. Thus, clothing, ornaments, and grave goods are good indicators of the deceased's social position. Robert Mainfort studied social stratification using 85 graves from the Fletcher Site cemetery in central Michigan. The Fletcher cemetery was used by northern Algonquin Indians, perhaps the Ottawa and Chippewa, from about 1740 or 1750 to 1765. Student archaeologists from Michigan State University excavated the site in 1967, 1968, and 1970. Mainfort, now an archaeologist with the State of Tennessee, was specifically interested in how the burials at the Fletcher Site reflected social stratification. The many European artifacts in the cemetery showed that the villagers were active trading partners with French fur traders who roamed the lakes and rivers of the Upper Midwest. Many graves contained silver bracelets and ear ornaments, iron woodworking tools, glass beads, iron knives, pistols, mirrors, and many other objects. The distribution of these objects through the cemetery was far from uniform. Some individuals owned many European artifacts, others had a few, one or two had none. Burial 70—an adolescent of unknown sex—was buried with 1 brass kettle, 33 decorative metal "tinkling" cones generally sewn on clothing, 1 brass projectile point, 4 loops of brass wire, 1 brass bell, 1 iron animal trap, 1 clasp knife, 1 "strike-a-light" for starting fires with a flint, 1 crooked knife, 2 silver plaques, 2 silver ear ornaments, 1 silver disk, 1 gunflint, 1 bone awl, 2 bone projectile points, 152 shell beads, 1,690 glass beads, and one woolen belt. Burial 64, however—a man, 25–40 years old—was buried with only two crooked knives. Burial 96, a woman between the ages of 25 and 40, was buried with nothing at all. Mainfort believed that "Those individuals who received the most copious grave furnishings are interpreted as representing the highest or most important social positions in the society." Thus, at the Fletcher Site cemetery, it appears that the numbers of grave goods found buried with the dead reflects the social stratification of one eighteenth-century Native American village.

One basic, stratified group studied by historical archaeologists is the class.

CLASS

Social scientists disagree about a precise definition of "class." Some say that a person's class membership has to do with their "life's chances," or their opportunity to acquire property, education, and material things. Others contend that class membership, and even life chances for that matter, have more to do with a person's relationship to production. Some people own factories and agricultural land, others work in them. In this social scheme, people are either owners (haves) or workers (have-nots). Many people equate class with income group.

In short, definitions abound. In one that is well known, anthropologist Marvin Harris defines "class" as a group of people who have a similar relationship to the structure of social control in a society and who possess similar amounts of power over the allocation of wealth, privilege, resources, and technology. An important point about classes is that an individual's membership in a particular class can change as they acquire (or lose) something of value in the society: wealth, power, a job, or education. Furthermore, men and women in a class system only know their position in a relative way. We may all have some idea whether we are in the upper, middle, or lower class, but we generally do not concern ourselves with whether we are part of the upper middle class or the lower upper class. What is important in historical archaeology is that specific pieces of material culture can sometimes be related to particular social classes.

Historical archaeologist Steven Shephard studied the relationship between material culture and class membership in Alexandria, Virgina. Beginning as a small trading post primarily for tobacco in the early 1730s, Alexandria soon grew into a major mercantile center. In its heyday, the city boasted a population stratified into classes that extended from enslaved African-Americans on the bottom to extremely wealthy planters and merchants on the top. Shephard examined three early nineteenth-century sites in the city, looking for material evidence of class membership. City records indicated that two sites could be classified as within the middle class (based on income and occupation), and one in the much poorer lower class. From the thousands of artifacts excavated by the city's permanent archaeological staff, Shephard decided to focus on ceramics because they can be easily studied in terms of quantity, quality, and variety. Throughout their lives, Alexandrian families usually purchased large quantities of ceramics. These pieces could be of vastly different quality, from fine imported wares to everyday kitchen pieces, in well-defined shapes and sizes. Examining a sample of about 1,300 bowls, cups, saucers, and plates from different neighborhoods, Shephard noticed that the middle-class households had a greater quantity and variety of dishes than did lower-class households. Middle-class families also had more matched pieces than poorer households, and of the matched pieces, the middle class had a greater variety of pieces.

Shephard's modest findings may seem somewhat obvious. Given our own personal knowledge of class differences, we can well imagine that men and women in a higher social position will have a greater variety of dishes than someone lower down the social ladder. Shephard's conclusion, however, that "the quantity and quality variables are the strongest correlates of class membership," provides an avenue of inquiry for others to follow. Quantities and qualities of artifacts are easy for historical archaeologists to document.

Obviously, one of the factors that influence the ability of class members to acquire certain dishes, or anything else for that matter, hinges on whether they can obtain them. We cannot buy what is not available, no matter how much we can afford it. We can expect the upper class to have a greater ability to obtain the goods they want. After all, they are generally "in control" (or at least know who is). But, if the elites want to live off the beaten path, far from highways or railroads, we may be willing to concede that they have trouble receiving some artifacts and commodities. But is this true?

Sherene Baugher and Robert Venables decided to test this idea by examining ceramic artifacts excavated at seven eighteenth-century sites in New York State. They chose two sites in the country, and five sites in New York City, two on Staten Island, three on Manhattan. They used historical records to establish that each site was inhabited by upper- or middle-class households. For example, one site was inhabited by Sir William Johnson, the English government's main liaison with the powerful Iroquois Indians. Less well known, but no less wealthy, people lived at the other sites. Having established the class affiliations of the sites' residents, Baugher and Venables compared the artifacts from each location. Like many archaeologists, they focused on the ceramic sherds. There were few differences between them. Each site contained the expensive porcelains and finely made white tablewares that are usually associated with eighteenth-century wealth. These ceramics were imported from England and the Far East. Baugher and Venables did observe a difference in the inexpensive tablewares, however, kitchen pieces made locally and purchased directly from the potters. It is likely that the households probably saw no reason to spend money importing mixing bowls, churns, and jars when they were easily available locally for less cost. Anyway, these pieces were for use in the kitchen, out of the public eye. Thus, it appears, at least for high-priced ceramic tablewares, that a household's location was less important than its class position and wealth. As Baugher and Venables said, "The buying power of a colonist, not the individual's proximity to a colonial city, determined what (and how much) the individual purchased." Then as now, class helps to shape what can be bought. Upper crust, colonial New Yorkers, regardless of address, could easily mimic the fashions of London and other European capital cities.

In a provocative and important essay published in 1988 and entitled "Steps to an Archaeology of Capitalism," archaeologist Robert Paynter states that historical archaeologists can do much more than simply identify the presence of classes at past archaeological sites. He proposes that historical archaeologists can make strong contributions to the very understanding of class. The potential to make this contribution exists because material culture plays such a large part in many theories of class.

Paynter's research is only in its infancy, but his ideas are intriguing. In discussing glass bottles—objects frequently found by historical archaeologists—Paynter states that the transition from mouth blowing to machine manufacture was more than simply a technological innovation. The development of bottle-making machines came about because labor strikes and work stoppages by glass blowers made the industry a risky one for factory owners. Bottle manufacturers sought to circumvent work-stopping labor problems by decreasing the number of "troublesome" employees. An automatic bottle maker was one clear way to do this. When put in this light, the bottle fragments found by historical archaeologists during excavation represent much more than a mere technological improvement; they symbolize the way one class—glass factory owners—reacted to the protests of another class—glass blowers. Much more remains to be done on the subject of class identification and meaning, but Paynter's research points in a new and interesting direction.

GENDER

Men and women constitute the two most basic groups in the vast panorama of human history. For years, archaeologists found it easy to speak about these two groups in simplistic terms. Prehistoric men hunted, so all stone arrowheads and spear points were "male" objects; women cooked, so all potsherds were "female" objects. Usually, scholars assumed that the "movers and shakers" of a society were men; they were responsible for cultural change and technological advancement. Women were behind the scenes: homemaking, weaving, and cooking.

Western convention recognizes only two sexes. We imagine sex to be based on physiology rather than on behavior. Not every culture, however, makes this assumption. The eighteenth-century Tahitians of the south Pacific recognized three sexes: male, female, and mahu. The mahu were permanent transvestites who were not regarded as oddities. Neither were they considered to be males or females. Visiting Europeans were horrified by the mahu. John Turnbull, who visited Tahiti in the early nineteenth century, described them in 1813 as "a set of men . . . whose open profession is of such abomination that the laudable delicacy of our language will not admit it to be mentioned." The famed William Bligh, captain of *H.M.S. Bounty,* later set adrift by his mutinous crew in 1788, said of one particular mahu, "The Women treat him as one of their Sex, and he observed every restriction that they do, and is equally respected and esteemed." Many Native American societies also recognized three sexes. Among the Crow of Montana, for instance, the berdache was the equivalent of the Tahitian mahu. Finds-Them-and-Kills-Them, a Crow berdache, dressed like a woman and performed the domestic chores of a woman. Other Crows saw him not as a deviant male, but as a member of a third sex.

Westerners also tend to equate sex with gender. Gender, rather than referring specifically to physical characteristics, relates to culturally prescribed behavior. Thus, among the Tahitians and the Crows, we Westerners would see two sexes/gender roles: males and females, with the mahu and berdache constituting deviant males. The Tahitians and the Crows, however, would see three gender roles: males, females, and recognized transvestites.

We took this short trip into sexual ethnography because a number of archaeologists are working diligently to dispel the Western perception of equating sex and gender. They propose that instead of simply adding women to their interpretations of the past, like eggs to a cake mix, archaeologists must learn to evaluate gender roles, gender systems, and gender ideologies. As historical archaeologist Donna Seifert puts it, "women are not defective men; pregnancy, childbearing, and nursing are not necessarily disabilities; women's behavior, experience, and history is not deviant behavior because it is not the same as men's." The study of gender is not just about women; it is about women and men interacting to create and maintain society. When we learn about women's roles in the past, we automatically also learn something about men's roles. Giving women a voice in the past empowers us to develop a deeper understanding of history and culture.

Consider, for example, Seifert's 1991 study of "Hooker's Division," the nineteenth-century red light section of Washington, DC. Hooker's Division was named for Major General Joseph Hooker, who as commander of the Army of the Potomac, in 1863, ordered the concentration of all of the city's prostitutes in one part of town. Hooker was forced into this drastic step by the city council. They were growing increasingly concerned about the burgeoning number of off-duty soldiers who were flooding the nation's capital with money in their pockets. Many of these troops, fresh off the farms of the Midwest and probably away from home for the first time, went looking for fully stocked saloons and fast women. History tells us that many of them found both in Hooker's Division.

Remarkably, even though prostitution is considered to be "the world's oldest profession," archaeologists before Seifert had not studied it. Rather than seeking to examine Hooker's Division as a way to learn about one particular group of women, Seifert chose to envision prostitution as a kind of gender relationship. In this setting, being a sexual partner is a job rather than an expectation of marriage. What permits prostitution to flourish are gender relationships and expectations in wider society.

When Seifert compared the artifacts excavated from the red light district, she found artifacts associated with clothing present in much greater quantity in Hooker's Division than at other, more purely residential parts of Washington. Most were buttons from a wide variety of garments, everything from fancy ladies' robes to everyday men's and women's shirts and coats. The excavators unearthed several men's trouser buttons, perhaps lost by the brothel porters. More likely, they were once the property of the young men who went into Hooker's Division with time on their hands and money in their pockets. (This is perhaps a delicate way of saying that these button-losing men may have been the clients!)

In addition to objects of clothing, objects of personal hygiene and adornment (mirrors, combs, and jewelry) occur more often in the red light district than at other, nearby residences. A jar of "Valentine's Meat Juice," for the cure of "social diseases," also says something about the health and concerns of the ladies in Hooker's Division.

Seifert's findings are important because they provide a voice to women too long absent from the archaeological story of the past. Her wider objective is perhaps more important, however, because she is studying a gender relationship. In this relationship, prostitutes work to support themselves and their families. Prostitution is not simply an aberrant whim that "just happens" to some women; it has economic and social roots that relate to gender roles in society.

In some cases, simply the act of demonstrating the presence of women at a site is enough to shake forever the foundations of once-cherished androcentric, or male-focused, interpretations. Archaeologists have recently done a superb job of placing women at sites where they have long been invisible. Logging camps, like military forts, are usually seen as a bastion of manhood. Lumberjacks, cut in the image of Paul Bunyan, go into virgin forests like soldiers to do battle with nature. With brute strength and force of will they turn trees into usable lumber. When women are mentioned in the historical records of the lumber industry, they are usually "in town" waiting, as one historian of logging says, "to separate the man from his hard earned money." Both written and oral histories project one, clear image of logging: it was a male-only activity.

After examining several photographs of logging camp residents and reading numerous historical records and reports, archaeologist Janet Brashler discovered without doubt that women were involved in logging. They lived in logging camps and were an integral part of the industry. Brashler based her research design on gender as an organizing principle of group relations. This allowed her to look beyond the all-male shanty camp that forms the basis for most of our modern images of logging. In looking specifically for women, she discovered the widespread use of family company camps and temporary family shanty camps. These camps were different-sized communities of loggers in which families lived together in the forests. Dogway, for example, was a temporary logging town established by the Cherry River Boom and Lumber Company, and inhabited from about 1910–1915 to 1927. At this abandoned town site, now in the Monongahela National Forest, in West Virginia, Brashler made numerous surface finds: intricately decorated transfer-printed dishes, cast iron stove parts, rusted barrel hoops and springs, and different-colored glass fragments. She also recorded crumbled brick chimneys, caved-in root cellars, old railway grades, and the locations of 60 old railroad cars that were converted into housing.

Brashler has clearly given a voice to the women of the Cherry River Boom and Lumber Company. Archaeologists interested in the gender relations of the logging industry face a challenge as they attempt, in Brashler's words, "to define more clearly the artifact assemblages found in family camps, single-gender camps, family shanty camps, camps with red-light districts, and camps where one or two women might have been present as the wives of the foreman or cook." How can the artifacts unearthed from logging sites be used to give voice to the women of the logging industry? Do the rusty tin cans, bent enameled metal plates and cups, broken glass bottles, and iron pot fragments represent logging-oriented gender roles?

Unfortunately, circumstances prevented Brashler from excavating the Monongahela logging camps. She had to work entirely with surface collections. Nonetheless, her research challenges us to look for women where we may least expect them.

We often assume that the earliest colonists and explorers from Europe were men. After all, Columbus took no women with him on his first or second voyages. Several archaeologists are rapidly changing this male-only view of colonialism. One is Florida archaeologist Bonnie McEwan, who is interested in empowering women in Spanish colonial society by documenting their presence at archaeological sites. History tells us that Spanish women engaged in numerous trades, from folk medicine to textile production, but that, in general, women were expected to be homemakers. In the sixteenth and seventeenth centuries, Spanish women generally came to the New World as the wives of wealthy aristocrats. These women had as their main responsibility the maintenance of the Spanish household.

The typical Spanish wife was usually ignored in colonial documents. Excavators, however, can find evidence of their presence in archaeological deposits. For example, at Puerto Real, Haiti, Charles Ewen found material evidence for the presence of women in the deposits of the sixteenth-century townsite. At a high-status residence, designated Locus 19, Ewen found a lace bobbin made of bone, a number of glass beads, a ring fashioned from jet (a dense, black coal), and a pendant in the shape of a unicorn. Nothing else is known of the woman, or women, who used the bobbin or wore the ring, pendant, and beads, but now that their presence is acknowledged, archaeologists can continue to search for them (see Chapter 11). Similarly, at a seventeenth-century Spanish mission site in Tallahassee, Florida, Bonnie McEwan has excavated objects similar to those found in Haiti: jet rings, metal sequins or beads, small brass rings, a quartz pendant in a teardrop shape.

In her research, McEwan has not only shown that women lived in colonial Spanish communities, she also has argued that Spanish wives had a dramatic role in shaping colonial society. Colonial Spanish wives made their impact felt through the Native American and African-American women domestics who worked in their homes. According to McEwan, Spanish women integrated domestic workers "into their culture through language instruction, religious indoctrination, and training in European traditions and mores." The continuity with Spain that colonial women sought in their colonial homes was impressed on their domestic servants because the Spanish wife was ultimately responsible for seeing that the home conformed to the Spanish ideal. Spanish women were thus on the front line of acculturation, bringing Spanish culture to non-Spaniards, and deciding which elements of non-Spanish culture to accept into their homes. Not only were Spanish women present in colonial New Spain, they also played an important role in bringing Spanish culture to the newly discovered continent.

The study of gender and gender roles is still in its archaeological infancy, but it offers great promise in overturning long-held stereotypes about men and women in recent history.

ETHNICITY

Before historical archaeologists turned to the study of class membership or gender relations, they studied ethnicity. Ethnicity was the first great sociological topic of historical archaeology.

The experts cannot agree on a precise definition of ethnicity any more than they can on class, except in the most general terms. An ethnic group is an assemblage of people who share enough physical and cultural characteristics to define themselves as "us," and everyone else as "them." Ethnicity refers to the characteristics the group accepts as pertinent to them. Ethnic groups can be "nationalities," such as the Croats and Serbs of today's war-torn Bosnia-Hercegovina, or "people," such as the Gypsies of Europe. In the United States, historical archaeologists have focused most of their attention on African, Hispanic, and Asian ethnic groups, although Europeans—Irish, Scottish, English, Germans—have also been examined.

For all its study by historical archaeologists, the correlation between ethnicity and artifacts remains poorly understood. Sherene Baugher and Robert Venables had explicit historical information about the ethnicity of the people who lived at four of the seven New York State sites they compared. Sir William Johnson, who lived farthest north, on the Mohawk River, was Irish; Robert Livingston, who lived on the Hudson, between Albany and New York City, was of Scottish and Dutch ancestry; Jacob Rezeau, who lived in the center of Staten Island, was French; and Christopher Billopp, who lived on the southern tip of Staten Island, was English. But Baugher and Venables were unable to observe any clear signs of ethnicity among the archaeological remains at the sites.

Lu Ann De Cunzo of the University of Delaware drew the same conclusion in her study of Paterson, New Jersey. De Cunzo examined the artifacts from six privies all dating to the nineteenth century. Paterson was founded in 1791 by the Society for the Establishment of Useful Manufacture. The town was the first planned manufacturing community in America and established with government support. Even though the town was not a great success at first, it soon became the destination of several immigrant groups, including those from the British Isles. The six privies studied by De Cunzo were associated with Irish and English settlers. She scrutinized the artifact collections from each privy, but found no clear evidence of Irish or English identity. She found no clay pipes with Irish slogans imprinted on them, no insignia related to Irish independence, nothing symbolizing pride in the British Empire. She saw no differences in the quantity and diversity of ceramic and glass objects in the privies. The medicine bottles, ceramic plates and cups, or liquor bottles indicated nothing particularly suggestive of ethnicity. In short, De Cunzo was unable to distinguish any material differences between historically documented Irish and English households. As she says, "The English and especially the Irish, maintained their ethnic identity through family and church ties and participation in voluntary ethnic associations, but like the Americans they strove for upward mobility and displayed the American 'ethic' of conspicuous consumption." In other words, both Irish and English immigrants strove to be "American" at the expense of any clear material expression of their ethnic diversity.

The New York and Paterson examples show just how hard it is to distinguish ethnic groups from household artifacts. For this reason, many researchers have turned to the study of "ethnic markers." Ethnic markers are individual artifacts or groups of artifacts that can undeniably indicate the presence of certain ethnic groups at archaeological sites.

The opium smoking pipe brought to America by nineteenth-century Chinese immigrants is a classic example of an ethnic marker. Opium pipe bowls have a dis-

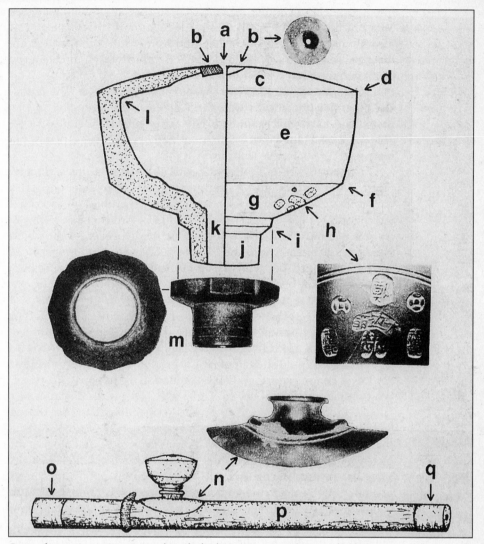

Parts of an opium pipe: a. smoking hole, b. insert, c. smoking surface, d. rim, e. side, f. shoulder, g. base, h. stamps, i. flange, j. stem, k. basal hole, l. rim joint, m. metal connector, n. saddle, o. end piece, p. pipe stem, q. mouth piece.

tinctive appearance, and once their characteristics are known, archaeologists can easily identify them. Made of either stone, such as jade, or pottery, the bowls resemble fancy doorknobs that have a hole, the "smoking hole," running downward through their center. This bowl, attached to a long pipestem, completed the opium pipe, or "pistol." Thus, opium pipes serve as a clear and obvious ethnic marker.

When Roberta Greenwood, then an archaeologist with the Los Angeles County Museum of Natural History, conducted research on Main Street in Ventura, California, during the 1970s, she used opium pipes as ethnic markers. She found small glass medicinal vials and opium pipe bowls in a mix of aboriginal and other nineteenth-century artifacts. These objects immediately signaled the presence of Chinese residents in the area. Greenwood's general expectation was that in a community that contained men and women of both Chinese and non-Chinese heritage, some artifacts could be singled out to represent each group. On the surface, her reasoning seems to make sense.

Greenwood found two archaeological features—a well and a trash pit—that she identified specifically with the Chinese. Well over half of the artifacts from these features were of Chinese origin. These objects included rice bowls, tea cups, ginger jars, and soy bottles. She identified ceramic cups, plates, bowls, and chamber pots as non-Chinese artifacts.

Greenwood thus argued that several kinds of artifacts, in addition to opium pipes, could be thought of as ethnic markers. Her pioneering research followed conventional wisdom and her assumptions seem difficult to criticize. Greenwood was following a new line of research, and she had no large body of information to consult. We must not criticize her too strongly because some objects truly may be associated specifically with the Chinese. Greenwood no longer holds the views she put forth in the 1970s. She, like all historical archaeologists, realizes that this kind of interpretation rests too strongly on an ethnic stereotype. For example, how can we ever assume that a porcelain tea cup or a soy bottle was just a Chinese artifact? This problem is perhaps most extremely expressed by the opium pipe bowl. Many people associate opium smoking only with the Chinese; pictures of Chinese men smoking opium are legion. Was, in fact, opium smoking strictly a Chinese habit?

In a study published in 1993, anthropologist Ruth Ann Sando and archaeologist David Felton report on their examination of the store records of the Kwong Tai Wo Company for the years 1871 to 1883. The precise location of the store is unknown, but it was somewhere in northern California. The 160 pages of records ended up in the Bancroft Library at the University of California in Berkeley. The purpose of Sando and Felton's study is to provide archaeologists with a more complete view of the kinds of material objects Chinese residents had available to them. They also researched the practice of opium smoking. The Kwong Tai Wo records not only offer information about the kinds of ceramic tablewares the Chinese bought and used, but they offer a rare, unspoken commentary on where the main profits of the business lay. For the 12 years covered by the account books, the total value of the ceramics mentioned is only $266.80. For the ten years from 1873 to 1883, the total value of the opium sold exceeded $2,850.

The Kwong Tai Wo store sold at least ten different kinds of opium, some with exotic names meaning "Abundant Luck," "Abundant Memory," and "Everlasting Peace." Can lids, bearing the names of these varieties, have been found at several archaeological sites in the American West. One thing Sando and Felton learned in their extensive research was that "Widespread use of opium was a prominent feature of life in America throughout the late 19th century, among both Chinese and non-Chinese alike." Although it is true that the Chinese generally took their opium by smoking, and that non-Chinese ingested theirs in medicines, many non-Chinese also smoked the substance. Thus, it is simplistic to argue that finding part of an opium pipe at an archaeological site necessarily means that Chinese were once present there.

Possible ethnic markers abound in the archaeological record. For example, Mark Leone (see Chapter 9) and his colleagues unearthed a steel comb at a site known as Gott's Court in Annapolis, Maryland. Gott's Court was an apartment house located about two blocks from the Maryland Statehouse. From 1906 until the mid-1930s, it was home to about 25 African-American households. The site was excavated as part of the interpretive project to understand and interpret the history and culture of historic Annapolis (see Chapter 12).

The excavators of Gott's Court discovered, for example, that the ceramic tablewares from the apartment building were diverse, a wide variety of vessel forms decorated with several kinds of unmatched patterns. Clearly, any table setting of these pieces would have looked disorganized and socially "inappropriate."

The ceramics from the site are certainly interesting, but what really attracted the attention of the archaeological team was the enigmatic comb. They searched through old catalogs and scoured archaeological site reports hoping that someone else had found one and could identify its function, but without success. When a photograph of the comb appeared in the *Washington Post,* an African-American housekeeper visited the laboratory and told the archaeologists that their mystery object was a hot comb used by African-Americans to straighten their hair. The archaeologists were overjoyed; their artifact had been identified. But there was still much to learn. They interpreted the comb as a way whereby African-Americans tried to integrate themselves into the job market. African-Americans with whom they spoke, however, said that this was not the case at all. The hot comb was used, they said, not as a tool of assimilation into white society, but rather as a way to ensure their cultural survival. By using the hot comb, African-Americans could make it appear as if they had been assimilated, when in fact this was not true. The use of the hot comb was simply a prudent way of negotiating the rules of white society. The hot comb is clearly an ethnic marker, but one that once had a deep symbolic meaning.

Do white clay smoking pipes proclaiming "Erin Go Bragh" (Ireland For Ever) symbolize Irish ethnicity? Does a blue bead found in a plantation cabin mean that it was worn by an African-American slave? Do the brightly colored yellow and red majolica ceramics from the Iberian Peninsula always signal the presence of Spanish colonialists? Reality is much more complicated, a matter of moving beyond common stereotypes. As Lu Ann De Cunzo's research in New Jersey demonstrates so well, ethnicity can be hidden and difficult to discover at archaeological sites. Even when census rolls, personal letters, and land deeds allow archaeologists to determine the ethnicity of the people who once lived at an archaeological site, the artifacts are rarely so forthcoming about their past owners' ethnicity.

RACE

Ethnicity and race are closely intertwined. Both present formidable challenges for the archaeological researcher, for both are difficult, and sometimes well nigh impossible, to identify in the archaeological record.

Most people tend to confuse race and ethnicity, so much so that the two have become practically synonymous in everyday speech. Even experts can sometimes make the mistake of confusing the two concepts. V. Gordon Childe, one of history's greatest, although eccentric, archaeological thinkers, said in 1926 that "The correlation of cultural with racial groups is generally hazardous and speculative." Childe actually meant "ethnic" groups, and his wording was unfortunate because he made this statement in his widely read *The Aryans: A Study of Indo-European Origins.* The book was so well known that it was eagerly read by the Nazis. Childe, a lifelong socialist, was never able to forget that they had misused his serious work in archaeological interpretation to justify their own pernicious deeds.

People in one group often use race to designate people in another group. People use ethnic terms to identify themselves because of some shared identity. Race is usually narrowly defined on the basis of one outward characteristic, most notably physical appearance. Today, modern anthropologists completely reject the term "race" as a valid human category, preferring instead to see human physical diversity simply as variety. In 1945, British anthropologist M. F. Ashley Montagu referred to race as humanity's "most dangerous myth."

Showing the fallacy of racial categories, however, does not necessarily mean that race can be ignored by historical archaeologists. Some people in the past did use racial categories to designate certain human groups, and we can well imagine that social behavior was affected by the usage. We know that ideas of racial inequality were common in American history, but can they be shown archaeologically?

In a boldly innovative paper presented in 1993, archaeologist Paul Mullins proposes that African-Americans, as part of the wider American consumer society, faced special challenges because of racism. African-Americans used mass-produced objects in certain unique ways. As he says, "In the face of racism, the ability to conduct, represent, and veil their communities was crucial to African America's cultural integrity and very survival." Accordingly, the purchase and use of material things by men and women of African descent "always was constrained by racism's myriad social discriminations, legal codes, informal barriers, and economic boundaries."

To support his hypothesis, Mullins used his excavations at the Maynard-Burgess House in Annapolis, Maryland. This property was occupied by two African-American families—first by the Maynards and then by the Burgesses—from 1847 until 1980. Mullins discovered that fish and other seafoods were important ways for African-Americans to circumvent the normal market. The faunal remains also show, however, that after the mid-nineteenth century, the Maynards relied less on such wild foods and more on foods from the market. By the beginning of the twentieth century, the household relied almost exclusively on professionally butchered meats. Similarly, the bottles from the house show that, by 1890, the Maynards were purchasing brand name foods and canning very little of their own food. Hundreds of fragments of tin cans and a large collection of bottles from professionally packaged foods—coupled with only two canning jars and one ceramic crock—combine to show that the Maynards had bought into the national market. Like most urban dwellers, they did not preserve their own foods anymore. They preferred instead to go to the store and buy them. Also, bottles from 26 nationally advertised brands of medicinal products—like mineral water and Bromo Seltzer—show that the May-nards relied on over-the-counter products rather than on home remedies.

Several pieces of ceramic tablewares lay amongst the glass bottles, butchered animal bones, and the medicine bottles. Interestingly, these dishes resembled those excavated at Gott's Court, Annapolis, mentioned above: they were not from matched sets. Mullins believe the African-Americans in Annapolis used a different strategy to obtain ceramic pieces. They may have purchased a few new vessels, but they probably obtained much of their tableware through barter and informal exchange. As one woman informant in Annapolis told the research team in 1991: "I don't remember us having any good china sets, you know . . . I think a lot of stuff was passed down from grandparents to parents." Mullins believed that the mix of ceramics found in the excavations at the Maynard-Burgess House "argues that everyday dining was a context in which the Maynard household felt little compulsion to aspire to dominant styles or project the appearance of assimilation." What this means is that African-Americans did not feel the need to appear to be a part of white society when they were at home and out of the public eye. Mullins believes that African-Americans bought into the American consumer society along with everyone else, but they were more likely to hide their affluence because of racist attitudes in society. As a result, the consumerism of African Americans was more like a tactic, "a richly textured effort to negotiate the contradictions of a society structured by racism and socioeconomic marginalization."

Mullins' study of the Maynard-Burgess House in Annapolis, Maryland, demonstrates how difficult the archaeological study of racism can be. There are no straightforward interpretations. The Maynards, like the men and women at Gott's Court, negotiated within white society in subtle ways that did not compromise their integrity. Hardly surprisingly, their methods of negotiation are difficult to identify today, for they were both complex and clandestine. We can only identify them from the dispassionate evidence of distinctive artifacts, which the negotiators bought, used, and threw away.

CLASS, GENDER, ETHNICITY, AND RACE

We have explored class, gender, ethnicity, and race as if they are all separate concepts. We have implied, perhaps, that these complex subjects can be extracted from society and put under a microscope individually. The separation of class, ethnicity, gender, and race is only a convenience, however, with little grounding in reality. Archaeologists, like all social scientists, must guard against "essentialism," the philosophical idea that some categories exist in all times and places. All notions of class, ethnicity, gender roles, and race have simply been created within a culture. Outside that culture, they would have no meaning.

We would all agree that no single individual is just an African-American, just a member of the middle class, or simply a woman. A person can be an African-American woman who belongs to the middle class, but she cannot occupy only one category. The reason is obvious: in a complex, highly stratified social organization, any single individual is a member of many groups. Historical archaeologists know this and are constantly trying to decide how best to study it. For example, in Steven Shephard's study of classes in Alexandria, Virginia, the middle-class households were headed by men who were European-American, often small slaveholders, and the nearby lower-class neighborhood was inhabited by free African-American unskilled laborers. The prostitutes in Hooker's Division researched by Donna Seifert were working-class individuals who were trying to feed their families; they were not simply women who had gone astray.

Class membership, gender role, ethnicity, and sometimes even race, are like the strings of a net; they are interconnected and inseparable. Nonetheless, the groups we have illustrated do provide a means for archaeologists of the historic period to organize their analyses and to frame their interpretations. A number of historical archaeologists have consciously tried to study intertwined social groups individually. A study often used by historical archaeologists comes from a southern plantation site.

John Otto, who excavated at Cannon's Point Plantation, St. Simons Island, Georgia, was one of the first historical archaeologists to attempt a study of an antebellum slave plantation as if it were composed of men and women who were not just slaves or slave owners, but who were members of several social groups at the same time.

Using his reading in history, historical sociology, and anthropology, Otto began by constructing a model of plantation society in the antebellum South. A central feature of this society was its social groups. Otto proposed that the inhabitants of plantations were members, at the same time, of at least three different social groups, which he termed "statuses." A "racial/legal status" in essence created two groups: free whites (planters and overseers) and unfree blacks (slaves). Three groups existed because of a "social status:" managers (planters), supervisors (overseers), and slaves (workers). An "elite/subordinate status" created two more groups: an elite (planters) and subordinates (overseers and slaves). The groups existed side by side. Each individual on the plantation belonged to three of them.

For Otto, it was an easy matter to associate different sites at Cannon's Point Plantation with planters, slaves, and overseers. The planter's house was located on the extreme northern end of the island, overlooking the salt marsh. As was typical of the slave-owning South, the planter's part of the site contained several buildings: his house, a detached kitchen, and a few small sheds and outbuildings. Nearby at Cannon's Point were a few, small, square slave quarters. These were probably reserved for slaves who worked in the master's house. Farther away and near the agricultural fields were the cabins of the field slaves. Between the field slaves' homes and those of the house servants was the overseer's cabin (Figure 10.1).

Having associated specific sites with slaves, overseers, and planters, Otto believed it would be possible to examine the artifacts unearthed from each site to learn how they reflected the three different "statuses" that existed within his model of plantation society. To learn the differences between his "racial/legal status" groups, he grouped together the artifacts found at the planter site and at the overseer site (because both were free whites). He then compared them with those unearthed at the slave site (because they were unfree blacks). To study the "social status" groups, he compared the three sites individually, and to investigate the

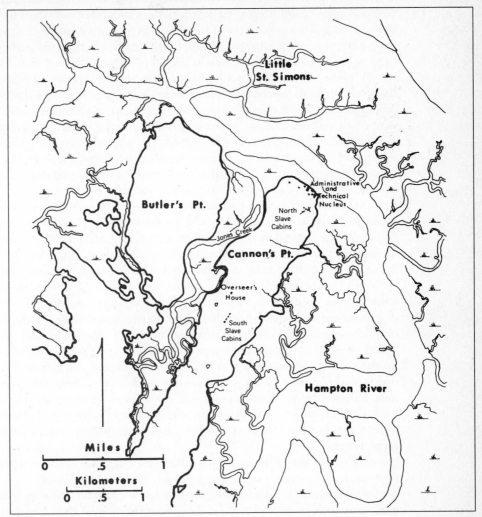

Figure 10.1 *Location of planter, overseer, and slave sites at Cannon's Point Plantation, St. Simons Island, Georgia, 1794–1860.*

"elite/subordinate status," he grouped the overseer and slave artifacts (the subordinates) and compared them with those from the planter site (the elite).

Otto's comparisons did show differences. For example, when he examined the liquor bottles from each of the three sites, he concluded that they represented the racial/legal status. The planter and the overseer sites contained more gin bottles than the slave quarters, but the latter contained more ale, port, and wine bottles. Food remains, however, reflected both the racial/legal status and the elite/subordinate status. The animal bones showed slaves were more dependent on wild animals than were either the white planter or overseer households. Wild species such as deer composed a full 45 percent of the slave meat diet. Although the planter ate fewer wild animals, the number of species in the bone sample from his house site was larger than that from either the overseer or the slave sites.

Ceramic vessel forms reflected the social status because each plantation group used a different variety of forms. In the planter deposits, flat wares—plates, deep plates for soup, and platters—constituted more than 80 percent of the ceramic collection. The excavations in the overseer's site yielded only 28 percent flat vessels; in the slave area only 19 percent of the ceramic vessels were in these forms. But, more than 40 percent of the vessels in the slave cabins were bowls; in the overseer deposits, 25 percent of the ceramics were bowls. Ceramic decoration, however, seemed to reflect the elite/subordinate status because the planter site had many more transfer-printed vessels than either the overseer or the slave sites. Thus, Otto shows that the three statuses can be identified in the archaeological deposits from Cannon's Point Plantation, but that some artifacts may signal different things. This diversity existed because plantation society was complex.

Archaeologist Lynn Clark was also interested in how archaeologists can learn about ethnicity and class and their interaction. Rather than to excavate, as Otto had done, she choose to study a common kind of material culture readily available above the ground, the gravestone. Clark, selecting more than 1,000 gravestones in Broome County, New York, was interested in testing the idea that ethnicity is associated with lower-class position. Her reasoning was that as ethnics climbed the social ladder in late nineteenth- and early twentieth-century America, they had to appear to give up their ethnicity. They had to assimilate into a mainstream American society that downplayed distinct European heritages. She thought that gravestones would be different within the lower class because the people would not have given up the symbols of their ethnicity. Because they would not be trying to assimilate, they would continue to use gravestone symbols that stressed their ethnic uniqueness. However, gravestones should become more alike in the middle class because these were the people who would have left their ethnic symbols behind. The ethnic groups who lived in Broome County were German-Jewish, Italian, Irish, and Slovak immigrants.

Clark's survey of the gravestones showed that ethnic groups and classes had a wide variety of options available to them. Traditionally, upper-class, white-collar workers established their lasting place in the social order by demonstrating their wealth and power. In a cemetery, the greatest display of wealth is the mausoleum, and before 1940, all of them in the cemeteries Clark studied were built by upper-class professionals or administrators. These people were either nonethnics or Irish in heritage. After the 1920s, however, upper-class nonethnics, Irish, and German Jews displayed their wealth less frequently on gravestones, but after about 1940, more blue-collar Italians built mausoleums to mimic the upper class. By the 1950s and 1960s, Italians were often building large mausoleums, but the upper class had stopped. Jewish graves were distinct by their widespread use of epitaphs, but particularly so after the 1930s.

Clark's work in "above-ground archaeology" shows how ethnicity and class are intertwined into a complex bundle that archaeologists can unravel only with the greatest difficulty. Today's archaeologists often find it impossible to decide whether people's actions were guided by their class position, ethnic affiliation, or some complex combination of both. When gender and concepts of race are thrown into the mix, archaeological solutions to the puzzles of past society become even more elusive. The creative research projects of Otto and Clark—and there are a growing number of archaeologist conducting such studies—show how difficult it is for archaeologists to attempt social analyses. Even historical archaeologists, who often have the benefit of documents, cannot count on making easy social interpretations. The archaeologist who tries to assign people from the past to groups is sure to encounter pitfalls. Class, gender, ethnicity, and race are important issues that will challenge historical archaeologists for years to come. They represent cutting-edge issues in the field for the foreseeable future.

CHAPTER
11

Historical Archaeology Around the World

"Everything that has happened since the marvelous discovery of the Americas—from the short-lived initial attempts of the Spanish to settle there, right down to the present day—has been so extraordinary that the whole story remains quite incredible to anyone who has not experienced it at first hand"

Bartolomé de Las Casas, 1542

In Chapter 1 we remarked that the modern world was shaped by compelling historical forces. The Age of Discovery, the African slave trade, and the Industrial Revolution—all played major roles in forging nation-states and mixed and mingled Western and non-Western cultures in every corner of the world. Anthropologist Eric Wolf has described this centuries-long process of globalization in his modern classic, *Europe and the People Without History,* published in 1982. He made the point that every human society was affected in one way or another by the expansion of Western civilization into the remotest corners of the globe. The past five centuries have seen the development of what historical sociologist Immanuel Wallerstein called the "modern world system." French historian Fernand Braudel described the "capitalist world-economy" that developed after about A.D. 1415 as "a fragment of the world, an economically autonomous section of the planet able to provide for most of its own needs." Braudel felt that the "links and exchanges" between the different parts of the world economy created a certain unity.

Since the late 1970s, experts have created a vast historical literature with an explicitly global perspective. One can easily get lost in the complications of these ideas and drown in an ocean of scholarly jargon. So, for the purposes of this book, we prefer to think of the contacts and associations maintained by Europeans in the world as "networks." Our inspiration comes from Eric Wolf, who defines modern world history as composed of "chains of causes and effects at work in the lives of particular populations." As Wolf aptly remarks: "The world of 1400 was already burgeoning with regional linkages and connections; but the subsequent spread of Europeans across the oceans brought the regional networks into worldwide orchestration, and subjected them to a rhythm of global scope." Men and women who, through their relations and contacts, interact as if in a web, can be said to constitute a "network."

After about 1415, many networks were global in scope. Many connections were ones of trade and exchange, of artifacts bartered for raw materials, manufactures for exotic baubles. In this chapter we take you on a tour of historical archaeology around the world, stopping here and there along the way to demonstrate the power and richness of the field. We focus on sites that tell us something about contacts between Europeans and non-Europeans during the European Age of Discovery. Of all the historical processes that have occurred since 1415, none have been more dramatic, more significant to modern history, than the multicultural contacts that developed from these centuries of Western exploration and colonization.

CULTURAL CONTACTS

The European Age of Discovery had a profound, often catastrophic, impact on indigenous peoples around the world. This "clash of cultures" has long intrigued anthropologists, who point out that the interactions were never one-sided. On a purely material level, Native Americans, Africans, and others were impressed by the durability of iron axes and the way that brass kettles could withstand intense heat without breaking, rapidly incorporating them into their daily lives. Many Mesoamerican peoples adopted Old World cereal crops, cattle, goats, and sheep without hesitation, seeing in them an immediate economic advantage. But the same societies were not simply users, they were givers as well. Native American farmers were the most expert agriculturalists of the sixteenth century. Europeans soon carried amaranth, potatoes, tomatoes, and tobacco back to the Old World. All are now commonplace across the globe.

The process of cultural and social interaction was extremely complex, often subtle. Many changes resulting from decisions made in good faith by one generation could have dramatic and dangerous effects on their descendants. For instance, the Khoi Khoi herders of the Cape of Good Hope at the southern tip of Africa were under such pressure to trade their cattle to the beef-hungry Dutch that they bartered away not only their surplus bulls, but also their cows. A generation later, many Khoi Khoi were without cattle, simply because they had no breeding stock.

Each side viewed the other through well-defined cultural binoculars. Some Maori of New Zealand considered Captain Cook and his men gods who came from across the horizon. Cook and his crew were horrified to find freshly butchered human bones in abandoned Maori camps, especially when their landings were opposed in many places. For generations, Europeans considered the Maori fierce cannibals, to the point that passing ships hesitated to land among them. All such multicultural contacts created, in the words of Australian anthropologist Nicholas Thomas, "mutual entanglements" and "shared histories." The Dutch dominated the Khoi Khoi herders of South Africa, just as the Spanish exploited the Zuñi pueblo dwellers in the American Southwest. In both cases, generations of increasingly complex transactions contributed to a tangled skein of history.

These indigenous peoples were affected by, as Braudel said, "the mighty shadow cast" over them by Western Europe, but they were not necessarily destroyed by it. What many Europeans took to be submission and acquiescence were in fact survival strategies. For example, many Aztec Indian communities in Mexico turned in on themselves and minimized their contacts with their new colonial masters, the Spanish. The Aztecs' conversion to Catholicism was actually a careful blending of cultural elements. They adapted their traditional religious beliefs and close-knit social ties to the realities of a new society, a society where they were economically marginal and on the bottom of the social ladder.

Blendings of European and indigenous cultures are reflected not only in surviving native belief systems and oral traditions, but also in subtle changes in artifacts of every kind. It is here that the archaeologist comes in, for very often judicious excavation and survey can reveal fascinating information about contacts between local groups and an expanding European-centered world system. The brief examples that follow provide instances in which archaeology has thrown light on complex cultural interactions.

PUERTO REAL, HAITI

Puerto Real was founded as a Spanish outpost in 1503, a scant 11 years after Columbus first landed in the Bahamas. Located on the northern coast of the island of Hispaniola, the settlement was less than 10 miles (16 km) southeast of Cape Haitian. The optimistic Spanish planned the colonial outpost as a mining settlement, as a base for exporting mineral wealth from the Indies. When local mineral outcrops proved unproductive, Puerto Real assumed the role of a way station for other mining ventures and became a port for the burgeoning slave trade. In 1519, the local people rose against the Spaniards in desperation. Hostilities continued sporadically for more than 20 years. The town's middle years were turbulent and uncertain. In the mid-sixteenth century, Puerto Real was often raided by pirates, who sometimes forced the inhabitants to trade with them at gunpoint. In 1562 a violent earthquake rocked the city. Shortly thereafter, in 1578, the Spanish authorities decided to move the residents of Puerto Real to a new town that would also house people from other Spanish outposts. By 1605, the Spanish had essentially given up on the western third of the island, leaving it to the French. This part of Hispaniola eventually became Haiti.

Archaeological research at Puerto Real has been supervised by Kathleen Deagan from the University of Florida. Her student Charles Ewen worked at the site in 1984–1985 and examined the effect of "the New World inhabitants and environ-

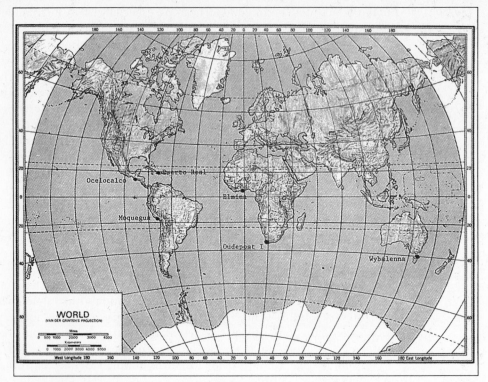

Archaeological sites mentioned in Chapter 11.

ment on the European colonists" (see Chapter 10). He knew that in 1514, Spanish-born residents of the settlement were less than 5 percent of the total population. Most were Indians. So he attempted to find material evidence for the creolization of the colonists' culture. He wanted to see how Spanish men and women were changed by the New World rather than to determine how they had changed it.

Ewen focused his efforts on a part of Puerto Real archaeologists call Locus 19. Earlier surveys of the town had revealed that this spot contained 57 distinct areas with masonry debris, probably the remains of houses. Ewen excavated in the center of Locus 19, and recovered not only more than 49,000 artifacts, but stone wall foundations, post holes, drains fashioned from brick, and a shallow trash midden (Figure 11.1). The artifacts included several kinds of European and non-European ceramics, glasswares, straight pins, brass buckles, decorative clasps from books, and ornaments, like the unicorn pendant we mentioned in Chapter 10.

Ewen hypothesized that, because there were so few Spanish living at the settlement, it was logical to expect them to enlist not only African slaves, but also local people in food preparation. The ceramics from Locus 19 convinced him that significant mixture of Spanish and indigenous cultures had indeed occurred. Locally made pottery accounted for 62 percent of the utilitarian, or kitchen, wares. The remainder were made in the Hispanic tradition. One pottery form, known, archaeologically, as "Christophe Plain," increased from 37 percent of the sample in the

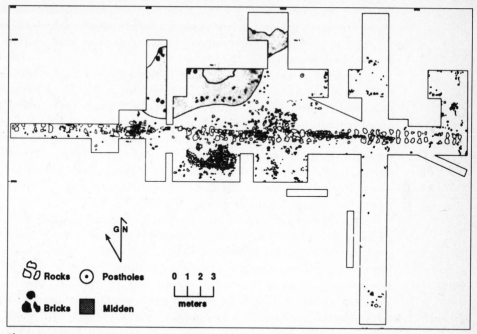

Figure 11.1 *Locus 19 at Puerto Real, Haiti, as excavated in 1985.*

early deposits to 40 percent in later times. Ewen theorizes this pottery style may be associated with African slaves. If so, then Africans also had a dramatic effect on the culture of the Spanish at Puerto Real.

Puerto Real's tablewares, such as plates, were never of indigenous manufacture. Ewen wonders if the colonial Spanish tried to project an image of cultural purity, when in fact they were learning many new things from the indigenous people around them. Only in private areas, away from public view, did local kitchen wares appear openly. If the same vessels imply division of labor along gender lines, then they mean that women were the first line of cultural exchange between the Spanish and the indigenous people of Hispaniola (see Chapter 10 for more discussion).

OCELOCALCO, MEXICO

The ways in which Native American cultures adapted to, or resisted, Spanish invasion and colonization has always fascinated archaeologists. Each culture chose its own strategy. Many, like the pueblo dwellers of the American Southwest, fought bitterly, hoped to drive out the invaders forever. Some sought to work with the Spanish when it became clear that violent resistance was pointless. In the Province of Soconusco, on the hot, humid Pacific coastal plain of Mexico, the natives became part of the Spanish commercial network through the cacao trade. Cacao is an evergreen tree whose seeds, or beans, are used to make cocoa and chocolate. So important was the plant that Mexican natives were allowed to pay their required tribute to the

Spanish Crown in cacao. They also bartered it with merchants to obtain a wide variety of European goods. Cacao was such a highly prized commodity that it allowed the men and women of Soconusco open access to objects made thousands of miles away in faraway Spain.

Ocelocalco was a predominantly Indian village occupied from about 1572 to 1767. When she excavated several buildings sites in the village in the mid-1980s, archaeologist Janine Gasco confirmed that the Indians were linked to the global Spanish trade network. Although most of the potsherds she found were locally made, her excavations also turned up pieces from far away. She unearthed fragments of tin-glazed majolica ceramics from Mexico, Guatemala, and Spain, porcelain from China, and metal and glass artifacts from outside the province. As was the case at Puerto Real, the locally made wares were reserved for kitchen use. Imported foreign wares were used specifically for serving food.

The European ceramics in the archaeological deposits provided clear evidence of the connection between Spain and Ocelocalco. What Gasco did not know was how traditional life had changed as a result of this connection. In the course of her investigation, however, she made a surprising find. Even though the people of Ocelocalco had access to Spanish objects and incorporated them into their daily lives, the objects "did not bring about a wholesale change in material culture." The natives used majolica plates, fashioned by Spanish potters who would never see the Americas, in the place of their traditional pottery. The ways that they used pottery for cooking and eating actually changed little from pre-contact times to the days of Spanish conquest. Metal tools quickly replaced chipped stone artifacts, but again, the change was not dramatic.

Gasco made a subtle but important point in her research. She did not dispute a widely accepted fact of colonial scholarship: that the impact of Europeans, in this case the Spanish, caused massive and often devastating social upheaval among indigenous peoples. However, she argued that the men and women of Ocelocalco were not simply overcome by Spanish culture. Their traditional culture did not fall apart immediately on contact. Instead, the local people accepted some aspects of Hispanic culture, rejected others, and modified still others. Gasco's findings, like those of Ewen at Puerto Real, portray conscious actions on the part of the native Mexicans.

MOQUEGUA VALLEY, PERU

Many Spanish colonial settlements were founded with specific economic objectives in mind, not only mining towns and haciendas, but wineries. They provide another fascinating window into the recent past. In a study conducted in the mid-1980s, American archaeologists Prudence Rice and Greg Smith, then from the University of Florida, examined a series of Spanish wineries, or bodegas, spread out along the Moquegua Valley in southern Peru. The Spanish established wineries in the New World both to meet their religious needs and for less noble purposes. They soon learned that wines traveled very poorly between Spain and Peru, so enterprising colonists attempted local production. The first Peruvian vineyards were established in the Moquegua Valley during the mid-sixteenth century. They soon prospered, supplying wine to all corners of Peru, even by pack animal into remote highland towns, especially to the silver mining center at Potosi. Peruvian wine also reached Mexico and Panama. These efforts at exportation, however, were not always appreciated. For example, in 1660 it was said that Peruvian wine caused "smallpox, measles, pneumonia, suppurating abscesses, typhus, fevers, diarrhoea, catarrh, boils, and hives." Nonetheless, the Moquegua vintners continued to produce wine in great quantities, until the mid-nineteenth century. In August 1868, a major earthquake shattered the valley, cracking or breaking thousands of fragile ceramic wine storage jars. From this time on, the valley's wine producers used oak barrels imported from Chile or the United States. Between 1879 and 1883, Chileans invaded the valley four times and wrecked havoc on the vineyards. The final straw came when aphids attacked the roots of the grape vines and ruined the industry by 1900.

Rice and Smith identified 130 separate wineries along a 16-mile (26 km) stretch of the Moquegua River. Many bodega sites still contained ruins of adobe workrooms, sheds, and sometimes even a chapel. Some could be identified by their empty courtyards. Others were littered with fragments of large, unglazed earthenware storage jars and other artifacts. Rice and Smith were pleasantly surprised to discover that storage jar sherds had dates etched directly into them. They observed 379 such dates, ranging from 1540 to 1866. Most fall within the 1736–1775 period, the dates that historical records cite as the major growth period of the Peruvian wine industry.

Rice and Smith's initial surveys of the Moquegua Valley, and their subsequent excavations in 1987, are doing much to refine the history of the Peruvian wine industry. Several varieties of Peruvian lead-glazed and tin-enameled ceramics in close association with imported European vessels and glasswares document the winemakers' connections with the wider world.

ELMINA, GHANA

European contacts with African societies were just as complex as those of the Spaniards in the Americas. As we have seen, the Portuguese were attracted to African coasts by gold and slaves, by trading ventures so profitable that they sought to control access to the interior by fortifying strategic locations. In 1482, a full decade before Columbus set foot in the Americas, the Portuguese Crown authorized the building of an imposing fort on the coast of modern Ghana in West Africa. This fort, named the Castle São Jorge da Mina, lies on a rocky headland, built to protect what the Portuguese hoped would be a lucrative gold trade with the interior. A small African community called Elmina was soon built under the castle walls, for it was Africans who actually controlled the trade with gold-mining peoples far inland. The Portuguese held on to the castle for 155 years, maintaining an ever-more-precarious control over the "gold coast" trade. Then the Dutch expanded their maritime trade at the expense of the Portuguese. They seized Portuguese possessions in northeastern Brazil and captured the West African castle in 1637. It proved a profitable investment for more than two centuries, until the Gold Coast was ceded to the British in 1872.

Fante people inhabited the area around Elmina before the Portuguese arrived, but other indigenous groups soon moved in, realizing the material advantage of living near an important European trading post. The size of the African community quickly swelled. By 1700, it had more than 1,000 stone houses and a population of perhaps as many as 15,000 residents. The townspeople, although culturally Fante, actually regarded themselves as a politically and even culturally distinct people. After a series of conflicts with these people, the British bombarded Elmina both from land and sea, destroying it on June 13, 1873. They leveled the town's ruins and used the site for a parade ground.

Happily for archaeologists, the site has remained undeveloped and available for excavation. Elmina thus offered a unique opportunity to examine the ways some Africans learned from and taught the Europeans who lived alongside them. Archaeologist Christopher DeCorse, now at Syracuse University, probed the settlement for several months in the mid-1980s. In all, he has excavated 3,011 square feet (271 sq m) and has exposed the foundations in another 600 square feet (54 sq m). These excavations yielded more than 100,000 artifacts. His research has permitted an intimate look into African-European interaction along the Gold Coast.

Most of the artifacts he excavated date to the eighteenth and nineteenth centuries. Many document connections between Elmina and the rest of the world. DeCorse found white clay tobacco pipes from England and the Netherlands, porcelain from China, and glass bottles from American patent medicines. He even discovered an almost whole, gray stoneware jug from Germany, brilliantly decorated with blue rosettes and ribbons. In its center are the letters "A R," referring to Queen Anne ("Anne Regina"), the English monarch from 1702 to 1714.

DeCorse's important research also documents cultural change in the cosmopolitan community beneath Elmina's walls. Many Africans and Europeans visited the fort, not only from overseas but from far in the interior. During some periods of the fort's history, Mande traders and Asante people from the interior were visible and active participants in the town's daily life. At other times, European slavers brought Africans from far inland both to labor locally and for export to Brazil and other parts of the New World.

The archaeology showed, however, that the people of Elmina were very selective in the changes they accepted. For example, the presence of buttons and buckles within the artifact collection attests to changes in dress styles. Slate pencils and writing slates show that at least some of the townspeople were literate. In contrast, European burial customs and cemeteries did not come into general use before 1873. People buried their dead under the floors of their houses. Burials were found beneath all the house floors DeCorse excavated, even in those having less than 12 inches (30 cm) of soil above bedrock. Many were associated with earthenware pots, perhaps ritual offerings.

DeCorse's excavations give us a picture of cultural continuity within an environment of continual economic and political change. The local Africans were indeed changed by regular contact with Europeans, but they also were not overwhelmed. They simply adapted to new circumstances in a conservative, logical way, adopted new artifacts and new customs when it was to their perceived advantage to do so.

OUDEPOST I, SOUTH AFRICA

It is a truism to say that the world of the 1990s is forged from deep historical roots. Nowhere is this truer than South Africa, where the complex politics of today result from centuries of interaction and misunderstanding between Europeans and Africans. We know much of these interactions from historical documents and oral traditions, but historical archaeology is rapidly filling in many gaps in the story.

When Portuguese captain Bartolemeu Diaz anchored in Mossel Bay, east of the Cape of Good Hope, South Africa, in 1488, he found himself in a peaceful and beautiful bay surrounded by green hills. Skin-clad herdsmen were grazing large cattle on the lush grass, but they fled for the interior at the sight of Diaz's ships. These herders were Khoi Khoi, nomadic cattle herders and foragers, people with the simplest of possessions, but a highly sophisticated adaptation to the unpredictable semitropical environment of the Cape. The Portuguese, and the Dutch who followed them, considered the Khoi Khoi little more than animals, people without an intelligible language or any recognizable religion. Sailors' tales recounted how they smeared themselves with rancid butter and how they could be smelt from 30 paces—upwind. The Europeans called them "Hottentots."

But the Khoi Khoi were vital to passing ships, for they supplied fresh meat to crews wrestling with scurvy. Because there was no gold to be found, they were left alone until 1652, when the Dutch East India Company founded a small fort at the Cape. The dynamics of interaction changed at once, for the newcomers were colonists, farmers in search of land and grass for grazing. They encroached on Khoi Khoi territories, restricted their movements, and forced them to trade more cattle, even their breeding stock. The Company told the colonists to "tolerate, negotiate, manipulate" the local people. They did so with such devastating effect that traditional culture of the Cape Khoi Khoi vanished within a century. The survivors eked out a living as ranch hands or domestic servants, or moved far inland.

The outlines of the story are well known, but many details remain a mystery. In 1984, Carmel Schrire, an archaeologist at Rutgers University, embarked on a study of Oudepost I, "Old Post," a small, stone fort that the Dutch built in 1669 to show the increasingly aggressive French that they "owned" the Cape. The French soon lost interest in the area, so the four to ten Dutchmen who lived at the post until 1732 spent their days trading with the neighboring Khoi Khoi. Schrire's work was to last four years and resulted in a major excavation of three buildings associated with Oudepost. Luckily, the region of the post has not seen much settlement after 1732, so the sites were undisturbed by recent activity.

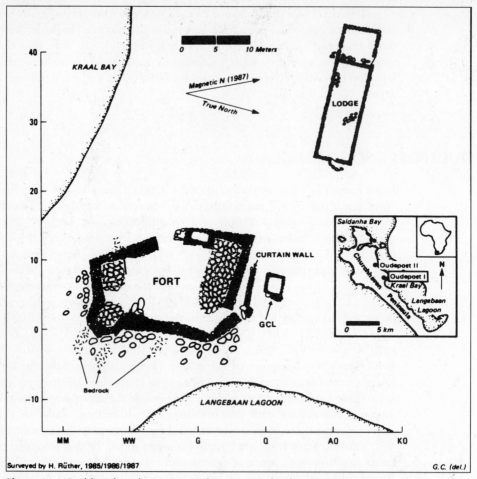

Figure 11.2 *Building foundations at Oudepost I, South Africa in 1987.*

Historical records mention the construction of the outpost, but only archaeo-logical research can provide precise details. There is no known map or plan of the remote post. Schrire's excavations revealed that the Dutch built three small build-ings on the beach at Oudepost I (Figure 11.2). One was an irregularly shaped fort that encompassed over 4,400 square feet (400 sq m). The second building, placed to the northwest, was a long, rectangular structure that measured 18.5 by 65.1 feet (5.6 by 19.8 m). Schrire found domestic artifacts and food remains here, as if it was the garrison barracks. The third edifice, located directly north of the fort, mea-sured only 9.3 by 10.6 feet (2.8 by 3.2 m). Its function is unknown. The Dutch con-structed the post buildings of rock collected from the sea shore. Schrire learned that the garrison did not deposit their refuse in one particular dump, but tossed it everywhere, leaving a broad layer of seventeenth-century glass, ceramics, gunflints, and metal throughout the site. The presence of Khoi Khoi pottery, stone tools, and

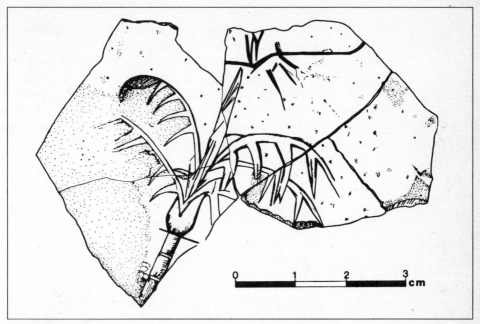

Figure 11.3 *Etched ostrich shell found at Oudepost I, South Africa.*

bone spear points in the midden deposits attest to their involvement in the outpost as well.

Historical records provide abundant evidence for interaction between the Khoi Khoi and the Dutch. For example, in 1670, the commandant reported that a small band of Khoi Khoi arrived to offer their services in fighting the French. In 1726, the post commandant, Jacob Titius, wrote, "The said Hottentot, having some cattle of his own, I hired for two years to take care of our sheep, on condition that he would be properly supplied with liquor and tobacco." Thus, as Schrire says, the issue is not whether the Khoi Khoi and the Dutch interacted at Oudepost, but to determine the nature of this interaction.

The faunal remains tell part of the story. Historical sources dwell on the importance of the cattle trade to the Dutch. Their relentless demand for meat, gained either by trade or theft, is thought to have put tremendous pressure on local Khoi Khoi groups. Cattle bones are indeed commonplace at Oudepost I. But the archaeological remains provide a more complete picture of Dutch subsistence. Instead of relying completely on sheep and cattle, they also encroached on the subsistence strategy of the Khoi Khoi. As Schrire says: "mounted frontier settlers lived off the land, shooting game for the pot, and . . . by doing so they invaded and preempted the hunter-gatherer niche" of the Khoi Khoi. Schrire's findings provide irrefutable proof of this Dutch strategy, as large numbers of fish, mammal, and bird bones were excavated in the fort's middens. In fact, domesticated species account for only about 28 percent of the animal bones found at the site.

Oudepost I offers not only insights into Dutch/Khoi Khoi interaction, but also a brief, albeit telling, glimpse into the thoughts of at least one Dutch member of the garrison. This unknown Dutch soldier has left us a tantalizing clue of his service at the post, well over 250 years ago. He etched a palm tree into an ostrich egg shell (Figure 11.3). Palms did not grow at the Cape in those days. Schrire imagines it being fashioned by a lonely soldier who pined for his days in warmer, more hospitable southeast Asia: "he embellished an ostrich egg with memories—his dreams mingling with reality, here, on the far African shore."

The Cape Khoi Khoi did not survive permanent European settlement in their homeland. Oudepost I flourished at a time when Dutch farmers were staking out ranches deep into Khoi territory, disrupting centuries-old seasonal movements that prevented the herders from overgrazing their large territories in the interior. By the late eighteenth century, the Cape Khoi Khoi were effectively extinct, the few survivors eking out precarious existences as ranch hands or at the margins of colonist society. Only early European records chronicle their fate and their culture, so researches like Schrire's fill in many details of day-to-day existence, of complex interactions that never appear in documents.

WYBALENNA, TASMANIA

British navigator Captain James Cook was a major figure in eighteenth-century history. He explored not only the Pacific and the Northwest Coast of North America, but circumnavigated New Zealand and made the first landing on the east coast of Australia, close to the site of modern Sydney, in 1770. Cook made fleeting contact with small numbers of Aborigines, explored the Great Barrier Reef, where he nearly lost his ship, and charted much of the eastern coast of a hitherto shadowy continent.

Australia was an enigmatic land, empty except for wandering hunters and foragers, an unexplored continent on the other side of the world. Britain was just about to lose her American colonies, once a convenient dumping ground for hardened criminals. So she turned to Australia as an alternative penal colony for those sentenced to "transportation for life." In 1778, 717 men and women offenders arrived at Port Jackson (later Sydney) to begin their sentences. A flood of convicts and colonists soon poured into the newly settled land, pushing aside or brutally exterminating the Aborigines in the process.

In 1803, a small party of convicts and soldiers landed at what is now Hobart, the capital of the island of Tasmania, to the south across the Bass Strait from Australia itself. At the time, an estimated 3,000 to 5,000 Aborigines lived on the island, having flourished there in complete isolation from the Australian mainland for at least 8,000 years. At first, the Aborigines melted into the interior, far from European outposts. But as the colonization of Tasmania took hold, incidents between Aborigines and settlers became more frequent. As the tentacles of white settlement spread inland and parties of convicts and sealers hunted kangaroos and sea mammals, the Aborigines turned hostile. Soon the settlers hunted them down and killed them on sight. By the 1830s, the military were conducting sweeps across the island, but the surviving 250 or so Aborigines simply melted into the bush and lived in hiding. Between 1832 and 1842, an eccentric bricklayer named George Augustus Robinson spent years contacting surviving groups, living with them, and gaining their trust. He persuaded the survivors to put themselves under European protection. They were shipped to windswept Flinders Island, 40 miles (64 km) off the northeastern corner of Tasmania, where they lived in a ramshackle community named Wybalenna. Hundreds of Tasmanian men, women, and children perished in enforced exile here over the next 14 years. The British euphemistically called Wybalenna the "aboriginal establishment on Flinders Island," but the Aborigines knew it as a vile prison camp.

In the early 1970s, archaeologist Judy Birmingham of the University of Sydney excavated this tragic settlement. She focused her investigation on the ways in which native Tasmanians accepted or rejected European attempts to transform them into Europeans. Using a map drawn in 1838 by the post's commandant, Birmingham's archaeological team was able to correlate visible surface scatters of rubble with once-functioning buildings (Figure 11.4). They identified military barracks, a hospital and surgeon's residence, a smith shop, the chaplain's home, prisoner's quarters, and the commandant's house. One of the most interesting architectural features of the site were the 20 or so "cottages" for the dispossessed Tasmanians.

Birmingham excavated five of these structures. She found them to be constructed in a line, abutting one another. A pair of small cottages, each about 12 by 16.5 feet (3.7 by 4.4 m) in size were situated on either side of a larger (15 by 16.6 feet; 4.6 by 5 m) cottage. Coincidentally, the dwellings were almost the exact size as many contemporary slave cabins in the American South. Like slave cabins, they were made of stone and brick.

The artifacts Birmingham and her crew unearthed at the Tasmanian camp include the full range of European items then available: glass bottles, English ceramics of several kinds, white clay smoking pipes, bone buttons, polished clay marbles. The presence of other objects—sandstone pounders and bronze-colored snail shells pieced for stringing—offer mute proof that at least some Aborigines did not instantly forget their traditional way of life once they moved to Wybalenna. In fact, Birmingham's analysis of the artifacts found within and around the cottages suggested that some members of the aboriginal community were more "Europeanized" than others. Some aboriginal men and women "strongly resisted the inroads of christianization, commercialization, and europeanization into their lifestyle and power base, and accepted selected features only—namely, those with recognizable advantages in their own lives."

Birmingham drew this somewhat startling conclusion from the artifacts found in her excavations. The remains from Cottages 7 and 8 are particularly instructive. They stood next to one another, yet exhibited completely different artifact inventories. Cottage 8 had many more European objects than Cottage 7. For instance, Cottage 7 contained only one clay pipe fragment, whereas 25 came from its surroundings. In contrast, the interior of Cottage 8 yielded ten pipe fragments, 45 outside. Blue and white English ceramics appeared in great number in Cottage 8, but only a few fragments were found associated with Cottage 7. Cottage 7 accounted for 27.3 percent of the bottle glass from the site; 72.6 percent came from Cottage 8. The artifact distributions from Cottages 7 and 8 appeared to send different cultural messages.

Birmingham compared the artifacts from the interior of the cabins with those on the exteriors. Then, after very carefully observing the way the artifacts were positioned in the ground, she proposed that the finds in Cottage 8 were swept from the

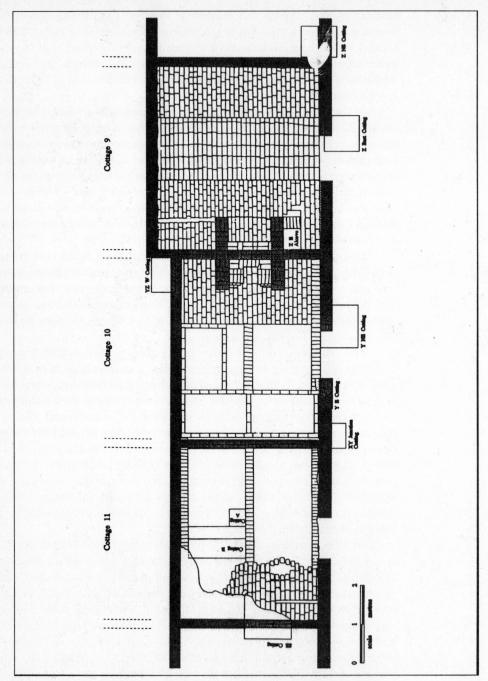

Figure 11.4 *Plan of Cottages 9, 10, and 11 at Wybalenna after excavation.*

interior to the exterior, making for a homogeneous collection. Surprisingly, she found no evidence of sweeping activity at Cottage 7. The occupants of Cottage 8 seem to have accepted nineteenth-century English ideas of cleanliness, whereas their neighbors did not. Birmingham believes that some of the cultural borrowings of the captive Tasmanians ran much deeper than the simple adoption of artifacts.

Conversely, the residents of Cottage 7 may have resisted acculturation as much as possible. The attempt to remain free of European influence is perhaps suggested by their diet, as portrayed by the excavated faunal remains. Cottage 7 accounted for 68 percent of the total bones collected from the site, whereas Cottage 8 only yielded 7 percent of them. The distribution of species in the cottages is also vastly different. Wallaby constituted a large part of the Cottage 7 remains, but significantly less in Cottage 8. Cottage 7 had wombat bones; Cottage 8 had none. These bones all indicate that the people in Cottage 7 hunted more than the residents of Cottage 8. The residents of Cottage 7 probably had a more traditional diet than did the people in Cottage 8.

Much remains to be learned about Wybalenna and the people who lived there, but Birmingham's excavations demonstrate the complexity of multicultural interactions, even as recently as the mid-nineteenth century. The Aborigines forced to live in this "aboriginal establishment," were victims of a kind of cultural genocide, in which the British sought to change the people forever. That some Tasmanians accepted foreign ways shows that the pressure to change was intense and powerful. That some did not so easily give up their traditional beliefs, attitudes, and way of life shows the strength and resilience of the Tasmanian culture.

The studies in this chapter are pioneer researches that offer new, and sometimes dramatic insights into the potential of historical archaeology as a way of studying complex interactions between Europeans and other societies. This potential gives us a starting point for Chapter 12, where we consider the historical archaeology of the future.

CHAPTER
12

The Past in the Present

"The absence of romance in my history will, I fear, detract somewhat from its interest; but I shall be content if it is judged useful by those inquirers who desire an exact knowledge of the past as an aid to the interpretation of the future"

Thucydides, 431–413 B.C.

Historical archaeology is the archaeology of ourselves, a field of research that spans many centuries. We use methods that can be applied with equal facility to medieval villages or land fills from modern industrial cities. It serves as a mirror into our own lives, and of those of people living only a few generations ago. For instance, University of Arizona archaeologist William Rathje has attracted wide attention for his archaeological studies of currently used urban landfills and trash dumps. Rathje has calculated that the Fresh Kills landfill on Staten Island, New York, is 25 times the size of the Great Pyramid of Khufu at Giza, Egypt, and 40 times the size of the Temple of the Sun at Teotihuacán, Mexico. He also has recovered hot dogs and other foodstuffs from landfills that date to the 1950s and discovered that newspaper almost never deteriorates when packed into the air-free environment of a landfill. Rathje's excavations have important bearing on such contemporary issues as recycling and garbage management, to say nothing of their potential in monitoring such exotica as cat food preferences in different urban neighborhoods.

Can one draw a line between past and present? When Congress enacted legislation establishing the National Register of Historic Places (sites deemed important enough to be protected from destruction) in 1976, it defined "antiquity" as 50 years from the present. Thus, in the year 2000, artifacts and buildings manufactured in 1950 will be classified officially as "ancient." This is a purely arbitrary definition, which is effectively meaningless except within a narrow legal context, simply because the recent past forms a continuum with the present. The continuum is cultural and social, political and economic, also technological. When archaeologist Jane Busch writes that "The tin can has played a significant role in American history and can play a significant role in archaeology," she is absolutely correct. Busch considers tin cans vehicles of history, easily dated by telltale signs of technological improvements in seals and seams. It is no coincidence that her study incorporates the "modern sanitary can," the kind we all bring home from the grocery store. Whether we like it or not, we are actors in the play.

In this chapter, we explore some of the roles of historical archaeology in the modern world, and ways in which one can become involved in the field.

LIVING ARCHAEOLOGY

Each of us is an actor in the unfolding history of the late twentieth century. As such, we are all "living history," archives crammed with memories of past events, of current experiences. Our daily doings, the people we meet, the objects with which we surround ourselves—all are history being lived in a very real way. It follows that historical archaeologists are part of the history they study. Ivor Noël Hume is a modern actor in the ongoing history of Colonial Williamsburg (see Chapter 6); Judy Birmingham is part of the history of Wybalenna (see Chapter 11). Because the line between "past" and "present" is blurred in historical archaeology, archaeologists of modern history cannot truly separate themselves from it. As anthropologist David Pilbeam said in the *Washington Post* in 1983, "We do not see things as they are, we see things as we are."

Nowhere is this truer than at living history exhibits, such as Plimouth Plantation, Massachusetts, which are popular, often international, tourist attractions. At Plimouth, for example, historical archaeologist James Deetz played a leading role in developing accurate plans for the reconstructed buildings. Plimouth is "inhabited" by men and women wearing period costumes. The "residents" are seen shoeing horses, carding and dying wool, cooking over large, blackened iron pots, and blowing delicate glass vases and bowls. The visitor experiences living history—a modern vision of life centuries ago, reconstructed from historical documents and archaeological research.

Living museums can be found all over the world. Henry Ford's Greenfield Village (see Chapter 3) is a well-known example. So is the Yorvik Viking Centre in York, England, where the daily life of a Anglo-Scandinavian town dating to A.D. 850–1050 has been recreated so vividly that even voices and smells are piped in. The visitor descends underground in a Disneyland-style car, passing through the centuries until one emerges in the Viking street. From the living community, the car travels through the excavations that reconstructed the town, then into the archaeological laboratory, a small display of important finds—there is even a "touching wall" of potsherds for children. Finally, the visitor emerges through the gift shop. Everything is calculated to entertain and enlighten, to make remote history

Figure 12.1 *Reconstruction of the slave quarters at Carter's Grove Plantation, Virginia.*

come alive. The visitor becomes part of history as part of learning about the past. Well over a million people visit Yorvik each year.

One of the most intriguing and recently conceived living museums in the United States is the slave quarters constructed at Colonial Williamsburg's eighteenth-century Carter's Grove Plantation. The Carter's Grove house, built between 1750 and 1755, is a huge brick mansion with a beautifully restored central stairway and baronial gardens. But the slave quarters tell a different story than the mansion. Or perhaps they only tell the story of economic wealth in a different way. The quarters are located about 800 feet (244 m) northwest of the mansion, partially screened by a row of trees. They consist of a cluster of four reconstructed wooden cabins with accompanying yards (Figure 12.1), their designs based on archaeological investigations. The largest building belongs to the slave foreman and his family. At the quarters buildings today, African-American men and women, dressed as slaves and "living" in the cabins, tell modern visitors a little of what it must have been like to have been a slave at Carter's Grove. The actors play their parts with telling passion, developing their stories partly from slave narratives collected during the 1930s.

However, because the actors undoubtedly put much of themselves into their historical performances, we can never truly say that what they do is just about the past. They are actors in our contemporary world using history to help us better understand slavery, racism, and discrimination. Their stories are powerful history lessons that take much of their strength from the reconstructed slave cabins. When faced with the physical reality of the cabins, visitors to the quarter are forced to confront America's slave past.

Another perspective on living history comes from an innovative series of archaeological projects conducted in Annapolis, Maryland, under the general direction of Mark Leone, of the University of Maryland. Using several eighteenth- and nineteen-century sites as a focus, Leone and his co-workers have developed a program that uses archaeological fieldwork to engage visitors to Annapolis. To ensure that the program is appealing, Leone hired a media consultant to help his team develop the best site tour possible. Their consultant, Philip Arnoult, director of the Theatre Project of Baltimore, first queried the archaeologists on what sorts of questions they typically received from visitors: How do archaeologists know where to look for sites? How do they employ objects for dating, and how do they use the knowledge they obtain? Armed with this information, he then worked with Leone and his team on the tour itself. Soon, more than 100 people a day were visiting the archaeological projects at Annapolis. In the summer and fall of 1982, 7,000 people toured the Victualling Warehouse Site alone. Built sometime before 1747, this warehouse was used to handle supplies for the Continental Army during the American Revolution.

The archaeologists at Annapolis learned three important elements of a successful tour. First, they discovered that the educational aspects of the projects must have as high a priority as the research itself. They could help eliminate two commonly held misconceptions: that archaeology is conducted by stuffy old men in pith helmets who are completely oblivious to the world around them, and that archaeologists are intent on stopping all construction projects in the name of science. Second, Leone and his team learned that the tours had to be structured. Both the path taken across the site by the visitors and the information they were told by their guide had to be consistent. At the same time, the archaeologists giving the tour must be willing to adjust their narrative in the light of new finds and to accommodate visitors' questions. In this sense, the archaeology became an interactive enterprise, with excavators and visitors almost equally engaged in the research. Finally, the Annapolis archaeologists found that archaeological research must not be presented as if it is only about the past. In Leone's words, "there must be a convincing tie to the present drawn out of the material from the past." At the Victualling Warehouse the archaeologists told the visitors of the site's interesting history. At the same time, though, they made certain that the visitors understood that the archaeology was seen by many of Annapolis' business owners as creating a tangible link between them and the historic business owners of the city. The story of the warehouse is but an early component of the total commercial history of the city.

Using this site-tour approach, the Annapolis archaeologists work diligently to draw visitors into the history of the town. Each visitor's place in history is in some ways as important as was that of Daniel Dulany, the owner of the Victualling Warehouse, who had his property seized by the government in 1781 because of his loyalist sympathies.

POLITICS AND HISTORICAL ARCHAEOLOGY

The idea that the "past" studied by historical archaeologists does not necessarily exclude the present raises an interesting and controversial question: does contemporary politics ever impinge on historical archaeological research? The subjects we address in Chapter 9—class, ethnicity, race, and gender—are all highly emotional, contemporary issues, so the archaeologist sometimes treads on potentially slippery political ground.

Governments and emerging states have long used archaeological research for various ends. The Nazis unashamedly used archaeology for political ends in the 1930s. Their program was dramatized in somewhat exaggerated form in the popular movie *Indiana Jones and the Raiders of the Lost Ark.* Indiana Jones thwarts evil Nazi archaeologists attempting to find the location of the all-powerful Ark of the Covenant so that they can use it in their scheme for world domination. The Nazis were fanciful depictions, but not without some basis in fact. In 1935, Heinrich Himmler, Hitler's head of the German police, including the Gestapo, created a research organization called Ahnenerbe, or "Ancestral Heritage." Much of this organization's "research" was more laughable than dangerous. For example, they really did try to find the Holy Grail (like *Indiana Jones and the Last Crusade*), they searched for Atlantis, they studied the history of German bread, and they believed that their early Germanic ancestors had learned to harness the energy of lightning and had used it as a weapon! The "scientists" of Ahnenerbe used their often-fudged archaeological findings to support their ideas of ethnic inferiority. In eastern Europe, they changed cultural chronologies to fit their theories of Nordic peoples as brilliant conquerors. Nazi archaeology had a well-defined agenda.

"History is written by the winners," as archaeologist Robert Paynter once wrote. It is the conquistadors' version of the Conquest of Mexico that dominate the history books, while the history and fate of the conquered Aztecs and other Native American groups are often ignored. We are now witnessing a profound change in our visions of history, fostered in part by a growing interest in non-Western history, and by indigenous peoples, who are reclaiming their heritage for themselves. They use archaeology to empower themselves and to educate their young people about the resilience of their traditional cultures. Some Australian Aborigine groups are using archaeology to tell their side of the continent's history. In New Zealand, the Maori are reclaiming their history very aggressively, both to foster cultural identity and to support land claims. Through such efforts, we can often acquire a much more sophisticated, multifaceted perception of history.

Several Native American groups in North America are pursuing active programs of heritage restitution. Many of the projects involve historical archaeology.

One such project was sponsored by the Northern Cheyenne of southeastern Montana to study the Outbreak of 1879.

The Outbreak came about as the result of a series of contacts between the U.S. government and the Northern Cheyenne, who lived in the southern Montana–northern Wyoming area. Cheyenne leaders agreed to sign the Medicine Lodge Treaty of 1867, but they did not understand that this meant they would be moved south to "Indian Territory," today's Oklahoma. Several prominent Cheyenne leaders protested the move, and in fact some of them went to Washington in 1872 to plead with President Grant to allow them to stay in their traditional homeland. Grant agreed to let them stay, but with Custer's defeat at the Little Bighorn, the Northern Cheyenne began to fear reprisals even though they were not involved in the battle. Under the leadership of Dull Knife and Little Wolf, the Northern Cheyenne sought a safe haven in the Big Horn Mountains. Their peace was short-lived because they were soon discovered and attacked by the U.S. cavalry. Faced with extreme hardship on the open plains if they fled, the Northern Cheyenne surrendered to the military at Fort Robinson, Nebraska, in April 1877. Tired of trying to feed themselves on a landscape that was becoming bare of their main food source, the bison, the Northern Cheyenne agreed to try life in Indian Territory. They moved there a couple of months later, but it was not long before more than two-thirds of their people were racked with fever and plague in the unfamiliar environment of Oklahoma. Desperate for relief, Dull Knife and Little Wolf led a group of their followers out of Oklahoma and toward their homeland in September 1878. The 353 Northern Cheyenne who fled, weak from sickness, knew that they would be pursued and killed or captured by the cavalry. Splitting into two groups, they kept up a running battle with the soldiers for several days. Little Wolf's band established a camp for the winter in northwestern Nebraska. Dull Knife's people, however, were persuaded to surrender to the cavalry at Fort Robinson, Nebraska. The conditions Dull Knife's band faced at Fort Robinson were little better than those in Oklahoma, and on the night of January 9, 1879, he led the famed Outbreak from the fort. Having taken with them only five rifles and several old pistols, Dull Knife's people could not put up much resistance, and 64 of them were killed. The cavalry sent most of the male leaders of the Outbreak to Dodge City, Kansas, for trial; they sent the rest of the Cheyenne to the Pine Ridge Agency in southwestern South Dakota. Dull Knife and his family escaped capture by hiding in a cave, but they were eventually taken to Pine Ridge as well. Dull Knife's people finally settled on the Tongue River Reservation in Montana, where they remain today.

The Northern Cheyenne have always told a different story of the break-out than that promulgated by military histories. Official accounts state that the Cheyenne used a northern route. The Cheyenne, relying on oral accounts passed from generation to generation, have always argued for a more southerly route. The routes are actually quite close to one another, and the controversy is seemingly unimportant—unless you are a Northern Cheyenne wanting to reclaim your heritage. They want to build a commemorative path along the escape route and a visitors' center in which to tell their side of the break-out. For too long, movies like *Cheyenne Autumn* have presented the story of the Cheyenne from the white perspective. Many Cheyenne believe that now is the time for them to present their own history. Settling on the route of the escape is one small way to begin to do this storytelling.

In 1987, Northern Cheyenne from Dull Knife Memorial College in Montana teamed up with Larry J. Zimmerman—an archaeologist at the University of South Dakota and a leader in promoting congenial relations between Native Americans and archaeologists—in an effort to use archaeology to find evidence of the escape route used over one hundred years before. The Native Americans provided geographical guidance and incorporated their traditional prayers and storytelling into the fieldwork. The archaeologists surveyed both routes for lead pistol balls, rifle bullets, and other telltale clues of hot pursuit. They found several lead pistol balls and rifle bullets in the southern route, but none along the officially sanctioned path. The Cheyenne were vindicated. In the words of project leader, J. Douglas McDonald, they "came to understand that their long-felt mistrust of archaeology might no longer be necessary. Both the archaeologists and the Northern Cheyenne learned that they can be natural allies, sometimes each possessing what the other needs."

THE PLUNDERED PAST

Archaeology is under siege all over the world. Deep plowing, industrial development, mining, and runaway urban sprawl, to say nothing of looters and vandals, are decimating the archaeological record everywhere. The historic and prehistoric past vanishes before our eyes with bewildering, tragic speed, to the point where one wonders if archaeology as a science will survive the onslaught. As we have emphasized again and again, the archaeological record is a finite resource. Once disturbed or destroyed, it is gone forever. The battle for the past is a war to the death. At stake is the survival of the priceless cultural heritage of all humankind.

National Geographic Society archaeologist George E. Stuart gave his assessment in 1989: "To me it is a miracle of miracles that any remnant of the human past has survived, for it seems that both nature and man are constantly engaged in the processes of obliteration." Stuart was talking both in general and specific terms. The battle is joined in urban building lots, along the rights-of-way of expanding freeways, in lush valleys about to be flooded by hydroelectric dams. But apart from industrial activity, mechanized agriculture, and destruction caused by the population explosion, plain human greed is always at work. Many people have a powerful, often illogical urge to collect and own the artifacts of the past, to display them on their mantles. Everything is grist to a fanatical collector's maw: beer cans, barbed wire, firearms—and ancient artifacts.

Slack Farm lies in western Kentucky, on the rich river floodplain near the confluence of the Ohio and Mississippi rivers. Between 200 B.C. and about A.D. 1650, a prosperous and growing Native American community dwelt in a small village here, fishing and foraging in the rich valley, later cultivating maize on nearby fertile soils. The closing centuries of Slack Farm's history straddle those critical centuries when Europeans were fanning westward across North America, spreading exotic diseases and unfamiliar trade goods before them. A scientific excavation at

Slack Farm or neighboring sites might yield not only imported European goods, but also critical information on the processes of contact between Native American and foreigner. But we will never find it, for every recognizable site of this age in the region has been looted by pothunters.

Slack Farm was the last undisturbed site, protected by a caring land owner. Then the farm changed hands. In 1987, ten men paid the property owner $10,000 for the right to lease the archaeological site on his land. They planned a massive treasure hunt during the months when the ground lay fallow between the fall harvest and the spring planting. By the time state authorities stepped in with a search warrant, the looters had dug 450 holes in the site, scattering pots and human bones over a pitted landscape that looked like a battlefield. They cared not a jot for history, just for fine artifacts as collectibles, and as commodities for sale. It was reported that one artifact, a smoking pipe fashioned in the shape of a human face, brought $4,500 from an artifact collector.

Faced with such overwhelming evidence of grave robbing, the police placed a cease and desist order on the ten men's activities. They were later charged with a misdemeanor, "desecration of a venerated object." The maximum penalty for this crime in Kentucky was a fine of $500 and a possible year in jail. However, four of the looters did not even live in Kentucky, and they could not be extradited for a misdemeanor. The Slack Farm scandal prompted the Kentucky Legislature to pass a law making it a felony to desecrate graves. Across the river in Indiana, however, the lawmakers chose a different course. There, the legislature tried to pass a law making it possible to fine grave robbers only for trespassing, which carries a possible penalty as low as $1. The bill narrowly missed passage, but its supporters say they will continue the fight to have the bill enacted someday. Putting it bluntly, they condone the rape of the past.

The Slack Farm desecration is but the tip of a scandalous iceberg. Every month brings a story of another important site destroyed, its contents sold to the highest bidder.

The Archaeological Market

All of this raises important ethical questions. Who, for example, owns the past? Humankind as a whole, the descendants of the owners (some of whom have been known to claim the right to auction off artifacts to the highest bidder), the current land owner, or the government? There are no easy answers, certainly in American society, which places a high premium on individual liberty and freedom of action.

Antiquities bring big money in the marketplace. In 1991, a *Time Magazine* article cited some glaring examples. On the night of February 2, 1990, masked gunmen attacked a storeroom housing artifacts from Herculaneum, the Roman town buried along with Pompeii by the eruption of Mount Vesuvius in A.D. 79. The robbers carefully selected 223 of the most precious artifacts from the Herculaneum collection. The items they stole were worth an estimated $18 million. In Amsterdam the following year, criminals stole 20 paintings from the Van Gogh Museum. These bandits were caught when their car got a flat tire, but the value of their heist was estimated at about $500 million. In Cambodia, the heads of Buddhist and

Hindu statues in the magnificent twelfth-century capital of Angkor have been sawn off their bodies for sale to collectors.

Art theft and artifact looting raise basic ethical issues for professional archaeologists. For example, many of the gold and copper artifacts, also sculpted pottery made by the Moche culture of the northern coast of Peru (A.D. 100–800) fetch thousands of dollars on the open market. Recently, a major controversy swirled around UCLA archaeologist Christopher Donnan, when he studied and published information on looted objects made by the Moche. Some experts thought that Donnan had made a serious error in professional judgment by seeming to condone looting and collecting. Donnan, however, tells a different story. As a scientist, and probably the leading authority on the Moche people, he defends his actions because they were motivated by the best intentions: to further document ancient Moche art and society. The stealing of artifacts is lamentable, but should archaeologists ignore the chance to learn from well-preserved, looted artifacts? As Donnan wrote in 1991, "It is tragic that looting takes place, and I know of no archaeologist who does not decry the loss of critical information that results. But to stand by when it is possible to make at least some record of whatever information can still be salvaged simply compounds the loss."

Looting is also a serious problem at historic sites, not only in the hands of developers, who seek, for example, to build houses on revered Civil War battlefields, but also from hobbyists. Although many of them throw up their hands in horror at the destruction at Slack Farm, they believe there is no harm in running metal detectors over historic sites in search of coins, military buttons, and other collectibles. After all, they argue, are there not historical documents, photographs, and even living people who remember historical sites? Many Civil War encampments and battlefields are plagued with collectors with a passionate urge to acquire and sell spent bullets or buttons. Bottle hunters tunnel into nineteenth-century trash heaps for patent medicine containers, old milk and beer bottles, and colorful glass flasks. Bottle hunters know, for example, that privies are prime locations for complete specimens. They use long steel probes to locate the soft fill of an abandoned toilet, then dig into it feverishly, destroying layer after layer of stratified data in quest of discarded glass. A collectibles market that pays hundreds, even thousands, of dollars for a single specimen fuels their searches.

Many well-respected and expert historical archaeologists maintain large artifact collections, acquired either by purchase, or in carefully controlled excavations. These are collections not to be admired, but to be used, not only to train students in artifact identification, but for comparative and dating purposes.

Archaeology began as treasure hunting, and many of the world's great museums acquired collections through excavations that were little more than glorified looting. No question, much has been saved for posterity through the acquisitive policies of early museum curators and wealthy collectors, at a time when archaeologists were few and far between and antiquities departments nonexistent in most countries. Today's collectors and antiquities dealers still argue passionately that they are saving the past by collecting it and venerating it, preserving it for future generations. These are specious arguments in a changed world where there are thousands of archaeologists, numerous museums, and a clear understanding of the importance of artifacts and their archaeological context in time and space. To their credit, many major museums have implemented tough acquisitions policies that insist on contextual information, policies designed to discourage looting. But the antiquities traffic continued unabated and will flourish as long as there are unscrupulous, unthinking people who believe that personal ownership is more important than history. Their philosophy is easily set down: I have taste, I have the money to indulge it, and as a tasteful, wealthy person, I have the individual right to own any part of the past I wish. Or do I?. . .

Who Owns the Past?

Should archaeological sites and artifacts be in private or public hands? Do any of us have the right to say that we own the past?

Although many governments have legislation that makes all archaeological sites, whether on private or public land, the property of the state, United States law effectively offers no protection to sites on privately owned land. As a nation, we place an enormous premium on individual rights and on individual ownership of the land and all on it. Technically, then, there was nothing, except his conscience, to prevent the owner of Slack Farm from selling the site on his land to the highest bidder. The looters were cited for desecrating graves, not for damaging an archaeological site. Although many of the most famous archaeological sites in North America, like, for example, Chaco Canyon or Mesa Verde in the Southwest, are under public ownership, hundreds of lesser historic locations are on private land, once commonplace locations, but places of great archaeological importance. The fur traders' post in South Dakota, the silver miner's cabin in Nevada, the tiny British outpost in Australia, all are as vital a part of the archaeological record as Slack Farm or Mesa Verde. The right to ownership of land and all on it carries with it important responsibilities, not only for conserving soil and water, or for proper erosion management, but for protecting historic sites as well. To their credit, many land owners recognize and accept these responsibilities, especially when they feel a strong historical identification with a site like a nineteenth-century barn—as, for example, is the case with many Western ranching properties. In many cases, the interests of the landowner, the historian, and the archaeologist coincide, where everyone has a responsibility for the site, for its preservation.

One of us (CEO) was involved in a project just like this in south Louisiana. He was contacted by the owners of the McIlhenny Company, the manufacturers of Tabasco Brand Pepper Sauce at Avery Island, Louisiana, since 1868. One of the oldest houses on the island is named Marsh House. Its precise date of construction is unknown, but it was a functioning residence by 1818. Over the years, the island was transformed from a sugar plantation to a hot sauce factory. Marsh House changed as well, eventually becoming a guest house and conference center for the McIlhenny Company, by the middle of the twentieth century an international corporation. In the mid-1980s, however, the house sustained a devastating fire that destroyed much of its superstructure. When restoration and renovation was planned for Marsh House, the McIlhenny Company, long known as a leader in promoting serious archaeology, called in Orser to conduct an archaeological testing program.

The company wanted to ensure that they did not destroy or damage any artifacts or earlier structural remains during the renovation process. The project was a complete success. As archaeologists, we were able to learn about antebellum life at Avery Island. The island was a typical sugar plantation. Slaves lived in small duplex cabins and labored in the cane fields or worked in the master's kitchen; the planters oversaw the slaves' labor, marketed the sugar the slaves produced, and lived in a large house, entertaining other planters as the occasion arose. The McIlhenny Company was true to its dedication to preservation. If academic research goals and corporate requirements could always be so closely linked, much could be learned about modern history and culture.

The Avery Island case is still the exception rather than the rule. The battle is far from over, for public attitudes toward even the recent past are more often couched in terms of financial worth and economic advantage rather than responsibility for the history of our forebears. There can be no compromise. All of us, collectively, own even the most insignificant records of the past, for they form part of our common cultural heritage, whether Native American or descendant of a conquistador, English colonist, or recent Polish immigrant. The past is all of ours, by right.

THE FUTURE OF HISTORICAL ARCHAEOLOGY

Where does the future of historical archaeology lie? Much depends on the success of our efforts to save the past for coming generations, on effective working partnerships between archaeologists and land owners and commercial enterprises, between Native Americans and students of the past. We can certainly predict that such partnerships will become more commonplace in the future, as all segments of society find it easier to join hands to protect the environment and the remains of those who enjoyed it before us.

Historical archaeology itself stands at an important crossroads, with the potential to add important, new theoretical models to the discipline, ones that will have far reaching impact not only on historic sites research, but on prehistoric archaeology as well. Many of these theoretical perspectives will revolve around fundamental issues both in historic and modern society—in the areas of cultural interaction, ethnic diversity, and changing gender roles. As we have emphasized many times, archaeology is unique in its ability to chronicle processes of cultural change over centuries, and sometimes over much shorter periods, even decades. These changes come down to us in material remains, in the form of architectural modifications and ever-shifting fashions in artifact style and design. The archaeological record is usually anonymous, a chronicle of working men and women going about their business day after day, year after year, leaving no record behind them except the most prosaic of artifacts and food remains. Such finds are the meat and drink of historical archaeology, a unique searchlight into the inner recesses of history. They allow us not only to find out about the lives of humble folk "without history," but about the intricate relationships between men and women, conquerors and the conquered, oppressors and the oppressed. If current trends continue, historical archaeologists will rewrite entire chapters of recent history by chronicling the relationships between the rulers and the ruled, the rich and the poor, even between different members of the family.

It will be historical archaeology that documents the complex interplay between African-Americans and plantation owners, between Spanish friars and Native Americans living in the shadow of mission walls, between English colonists and Maori groups in New Zealand. As we move into an era when we study world history from an increasingly global perspective, we will think of the Age of Discovery, of the Industrial Revolution, as complicated developments that involved ever-changing relationships not only between European nations, but between a myriad of human societies large and small in every corner of the world. Unraveling the complexities of these relationships will require multidisciplinary research, not only conventional documents and oral histories, but genetic and linguistic inquiries, anthropological investigations, and a truly global form of historical archaeology that studies both the expansion of European culture and indigenous responses to external contact. Historical archaeology is already a multidisciplinary enterprise; it will become even more so in an era when multicultural perspectives on recent history are assuming ever-greater importance.

Future definitions of history cannot be confined to the narrow universe of documents, and perhaps oral tradition. They must encompass a broad range of disciplines, each with their own contribution to make to a multicultural past. Archaeology will be one of them.

BEING EDUCATED IN HISTORICAL ARCHAEOLOGY

How can one become a historical archaeologist, embark on a career in a new and burgeoning field? A growing number of universities around the world are beginning to offer professional training in the subject, but few historical archaeology programs now exist. Some programs, such as the one at Michigan State University, are well established; others, such as the one at the University of Sydney in Australia, are relatively new. The lack of programs dedicated to historical archaeology relates to the newness of the field. However, historical archaeology is a field in which career opportunities will open up in coming years, especially as multidisciplinary curricula gain in popularity.

To become a professional archaeologist requires a minimum of an MA, and to do serious research and teach at the university level, a PhD. At the undergraduate level, even at a university that does not offer a degree in historical archaeology, it is possible to learn enough to obtain admission into a good MA or PhD program. Our advice is to declare a major in anthropology, then design your curriculum, as much as you can, around courses in anthropology, archaeology, history, and geography. Take as much cultural anthropology as possible, for courses in this field will give you a grounding in cultural diversity on a global level and help you develop an anthropological perspective, a background in theories of culture.

In terms of archaeology itself, you should focus on method and theory. The more you can learn about excavation methods and past archaeologists' theories, the better prepared you will be for future graduate seminars. Courses in historiography, archival research methods, and oral history, as well as survey offerings in regional and world history, will stand you in good stead as you develop your skills in historical research methods. Your studies in geography should include courses in cultural geography, landscape design, settlement analysis, and even cartography. Geographers can teach you about vernacular architecture, about ways of analyzing spatial arrangements of people, and how to read a landscape.

If seriously interested in applying to graduate school, you should plan, while an undergraduate, to attend an archaeological field school. These are actually university and college courses where the classroom is an archaeological site; the pens and papers are trowels and shovels. Field schools in prehistoric archaeology have been around since at least the 1930s, but the number of field schools in historical archaeology is burgeoning today. Both the Society for Historical Archaeology and the Archaeological Institute of America maintain lists of field schools, and *Archaeology Magazine* publishes information about archaeological field schools regularly. Also, consult your instructors. They may know of local field schools, or be able to steer to you information sent to their department. A field school is a wonderful opportunity both to gain practical field experience, and also to find out whether you have an aptitude for fieldwork. Far better to test yourself in the field before you apply to graduate school, for archaeological excavation and survey can be tough, demanding work, which is not for everyone.

Professional training in historical archaeology, or in any kind of archaeology for that matter, comes from MA and PhD programs at major universities. Anyone seeking to become a professional researcher and university teacher must obtain a PhD, a process that can take up to seven years or more, involving the execution of a major piece of original research. Increasing numbers of people are electing to take a Masters in archaeology, frequently specializing in conservation, cultural resource management, and other topics with a strong resource management emphasis. Many of these graduates go into government departments or into the environmental industry. The choice of a graduate program depends on many variables, among them the quality and interests of the faculty, the kind of historical archaeology you wish to pursue (For example, there is no point in applying to a program interested in Hispanic colonial problems when your interests lie in English colonists in New England), and your methodological and theoretical interests. Again, you should rely heavily on the advice of your undergraduate advisers, who have contacts in the field, and know which departments are best for your purposes.

Finally, and most important: do not contemplate a career in historical archaeology unless you have a passionate interest in the subject and a real commitment to the past. This is not a field for the lukewarm enthusiast, or for those who hanker after undemanding job security. All archaeological jobs require unlimited enthusiasm, abundant energy, the ability to tolerate discomfort and low salaries, and, above all, passion and a sense of humor. For those who meet these criteria, there are few more satisfying jobs on earth.

What kind of professional training do you need? The Society of Professional Archaeologists (SOPA) is an organization that promotes the highest standards of archaeological research. As part of their program of advancing professionalism, they have created a rigid set of guidelines to judge the qualifications of archaeologists. An applicant who is judged to meet their standards is listed in an annual directory available to government and private organizations, who wish to hire an archaeologist. To meet SOPA's requirements for historical archaeology, the applicant "must document a minimum of one year of field and laboratory experience, including 24 weeks of field work and eight weeks of laboratory work under supervision of a professional historical archaeologist on sites and artifacts of an historic period, and 20 weeks in a supervisory or equally responsible capacity." In addition, the applicant must prove that they have been the author of a serious, scientific report of investigation, and have prepared a scholarly work on the level of an MA thesis or PhD dissertation. The guidelines are tough for a good reason. Archaeological sites are a nonrenewable resource; once they are destroyed, they are gone forever. As such they deserve nothing but professional attention.

JOBS IN HISTORICAL ARCHAEOLOGY

There are far more archaeologists than there are paying jobs in the field, so the employment picture is always tight, especially in academia in an era of declining resources. Time was when most archaeologists worked in universities and colleges, teaching during the academic year, perhaps running field schools or doing research during the summers. During the past quarter century, the employment picture has changed completely, as more and more professional opportunities for archaeologists open up in government, in nonprofit organizations, and in private companies conducting environmental research and cultural resource management. Many archaeologists work in administrative positions in the National Park Service and Parks Canada, as state archaeologists managing the National Register of Historic Places, or as park rangers—to mention only a few careers. These are areas where trained historical archaeologists are highly competitive, because of their broad, multidisciplinary training, not only in archaeology, but in historiography, historic preservation, and anthropology. Museums and historical societies also offer chances to acquire on-the-job training, and sometimes paid employment.

HISTORICAL ARCHAEOLOGY
AND THE LOCAL HISTORICAL SOCIETY

Historical societies are the backbone of local history in the United States and other countries. Some are humble organizations, mainly devoted to genealogical research. Others support museums and archives, and maintain active publication programs, lecture series, and many services for their membership. The larger societies employ professional administrators and historians and maintain active liaisons with local universities and colleges, to say nothing of adult education programs. Most historical societies are invaluable resources for archaeologist and student alike, especially groups deeply involved in historic preservation and research into local history. In many cases, such organizations realize the importance of historical archaeology and see its relevance to understanding more of their community's history. They sometimes sponsor scientific archaeological digs, often working in close association with a professional archaeologist from a local university or college. These kinds of projects are especially rewarding because they acquaint nonarchaeologists with the profession in a very real way.

A perfect example of this kind of project occurred in 1992 in Bloomington, Illinois. Historical archaeologists Mark Groover, Melanie Cabak, and David Babson, then with Illinois State University, worked closely with members of the Bloomington-Normal Black History Group on the excavation of the Wayman African Methodist Episcopal Church and Parsonage. The Bloomington-Normal Black History Group is an organization of local citizens interested in promoting an understanding of African-American history in these two central Illinois towns. The group is sponsored the by McLean County Historical Society in Bloomington. Organized in 1843, the Wayman A.M.E. Church has long been a focal point of African-American religious expression. Groover, Cabak, and Babson organized three excavations on the historic church site with the help of 21 volunteers. Some of them were young adolescents, many members of the black history club. The dig was spectacularly successful, recovering hundreds of artifacts used at the church. Some of the most interesting artifacts relate to health. Medicine bottles found at the site convinced Groover and his team that the church was used as a place to dispense medicines to the parishioners. Historical records even showed that a doctor once lived in the church's residence. In the nineteenth century, the church was apparently an important provider of health care to the African-American community, and the church yard was the scene of many social gatherings. In this case, limited excavation conducted with the assistance of a historical group did much to confirm theories about the changing role of the church in local African-American life.

Historical societies are a vital resource for historical archaeology, with open-ended potential for all kinds of exciting research and preservation projects that can be used to train competent fieldworkers and sustain popular enthusiasm about the past. All archaeology, by its very nature, seems a luxury in a world beset by catastrophic social problems and nationalist rivalries. Yet it most emphatically is not, for it offers one of the few ways science has of studying and understanding human biological and cultural diversity over long periods. Most of you, dear readers, will never become professional archaeologists, nor should you. Hopefully, these pages will spark in you an interest in the past, so that you enjoy it and make it part of your life for the rest of your days. All of us enjoy a magnificent cultural legacy from the remote and not-so-remote past, a past that each generation must preserve for their children and grandchildren. So, please, whatever your interest in archaeology and history, please do all you can to save the past for the future. Future generations will censure us if we do not.

Here are some guidelines for us all:

- Treat every archaeological site and artifact as a finite resource that, once destroyed, can never be replaced.
- Report all archaeological discoveries to responsible archaeological authorities (archaeological surveys, museums, university or college departments, government agencies).
- Obey all laws relating to archaeological sites.
- Never dig a site without proper training or supervision.
- Never collect archaeological finds from any country for your private collection or for profit.
- Respect modern and prehistoric burial grounds, many of which have deep spiritual significance.

USEFUL ADDRESSES

Here are four addresses where you can obtain information about archaeological activities, field schools, and volunteer excavations:

Society for Historical Archaeology
P. O. Box 30446
Tucson, AZ 85751

Archaeological Institute of America
Box 1901, Kenmore Station
Boston MA 02215

Archaeology Magazine
135 William Street
New York, NY 10038

Society for American Archaeology
Railway Express Building
980 2nd Street NE Suite 12
Washington, DC 20002

In this brief introduction to historical archaeology, we have tried to communicate the excitement of this emerging field. We showed in Chapter 2 that historical archaeology is not a discipline with a long and venerable history. Compared with other kinds of archaeology, it is only an infant. Its very youth gives historical archaeology vitality. The field is exciting, and historical archaeologists are pushing current knowledge to the limit, challenging old interpretations, creating new ones. We have known all along that some of what we were writing would be refined and sometimes even refuted by future excavations. The rapid accumulation of knowledge in a field as new as historical archaeology is inevitable. We are not troubled that some of what we have written will be corrected by our colleagues or even replaced with better and more complex examples. On the contrary, we are excited by it. Even in the social sciences, scientific knowledge is a process of researching, writing, researching anew, and writing again. Change is occurring quickly in historical archaeology. New sites are being excavated all the time, and increasing numbers of students are being introduced to our field. Historical archaeologists are exploring parts of the world that only recently were blank territories on the map of archaeological knowledge. If you are fascinated by the archaeology of modern history and are enthused by its promise, then we welcome you to historical archaeology with open arms.

Guide to Further Reading

The references that follow are necessarily selective, but will give you access to the more technical literature of historical archaeology. Brian Fagan's *Archaeology: A Brief Introduction*, 5th ed., (New York: HarperCollins, 1994), and any one of several comprehensive method and theory texts on the market, will provide you with excellent background to the general principles of archaeology. Much of the literature of historical archaeology appears in professional journals or in reports of extremely limited distribution. We recommend that you consult an expert before attacking the more specialist literature. For your convenience, however, we include the archaeological works we have used for each chapter, as well as more general background readings.

GENERAL WORKS ON HISTORICAL ARCHAEOLOGY

The classic short account of historical archaeology is James Deetz's well-written *In Small Things Forgotten: The Archaeology of Early American Life* (Garden City, NY: Anchor Press/Doubleday, 1977). Ivor Noël Hume, *Historical Archaeology* (New York: Alfred A. Knopf, 1972) is a somewhat outdated, but elegant work which focuses on European-American sites. The same authors' *The Virginia Adventure* (New York: Alfred A. Knopf, 1994) is a fascinating account of historical archaeology at Roanoke and Jamestown. Some more specialized edited volumes include: Lisa Falk (ed.), *Historical Archaeology in Global Perspective* (Washington DC: Smithsonian Institution Press, 1991); Mark P. Leone and Parker Potter, Jr. (eds.), *The Recovery of Meaning: Historical Archaeology in the Eastern United States* (Washington DC: Smithsonian Institution Press, 1988); Randall H. McGuire and Robert Paynter (eds.), *The Archaeology of Inequality* (Oxford: Basil Blackwell, 1991); Robert L. Schuyler (ed.), *Historical Archaeology: A Guide to Substantive and Theoretical Contributions* (Farmingdale, NY: Baywood, 1978). Stanley South, *Method and Theory in Historical Archaeology* (New York: Academic Press, 1977); and Stanley South (ed.), *Research Strategies in Historical Archaeology* (New York: Academic Press, 1977) cover more theoretical issues. For post-medieval archaeology in Great Britain, consult David Crossley, *Post-Medieval Archaeology in Britain* (Leicester: Leicester University Press, 1990). Case studies are beginning to appear in historical archaeology. Two recent ones are: Kenneth L. Feder, *A Village of Outcasts: Historical Archaeology and Documentary Research at the Lighthouse Site* (Mountain View, CA: Mayfield, 1994), and Janet D. Spector, *What This Awl Means: Feminist Archaeology at a Wahpeton Dakota Village* (St. Paul: Minnesota Historical Society Press, 1993). A workbook for historical archaeology students has recently been published: Russell J. Barber's *Doing Historical Archaeology:*

Exercises Using Documentary, Oral, and Material Evidence (Englewood Cliffs, NJ: Prentice-Hall, 1994).

MAJOR JOURNALS COVERING HISTORICAL ARCHAEOLOGY

The major English-language journals dealing solely with historical archaeology are *Historical Archaeology* (published in the United States by the Society for Historical Archaeology), *Post-Medieval Archaeology* (published in England by the Society for Post-Medieval Archaeology), and *The Australasian Journal of Historical Archaeology* (published by The Australasian Society for Historical Archaeology). The Historical Archaeology Research Group of the University of Cape Town, South Africa, issues a newsletter entitled *Crossmend*. Most major archaeological journals do not regularly publish articles about historical archaeology, although contributions occasionally appear in *American Antiquity* and *Antiquity*.

CHAPTER 1: WHAT IS HISTORICAL ARCHAEOLOGY?

The issues explored in this chapter are discussed, usually superficially, in most of the books mentioned above. For the use of written records in historical archaeology consult Mary C. Beaudry (ed.), *Documentary Archaeology in the New World* (Cambridge: Cambridge University Press, 1988) and Barbara J. Little (ed.), *Text-Aided Archaeology* (Boca Raton, FL: CRC Press, 1992).

Historiography has generated an enormous literature. Two classics: Marc Bloch, *The Historian's Craft*, trans. Peter Putnam (New York, Vintage, 1953) and Edward Hallet Carr, *What Is History?* (New York: Alfred A. Knopf, 1961). A similar work, written by a respected archaeologist, is V. Gordon Childe, *History* (London: Cobbett Press, 1947). More recent essays include: R. F. Atkinson, *Knowledge and Explanation in History: An Introduction in the Philosophy of History* (London: Macmillan, 1978); Daniel J. Boorstin, *Hidden History* (New York: Harper and Row, 1987) and David Hackett Fischer, *Historians' Fallacies: Toward a Logic of Historical Thought* (New York: Harper and Row, 1970). A wonderful book by a historian that makes explicit use of historical archaeology is T. H. Breen, *Imagining the Past: East Hampton Histories* (Reading, MA: Addison-Wesley, 1989). Eric Wolf, *Europe and the People Without History* (Berkeley: University of California Press, 1984) is indispensable on the Age of Discovery and issues of interconnectedness.

Specialist literature:

Adams, William H., *Silcott, Washington: Ethnoarchaeology of a Rural American Community*. Reports of Investigation 54. (Pullman: Laboratory of Anthropology, Washington State University, 1977).

Armstrong, Douglas V., *The Old Village and the Great House: An Archaeological and Historical Examination of Drax Hall Plantation, St. Ann's Bay, Jamaica*. (Urbana: University of Illinois Press, 1990).

Haggett, Peter, *The Geographer's Art*. (Oxford: Basil Blackwell, 1990).

Hogarth, David G., *Authority and Archaeology: Sacred and Profane.* (London: John Murray, 1899).

Schmidt, Peter R., *Historical Archaeology: A Structural Approach in an African Culture.* (Westport, CT: Greenwood, 1978).

Schuyler, Robert L., Historical Archaeology and Historic Sites Archaeology as Anthropology: Basic Definitions and Relationships. *Historical Archaeology* 4(1970):83–89.

Schuyler, Robert L., Parallels in the Rise of the Various Subfields of Historical Archaeology. *Conference on Historic Site Archaeology Papers* 10 (1977):2–10.

CHAPTER 2: A BRIEF HISTORY OF HISTORICAL ARCHAEOLOGY

We wrote this chapter using the specialist literature. Father Martin's excavations at Sainte Marie appear in Kenneth E. Kidd's *The Excavation of Ste. Marie I* (Toronto: University of Toronto Press, 1949), and mention of Hall's excavations can be found in Deetz's "Late Man in North America: Archaeology of European Americans," in *Anthropological Archaeology in the Americas* (Washington, DC: Anthropological Society of Washington, 1968) pp. 121–130. In addition to Leone and Potter's *The Recovery of Meaning,* and McGuire and Paynter's *The Archaeology of Inequality,* already mentioned, case studies in contemporary historical archaeology can be found in the special issue of *Historical Archaeology* "Meanings and Uses of Material Culture," Barbara J. Little and Paul A. Shackel (eds.), 26(1992) 26:3. Additional archaeological studies of gender can be found in Dale Walde and Noreen D. Willows (eds.), *The Archaeology of Gender: Proceedings of the Twenty-Second Annual Conference of the Archaeological Association of the University of Calgary,* (Calgary: University of Calgary, 1991), and in Cheryl Claasen (ed.), *Exploring Gender Through Archaeology: Selected Papers from the 1991 Boone Conference* (Madison, WI: Prehistory Press, 1992).

Specialist literature:

Baker, Vernon G., *Historical Archaeology at Black Lucy's Garden, Andover, Massachusetts: Ceramics from the Site of a Nineteenth Century Afro-American* (Andover, MA: Philips Academy, 1978).

Beaudry, Mary C. and Stephen A. Mrozowski (eds.), *Interdisciplinary Investigations of the Boott Mills, Lowell, Massachusetts, Volume I: Life at the Boarding Houses, A Preliminary Report.* (Boston: National Park Service, 1987).

Binford, Lewis R., Archaeology as Anthropology. *American Antiquity* 28(1962):217–225.

Cohn, Bernard S., An Anthropologist Among the Historians: A Field Study. *The South Atlantic Quarterly* 61(1962):13–28.

Deagan, Kathleen, Avenues of Inquiry in Historical Archaeology. In *Advances in Archaeological Method and Theory,* vol. 5, Michael B. Schiffer (ed.), pp. 151–177. (New York: Academic Press, 1982).

Fish, Carl Russell, Relation of Archaeology and History. *Proceedings of the State Historical Society of Wisconsin at the Fifty-Eighth Annual Meeting Held October 20, 1910,* pp. 146–152. (Madison: State Historical Society of Wisconsin, 1911).

Fontana, Bernard L., On the Meaning of Historic Sites Archaeology. *American Antiquity* 31(1965):61–65.

Greenman, Emerson F., *Old Birch Island Cemetery and the Early Historic Trade Route, Georgian Bay, Ontario.* (Ann Arbor: University of Michigan Press, 1951).

Hagen, Richard S., Back-Yard Archaeology at Lincoln's Home. *Journal of the Illinois State Historical Society* 44 (1951):340–348.

Hardesty, Donald C., *The Archaeology of Mining and Miners: A View from the Silver State* (Tucson, AZ: Society for Historical Archaeology, 1988).

Harrington, J. C., Archaeology as an Auxiliary Science of American History. *American Anthropologist* 7 (1955):1121–1130.

——— *New Light on Washington's Fort Necessity.* Richmond, VA: Eastern National Park and Monument Association, 1957).

Hodder, Ian, *Reading the Past: Current Approaches to Interpretation in Archaeology.* (Cambridge, England: Cambridge University Press, 1986).

Isaac, Rhys, *The Transformation of Virginia, 1740–1790.* (Chapel Hill: University of North Carolina Press, 1982).

Jelks, Edward B., Archaeological Explorations at Signal Hill, Newfoundland, 1965–1966. *Canadian Historic Sites: Occasional Papers in Archaeology and History,* no. 7 (Ottawa: National Historic Sites Service, 1973).

Kidd, Kenneth E., *The Excavation of Ste. Marie I* (Toronto: University of Toronto Press, 1949).

Leone, Mark P., Interpreting Ideology in Historical Archaeology: Using the Rules of Perspective in the William Paca Garden in Annapolis, Maryland. In *Ideology, Power, and Prehistory,* Daniel Miller and Christopher Tilley (eds.), pp. 25–35. (Cambridge, England: Cambridge University Press, 1984).

South, Stanley, *Method and Theory in Historical Archaeology.* (New York: Academic Press, 1977).

Wheaton, Thomas R. and Patrick W. Garrow, Acculturation and the Archaeological Record in the Carolina Lowcountry. In *Archaeology of Slavery and Plantation Life,* Theresa A. Singleton (ed.), pp. 239–259. (Orlando: Academic Press, 1985).

Woolworth, Alan and Raymond Wood, The Archaeology of a Small Trading Post. *River Basin Survey Papers, Bulletin 176* (Washington, DC: U.S. Government Printing Office, 1960)

Yentsch, Anne, Chesapeake Artefacts and Their Cultural Context: Pottery and the Food Domain. *Post-Medieval Archaeology* 25(1991):25–72.

CHAPTER 3: HISTORICAL CULTURE

Anthropologists have written numerous books about the history, nature, and future directions of their discipline. An excellent and very readable history of anthropology: Annemarie de Waal Malefijt, *Images of Man: A History of Anthropological Thought* (New York: Alfred A. Knopf, 1974). A more complete synthesis: Fred W. Voget's *A History of Ethnology* (New York: Holt, Rinehart, and Winston, 1975). Good collections of readings in anthropology are Paul Bohannan and Mark Glazer (eds.), *High Points in Anthropology* (2nd ed., New York: Alfred A. Knopf, 1988) and Johnnetta B. Cole (ed.), *Anthropology for the Nineties: Introductory Readings* (New York: The Free Press, 1988).

For archaeology as anthropology see Guy Gibbon's *Anthropological Archaeology* (New York: Columbia University Press, 1984). An older source: Mark P. Leone (ed.), *Contemporary Ar-*

chaeology: A Guide to Theory and Contributions (Carbondale: Southern Illinois University Press, 1972).

Classic articles on ethnographic analogy and the direct historical approach include: Robert Ascher, "Analogy in Archaeological Interpretation." *Southwestern Journal of Anthropology* 17(1961):317–325; and Julian H. Steward, "The Direct Historical Approach to Archaeology," *American Antiquity* 7(1942):337–343. The use of analogy in historical archaeology: Charles E. Orser, Jr., "Ethnohistory, Analogy, and Historical Archaeology." *Conference on Historic Site Archaeology Papers* 13 (1972):1–24; and Robert L. Schuyler. "The Use of Historic Analogs in Archaeology." *American Antiquity* 33(1968):390–392. Analogical reasoning in archaeology: P. Nick Kardulias. "Estimating Population at Ancient Military Sites: The Use of Historical and Contemporary Analogy." *American Antiquity* 57(1992):276–287.

Research designs and sampling are controversial issues. Research designs are discussed in Lewis R. Binford, "A Consideration of Archaeological Research Design," *American Antiquity* 29 (1963):425–441. Sampling: James W. Mueller (ed.), *Sampling in Archaeology* (Tucson: University of Arizona Press, 1975). Another good source: Stephen Plog, Fred Plog, and Walter Wait, "Decision Making in Modern Surveys," in *Advances in Archaeological Method and Theory*, *Vol. 1,* Michael B. Schiffer (ed.), pp. 383–421. (New York: Academic Press, 1976). A good source for the use of new technologies for evaluating areas thought to contain archaeological sites: W. J. Judge and L. Sebastian (eds.), *Quantifying the Present and Predicting the Past: Theory, Method, and Application of Archaeological Predictive Modeling.* (Washington: Government Printing Office, 1988).

Many books and articles discuss historic preservation. One book heavily slanted toward archaeology is Thomas F. King, Patricia Parker Hickman, and Gary Berg (eds.), *Anthropology in Historic Preservation: Caring for a Culture's Clutter* (New York: Academic Press, 1977). Two good books about the preservation of historical buildings, towns, and environments: Antoinette J. Lee (ed.), *Past Meets Future: Saving America's Historic Environments* (Washington: Preservation Press, 1992); and Arthur P. Ziegler, Jr. and Walter C. Kidney, *Historic Preservation in Small Towns: A Manual of Practice* (Nashville: American Association for State and Local History, 1980).

Specialist literature:

Beattie, Owen and John Geiger, *Frozen in Time: Unlocking the Secrets of the Doomed 1845 Arctic Expedition* (New York: Penguin, 1987).

Binford, Lewis R., Smudge Pits and Hide Smoking: The Use of Analogy in Archaeological Reasoning. *American Antiquity* 32(1967):1–12.

Boorstin, Daniel, *Hidden History* (New York: Harper and Row, 1987).

Fox, Richard Allan, Jr., *Archaeology, History, and Custer's Last Battle: The Little Bighorn Reexamined* (Norman: University of Oklahoma Press, 1993).

Handler, Jerome S. and Frederick W. Lange, *Plantation Slavery in Barbados: An Archaeological and Historical Investigation* (Cambridge: Harvard University Press, 1978).

Harrington, Spencer P. M., Bones and Bureaucrats: New York's Great Cemetery Imbroglio. *Archaeology* 46, 2 (1993):28–38.

Heite, Edward F., *Archaeological Data Recovery on the Collins, Geddes Cannery Site, Road 356A, Lebanon, North Murderkill Hundred, Kent County, Delaware.* (Wilmington: Delaware Department of Transportation, 1990).

Kelly, Roger E. and Marsha C. S. Kelly, Arrastras: Unique Western Historic Milling Sites. *Historical Archaeology* 17, 1 (1983):85–95.

Kidder, A. V., *An Introduction to the Study of Southwestern Archaeology, with a Preliminary Account of the Excavations at Pecos.* (New Haven: Yale University Press, 1924).

Lamb, Teresia A., *Preliminary Archaeological Reconnaissance and Assessment of Destrehan Plantation, St. Charles Parish, Louisiana.* (New Orleans: Archaeological and Cultural Research Program, University of New Orleans, 1983).

Lewis, Kenneth E. and Helen W. Haskell, *The Middleton Place Privy: A Study of Discard Behavior and the Archaeological Record.* Research Manuscript 174. (Columbia: South Carolina Institute for Archaeology and Anthropology, 1981).

Mrozowski, Stephen A., "Historical Archaeology as Anthropology." *Historical Archaeology* 22 (1988) 1:18–24.

Munson, Patrick J., Comments on Binford's "Smudge Pits and Hide Smoking: The Use of Analogy in Archaeological Reasoning." *American Antiquity* 34(1969):83–85.

Murray, Jeffrey S., The Mounties of Cypress Hill. *Archaeology* 41, 1(1988):32–38.

Pastron, Allen G., William C. Hoff's Gold Rush Emporium: Bonanza from Old San Francisco. *Archaeology* 41, 4 (1988):32–39.

——— On Golden Mountain. *Archaeology* 42, 4 (1989):48–53.

Reinhart, Theodore R. (ed.), *The Archaeology of Shirley Plantation.* (Charlottesville: University Press of Virginia, 1984).

Scott, Douglas D., Richard A. Fox, Jr., Melissa A. Connor, and Dick Harmon, *Archaeological Perspectives on the Battle of the Little Bighorn* (Norman: University of Oklahoma Press, 1989).

Starbuck, David R. and Mary Bentley Dupré, Production Continuity and Obolescence of Traditional Red Earthenwares in Concord, New Hampshire. In *Domestic Pottery of the Northeastern United States, 1625–1850,* Sarah Peabody Turnbaugh (ed.), pp. 133–152. (Orlando: Academic Press, 1985).

Tuck, James, A Sixteenth-Century Whaling Station at Red Bay, Labrador. In *Early European Settlement and Exploration in Atlantic Canada,* G. M. Story (ed.), pp. 41–52. (St. John's: Memorial University of Newfoundland, 1982).

Tylor, Edward Burnett, *The Origins of Culture, Part I of "Primitive Culture."* (New York: Harper and Row, 1958).

Upward, Geoffrey C., *A Home for Our Heritage: The Building and Growth of Greenfield Village and Henry Ford Museum, 1929–1979.* (Dearborn, MI: Henry Ford Museum Press, 1979).

CHAPTER 4: HISTORICAL ARTIFACTS

Many authors have discussed material culture. Some relevant studies and essays include: Leland Ferguson (ed.), *Historical Archaeology and the Importance of Material Things* (California, PA: Society for Historical Archaeology, 1977); Ian M. G. Quimby (ed.), *Material Culture and the Study of American Life* (New York: W. W. Norton, 1978); and Thomas J. Schlereth (ed.), *Material Culture Studies in America* (Nashville: American Association for State and Local History, 1982). See also: Arthur Asa Berger, *Reading Matter: Multidisciplinary Perspectives on Material Culture* (New Brunswick, NJ: Transaction, 1992); Mihaly

Csikszentmihalyi and Eugene Rochberg-Halton, *The Meaning of Things: Domestic Symbols and the Self* (Cambridge: Cambridge University Press, 1981); Chandra Mukerji, *From Graven Images: Patterns of Modern Materialism* (New York: Columbia University Press, 1983); Robert Blair St. George (ed.), *Material Life in America, 1600–1860* (Boston: Northeastern University Press, 1988); and Thomas J. Schlereth, *Artifacts and the American Past* (Nashville: American Association for State and Local History, 1980) and *Cultural History and Material Culture: Everyday Life, Landscapes, Museums* (Ann Arbor, MI: UMI Research, 1990). Two wonderful anthropological studies of material objects are Mary Douglas and Baron Isherwood, *The World of Goods* (New York: Basic, 1979) and Nicholas Thomas, *Entangled Objects: Exchange, Material Culture, and Colonialism in the Pacific* (Cambridge: Harvard University Press, 1991).

Artifacts in historical archaeology: a good starting point is Ivor Noël Hume's *A Guide to Artifacts of Colonial America* (New York: Alfred A. Knopf, 1969). The complexities of the subject are well covered in Richard A. Gould and Michael B. Schiffer (eds.), *Modern Material Culture: The Archaeology of Us* (New York: Academic, 1981); Daniel Miller's *Material Culture and Mass Consumption* (Oxford, England: Basil Blackwell, 1987) and Suzanne Spencer-Wood's edited volume *Consumer Choice in Historical Archaeology* (New York: Plenum, 1987).

Makers' marks on ceramics and glass: Geoffrey A. Godden, *Encyclopaedia of British Pottery and Porcelain Marks* (New York: Bonanza, 1964) and Julian Harrison Toulouse, *Bottle Makers and Their Marks* (New York: Thomas Nelson, 1971). American pottery marks: William C. Gates and Dana E. Ormerod's, "The East Liverpool Pottery District: Identification of Manufacturers and Marks," *Historical Archaeology* 16 (1982) 1–2; and Ralph M. and Terry H. Kovel, *Dictionary of Marks: Pottery and Porcelain* (New York: Crown, 1953). Books on makers' marks exist for many different classes of artifacts, many of them from small presses, often geared to antique collectors. One example: Malcolm A. Rogers, *American Pewterers and Their Marks* (Southampton, NY: Cracker Barrel Press, 1968).

Specialist literature:

Becker, Carl L., What Are Historical Facts? *Western Political Quarterly* 7(1955):327–340.

Cotter, John, *Archaeological Excavations at Jamestown Colonial National Historical Park* (Washington, DC: National Park Service, 1958).

Deagan, Kathleen, *Spanish St. Augustine: The Archaeology of a Colonial Creole Community.* (New York: Academic Press, 1983).

Deetz, James F., Scientific Humanism and Humanistic Science: A Plea for Paradigmatic Pluralism in Historical Archaeology. *Geoscience and Man* 23(1983):27–34.

Gradwohl, David M. and Nancy M. Osborn, *Exploring Buried Buxton: Archaeology of an Abandoned Iowa Coal Mining Town with a Large Black Population.* (Ames: Iowa State University Press, 1984).

Lehmer, Donald J., *Introduction to Middle Missouri Archaeology.* (Washington, DC: National Park Service, 1971).

Lief, Alfred, *A Close-Up of Closures: History and Progress.* (New York: Glass Container Manufacturers Institute, 1965).

Martin, Ann Smart, The Role of Pewter as Missing Artifact: Consumer Attitudes Toward Tablewares in Late 18th Century Virginia. *Historical Archaeology* 23, 2(1989):1–27.

Monks, Gregory G., Architectural Symbolism and Non-Verbal Communication at Upper Fort Garry. *Historical Archaeology* 26, 2(1992):37–57.

Orser, Charles E., Jr., *The Material Basis of the Postbellum Tenant Plantation: Historical Archaeology in the South Carolina Piedmont.* (Athens: University of Georgia Press, 1988).

Pendergrast, Mark. *For God, Country, and Coca-Cola: The Unauthorized History of the Great American Soft Drink and the Company that Makes it.* (New York: Scribner's, 1993).

Phillippe, Joseph S., *The Drake Site: Subsistence and Status at a Rural Illinois Farmstead.* (Normal, IL: Midwestern Archaeological Research Center, Illinois State University, 1990).

Schlereth, Thomas J., Material Culture Studies in America, 1876–1976. In *Material Culture Studies in America,* Thomas J. Schlereth (ed.), pp. 1–75. (Nashville: American Association for State and Local History, 1982).

Shackel, Paul A., *Personal Discipline and Material Culture: An Archaeology of Annapolis, Maryland, 1695–1870* (Knoxville: University of Tennesee Press, 1993).

Stewart-Abernathy, Leslie C., *The Moser Farmstead* (Fayetteville, AR: Arkansas Archaeological Survey, 1986).

Thomas, David Hurst, Saints and Soldiers at Santa Catalina: Hispanic Designs for Colonial America. In *The Recovery of Meaning: Historical Archaeology in the Eastern United States,* Mark P. Leone and Parker B. Potter Jr. (eds.), pp. 73–140. (Washington, DC: Smithsonian Institution Press, 1988).

CHAPTER 5: TIME AND SPACE

Context, time, and space are central concepts discussed by any basic archaeological method and theory textbook, such as Fagan's companion volume to this one. David Lowenthal's *The Past is a Foreign Country* (Cambridge: Cambridge University Press, 1985) offers a fascinating commentary on the meaning of time to modern society.

Association, superposition, relative chronology, and dating methods in archaeology: See any basic text for up-to-date descriptions of the various methods or consult an older sourcebook: Joseph W. Michels, *Dating Methods in Archaeology* (New York: Seminar Press, 1973). Site formation processes: Michael B. Schiffer's *Formation Processes of the Archaeological Record* (Albuquerque: University of New Mexico Press, 1987).

Space and settlement archaeology: three older, but still very good, studies are K. C. Chang (ed.), *Settlement Archaeology* (Palo Alto, CA.: National Press, 1968); David L. Clarke (ed.), *Spatial Archaeology* (London: Academic Press, 1977); and Ian Hodder and Clive Orton, *Spatial Analysis in Archaeology* (Cambridge: Cambridge University Press, 1976). A good settlement study in historical archaeology: Michael J. O'Brien, *Grassland, Forest, and Historical Settlement: An Analysis of Dynamics in Northeast Missouri* (Lincoln: University of Nebraska Press, 1984).

Proxemics: Edward T. Hall, *The Hidden Dimension* (Garden City, NY: Doubleday, 1966). A recent archaeological discussion of how humans learn about space is Thomas Wynn, *The Evolution of Spatial Competence* (Urbana: University of Illinois, 1989). An archaeological treatment of proxemics: Ruth Tringham (ed.), *Territoriality and Proxemics: Archaeological and Ethnographic Evidence for the Use and Organization of Space* (Andover, MA: Warner Modular, 1973).

Specialist literature:

Biddle, Martin, The Rose Revisited: A Comedy (?) of Errors. *Antiquity* 63(1989):753–760.

Binford, Lewis R., A New Method of Calculating Dates from Kaolin Pipe Stem Fragments. *Southeastern Archaeological Conference Newsletter* 9, 1(1962):19–21.

Catts, Wade P. and Jay F. Custer, *Tenant Farmers, Stone Masons, and Black Laborers: Final Archaeological Investigations of the Thomas Williams Site, Glasgow, New Castle County, Delaware.* (Wilmington: Delaware Department of Transportation, 1990).

Cotter, John L., Daniel G. Roberts, and Michael Parrington, *The Buried Past: An Archaeological History of Philadelphia* (Philadelphia: University of Pennsylvania Press, 1992).

Harrington, J. C., Dating Stem Fragments of Seventeenth and Eighteenth Century Clay Tobacco Pipes. *Quarterly Bulletin of the Archaeological Society of Virginia* 9, 1(1954):10–14.

Heighton, Robert F. and Kathleen A. Deagan, A New Formula for Dating Kaolin Clay Pipestems. *Conference on Historic Site Archaeology Papers* 6(1972):220–229.

Kent, Susan, *Analyzing Activity Areas: An Ethnoarchaeological Study of the Use of Space.* (Albuquerque: University of New Mexico Press, 1984).

Noël Hume, Ivor, *Martin's Hundred: The Discovery of a Lost Colonial Virginia Settlement* (New York: Delta, 1983)

Orrell, John and Andrew Gurr. What the Rose Can Tell Us. *Antiquity* 63(1989):421–429.

Praetzellis, Mary and Adrian Praetzellis, *The Mary Collins Assemblage: Mass Marketing and the Archaeology of a Sacramento Family.* (Rohnert Park, CA: Anthropological Studies Center, Sonoma State University, 1990).

————— *"For a Good Boy": Victorians on Sacramento's J Street.* (Rohnert Park, CA: Anthropological Studies Center, Sonoma State University, 1990).

Robinson, William J., Tree-Ring Studies of the Pueblo de Acoma. *Historical Archaeology* 24, 3(1990):99–106.

South, Stanley, Evolution and Horizon as Revealed in Ceramic Analysis in Historical Archaeology. *Conference on Historic Site Archaeology Papers* 6(1972):71–116.

CHAPTER 6: SITE SURVEY AND LOCATION

Much of the information covered in this chapter can be found in Noël Hume's *Historical Archaeology.* The application of subsurface surveying techniques in archaeology: Don H. Heimmer, *Near-Surface, High Resolution: Geophysical Methods for Cultural Resource Management and Archaeological Investigations* (Denver: Interagency Archaeological Services, National Park Service, 1992). Although much of the presentation is technical, this book has a comprehensive bibliography with many sources directly related to historical archaeology. It even contains advertisements for the equipment needed to conduct subsurface surveys!

General books about subsurface surveying in archaeology include Anthony Clark's *Seeing Beneath the Soil: Prospecting Methods in Archaeology* (London: Batsford, 1990) and Irwin Scollar's *Archaeological Prospecting, Image Processing, and Remote Sensing* (Cambridge, England: Cambride University Press, 1989). Also useful is the British journal *Archaeometry.*

Specialist literature:

Arnold, J. Barto III, Marine Magnetometer Survey of Archaeological Materials near Galveston, Texas. *Historical Archaeology* 21, 1(1987):18–47.

Arnold, J. Barto III, G. Michael Fleshman, Curtiss E. Peterson, W. Kenneth Stewart, Gordon P. Watts, Jr., and Clark P. Weldon, USS *Monitor:* Results from the 1987 Season. *Historical Archaeology* 26, 4(1992):47–57.

Bailey, Richard N., Eric Cambridge, and H. Denis Briggs, *Dowsing and Church Archaeology* (Wimborne, Dorset: Intercept, 1988).

Benn, David W. (ed.), *Big Sioux River Archaeological and Historical Resources Survey, Lyon County, Iowa: Volume I.* (Springfield: Center for Archaeological Research, Southwest Missouri State University, 1987).

Bevan, Bruce W., David G. Orr, and Brooke S. Blades, The Discovery of the Taylor House at the Petersburg National Battlefield. *Historical Archaeology* 18, 2(1984):64–74.

Costello, Julia G. and Phillip L. Walker, Burials from the Santa Barbara Presidio Chapel. *Historical Archaeology* 21, 1(1987):3–17.

Ellwood, Brooks B., Electrical Resistivity Surveys in Two Historical Cemeteries in Northeast Texas: A Method for Delineating Burial Shafts. *Historical Archaeology* 24, 3(1990):91–98.

Kenyon, Jeff L. and Bruce Bevan, Ground-Penetrating Radar and Its Application to a Historical Archaeological Site. *Historical Archaeology* 11(1977):48–55.

Mason, Randall J., An Unorthodox Magnetic Survey of a Large Forested Historic Site. *Historical Archaeology* 18, 2(1984):54–63.

Noël Hume, Ivor, *Archaeology and Wetherburn's Tavern* (Williamsburg: Colonial Williamsburg Foundation, 1969).

Synenki, Alan T. (ed.), *Archaeological Investigations of Minute Man National Historical Park, Volume I: Farmers and Artisans of the Historical Period.* (Boston: National Park Service, 1990).

von Frese, Ralph R. B., Archaeomagnetic Anomalies of Midcontinental North American Archaeological Sites. *Historical Archaeology* 18, 2(1984):4–19.

von Frese, Ralph R.B., and Vergil E. Noble, Magnetometry for Archaeological Exploration of Historical Sites. *Historical Archaeology* 18, 2(1984):38–53.

Weymouth, John W. and William I. Woods, Combined Magnetic and Chemical Surveys of Forts Kaskaskia and de Chartres Number 1, Illinois. *Historical Archaeology* 18, 2(1984):20–37.

CHAPTER 7: PRE-EXCAVATION FIELDWORK: DOCUMENTS, INTERVIEWS, BUILDINGS

Several good books on historical methods have been written by trained historians. Older examples: Mary Sheldon Barnes, *Studies in Historical Method* (Boston: D.C. Heath, 1896); Gilbert J. Garraghan, *A Guide to Historical Method* (New York: Fordham University Press, 1946). A more recent manual: Robert Jones Shafer (ed.), *A Guide to Historical Method*, 3rd ed. (Homewood, IL: Dorsey, 1974). Also of use is the undergraduate manual: Norman F. Cantor and Richard I. Schneider, *How to Study History* (New York:

Thomas J. Crowell, 1967). For general comments, you may wish to consult Jacques Barzun and Henry F. Graff, *The Modern Researcher*, 4th ed. (San Diego: Harcourt Brace Jovanovich, 1985). The journal *Historical Methods* is also a useful source.

Oral history: Willa K. Baum's *Oral History for the Local Historical Society, 3rd ed.* (Nashville: American Association for State and Local History, 1987) is an excellent starting point. It includes step-by-step instructions by someone who knows a great deal about conducting oral history interviews. Transcribing techniques: Willa K. Baum, *Transcribing and Editing Oral History* (Nashville: American Association for State and Local History, 1977) and Mary Jo Deering, *Transcribing Without Tears: A Guide to Transcribing and Editing Oral History Interviews* (Washington, DC: George Washington University Library, 1976). Louis Gottschalk, Clyde Kluckhohn, and Robert Angell, *The Use of Personal Documents in History, Anthropology, and Sociology* (New York: Social Science Research Council, 1945), and Jan Vansina, *Oral Tradition as History* (Madison: University of Wisconsin Press, 1985) discuss oral interviewing as anthropology and history.

The definitive source on HABS/HAER documentation and surveying is John A. Burns (ed.), *Recording Historic Structures* (Washington, DC: American Institute of Architects Press, 1989).

Specialist literature:

Baker, T. Lindsay and Billy R. Harrison, *Adobe Walls: The History and Archaeology of the 1874 Trading Post.* (College Station: Texas A & M University Press, 1986).

Breen, T. H., *Imagining the Past: East Hampton Histories* (Reading, MA: Addison-Wesley, 1989).

Davidson, James West and Mark Hamilton Lytle, *After the Fact: The Art of Historical Detection.* (New York: Alfred A. Knopf, 1982).

Jurney, David H. and Randall W. Moir (eds.), *Historic Buildings, Material Culture, and the People of the Prairie Margin.* (Dallas: Archaeology Research Program, Southern Methodist University, 1987).

Landers, Jane, *Fort Mose, Gracia Real de Santa Teresa de Mose: A Free Black Town in Spanish Colonial Florida.* (St. Augustine: St. Augustine Historical Society, 1992).

Worthy, Linda H., *All That Remains: The Traditional Architecture and Historic Engineering Structures, Richard B. Russell Multiple Resource Area, Georgia and South Carolina.* (Atlanta: National Park Service, 1983).

CHAPTER 8: ARCHAEOLOGICAL FIELDWORK: FIELD AND LABORATORY

We lack an up-to-date field manual for New World archaeologists, so most people consult more general, often European, sources. Two good places to begin are Philip Barker's *Techniques of Archaeological Excavation,* 2nd ed. (New York: Universe, 1982), and Martha Joukowsky's *A Complete Field Manual of Field Archaeology: Tools and Techniques of Field Work for Archaeologists* (Englewood Cliffs, NJ: Prentice-Hall, 1980). Ivor Noël Hume's *Historical Archaeology,* already cited, is a classic, though somewhat outdated, source on fieldwork for historical archaeologists.

Field reports mentioned in the text: William Lees' study of Limerick Plantation appeared as *Limerick, Old and In the Way: Archaeological Investigations at Limerick Plantation* (Columbia: South Carolina Institute of Archaeology and Anthropology, 1980). Fort Southwest Point: Samuel D. Smith (ed.), *Fort Southwest Point Archaeological Site, Kingston, Tennessee: A Multidisciplinary Interpretation* (Nashville: Tennessee Department of Environment and Conservation, Division of Archaeology, 1993).

An excellent, easy-to-read book about simple artifact conservation is Per E. Guldbeck's *The Care of Historical Collections: A Conservation Handbook for the Nonspecialist* (Nashville: American Association for State and Local History, 1972). The Wolstenholme Towne helmets: Ivor Noël Hume, "First Look at a Lost Virginia Settlement," *National Geographic* 155, 6(1979):734–767; and "New Clues to an Old Mystery," *National Geographic* 161, 1(1982):52–77. Wolstenholme Towne is described in the same author's *Martin's Hundred* mentioned above.

For the basics of archaeological typology, you should consult widely available college texts. The Potomac Typological System, POTS, appeared in Mary C. Beaudry, Janet Long, Henry M. Miller, Fraser D. Neiman, and Garry Wheeler Stone, "A Vessel Typology for Early Chesapeake Ceramics: The Potomac Typological System," *Historical Archaeology* 17, 1(1983):18–43.

Specialist literature:

Crader, Diana C., The Zooarchaeology of the Storehouse and the Dry Well at Monticello. *American Antiquity* 49(1984):542–558.

——— Slave Diet at Monticello. *American Antiquity* 55(1990):690–717.

Herskovitz, Robert M., *Fort Bowie Material Culture* (Tucson: University of Arizona Press, 1978).

Reitz, Elizabeth J. and C. Margaret Scarry, *Reconstructing Historic Subsistence with an Example from Sixteenth-Century Spanish Florida.* (Tucson, AZ: Society for Historical Archaeology, 1985).

Stone, Lyle M., *Fort Michilimackinac, 1715–1781: An Archaeological Perspective on the Revolutionary Frontier* (East Lansing: The Museum, Michigan State University, 1974).

CHAPTER 9: EXPLAINING THE HISTORICAL PAST

Articles dealing with the development of historical archaeology up to 1978 can be found in Schuyler's *Historical Archaeology*. Humanistic studies: Robert Ascher and Charles H. Fairbanks, "Excavation of a Slave Cabin: Georgia, U.S.A., *Historical Archaeology* 5 (1971):3–17; William M. Kelso, *Kingsmill Plantations, 1619–1800: Archaeology of Country Life in Colonial Virginia* (Orlando: Academic Press, 1984). Scientific studies: Stanley South, *Method and Theory in Historical Archaeology;* Kenneth E. Lewis, *Camden: A Frontier Town in Eighteenth-Century South Carolina* (Columbia: South Carolina Institute of Archaeology and Anthropology, 1976). Studies by Deetz are: "Material Culture and Worldview in Colonial Anglo-America," in Leone and Potter's *The Recovery of Meaning*, pp. 219–233, and in his *In Small Things Forgotten*. His most recent, and less structuralist, book, is *Flowerdew Hundred: The Archaeology of a Virginia Plantation, 1619–1864* (Charlottesville: University Press of Virginia, 1993). Henry Glassie's book was published as

Folk Housing in Middle Virginia: A Structural Analysis of Historic Artifacts (Knoxville: University of Tennessee Press, 1975). Martin Hall's paper on Cape Town, South Africa, appears as "Small Things and the Mobile, Conflictual Fusion of Power, Fear, and Desire," in *The Art and Mystery of Historical Archaeology: Essays in Honor of James Deetz*, Anne Elizabeth Yentsch and Mary C. Beaudry (eds.), pp. 373–399. (Boca Raton, FL: CRC Press, 1992). Mark Leone's principal paper is: "The Georgian Order as the Order of Merchant Capitalism in Annapolis, Maryland," in Leone and Potter's *The Recovery of Meaning*, pp. 235–261. His paper on Mormon fences is "Archaeology as the Science of Technology: Mormon Town Plans and Fences," in *Research and Theory in Current Archaeology*, Charles Redman (ed.), pp. 125–150. (New York: John Wiley and Sons, 1973). Also extremely useful is Paul A. Shackel's, *Personal Discipline and Material Culture* mentioned above. An important statement on critical theory as it can be applied to historical archaeology is: Mark P. Leone, Parker B. Potter, Jr., and Paul A. Shackel, "Toward a Critical Archaeology," *Current Anthropology* 28(1987):283–302.

CHAPTER 10: THE ARCHAEOLOGY OF MODERN GROUPS

Class, ethnicity, gender, and race have generated a vast literature. The following are useful for our purposes: William C. McCready, *Culture, Ethnicity, and Identity: Current Issues in Research* (New York: Academic Press, 1983); H. Edward Ransford, *Race and Class in American Society: Black, Chicano, Anglo* (Cambridge, MA.: Schenkman, 1977); Peter I. Rose, *They and We: Racial and Ethnic Relations in the United States* (New York: Random House, 1981); and Stephen Steinberg's *The Ethnic Myth: Race, Ethnicity, and Class in America* (Boston: Beacon Press, 1989). These books, and the sources they cite, give an ample introduction to the topic of social groups. Marvin Harris' definition comes from his introductory textbook *Culture, People, and Nature: An Introduction to General Anthropology*, 4th ed., (New York: Harper and Row, 1985)

Specialist literature:

Baugher, Sherene and Robert W. Venables, Ceramics as Indicators of Status and Class in Eighteenth-Century New York. In *Consumer Choice in Historical Archaeology*, Suzanne M. Spencer-Wood (ed.), pp. 31–53. (New York: Plenum Press, 1987).

Brashler, Janet G., When Daddy was a Shanty Boy: The Role of Gender in the Organization of the Logging Industry in Highland West Virginia. *Historical Archaeology* 26, 4(1991):54–68.

Clark, Lynn, Gravestones: Reflections of Ethnicity or Class? In *Consumer Choice in Historical Archaeology*, Suzanne M. Spencer-Wood (ed.), pp. 383–395. (New York: Plenum Press, 1987).

De Cunzo, Lu Ann, *Economics and Ethnicity: An Archaeological Perspective on Nineteenth Century Paterson, New Jersey*. Ph.D. dissertation, University of Pennsylvania, Philadelphia.

Greenwood, Roberta S., The Chinese on Main Street. In *Archaeological Perspectives on Ethnicity in America: Afro-American and Asian American Culture History*, Robert L. Schuyler (ed.), pp. 113–123. (Farmingdale, NY: Baywood, 1980).

McEwan, Bonnie G., The Archaeology of Women in the Spanish New World. *Historical Archaeology* 26, 4(1991):33–41.

Mainfort, Robert C., Jr., *Indian Social Dynamics in the Period of European Contact: Fletcher Site Cemetery, Bay County* (East Lansing: The Museum, Michigan State University, 1979).

Mullins, Paul R., "A Bold and Gorgeous Front": The Contradictions of African America and Consumer Culture, 1880–1930. Unpublished paper presented at the School of American Research, Sante Fe, October, 1993.

Otto, John Solomon, Race and Class on Antebellum Plantations. In *Archaeological Perspectives on Ethnicity in America: Afro-American and Asian American Culture History,* Robert L. Schuyler (ed.), pp. 3–13. (Farmingdale, NY: Baywood, 1980).

Paynter, Robert, Steps to an Archaeology of Capitalism: Material Change and Class Analysis. In *The Recovery of Meaning: Historical Archaeology in the Eastern United States,* Mark P. Leone and Parker B. Potter, Jr. (eds.), pp. 407–433. (Washington, DC: Smithsonian Institution Press, 1988).

Sando, Ruth Ann and David L. Felton, Inventory Records of Ceramics and Opium from a Nineteenth-Century Chinese Store in California. In *Hidden Heritage: Historical Archaeology of the Overseas Chinese,* Priscilla Wegars (ed.), pp. 151–176. (Amityville, NY: Baywood, 1993).

Seifert, Donna J., Within Sight of the White House: The Archaeology of Working Women. *Historical Archaeology* 26, 4(1991):82–108.

Shepherd, Steven J., Status Variation in Antbellum Alexandria: An Archaeological Study of Ceramic Tableware. In *Consumer Choice in Historical Archaeology,* Suzanne M. Spencer-Wood (ed.), pp. 163–198. (New York: Plenum Press, 1987).

Wylie, Jerry and Richard E. Fike, Chinese Opium Smoking Techniques and Paraphernalia. In *Hidden Heritage: Historical Archaeology of the Oversees Chinese,* Priscilla Wegars (ed.), pp. 255–303. (Amityville, NY: Baywood, 1993)

CHAPTER 11: HISTORICAL ARCHAEOLOGY AROUND THE WORLD

Eric Wolf, *Europe and the People without History* (Berkeley: University of California Press, 1982) is a fundamental source for this chapter. A more popular account focusing on a variety of groups: Brian Fagan, *Clash of Cultures* (New York: W. H. Freeman, 1984). We used the following case studies in this chapter:

Birmingham, Judy, *Wybalenna: The Archaeology of Cultural Accommodation in Nineteenth Century Tasmania* (Sydney: Australian Society for Historical Archaeology, 1992).

DeCorse, Christopher R., Excavations at Elmina, Ghana. *Nyame Akuma: A Newsletter of African Archaeology* 28(1987):15–18.

———— Historical Archaeological Research in Ghana, 1986–1987. *Nyame Akuma* 29(1987):27–31.

Ewen, Charles R., *From Spaniard to Creole: The Archaeology of Cultural Formation at Puerto Real, Haiti* (Tuscaloosa: University of Alabama Press, 1991).

Gasco, Janine, Material Culture and Colonial Indian Society in Southern Mesoamerica: The View from Coastal Chiapas, Mexico. *Historical Archaeology* 26, 1(1992):67–74.

Posnansky, Merrick and Christopher R. DeCorse, "Historical Archaeology in Sub-Saharan Africa: A Review." *Historical Archaeology* 20, 1(1986):1–14.

Rice, Prudence M. and Greg C. Smith, The Spanish Colonial Wineries of Moquegua, Peru," *Historical Archaeology* 23, 2(1989):41–49.

Schrire, Carmel, The Historical Archaeology of the Impact of Colonialism in Seventeenth-Century South Africa. In *Historical Archaeology in Global Perspective,* Lisa Falk (ed.), pp. 69–96. (Washington, DC: Smithsonian Institution Press, 1991)

———— Digging Archives at Oudepost I, Cape, South Africa. In *The Art and Mystery of Historical Archaeology,* Anne Elizabeth Yentsch and Mary C. Beaudry (eds.), pp. 361–372. (Boca Raton, FL: CRC Press, 1992).

CHAPTER 12: THE PAST IN THE PRESENT

United States legislation appears in King, Hickman, and Berg's *Anthropology in Historic Preservation,* already cited, pp. 199–302, and in Philip Speser and Kathleen Reinburg, *Federal Archaeology Legislation: A Compendium, Vol. 4* (Washington: Foresight Science and Technology, 1986). Copies of this legislation are readily available in all states at the office of the state archaeologist.

Site visitation at Annapolis is covered in: Mark Leone "Method as Message: Interpreting the Past with the Public," *Museum News* 62, 1(1983):34–41, and in Parker B. Potter, Jr., *Public Archaeology in Annapolis: A Critical Approach to History in Maryland's Ancient City.* (Washington, DC: Smithsonian Institution Press, 1994). An important statement of the program appears, with the comments of critics and supporters, in Leone, Potter, and Shackel, "Toward a Critical Archaeology," mentioned above. A critique of the Carter's Grove slave quarters appears in Terrence W. Epperson's "Race and the Disciplines of the Plantation," *Historical Archaeology* 24, 4(1990):29–36.

Political uses of archaeology: An excellent starting point is Peter Gathercole and David Lowenthal (eds.), *The Politics of the Past,* (London: Unwin Hyman, 1990). This book contains information about the Nazis' program of "archaeology," as well as information about the efforts of several indigenous groups to reclaim their histories.

Site destruction, vandalism, and looting: Ian Graham, "Looters Rob Graves and History," *National Geographic* 169, 4(1986):452–461; George E. Stuart, "The Battle to Save Our Past," *National Geographic* 175, 3(1989):392–393; Brian Alexander, "Archaeology and Looting Make a Volatile Mix," *Science,* 250(1990):1074–1075; James Walsh, "It's a Steal," *Time* 138, 21(1991):86–88; Christopher B. Donnan, "Archaeology and Looting: Preserving the Record," *Science* 251(1991):498. A good overview of the Slack Farm controversy is Harvey Arden's "Who Owns the Past?" *National Geographic* 175, 3(1989):376–392.

Controversies over artifact collecting: Gillett B. Griffen, "In Defense of the Collector," *National Geographic* 169, 4(1986):462–465; and Colin Renfrew, "Collectors are the Real Looters," *Archaeology* 46, 3(1993):16–17.

Job opportunities and training in historical archaeology: Your best source is a professional archaeologist, but a short booklet, *Opportunities in Historical Archaeology,* is still available from the Society for Historical Archaeology.

Other sources used in preparing this chapter are: Jane Busch, "An Introduction to the Tin Can," *Historical Archaeology* 15, 1(1981):95–104; J. Douglas McDonald, Larry J. Zimmerman, A. L. McDonald, William Tall Bull, and Ted Rising Sun, "The Northern Cheyenne Outbreak of 1879: Using Oral History and Archaeology as Tools of Resistance." In *The Archaeology of Inequality*, Randall H. McGuire and Robert Paynter (eds.), pp. 64–78. (Oxford: Basil Blackwell, 1991); and Charles E. Orser, Jr., *Historical Archaeology at Marsh House (Residence Hill Site, 16IB130), Avery Island, Louisiana.* (Avery Island: Avery Island, Inc., 1987).

Glossary

This glossary gives informal definitions of key words and ideas in the text. It is not a comprehensive dictionary of historical archaeology. Jargon is kept to a minimum, but a few technical expressions are inevitable. Some terms commonly used in archaeology but not specifically described in this book are also included here for convenience.

absolute dating: Dating in calendar years before the present; chronometric dating.

activity area: A patterning of artifacts in a site indicating that a specific activity, such as stone toolmaking, took place.

activity set: A set of artifacts that reveals the activities of an individual.

Age of Discovery: The period of Western expansion, c. A.D. 1415 to about 1800.

analogy: A process of reasoning whereby two entities that share some similarities are assumed to share many others.

analysis: A stage of archaeological research that involves describing and classifying artifactual and nonartifactual data.

anthropology: The study of humanity in the widest possible sense. Anthropology studies humanity from the earliest times up to the present, and it includes cultural and physical anthropology, anthropological linguistics, and archaeology.

antiquarian: Someone interested in the past who collects and digs up antiquities unscientifically, in contrast to the scientific archaeologist.

archaeological context: See **context.**

archaeological culture: A group of assemblages representing the surviving remains of an extinct culture.

archaeological data: Material recognized as significant as evidenced by the archaeologist and collected and recorded as part of the research. The four main classes of archaeological data are artifacts, features, structures, and food remains.

archaeological reconnaissance: Systematic attempts to locate, identify, and record the distribution of archaeological sites on the ground and against the natural geographic and environmental background.

archaeological theory: A body of theoretical concepts providing both a framework and a means for archaeologists to look beyond the facts and material objects for explanations of events that took place in the past.

archaeological unit: Arbitrary unit of classification set up by archaeologists to separate conveniently one grouping of artifacts in time and space from another.

archaeologist: Someone who studies the past using scientific methods, with the motive of recording and interpreting ancient cultures rather than collecting artifacts for profit or display.

archaeology: A special form of anthropology studying extinct human societies or extinct phases of surviving cultures using material remains. The objectives of archaeology are to construct culture history, reconstruct past lifeways, and study cultural process.

archaeomagnetic dating: Chronometric dating using magnetic alignments from buried features, such as pottery kilns, which can be compared with known fluctuations in the earth's magnetic field and produce a date in years.

Archaic: In the New World, a period when hunter-gatherers were exploiting a broad spectrum of resources and may have been experimenting with agriculture.

area excavation: Excavation of a large, horizontal area, usually used to uncover houses and settlement patterns.

artifact: Any object manufactured or modified by human beings.

assemblage: All the artifacts found at a site, including the sum of all subassemblages at the site.

association: The relationship between an artifact and other archaeological finds at a site.

attribute: A well-defined feature of an artifact that cannot be further subdivided. Archaeologists identify types of attributes, including form, style, and technology, to classify and interpret artifacts.

attribute analysis: Analyzing artifacts using many of their features. Usually these attributes are studied statistically to produce clusters of attributes that can be used to identity statistical classes of artifacts.

burial site: An archaeological site once used for burying the dead, especially cemeteries.

cambium: A viscid substance under the bark of trees, in which the annual growth of wood and bark takes place.

ceramics: Objects of fired clay.

chronological types: Types defined by form that are time markers.

chronometric dating: Dating in years before the present; absolute dating.

class: Two definitions: In archaeology, a general group of artifacts, like "bottles," which will be broken down into specific types, like "wine bottles" and so on. In a wider context, a group of people who have a similar relationship to the structure of social control in a society, and who possess similar amounts of power over the allocation of wealth, privilege, resources, and technology.

Classical archaeologist: A student of the classical civilizations of Greece and Rome.

classification: The ordering of archaeological data into groups and classes, using various ordering systems.

cognitive archaeology: A theoretical approach to archaeology concerned with patterns behind material culture.

commodity: An object created for exchange and trade.

community: In archaeology, the tangible remains of the activities of the maximum number of people who together occupy a settlement at any one period.

component: An association of all the artifacts from one occupation level or chronological period at a site.

conservation archaeology: Another name for cultural resource management.

context: The position of an archaeological find in time and space, established by measuring and assessing its associations, matrix, and provenience. The assessment includes study of what has happened to the find since it was buried in the ground.

core borer: A hollow tubelike instrument used to collect samples of soils, pollens, and other materials from below the surface.

cranial: Of or pertaining to the skull (cranium).

critical theory: A theoretical approach to archaeology that assumes that archaeologists have an active impact on their society.

crop marks: Differential growth in crops and vegetational cover that reveals the outlines of archaeological sites from the air.

cross-dating: Dating of sites by objects of known age, or artifact association of known age.

cultural anthropology: The aspect of anthropology focusing on cultural facets of human societies (a term widely used in the United States).

cultural evolution: A theory similar to that of biological evolution, which argues that human cultures change gradually throughout time, as a result of a number of cultural processes.

cultural materialism: A combination of critical theory and materialism in historical archaeology.

cultural process: A deductive approach to archaeological research that is designed to study the changes and interactions in cultural systems and the processes by which human cultures change throughout time. Processual archaeologists use both descriptive and explanatory models.

cultural resource management: The conservation and management of archaeological sites and artifacts as a means of protecting the past.

cultural system: A perspective on culture that thinks of culture and its environment as a number of linked systems in which change occurs through a series of minor, linked variations in one or more of these systems.

culture: Human culture is a set of designs for living that help mold our responses to different situations. It is our primary means of adapting to our environment. A "culture" in archaeology is an arbitrary unit meaning similar assemblages of artifacts found at several sites, defined in a precise context of time and space.

culture area: An arbitrary geographic or research area in which general cultural homogeneity is to be found.

culture history: An approach to archaeology assuming that artifacts can be used to build up a generalized picture of human culture and descriptive models in time and space and that these can be interpreted.

datum point: A location from which all measurements on a site are made. The datum point is tied into local survey maps.

deduction: A process of reasoning that involves testing generalizations by generating hypotheses and testing them with data. Deductive research is cumulative and involves constant refining of hypotheses. Contrasts with inductive approaches where one proceeds from specific observations to general conclusions.

demography: The study of population.

dendrochronology: Tree-ring chronology.

descriptive types: Types based on the physical or external properties of an artifact.

direct historical analogy: Analogy using historical records or historical ethnographic data.

direct historical approach: Archaeological technique of working backward in time from historic sites of known age into earlier times.

discourse: The interaction between material objects, written texts, and spoken words.

domestic site: Site where household domestic activities take place.

dowsing: Locating archaeological sites using movements of a stick, a technique that can only be used by relatively few people, who have the "touch."

epiphysis: The articular end of a long bone, which fuses at adulthood.

ethnic group: An assemblage of people who share enough common physical and cultural characteristics to define themselves as a group perceived as different from others.

ethnicity: The characteristics an ethnic group accepts as pertinent to them.

ethnoarchaeology: Living archaeology, a form of ethnography that deals mainly with material remains. Archaeologists carry out living archaeology to document the relationships between human behavior and the patterns of artifacts and food remains in the archaeological record.

ethnobotany: The study of ancient plant remains.

ethnography: A descriptive study, normally an in-depth examination of a culture.

ethnohistory: Study of the past using non-Western, indigenous historical records, and especially oral traditions.

ethnology: A cross-cultural study of aspects of various cultures, usually based on theory.

evolutionary archaeology: An explanatory framework for the past that accounts for the structure and change in the archaeological record.

excavation: The digging of archaeological sites, removal of the matrix and observance of the provenance and context of the finds therein, and the recording of them in a three-dimensional way.

exchange system: A system for exchanging goods and services between individuals and communities.

experimental archaeology: The use of carefully controlled modern experiments to provide data to aid in interpretation of the archaeological record.

feature: An artifact such as a house or storage pit, which cannot be removed from a site; normally, it is recorded only.

form: The physical characteristics—size and shape or composition—of any archaeological find. Form is an essential part of attribute analysis.

form analysis: Analysis of artifacts based on the assumption that the shape of a pot or other tool directly reflects its function.

formation processes: Humanly caused or natural processes by which an archaeological site is modified during or after occupation and abandonment.

foot (or pedestrian) survey: Archaeological reconnaissance on foot, often with a set interval between members of the survey team.

formula dating: Absolute dating using artifact attributes, especially applied to pipe stems and ceramics.

functionalism: The notion that a social institution within a society has a function in fulfilling all the needs of a social organism.

functional type: Type based on cultural use or function rather than on outward form or chronological position.

geographic information systems: Computer-generated mapping systems that allow archaeologists to plot and analyze site distributions against environmental and other background data derived from remote sensing, digitized maps, and other sources.

general systems theory: The notion that any organism or organization can be studied as a system broken down into many interacting subsystems, or parts; sometimes called cybernetics.

ground-penetrating radar: See Pulse Radar.

HABS/HAER survey: Historic American Buildings Survey/Historic American Engineering Record, standards for historic surveys of buildings in the United States.

half-life: The time required for one half of a radioactive isotope to decay into a stable element. Used as a basis for radiocarbon and other dating methods.

hieroglyphs: Ancient writing form with pictographic or ideographic symbols; used in Egypt, Mesoamerica, and elsewhere.

historical archaeology: The study of archaeological sites from the modern period in conjunction with historical records and other kinds of information. It is sometimes called historic sites archaeology.

historical structuralism: An approach to historical archaeology that tries to discover the hidden themes and relations in a culture.

historiography: The study of how history is written.

history: Study of the past through written records.

hominid: A member of the family *Hominidae,* represented today by one species, *Homo sapiens.*

horizon: A widely distributed set of culture traits and artifact assemblages whose distribution and chronology allow one to assume that they spread rapidly. Often, horizons are formed of artifacts that were associated with widespread, distinctive religious beliefs.

horizontal (area) excavation: Archaeological excavation designed to uncover large areas of a site, especially settlement layouts.

household unit: An arbitrary archaeological unit defining artifact patterns reflecting the activities that take place around a house and assumed to belong to one household.

humanistic historical archaeology: Archaeological research intended to complement the humanistic side of history.

ideology: The knowledge or beliefs developed by human societies as part of their cultural adaptation.

induction: Reasoning by which one proceeds from specific observations to general conclusions.

industrial archaeology: The study of sites of the Industrial Revolution and later.

industrial site: In historical archaeology, a site where manufacturing of commodities takes place.

inorganic materials: Material objects that are not part of the animal or vegetable kingdom.

interpretation: The stage in research at which the results of archaeological analyses are synthesized and we attempt to explain their meaning.

kinship: In anthropology, relationships between people that are based on real or imagined descent or, sometimes, on marriage. Kinship ties impose mutual obligations on all members of a kin group; these ties were at the core of most prehistoric societies.

leaching: Water seeping through the soil and removing from it the soluble materials.

lineage: A kinship group that traces descent through either the male or female members. In a lineage, direct ancestry to a lineage founder is known.

magnetometer: A subsurface detection device that measures minor variations in the earth's magnetic field and locates archaeological features before excavation.

markers' marks: Manufacturing marks etched or stamped onto mass-produced ceramics, glassware, and metals. Also called "hallmarks."

material culture: Normally refers to technology and artifacts.

materialism: Theoretical perspectives where the reality of physical matter takes precedence over ideas and thought processes.

mean ceramic dating formula: A formula used for dating ceramics by their date ranges of manufacture.

military site: An archaeological site where military activities took place, usually a battlefield or fort.

mitigation: In archaeology, measures taken to minimize destruction on archaeological sites.

model: A theoretical reconstruction of a set of phenomena, devised to understand them better. Archaeological models can be descriptive or explanatory.

multipurpose site: An archaeological site where many different activities took place.

natural transformations: Changes in the archaeological record resulting from natural phenomena that occur after the artifacts are deposited in the ground.

natural type: An archaeological type coinciding with an actual category recognized by the original toolmaker.

neighborhood: A group of households within a well-defined area.

oral tradition: Historical traditions, often genealogies, passed down from generation to generation by word of mouth.

ordering: In archaeology, the arranging of artifacts in logical classes and in chronological order.

organic materials: Materials such as bone, wood, horn, or hide that were once living organisms.

Paleolithic: The Old Stone Age.

paleontology: The study of fossil (or ancient) bones.

palynology: Pollen analysis.

physical anthropology: Basically, biological anthropology, which includes the study of fossil human beings, genetics, primates, and blood groups.

Pleistocene: the last major geological epoch, extending from about two million years ago until about 11,000 B.C. It is sometimes called the Quaternary, or the Great Ice Age.

pontil scar: The characteristic mark left on the base of glass vessels by breaking off the glass blower's rod.

postprocessual archaeology: Theoretical approaches to archaeology that are critical of processual archaeology and that emphasize social factors in human societies.

POTS: Potomac Typological System, a system for classifying ceramics used in the Chesapeake Bay area of Virginia and Maryland.

potsherd: A fragment of a clay vessel.

prehistory: The millennia of human history preceding written records. Prehistorians study prehistoric archaeology.

primary context: An undisturbed association, matrix, and provenance.

primary source: An original historical source, like a letter.

privy: A toilet.

probate records: A record of a dead individual's estate, an important source of historical information.

process: In archaeology, the process of cultural change that takes place as a result of interactions between a cultural system's elements and the system and its environment.

protohistoric: See Secondary Prehistory.

provenience: The position of an archaeological find in time and space, recorded three-dimensionally.

proximal: Opposite to distal: the end of a bone nearest to the skeleton's center line.

radiocarbon dating: An absolute dating method based on measuring the decay rate of the carbon isotope, carbon 14, to stable nitrogen. The resulting dates are calibrated with tree-ring chronologies from radiocarbon ages into dates in calendar years.

redistribution: The dispersal of trade goods from a central place throughout a society, a complex process that was a critical part of the evolution of civilization.

region: A geographically defined area in which ecological adaptations are basically similar.

relative chronology: Time scale developed by the law of superposition or artifact ordering.

remote sensing: Reconnaissance and site survey methods using such devices as aerial photography to detect subsurface features and sites.

research design: A carefully formulated and systematic plan for executing archaeological research.

resistivity survey: Measurement of differences in electrical conductivity in soils, used to detect buried features such as walls and ditches.

Sanborn maps: Maps produced by the D. A. Sanborn National Insurance Diagram Bureau (later, the Sanborn Map and Publishing Company) beginning in the mid-nineteenth century. These maps show the location and construction type of all buildings in the town or city mapped.

scanner imagery: A method of recording sites from the air using infrared radiation that is beyond the practical spectral response of photographic film. Useful for tracing prehistoric agricultural systems that have disturbed the topsoil over wide areas.

science: A way of acquiring knowledge and understanding about the parts of the natural world that can be observed. A disciplined and highly ordered search for knowledge carried out systematically.

secondary context: A context of an archaeological find that has been disturbed by subsequent human activity or natural phenomena.

secondary prehistory: The time when literate people came in contact with and wrote about nonliterate peoples. Often termed "protohistoric."

secondary source: A historical source that itself draws on primary sources.

selective excavation: Archaeological excavation of parts of a site using sampling methods or carefully placed trenches that do not uncover the entire site.

settlement archaeology: Investigation of ancient settlement patterns.

settlement pattern: Distribution of human settlement on the landscape and within archaeological communities.

site: Any place where objects, features, or other finds manufactured or modified by human beings are found. A site can range from a living site to a quarry site, and it can be defined in functional and other ways.

site plans: Specially prepared maps for recording the horizontal provenience of artifacts, food remains, and features. They are keyed to topographic maps.

site survey: Collection of surface data and evaluation of each site's archaeological significance.

slip: Fine, wet clay finish applied to the surface of a clay vessel before its firing and decoration.

social anthropology: The British equivalent of cultural anthropology, with emphasis on sociological factors.

sociocultural: Combining social and cultural factors.

soil phosphate analysis: Measuring phosphate levels in the soil to detect the presence of human settlement.

sonar: Underwater detection using sound waves.

spectrographic analysis: Chemical analysis that involves passing the light from a number of trace elements through a prism or diffraction grating that spreads out the wavelengths in a spectrum. This enables one to separate the emissions and identify different trace elements. A useful approach for studying metal objects and obsidian artifacts.

stratification: The formation by natural processes of geological layers. Also used in archaeology to refer to the formation of social classes in human societies.

stratigraphy: Observation of the superimposed layers in an archaeological site.

stratum: A single layer of soil or a social level.

structuralism: A perspective that attempts to discover the hidden themes and relations in a culture.

style: In an evolutionary context, a means of describing forms that do not have detectable selective values.

stylistic analysis: Artifact analysis that concentrates not only on form and function, but on the decorative styles used by the makers—a much-used approach to ceramic analysis.

subassemblage: Association of artifacts denoting a particular form of prehistoric activity practiced by a group of people.

subsurface testing: Any small-scale archaeological excavation.

surface survey: The collection of archaeological finds from sites, with the objective of gathering representative samples of artifacts from the surface. Surface survey also establishes the types of activity on the site, locates major structures, and gathers information on the most densely occupied areas of the site that could be most productive for total or sample excavation.

synthesis: The assemblage and analysis of data preparatory to interpretation.

taxonomy: An ordered set of operations that results in the subdividing of objects into ordered classifications.

technological analysis: Study of technological methods used to make an artifact.

temper: Coarse material such as sand or shell added to fine pot clay to make it bond during firing.

tempering: A process for hardening iron blades, involving heating and rapid cooling. Also, material added to potters' clay.

test pit: An excavation unit used to sample or probe a site before large-scale excavation or to check surface surveys.

text-aided archaeology: see Historical Archaeology.

three-age system: A technological subdivision of the prehistoric past developed for Old World prehistory in 1806.

topographic maps: Maps that can be used to relate archaeological sites to basic features of the natural landscape.

total excavation: Complete excavation of an archaeological site. Usually confined to smaller sites such as burial mounds or campsites.

trace elements: Minute elements found in rocks that emit characteristic wavelengths of light when heated to incandescence. Trace-element analysis is used to study the sources of obsidian and other materials traded over long distances.

tradition: Persistent technological or cultural patterns identified by characteristic artifact forms. These persistent forms outlast a single phase and can occur over a wide area.

transformational processes: Processes that transform an abandoned settlement into an archaeological site through the passage of time. These processes can be initiated by natural phenomena or human activity.

type: In archaeology, a grouping of artifacts created for comparison with other groups. This grouping may or may not coincide with the actual tool types designed by the original manufacturers.

underwater archaeology: Study of archaeological sites and shipwrecks beneath the surface of the water.

uniformitarianism: Doctrine that states the earth was formed by the same natural geological processes that are operating today.

unit: In archaeology, an artificial grouping used for describing artifacts.

use–wear analysis: Microscopic analysis of artifacts to detect signs of wear through use on their working edges.

vertical excavation: Excavation undertaken to establish a chronological sequence, normally covering a limited area.

votive: Intended as an offering as a result of a vow.

zooarchaeology: The study of animal remains in archaeology that provides information about subsistence practices and past environments.

Credits

54	Charles P. Mountford. © National Geographic Society
58	From the collections of Henry Ford Museum & Greenfield Village
61	Middleton Place Foundation
62	Hume, Ivor Noel. Historical Archaeology (New York: Alfred A. Knopf, 1969)
63	Library of Congress
64	Ned Heite

Chapter 4

73	U.S. Forest Service
77	Courtesy of the Trustees of the Wedgwood Museum, Barlaston, Staffordshire, England
78	Coca-Cola USA
80	Godden, Geoffrey A. Encyclopedia of British Pottery and Porcelain Marks (New York: Bonanza, 1964)
81	Godden, Geoffrey A. Encyclopedia of British Pottery and Porcelain Marks
82	Department of Anthropology, University of Minnesota
84	U.S. Patent Office
87	Phillippe, Joseph S. The Drake Site: Subsistence and Status at a Rural Illinois Farmstead (Normal, IL: Midwestern Archaeological Research Center, 1990)
92	Shackel, Paul A. Personal Discipline and Material Culture: An Archaeology of Annapolis, Maryland, 1696–1870 (Knoxville: University of Tennessee Press, 1993)

Chapter 5

99	Colonial Williamsburg Foundation
101	Charles Orser
102	Graphic by Adrian Praetzellis and Nelson Thompson. Praetzellis, Mary; Praetzellis, Adrian: For a Good Boy: Victorians on Sacramento's J Street (Rohnert Park, CA: Anthropological Studies Center, Sonoma State University, 1990)
103	Colonial Williamsburg Foundation
104	Hume, Ivor Noel, A Guide to Artifacts of Colonial America (New York: Alfred A. Knopf, 1972)
105	Harrington, J. C. Dating Stem Fragments of Seventeenth and Eighteenth Century Clay Tobacco Pipes, 1954
109	North Carolina Department of Cultural Resources
110	North Carolina Department of Cultural Resources
111	Kent, Susan. Analyzing Activity Areas: An Ethnoarchaeological Study of the Use of Space (Albuquerque: University of New Mexico Press, 1984)
112	Granger
116	Koch, Augustus. Bird's-Eye View of the City of Sacramento, State of California (San Francisco: Britton & Rey, 1870)

117	Graphic by Adrian Praetzellis and Nelson Thompson. Praetzellis, Mary; Praetzellis, Adrian: For a Good Boy: Victorians on Sacramento's J Street. (Rohnert Park, CA: Anthropological Studies Center, Sonoma State University, 1990)
119	Charles Orser

Chapter 6

122	Sean Smith/The Guardian
123	Colonial Williamsburg Foundation
127	Minute Man National Historic Park
128	Bibliotheque Service Hydrographic, Paris, France #C4040–24.
129	William L. Clements Library
131, 132, 133	Contribution #8, Chaco Center, NPS and University of New Mexico
134	F. Terry Norris, U.S. Army Corps of Engineers
138	J. W. Weymouth; W. I. Woods. Combined Magnetic and Chemical Surveys of Forts Kaskaskia and de Chartres Number 1, Illinois. (Historical Archaeology, vol. 18, number 2, 1984)

Chapter 7

147	Panhandle Plains Historical Society
148	Library of Florida History, University of Florida
149	National Museum of the American Indian, Smithsonian Institution
151 (top)	The Kansas State Historical Society
151 (bottom)	The Kansas State Historical Society
154 (top)	HABS Collections, Library of Congress
154 (bottom)	HABS Collections, Library of Congress

Chapter 8

160	South Carolina Institute of Archaeology and Anthropology
164	Quarterly Bulletin of the Archaeological Society of Virginia 46(1), 1991
168	Tennessee Division of Archaeology
169	Tennessee Division of Archaeology
171	Tennessee Division of Archaeology
172	Tennessee Division of Archaeology
173 (top)	Tennessee Division of Archaeology
173 (bottom)	Tennessee Division of Archaeology
178	Mary C. Beaudry, Janet Long, Henry M. Miller, Fraser D. Nelman, Garry W. Stone. A Vessel Typography for Early Chesapeake Ceramics: The Potomac Typological System (Historical Archaeology 17:1, 1983)

Chapter 9

184	Archives, Virginia Department of Historic Resources
185	Archives, Virginia Department of Historic Resources
187	South, Stanley: Method and Theory in Historical Archaeology (New York: Academic Press, 1977)
188	University of South Carolina Institute of Archaeology and Anthropology
189	University of South Carolina Institute of Archaeology and Anthropology
192	Grunnitus, Monkmeyer
194	Plimouth Plantation
195	Anne Yentsch from Yentsch, A E., Beaudry, M. C., eds.: The Art and Mystery of Historical Archaeology: Essays in Honor of James Deetz. (Boca Raton: CRC Press, 1992)

Chapter 10

201	Massachusetts Bureau of Statistics of Labor
211	Wylie, Jerry, Fike, Richard E. Chinese Opium Smoking Techniques and Paraphenalia, in Hidden Heritage: Historical Archaeology of the Overseas Chinese. Priscilla Wegarsm, ed. (Amityville, NY: Baywood Publishing Company, Inc. 1993)
217	J. S. Otto. Cannon's Point Plantation, 1794–1860: Living Conditions and Status Patterns in the Old South (Orlando: Academic Press, 1984)

Chapter 11

222	Charles Orser
223	Charles R. Ewen. From Spaniard to Creole: The Archaeology of Cultural Formation at Puerto Real, Haiti (Tuscaloosa: University of Alabama Press, 1991)
228	H. Ruther
229	Schrire, Carmel. The Historical Archaeology of the Impact of Colonialism in Seventeenth-Century South Africa. From: Historical Archaeology in Global Perspective, Lisa Falk, ed. (Washington, DC: Smithsonian Institution Press, 1991)
232	State Library of New South Wales

Chapter 12

237	Colonial Williamsburg Foundation

Index

PAVILLON DENON

LOUVRE
PARIS

Newsweek/GREAT MUSEUMS OF THE WORLD

NEW YORK, N.Y.

**GREAT MUSEUMS
OF THE WORLD**

Editorial Director—Carlo Ludovico Ragghianti
Assistant—Giuliana Nannicini
Translation and Editing—Editors of ARTNEWS

LOUVRE
PARIS

Texts by:

Gigetta Dalli Regoli
Decio Gioseffi
Gian Lorenzo Mellini
Licia Ragghianti Collobi
Pier Carlo Santini

Design:

Fiorenzo Giorgi

Published by

NEWSWEEK, INC.
& ARNOLDO MONDADORI EDITORE

Library of Congress Catalog Card No. 68-19927

© 1967—Arnoldo Mondadori Editore—CEAM—Milan

© 1967—Photographs Copyright by Kodansha Ltd.—Tokyo

All rights reserved. Printed and bound in Italy

DEDICATION FROM THE LOUVRE

JEAN CHATELAIN
Director of the Museums of France

The space reserved in this series for the great French museums, the Louvre, the Musée National d'Art Moderne and the Guimet (Oriental art) would alone justify my gratitude, as Director of French museums. The scope and audacity of the project is equal to its usefulness, and the last quality will be immediately apparent to a knowledgeable public: sophisticated art lovers, critics and curators, for whom this vast editorial endeavor will facilitate comparisons and confrontations between objects and works of art distributed through the world's great museums.

In more general terms, the proliferation of publications devoted to museums offers, when they are of high quality, one of the most powerful means of combating the major obstacle to the complete efficiency of museums: that is, the general public's distrust, based upon ignorance of the museums' role and usefulness. The material conditions for a greater use of museums have now been met in all highly developed countries. The rise of standard of living and of education, the increase in leisure time, the growing possibilities for travel—all these factors should contribute to creating a potential museum public, not only much larger, but far more varied than that of the past. But in the eyes of a large sector of this potential public, the museum too often seems a secret world, a place restricted to a few initiates where they are afraid to enter in fear of being, or seeming to be, ignorant. Every publication of quality devoted to museums contributes to the dissipation of this fear.

However, there is no question, even for those in charge of museums, of considering attendance an end in itself: the full growth of mankind remains the only objective of any real value. But we believe profoundly that, from now on, and still more in the future, the museum will be one of the means whereby man, at the end of the twentieth century, will achieve this growth, while maintaining a balance between his material well-being and intellectual and moral satisfactions. Progress in modern technology frees us more each day from the condition which burdened our fathers, bringing a constant stream of new improvements to man's environment. But this progress is accompanied by growing uniformity, as well as by a moral and emotional drain. Let us take aviation as an example of a modern technique. With ever increased speed, we fly from one international airport to another, but the two look so much alike that it seems hardly worthwhile to have made the trip. And as for the mechanism of the airplane, it is comprehensible only to the specialized technician. This schism threatens every material area of life. Thus we must concern ourselves now with a taste for the humane, so that our children will be able to preserve it in the better world which will be theirs. They must be able to retrace the long efforts expended through the centuries to arrive at the year 2000. We must preserve for them, in the midst of material comforts, a taste for things which are simply beautiful or moving, whether they be masterpieces which have survived the years, a craftsman's humble tools or the imperfect attempts made by a rudimentary machine. The role of the museum is to preserve all those things which bear witness to the slow evolution of man and to his constant search for the beautiful and useful. Their directors must guard against the kind of pride which insists that everything which contributes to the progress and attendance of museums, contributes, at the same time, to the improvement of man's destiny. But museums are the invaluable humanizing elements of tomorrow's society.

PREFACE

RENÉ HUYGHE
of the French Academy

Culture—by which I mean humanist culture—was born on that day when the Latin tongue affirmed with Terence: "Nothing human is foreign to me." Some twenty centuries later, a painter this time, and a Fleming, Rubens, gave this thought still more resonance by proclaiming: "I consider the entire world my homeland." In every country of the world, the museum, using the international language of art which, needing no translation, addresses itself to the sight, mind and heart of each, echoes this teaching.

The nucleus of any museum is, naturally, its national art, since there is no life force which is not nourished by roots. But as the tree grows and reaches out, it climbs, spreading in the open air, and within this space, sees the circle of its own horizon widen with its growth. And so it is with man. Like the human spirit, the museum spreads its branches, first towards its sister civilizations, then neighboring ones, then foreign, and, finally, towards those most remote and exotic. Its pediment should be inscribed with the words of Rubens, with this slight change: "I consider the entire world my culture."

If there is one museum which can unquestionably make such a proclamation of faith, it is the Louvre. Fruit of French civilization, this crossroads where all races—Mediterranean, Northern and Eastern— have mingled, always has stood for openness and mutual understanding. The Louvre has always resisted the modern tendency towards specialization; within this immense palace whose arms enfold the grassy Tuileries, reaching to the far side of the Place de la Concorde, to the Jeu de Paume, where the Impressionists are hung, it houses the treasure of centuries and nations. Beginning with ancient Egypt, at the moment when an agrarian civilization emerged from the limbo of prehistory, its masterpieces proliferate until, with the modern period, the museum refuses a commitment to current trends and their uncertainties, preferring to wait until time and history make a choice. Always in search of the rare object, the Louvre, in spite of the co-existence of important specialized museums in the Paris region, such as the Guimet or Cernuschi, boasts its own collection of Oriental art. And having the Musée des Arts Décoratifs within its very perimeter makes it possible to juxtapose the décors of life with those masterpieces which history has claimed as the highest achievements of each period. It is a gigantic "complex," as today's term has it, where man's efforts to leave a trace, a legacy upon which his major successes would be inscribed, commingle and complete one another in ever-renewed waves. A gigantic unity where, as we look closely, we see a unity in depth and where, thanks to the close association of what might have been separate museums, and which is now only a rich diversity of "departments," the press of humanity traces its path through the centuries, veering from left to right, but without ever abandoning the common bed-rock from which the tide of man's immense aspiration surges to realize the best within himself. The visitor must pass through numberless galleries in order finally to become aware of that *"élan vital"* of Bergson, of that ardent search whose apparent goals may vary, but which, in its totality, only passes through diverse transformations to reach an exaltation of quality itself—the ultimate rationale of man perhaps—and in any case, his certain attribute.

The museum is pre-eminently an instrument of culture, and culture essentially consists of transcending oneself, to become concerned with what is external to the ego. Since Kant, we have been aware that art was one of the most characteristic expressions of culture, since it is the image of man's most *disinterested* activity. This progressive conquest by which man overcomes his nature and, within the limits of his daily routines, surmounts immediate and direct self-interest, through growing powers of transcendance from animal to man, to reach, finally, that superior degree which we call humanism—these are the stages we can follow through a museum like the Louvre.

Its point of departure was the desire of the Kings of France, a desire nourished by Greed, to establish a collection: and its "seed" may be discerned in its library, so rich in illuminated manuscripts, formed by Charles V in the old Louvre itself, his own palace, which then occupied the southwest corner of the present *Cour Carrée*. With Francis I, we come to the "collector's cabinet," comprising several masterpieces by contemporary Renaissance masters, some of whom were court painters, and foremost of these, Leonardo da Vinci, who died in Francis' castle at Amboise.

The simultaneous acquisition of antique art at this time began to broaden the collection, starting a trend whose peak would be reached under Louis XIV—the study of classical sources and copies of antique culture which dominated the West at that time. Through a policy of individual purchases, combined with the acquisition of international collections already formed by rich private citizens, such as Jabach, the King of France acquired representative objects, landmarks in the development of a civilization upon whose summit he considered himself poised, its progress unfolding from the Age of Pericles to Papal Rome.

Doubt and anxiety appeared in the form of those masterpieces of Venetian art whose political and economic history bridged two different worlds: Central Europe and the northern Germanic world, called "barbaric" by the ancients, and as such, duly ignored, and the East, with Constantinople as its frontier city. From the end of the seventeenth century and the reign of Louis XIV, a new taste began to insinuate itself, one which would entail a change of values and the collapse of old boundaries; a mounting admiration for Northern art, the Dutch and Flemish, whose works would reveal a spirit altogether different from that of the Latins, even while they preached the same lessons.

Thus, those tendencies gathered force which would finally erupt in the nineteenth century, giving birth to Romanticism. France, discovering her solidarity with Northern Europe, tried to lay claim to that area within her own past closest to the contemporary spirit: Medieval art, and especially the Gothic, whose name, however erroneous, was sufficiently indicative of its attraction. The concept of "national antiquities" was exemplified by the Musée des Monuments Français, established during the Revolution, and whose beginnings would soon form the nucleus of the Department of Modern Sculpture in the Louvre. Henceforth, the boundaries of Western culture would be dim; later they would dissolve altogether. Classical Antiquity lost its monopoly on the origins of art, as archeology discovered a territory far more vast. First Egypt, then Mesopotamia, at first known through Assyrian art, revealed those antecedents through which Western art had come into contact with the East. Thanks to French scholars, to their expeditions and excavations, the Louvre could add departments of Egyptology and Assyriology.

Thus the groundwork was laid for the discovery of Oriental civilization, the work of the last half of the nineteenth century: its main impetus was the opening of Japan to foreigners and the ensuing trade which resulted. An important collection of Japanese prints was added to the Drawings Department. It was also at this time that the Louvre yielded to the pressure of still farther reaching curiosity. Interest in so-called primitive societies, Pre-Columbian and African, finally required, at the beginning of the twentieth century, the creation of specialized museums.

In the meantime, another important change had come about. The Royal Collection, gradually opened to visitors, was, in the course of the eighteenth century, transformed into a public museum. The Gallery of Marie de' Medici, painted by Rubens for the Queen Mother's palace in the Luxembourg Gardens (and today in the Louvre) became, under Louis XV, accessible to artists and art lovers at regular visiting hours. It remained for the Revolution to make this change official, by establishing a public Louvre, belonging to the nation and open to all. At this time, it was constituted along the lines of its present organizational structure, and in the nineteenth century several generations of curators were to fill in the outlines of a program of almost world-wide dimensions, but in which the East was still only summarily represented by Islamic art and Japanese prints. The Louvre remains the center of a circle of Parisian museums gravitating around it (it also houses the offices of the Direction of French Museums) which in their totality combine to give a picture of the whole sweep of civilization.

What can we retain from such a vast and complex picture? What guideline is there to follow? Above all else, it is the life spirit of art which we hope to grasp in such a confrontation with time and space. Egypt and Mesopotamia emerge from pre-history, as their societies become organized into agrarian civilizations, whose stability and cumulative revenue made possible the founding of cities, and finally, 11 of the State. In these river valleys, where irrigation is the source of fertility, the primordial problem is one of property: at first, the regulation of agriculture, then the establishment of a system of taxation, the basis of government resources. The primordial science thus became geometry, which organized the division of surfaces and facilitated the re-constitution of fields after flooding.

The most ancient art form serves to evoke religious or historical scenes which constitute a rationale for the image. The problem became one of striking an appropriate balance between respect for the life thus evoked and the simplified order of its depiction. In different, though parallel ways, Egypt and Mesopotamia each resolves this problem in the third century B.C. The scenes of daily life with which artists under the Pharoahs immortalized tomb walls with chisel or brush reveal that same harmony between the perceived and the conceptual that we find in the reliefs of hunting and battle scenes which seventh to ninth century B.C. Assyrian artists carried to their highest point of refinement.

Both civilizations heavily influenced the beginnings of Greek art. Nor should we forget the example provided by the statues of Assyrian Kings. It was Egypt, nonetheless, which first explored the spirit which would reach perfection under Hellenic skies. The Egyptian artist, constrained to repeat subjects fixed and unchangeable in their every detail, was obliged to concentrate all effort, all creative power upon the quality of his work, in the movement of delicacy of the line through which he expressed himself. Thus, to the ordered perfection of form and surface, developed by Greek artists, to the suppleness and freedom allowed them by the birth of the city-state, Egypt was the first to add that subtlety and harmony through which an artist attains the full measure of his powers. Later, at the other end of the earth, Japanese artists would triumph with an equally sublime fusion of craft and spirit.

What was the contribution of Greece? For one, the element of independence. Every citizen was free and thus competed freely within the City. The Greek learned initiative. From more or less perfect imitation, he moved to invention, as much in the objectives of his art (opening a wider area to reality) as in his style (making possible esthetic experiment) and creation. From then on, Greek art was no longer burdened by dogma and tradition, but subject to intellectual examination. The Greek artist questioned art and nature. Conceiving beauty, he forced himself to define it. What had previously been only intuitive, became lucid. Art thus benefited from its new state of consciousness and from the experimentation stimulated by new awareness.

Gradually, Greek art was superseded by Roman, which imitated and copied Greek works, with particular emphasis on their more materialized, naturalistic elements. And, by the same token, the unique aura of quality, the mark of classical genius, evaporated from the Roman copies. Inversely, late Roman art was characterized by a preoccupation with the inner life, which gradually supplanted the search for plastic harmony. The philosophers of the late antique world gave precedence to personal problems of man's destiny, as religion became permeated by currents of mysticism which radically changed its logical structure. Thus the ground was prepared for the seeds of Christianity coming from Judea, in the Eastern Mediterranean. The new faith infiltrated, absorbed and finally overturned the domain of the Roman Empire, replacing the realistic, rational spirit, implanted by Greco-Roman antiquity, with a spiritual fervor, strongly colored by the East. Subsequently, the center of the Western Empire was transferred from Rome to Constantinople, which then became the capital of the Byzantine Empire. For more than ten centuries, the remains of the classical tradition were, in diluted form, absorbed into an art where spiritual realities would henceforth count for more than the realities of the visible world; moreover, this turn towards the East was accentuated by the proximity of Persia, the ancient adversary of Rome, where the last vestiges of Mesopotamian civilization were perpetuated, interwoven with Far Eastern influences carried from China by the route of the silk trade. Such was the new Christian art under the aegis of Byzantium.

The westernmost part of the Mediterranean, however, would remain bound to Europe, and, after the great leveling and vast fusions of the Barbarian invasions, gathered its forces to establish an autonomous Christian civilization which we know as the Middle Ages.

A first Carolingian "Renaissance" in the ninth century tried to bring some coherent order to the surviving elements of antiquity, and acknowledged as valuable sources the contributions of barbarian civilization to areas such as metalwork. In the following century, despite the wave of Eastern influence reinforced first by pilgrimages to the Holy Land, then by the Crusades, the stifled voice of Latin civilization arose with renewed energy. The results of this rebirth was Romanesque art, in which ancient, restored Roman structures were welded to a sculptural repertory in which barbaric elements were joined to those of declining Byzantium and emergent Islam.

But in this opposition of Western civilization reborn and an Eastern world characterized by the Islamic conquest of Byzantium, Europe was the galvanizing force. And this time it was Northern elements,

12

superseding the Latin heritage, which played the more active and creative role. From the beginning of the twelfth century, a new style and spirit predominated, which we call, however inaccurately, Gothic, and whose center was the Ile-de-France. Here the force and vitality, as seen in its architecture and images which turned progressively towards a rediscovery of nature, enveloping the old formalist cult, imbuing it with new intensity and dynamic: the spiritual life of Christianity encountered a source of expression commensurate with its nature.

Soon Europe, under the leadership of an Italy avid to reclaim past glory, would feel equal to the task of rebinding herself to the tradition of classical antiquity and to revive within this new civilization the spirit which had forged the ancient grandeur of the West. Painting emerged and asserted itself in the course of the declining Middle Ages; its role then had been a modest one, limited to miniatures and to a few frescoes. The dominant religion had enlisted the best talents in a campaign for the beautification of its churches. And there, the art of mosaic, Byzantine in origin and translated to Italy, of stained glass, the magical development of a barbarian art, and, again, of tapestry, were, in the North, subsidiary to architecture. The devout were absorbed by a common faith and preferred those arts better adapted to a collective scale. Then, with the thirteenth century, the rise of the bourgeoisie gave new directions to art; with hard-won material wealth, and the sense of personal property, art returned to a worldly and human level. The painting, property or gift of a corporation, was soon to become more and more often a private possession, the pride and delight of its owner, and thus assumed a growing importance. And with this change, painting began to reign supreme.

In the fourteenth and fifteenth centuries, however, Italy and the Northern countries manifested these changes differently. Medieval Italy was dominated by Byzantine influences, which had carried the spiritual inspiration and ascetic aspects of Christianity to their highest degree. Mosaics, schematic and sanctified with their shimmering gold backgrounds, suggested the approach of the divinity. Italian painting thus had the task of placing these theological abstractions within reality, returning these schema to a world of volumes and space. Naturally, this new art sought the positive forms which it needed to reincarnate them from the still-viable traditions of Greco-Roman sculpture. From the spiritualized abstractions of Byzantium, Italian art moved uninterruptedly towards those structures which reason brilliantly conceived and then generalized. The Virgin of Cimabue indicates the brilliance with which this transition was accomplished. Like Giotto in the next generation, these artists had not abandoned a world dominated by the intellect; they simply modified the concepts of theocentric transcendance with more rational evidence.

In the Northern countries, the other pole of European art, this departure created special problems: their artists had also been formed by a Middle Ages bathed in Christian fervor, in which every attribute of the visible world was a symbol of God. But here, more than elsewhere, and particularly in the Low Countries, where the cloth-trade played a dominant economic role, material realities had imparted to faith a more concrete consistency, very close to the things of this world and their presence. Since the thirteenth century, the Middle Ages had inclined towards a growing realism. One might say that throughout the Western world, a natural movement of gravity led from the divine to the human level, but in Northern Europe, this movement was conceived as a vindication of the senses and of external observation. Italy, however, nourished by the sense of her antique past as the highest point of civilization, saw in the Renaissance the occasion to revive pagan culture (as witness, for example, the *Parnassus* of Mantegna, or the *Apollo and Marsyas* of Perugino) and interpreted this movement on an intellectual plane, as a flowering of intelligence in all its forms.

The Flemish found their mode of expression at the beginning of the fifteenth century with the art of Jan van Eyck and his new discoveries in oil technique, which made possible an illusionist rendering of the material aspect of the universe. At the beginning of the sixteenth century, Quentin Metsys demonstrates, in *Portrait of a Moneychanger and his Wife,* how quickly the evolution had taken place; brilliant rendering is placed at the service of a concrete vision and specific interest. The way was opened for Dutch naturalism of the seventeenth century and the subtle, rigorous recording of everyday existence. The genius alone could occasionally assert the individual spark of his own sensibility, to transform the flatness of reality by the crystalline purity of the soul which perceived it: such an artist was Jan Vermeer of Delft.

When Italy turned to the same problems of transcribing the visual world, she interpreted their solution less as a tribute to the powers of vision than as an exaltation of those of intelligence, capable of solving problems in every domain. For it was intellect which organized and constructed the forms designed to render volume, intellect which organized and constructed perspective, devised to translate the breadth and depth of space wherein these volumes would be placed. In Italian painting as well, geo- 13 metric analysis often took precedence over optical analysis, as seen, for example, in the fifteenth-century *Rout of San Romano* of Paolo Uccello. This rigor, the basis for Leonardo Da Vinci's observation that painting is a "cosa mentale" was nonetheless tempered by two factors: one, inherited from the near medieval past was the continuation of that moving tenderness of divine revelation, disseminated by the Gothic influence and present to a greater degree in Sienese art whose more emotive genius found its most typical expression in Simone Martini than in Florentine painting, where genius assumed more intellectual form, exemplified by the art of Ghirlandaio whose charm is invested with intense fervor. The other factor was the inevitable influence of Northern painting, whose scientific technique Italian artists, like Antonello da Messina and Giovanni Bellini (Mantegna's brother-in-law) were proud to have acquired for their own.

Thus the way was prepared for that great flowering of Italian art which took place in the sixteenth century, the High Renaissance. Italian artists joined the sources of optics, developed by the North, to the intellectual organization unique to their own tradition. Yet at the same time, this art retained the sense of transcendance which, reaching towards God in past centuries, now tended towards a more worldly interpretation: the search for quality as expressed by an ideal of beauty.

In the works of three great masters, these elements are fused and carried to their culminating point of genius. The eldest was Leonardo da Vinci, whose youth was formed by the fifteenth century, and in whose art all the possibilities of painting were subjected to the domination of the human mind, conscious and proud of its powers, daring even to extend them to that farthest realm where only intuition and the unconscious were thought to reside. The *Mona Lisa* penetrates the enigma of being, respected in all its indefinable nature. Leonardo still stirs the shadowy regions, expressive of his magic. Raphael, on the other hand, makes the purest light unequivocally reveal the harmonies of body and soul. His *Portrait of Baldassare Castiglione* is the quintessential humanist. But with the art of the third giant, Michelangelo, we already hear the rumblings of discontent, a need to burst every limitation, as we can see in his *Slave,* strangled by his crushing burden. The unquenchable yearning of the Baroque, soon to supersede Classicism throughout Europe and to rekindle the stormy passions of life, was already beginning to emerge.

A closer link between Northern and Mediterranean Europe was created, at this same period, by Venetian painting, the northernmost school of Italian art. Imbued more than the others by the spirit of the East, Venice, whose seaport led to the Orient, was also an outlet for the Germanic countries. Dürer, the greatest German painter of the Renaissance, made several long visits there. Like Flanders, with whom it enjoyed close relations, Venice was ruled by a mercantile patrician class. It was Venetian artists who shattered the boundaries of Italian genius, with its tendency to be limited by pure intelligence. Here, conversely, an insatiable taste developed for material splendors—the richness of flesh, fabrics, color and light. But where the North had taught them to copy with veracity, Venice, having once absorbed this fifteenth-century lesson, transformed it by means of such opulent additions to the painting itself as colored glass inlays. Among the great High Renaissance painters, it was Corregio of Parma who could most subtly evoke this shiver of sensuality. From Giorgione, who died prematurely, to his friend Titian, who dominated the century, to Veronese, inventor of tonal harmonies hitherto unimagined in their coloristic brilliance and silvery sheen, to Tintoretto, whose frustrated and tormented genius seems to usher in the age of modern anxiety—these painters all revealed an art whose repercussions would be enormous for the destiny of painting: henceforth, painting would have to discover within itself those riches which previously it had been content to transcribe. And no painter exemplifies this discovery with as much coloristic subtlety and technical daring as Velazquez.

Venice, however, had still other contributions to make. From the very beginning of the sixteenth century, Giorgione had shown that art could be the most secretive, as well as most profound expression of the artist's personality, and the orchestration of colors and light could, as in music, be the emanations of a soul. His *Concert Champêtre* reveals a universe born of the artist's dreams, to which he has given himself and through which he appears to others. Somewhat later than Giorgione, a more solitary and bitter genius, El Greco, moving from Greece to Venice before settling in Spain, created works of such violently personal vision that for a long time they were considered merely bizarre and ignored as such.

It was only with the seventeenth century that these newly liberated forces were to reveal all their potential. In Italy, at the very start of the century, Caravaggio abruptly broke with the Renaissance ideal of formal beauty. Thus the way was paved for a new art form: in Flanders, Rubens substituted the flood of life in all its lyricism for the scientific harmony of form, in that same Baroque direction begun by Michelangelo; in Holland, Frans Hals expressed this verve with a technique so boldly modern as to surpass the Venetians in its freedom; here, too, Rembrandt exhausting every resource of personal vision, revealed what a powerful and profound nature could leave the world through its own imprint—a breadth and significance which shattered and eclipsed the literal sense of vision. Reworked, recreated, this vision became nothing less than the soul made manifest in all its unknown power to discover in the depths of itself that spiritual retreat which it had sought since the Middle Ages within a communal faith, and for which the Renaissance had substituted the organization of intellectual and positive resources of tangible reality.

Thus each school of European painting had its turn at the center of the stage as, in turn, the contribution of each became more highly evolved. Until this time, French painting had played more of a mediating role. Midway between Italy and the North, French art had, during the Middle Ages and the reign of the Gothic, dominated the Northern regions of Europe; its "primitive" painters were more allied to the Flemish esthetic, while bringing to this tradition their own qualities of delicacy and tenderness. In the south, however, French painting displayed its particular aptitude to participate in the Mediterranean genius, as we can see in the almost Spanish accents of the Avignon *Pietà*.

The French vocation for psychology may be seen in the work of a brilliant series of portraitists. Fouquet, formed by the traditions of Italy where he had studied, was the most highly representative in the fifteenth century. In the sixteenth, affinities with Northern realism became, especially with Clouet, more sharply defined. From then on, the intermediate position of France allowed her to turn to the growing prestige of the Italian High Renaissance for lessons in harmony, to which, with the School of Fontainebleau, France added the pronounced elegance of her own tradition. This appropriation of classical territory became still more defined in the seventeenth century when the two greatest French painters, Poussin and Claude Lorrain settled in Rome. That spiritual realism, however, in which the national equilibrium found its expression, was represented by the Le Nain brothers, by Georges de La Tour (influenced by Caravaggio and only recently discovered) and by French still-life painting.

In the seventeenth century, a change in direction made it possible for French painting, threatened by desiccation, to turn towards Rubens and to Flemish art, finding, so to speak, an antidote in the life and lyricism of the North. Boucher confined himself to conferring a new sensual vitality upon a classical repertory, but his disciple, Fragonard, with more audacity still, borrowed as much from Rubens as from Rembrandt. And the painting of Chardin brings together all the resources of a newly liberated pictorial craft applied to the traditions of familiar realism.

Nonetheless France, now moving to the cultural forefront, whose influence spread increasingly throughout Europe, was still to make her major contribution to Western art. Her psychological vocation, ever more refined, was the genesis of the marvel which is French portraiture, whether painting or sculpture. Through it, she would achieve the perfect fusion of two recent revelations which had shaken European art: this vocation consciously sought to express the individual in those areas which seemed to defy revelation, and to this end, it forged a language whose pictorial technique created a new domain. From the very beginning of the eighteenth century, and even before the death of Louis XIV, Watteau had revealed himself, in this double role, to be an innovator as astounding as had been Giorgione, his predecessor by two centuries. Watteau's example was not to be understood immediately. The nineteenth century, on the contrary, began by the attempt to revive the classical disciplines, as exemplified by the art of David and his disciple, Ingres. Baron Gros provided a counter-current to this Neo-Classicism, and finally, Géricault galvanized these spiritual outpourings and Romanticism reached its plenitude. Another painter, Delacroix, united classical reflection with Romantic passion to nourish a lyric power illuminating an ardent soul consumed by torment and yearning, at the same time that this painter's interest in the exotic breached the boundaries of traditional culture.

Delacroix's art was superseded by Realism which leaned heavily upon scientific discoveries and a triumphant positivism. From Millet's epic vision to the substantial Courbet, this movement reassured itself, through a patient observation of reality, that it was doomed. The Impressionists, whose goal had been to extend Realism, ended by exhausting it. The role of energy, that particular element of contemporary life, was just then revealed to them, exciting their interest in its most visible expression —light. In the mid-nineteenth century, Corot became the most delicate bard of light, reflecting the exquisite and dreamy sensibility incarnate in his figures and landscapes. Under the impetus of Corot, the Impressionists sacrificed everything to the investigation of light first begun by Claude Lorrain. Degas was followed by Toulouse-Lautrec who, resisting this trend, continued to explore the possibilities of realism by consecrating it to the observation of contemporary life, and by endowing this realism with the mordancy which gives his art its particularly modern stamp. Change had also come about with Manet, an older painter, who both transformed Impressionism and was influenced by it, 15 while, at the same time, remaining faithful to a classical construction of space. In the following generation, Camille Pissarro still retained a rustic density inherited from Millet. It was, however, Claude Monet, above all, who atomized the universe, hurling it into a chromatic vibration in which form and matter were definitively dissolved. From then on, the real had lost its reality: the traditional scaffolding of painting had collapsed.

Consequently, painting now had to be reconstructed. Renoir, already allied to tradition through his admiration for Rubens and Delacroix, remained faithful to the carnal architecture of the body and exalted it. The Post-Impressionists, led by Paul Cézanne, while yielding nothing of the Impressionists' optical veracity, returned painting to its pure elements: form and color, and by expressing one through the other, proved each to possess a unique force distinct from imitation. From this revelation were to emerge Cubism and abstract art. Gauguin's contribution carried him a step further, proving that form and color could be used in all combinations, thus breaking the shackles of truth, as measured by the familiar appearance of things, and devoting his art, instead, to expressive force, to reveal the inner world of the artist. His contemporary, van Gogh forged ahead in this same direction, casting colors and forms into a burning brazier where, flaming and twisting, their fire illuminated the tormented bursts of the artist's sensibility.

Everything was ready for a new era in art, an era in which the artist would have the freedom to find grandeur outside of his own past and his own traditions.

ANCIENT EGYPT

SEATED SCRIBE. *V Dynasty.*

This famous statue of an unnamed scribe was discovered in the course of a disorganized excavation conducted by the famous 19th-century French Egyptologist Auguste Edouard Mariette at Sakkara. In 1921, it was found to bear a close resemblance to a seated statue of the monarch Kai which had been shipped to the Louvre after the same excavation. This Egyptian official has thus survived in two monuments.

The statue is considered one of the masterpieces of Egyptian art. On the one hand it is intensely realistic, particularly in the level gaze of the eyes, which are inlaid with highly polished hard stone. On the other hand, and in striking contrast to this realism, the sculptural forms are severely geometric. The figure is adamantly frontal, preserving something of the original four-sided block of stone from which it was cut. It is as if the artist had thought in terms of four juxtaposed bas-reliefs instead of a monument in the round. This peculiarly Egyptian attitude toward the block leaves its traces in almost all Egyptian sculpture, and is evident, for example, in the flat planes of the scribe's back.

Egyptian art is characterized by the artists' attempts to seek out and depict a figure's most typical or most significant view. Hence we find profile heads with eyes shown frontally, and frontal torsos with legs and arms in profile. This approach is connected with man's normal vision and is always present to a greater or lesser extent in primitive arts. Yet one cannot call Egyptian art "primitive." It is with civilizations of the ancient periods that certain rules for principal views (in painting and for reliefs) and for frontality (in sculpture in the round) become binding. These two aspects stem from one and the same phenomenon, based on a new need for architectonic order and pictographic clarity. The mastabas and pyramids of Old Kingdom Egypt expressed this need for geometric and architectonic order, while the development of hieroglyphic writing did the same for pictographic, narrative clarity. From then on, the canon affected every branch of Egyptian art, its repertory lasting for millennia. The sculptor of the V dynasty, however, while working in a tradition which was already centuries old, was not subdued completely by the system. He accepted parts of the code, but he felt free enough to make a few choices on his own, filling out a given scheme with his own esthetic experience. Thus he was able to add realist touches to the otherwise abstract figure of the Seated Scribe.

HEAD OF KING DEDEFRE. *IV Dynasty.*

King Dedefre's portrait, while as realistic as the representations of courtiers in the Old Kingdom, differs from them in its smooth, firm

Seated Scribe
V Dynasty (2563–2423 B.C.):
circa 2500 B.C.
Painted limestone; 21″ high
From Sakkara.

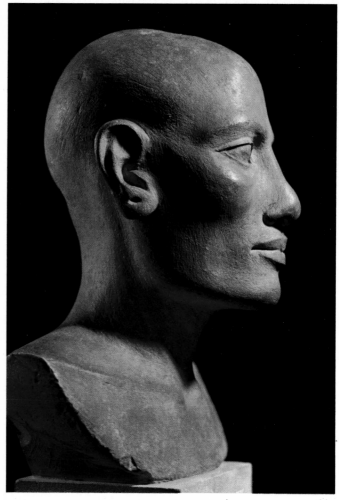

modeling. His royal crown *(nemsit),* with the emblematic snake *(ureus)* rising above the headband, imparts a Cubistic quality to the head with a suggestion of architectonic modules.

HEAD OF A YOUNG MAN (THE SALT HEAD). *IV Dynasty (?).* The so-called Salt Head—named after its former owner—has been dated to periods as much as 14 centuries apart, a startling difference of opinion which is explicable only in the case of an art like Egypt's, where the artistic language crystallized at the dawn of its history and remained uninflected by the passing of the centuries. This head is problematic because of its relative independence of the Egyptian esthetic code. It has a naturalism characteristic of just two phases in Egyptian art—the Old Kingdom, with its nascent realism, and the Amarna phase, with its markedly realistic trend. The Salt Head seems to fit better into the second of the two because of its "life-mask" quality typical of certain works from the Amarna epoch.

GIRL WITH A LOTUS. *V Dynasty (?).*
This representation of a girl smelling a flower exemplifies the technique

Above:

Head of a Young Man
IV Dynasty (2723–2563 B.C.) or Amarnian period (second quarter of XIV century B.C.) Painted limestone; 13 1/4″ high. Origin unknown; formerly in the Salt collection, thus known as the "Salt Head."

Left:

Head of King Dedefre, Cheop's Brother and Immediate Successor
IV Dynasty; XXVII century B.C.
Red Sandstone; 11″ high
From Aburoash.

Girl with Lotus
V Dynasty (?)
Painted limestone; 21″ high.

20

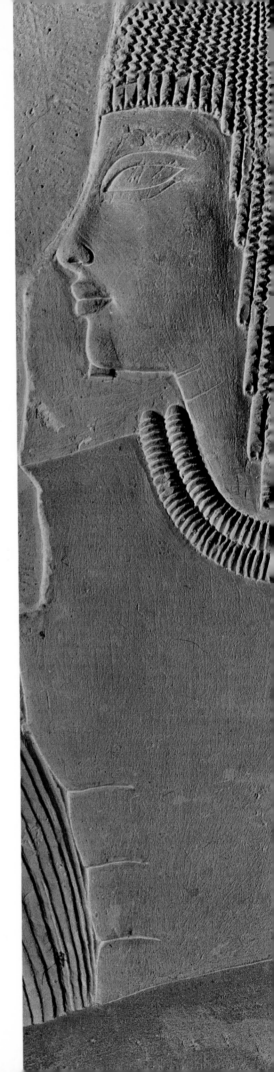

of incised relief work, a favorite medium in Egyptian art. Rather than projecting from the background, the body receives the dimension of depth only by the incision of its outlines. This gives the figure an abstract quality akin to the effect achieved by modern solar photography and emphasizes the contour lines, which assume a fluid elegance almost independent of the body.

REHERKA AND MERSANKH. *V Dynasty.*

A characteristic Old Kingdom type of statue is the family group, in which the figures were conceived as separate entities and juxtaposed. There is also the "false" group, in which two statues representing the same person are paired. In the latter, the image has become a definitive symbol: no longer are two "objects" occupying the same space, but an idea is repeated twice within the same context. The group Raherka and Mersankh, on the other hand, is distinguished by a more explicit intention to represent reality by giving the pair a more naturalistic appearance, with the woman leaning confidently on the man.

AMENMES AND HIS WIFE. *XVIII Dynasty.*

Amenmes' funerary relief, datable around the Amarna period, typifies the Theban school in the New Kingdom. The stylistic conventions clearly belong to the code developed in the Old and Middle Kingdoms, yet they are confined here by a discipline which was previously absent.

22

*Pharaoh Taharka Offering Two Wine Cups
to the Falcon God Hemen*
XXV "Ethiopian" Dynasty (circa 689–
680 B.C.) Schist, wood, bronze (the base is
covered with silver, the falcon is gilded); 7 4/5″
high, 4″ wide, 10 1/4″ long.

The originality of the work lies in the subtle variations on the traditional rhythmic composition and design. Here, as in the relief of the Girl with a Lotus, we can appreciate the elegance of the outline and the clarity of incision.

THE PHAROAH TAHARKA OFFERING TWO WINE CUPS TO THE FALCON GOD HEMEN. *XXV Dynasty.*

Bronze sculpture which flourished in Mesopotamia, appears later in Egypt than elsewhere in the Near East. Small bronzes are common in Egypt only after the XXII Dynasty, and are often inlaid with precious metals or decorated with gold leaf.

PREPARATIONS FOR A BANQUET. *V Dynasty.*

The detail illustrated here comes from a series of reliefs which decorated the walls of the funerary chapel of the Mastaba of Akhuthotep. Banquet scenes like this were conventional in Egyptian funerary art, and they served to project earthly pleasures into the afterlife. Apparently Akhuthotep died before the decoration of his chapel was finished. The registers above the portion illustrated here still bear traces of squared-off guidelines which served either as a guide for enlarging a smaller drawing of the banquet scene or as modules for an artist working with canonical proportions. Either possibility demonstrates the academism of pharaonic art, which, more than in any other art, tied artists to traditions established by the past. Yet at the same time Egyptian art was not static. To the casual observer there may be no difference between this work and that of the New Kingdom, but closer examination of this relief compared to that of Amenmes is instructive. Two butchers grasp the leg of an ox and one of them slices it with a large knife. Their torsos are shown in profile from the shoulder down, while Amenmes' torso is shown frontally; at the same time the legs and heads of all three are in profile. The attempt to show the butchers in complete profile heightens the strong diagonals of the composition, which combine with the rectilinear forms of the bodies and the curves of the animal's leg to create a subtle interplay of linear motifs and triangular spaces.

Preparations for a Banquet
Detail from reliefs in the funerary chapel
of the Mastaba of Akhuthotep
V Dynasty
Painted limestone; 14″ high.

25

ROYAL HEAD. *XVIII Dynasty*.
A typical product of the Amarna period, this wooden head decorated the top of a harp. The styles characteristic of this period were connected with the religious reforms of Amenhotep IV—Ikhnaton. The term "expressionistic" has often been applied to the monuments of this period because of their curious combination of realistic with stylized linear elements. The head illustrated here resembles official portraits of the Pharaoh, whose physical abnormality may have formed the basis for the experimental stylization typical of the Amarna period. It is the product of a refined art, with its delicate interplay of soft curves and long smooth planes, expressing something akin to the European decorations of the late nineteenth-century Art Nouveau period.

ROYAL HEAD. *XVIII Dynasty*.
This head of a young Pharaoh is covered with two glazes of blue faience. If, as is probable, this is a head of Tutenkhamon, it would be one of the most typically Amarnian works of his brief reign. Especially characteristic is the oblique slant of the enormous almond eyes, which, as in the art of the Extreme Orient, is more a stylistic than a racial trait, its source lying in a keen feeling for the sophistications of linear design.

SPHINX FROM TANIS. *Middle Kingdom*.
The Hyksos king Apopi, Meneptah (son of Rameses II), and Seshonk I (XXII Dynasty) in turn usurped the colossal Sphinx of Tanis which dates from the Middle Kingdom (reigns of Sesotri III and Amenemhet III) as well as other examples from the same era. Ancient as this stone representation is, the iconography of the sphinx is even older.

Above:

Royal Head
End of XVIII Dynasty
Opaque two-toned glass (formerly inlaid with stone and metal); 3 1/2″ high.

Left:

Royal Head
End of XVIII Dynasty
Ornament in colored wood for top of a harp (formerly inlaid with stone and metal in the eye sockets and eyebrows); height of entire piece 7 1/4″ of which about 3″ were inserted in the neck of the instrument. From Tell el Amarna; acquired by the Louvre in 1932.

Sphinx from Tanis
Middle Kingdom
Red granite; 81″ high, 136″ long.

26

OSTRAKON: RAMESSIDE HEAD WITH THE ATTRIBUTES OF OSIRIS. *XX Dynasty.*

The Greek work *ostraka* (meaning sherd or shell) is used to designate stone scraps or fragments on which Egyptian artists made sketches of preparatory designs, and these have been found in relatively large numbers. They probably were studies for paintings, rather than sculpture, as the summary indications of color suggest. In general these sketches are merely outlines, similar to those traced on walls preceding the execution of stone reliefs.

The drawing illustrated here demonstrates the characteristic graphic mannerism of the XIX Dynasty, the origin of which might be connected with the linearism of Amarnian art. The nose has the characteristic curving profile and the eye is reduced to an elegant ornamental motif. It is no longer schematic, as the Egyptian canon demanded, but hints at a more naturalistic profile.

THE SINGER OF AMON, ZEDKHONSUAUFANKH, PLAYS THE HARP BEFORE THE GOD HARMAKHIS. *New Kingdom.*

The singer, on his knees before the seated figure of the god, plays a harp decorated with a royal head. The man's face is depicted in the expressionistic manner of the Amarna period, both in the interplay of curve and plane and in the realistic feature of the open mouth holding its note for all eternity. The colors are elementary—a white background, with areas of red-orange, dark green and yellow—but the brushwork is fluid and easy, so that the outlines and the bodies they define blend into a whole.

The Singer of Amon, Zedkhonsuaufankh, Plays the Harp before the God Harmakhis
New Kingdom
Painted wood; 11 1/2″ high.

Ostrakon: Ramesside Head with the Attributes of Osiris
XX Dynasty (1200–1085 B.C.)
Sketch in red and black for a wall decoration;
limestone; 8 1/3″ high.

28

Statue of the Chancellor Nakht
Middle Kingdom, XII Dynasty
(1991–1786 B.C.)
Painted wood (inlaid eyes); 69″ high.
From Assiut.

STATUE OF THE CHANCELLOR NAKHT. *XII Dynasty.*
The statue of Nakht is one of the most remarkable pieces of wooden sculpture preserved from the Middle Kingdom. It retains traces of original polychromy and is almost completely covered by red paint. The rigid frontality of the figure follows the tradition of Old Kingdom sculpture. In comparison with Memphis statuary, this statue demonstrates a tighter synthesis of volumes, avoiding any unnecessary deviation from pure geometric forms. Thus the roundness of the head is accentuated by its smoothness (hair was probably painted on), and the nose has no nostrils. Similarly, the long skirt with its stiff apron forms a truncated pyramid and reflects an architectural feeling for geometric form. The arms hang stiffly at the sides of the body, yet the artist has injected a certain naturalism in the gesture of the right hand, which pulls the garment aside hiding the thumb in a crease of the cloth.

TORSO OF ISIS. *Ptolemaic Period.*
The torso is undoubtedly a fragment of a statue of Isis. The frontality of the figure, left leg advancing slightly, the stiffly hanging arms, the round breasts and the exaggerated height of the stomach are entirely in keeping with the Egyptian artistic tradition. Yet if one compares this work with a torso from the Amarna period, the influence of Greek art becomes evident. The drapery, knotted below the breasts and falling down the body between the legs, is depicted with a certain plasticity not apparent in the Amarna torso, where the lines are incised rather than modeled. This statue is not, however, a product of a colonial art, nor is it a Greek version of a traditional Egyptian work, a copy done by someone with antiquarian interests. It is a product of an indigenous culture which was becoming increasingly Hellenized in spite of a desire to remain faithful to Egyptian tradition.

FEMALE TORSO. *XVIII Dynasty.*
The fragment illustrated here is typical of the Amarna style, not as much for the linear quality of the drapery as for the prominent stomach and thighs. The former motif goes back to the dawn of Egyptian art, and in the course of the XVIII Dynasty found wide expression and numerous modifications. The latter shows an attempt to project horizontal and vertical lines into a third dimension, rounding the surface of the relief as if it were a portion of the body of a vase. This feature also characterizes pharaonic iconography, and its source has been sought in the supposed physical deformation of Ikhnaton. It could lie, however, in the artists' deliberate rebellion against the traditionally contained, almost columnar forms of Egyptian art; the result of this rebellion found an analogy in the ideal of the "pregnant nude," which also characterized European art in the late Gothic period.

Torso of Isis
Ptolemaic Period (Greek-Alexandrian)
330–30 B.C.
Diorite sculpture in the round; 27 1/4″ high.

Female Torso
End of XVIII Dynasty (1370–60 B.C.)
Red quartz; 11 4/5″ high.
Probably from Tell el Amarna

31

HEAD OF A PRINCESS. *XVIII Dynasty.*

The extraordinary refinement and surprising versatility of the Amarna period attains full expression in this fragment found in Tell el Amara, dating from the end of Ikhnaton's revolution (more precisely, between the reigns of Ikhnaton and Tutenkhamon, 1358 B.C.). The asymmetry of the wig, apparently characteristic of children's hair fashions, stands in contrast to the symmetry and geometric precision of the face. The cheeks seem as if traced out by a compass, and the hairline forms the third side of an equilateral triangle with curved sides. The curve of the chin is echoed by the curve of the lips, and the arching eyesockets repeat the flare of the nostrils. Thus the artist in his own way has reaffirmed the Egyptian principles of reducing human features to an esthetic formula.

SARCOPHAGUS OF DJEDKHONSOUIOUFANKH. *XXVI Dynasty.*

The most ancient mummies had faces painted on the wrappings around the deceased persons' heads. Later the sarcophagus itself, like the wrappings, was given the form of the mummy and painted with human features. Often the mummy was contained in multiple sarcophagi, each one shaped like the body and painted. Wooden anthropomorphic sarcophagi generally date no earlier than the New Kingdom. The painted decoration is always religious in character, depicting the soul's voyage to the afterlife and the deities it will meet, as well as the judgment to which it must submit. The Egyptians also wrote various exorcisms and entire chapters of *The Book of the Dead* are devoted to sarcophagi. Apart from their religious significance, they are extraordinary artistic creations, their anthropomorphic character abstracted and reduced to an elegant stylization. The mummy became an idol, covered with a lively polychrome decoration executed by an artist with a sure sense of composition and a profound understanding of the medium he was using.

NECKLACE OF THE PHARAOH PINEDJEM. *XXI Dynasty.*

Egyptian artists took pleasure in ornamental design for its own sake, and consequently they found jewelry a most satisfactory medium for expression. The jewelry of the New Kingdom, which includes the famous treasure of Tutenkhamon, excels in its refinement, technical precision and thoughtful juxtaposition of enamel, precious stones and gold. Pinedjem's necklace demonstrates the high level of workmanship in the exquisitely fine links of the triple chain, the elegant pendants and the plaque decorated with a sacred scarab crowned by the solar disk.

Head of a Princess
End of XVIII Dynasty
Limestone; 6″ high.
From Tell el Amarna.

Sarcophagus of Djedkhonsouioufankh
XXVI Dynasty (circa 660–525 B.C.)
Mummy cover. Sculptured wood,
stucco and polychrome; 63″ long.

33

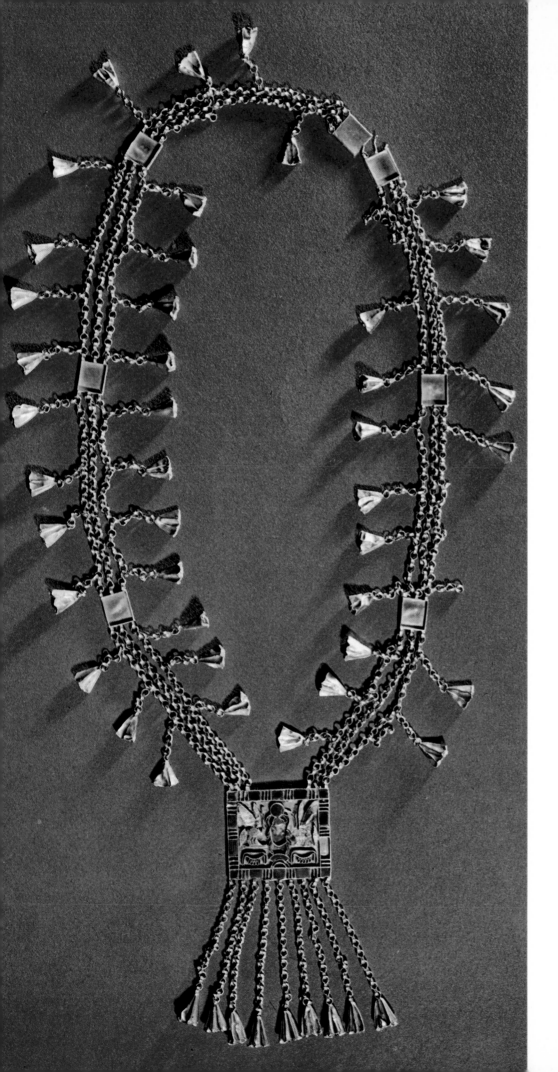

Necklace of the Pharaoh Pinedjem
End of New Kingdom, Thebes, XXI
Dynasty; circa 1030 B.C.
Necklace with flower-shaped pendants
and rectangular centerpiece. Gold and
silver and lapis lazuli; 19 3/5″ long.

ASIA MINOR

Goddess of Fertility
Second half of Third Millennium B.C.
Terra-cotta placque with red varnish;
25″ high. From Cyprus.

GODDESS OF FERTILITY. *Third Millennium B.C.*
During the Bronze Age, Cyprus was inhabited by a civilization closely related to the contemporary cultures of the Anatolian coast and the region of Syria, and at the same time profited from certain links with the Aegean. This island civilization produced the little goddess illustrated here, one of the oldest examples of a class characterized by the geometric stylization of the human figure. Only the ears and the tip of the nose project from the flat rectangular stone surface. The borders of the garment, the necklaces and arms are indicated by simple incision, while the eyes, nostrils, the mouth, the hands and the "pearls" of the necklaces are indicated by small holes punched in the surface. The idol is the expression of an abstract style, the result of a considered rather than casual composition, stemming from the magic and arcane symbolism of a prehistoric civilization. The contemporary Surrealist Max Ernst, in his recent *Ubu Father and Son,* probably had in mind this kind of idol and the impressiveness of its magical abstraction.

STELE OF NARAMSU'EN. *End of the Third Millennium B.C.*
The Akkadians ruled Mesopotamia without seriously disrupting Sumerian culture during the two centuries between the Proto-Dynastic and the Late Sumerian periods. Akkadian sculptors, however, when faced with the heavy, rough figure style of the older civilization (which did influence them at times) and the stiff formality of its representations in relief, proved themselves closer, more attentive observers of nature than were their Sumerian counterparts. The Stele of Naramsu'en is an exceptional monument, and is probably the oldest work of art we know in which the artist attempted to represent the idea of space. He clearly intended to show a natural, realistic relationship between the human figures and their topographical setting rather than succumbing to a traditional stylization. His task was rendered easier in part by the conformation of the place represented, a mountainside; and by the scene shown, an assault by the Akkadians on a hill tribe. The foothills appear as undulating lines building up to the mountain peak. Thus the sculptor had an excuse for showing one figure on top of the other. In a normal representation of a crowd standing in a flat area, artists traditionally projected the idea of several rows of people using this same disposition, without the visual rationale of a sloping terrain. Similarly, the sculptor gave a certain movement to the background by placing various warriors on successively higher foothills. He indicates that the higher a person is the farther away he is from the viewer by showing him behind someone on a foothill lower in the relief. The sculptor has not yet reached the point of showing that mountains and hills can hide or half-hide human figures. For this sophistication, one must wait another 19 centuries until the appearance of the Argonaut Krater (also in the Louvre).

Stele of the Victory of Naramsu'en,
King of Akkad
Sippar: period of Akkadian Rule; phase III,
circa 2389–2353 B.C. Pink sandstone; 78 4/5″
high, 41 1/3″ wide. Commemorative stele from
Susa; taken as war plunder in XII century B.C.
by King Shutruknahhunte, after the Babylonian
conquest of Sippar and other cities.

THE PRIEST ABIHIL OF THE TEMPLE OF ISHTAR.

Third Millennium B.C.

The bearded and bald Abihil wears the sheepskin skirt typical of the Sumerians in this period. He sits on a wicker stool, his hands clasped in prayer. The small size of the statue, its compactness and geometric rotundity is typical of the Proto-Dynastic epoch, and more particularly of the Fara period, of which this is one of the finest works known. Also characteristic are the large eyes, rendered intense and piercing by the inlaid colored stone. Although this statue is conceived frontally, it seems less rigidly confined by its four-sided approach than the Seated Scribe from Egypt. The curves and planes of the body are rounded off, giving the figure a rotund appearance, disguising the fact that, as in Egypt, the artist thinks in terms of two-dimensional surfaces joined together to create a third dimension.

38

The Priest Abihil of the Temple of Ishtar at Mari
Predynastic epoch, Fara phase (ancient Shurupak in Sumer): circa 2900–2685 (?) B.C. Detail of seated figure. Alabaster with bitumen inlays (eyebrows) and lapis lazuli (eyes); 20 3/5″ high. From Mari, now called Tell-Hariri on the Euphrates.

VOTIVE TABLET OF URNANSHE. *III Millennium B.C.*

In this Sumerian votive tablet, the ruler Urnanshe is depicted twice, each time followed by the diminutive figure of a servant. In the upper register, he carries a basket on his head filled with materials for the construction of a temple; in the lower, he is shown seated on a throne. Before him stand his numerous children, four above and four below, identified by their respective names. It is not clear who is the personage of larger size preceding the children in the upper row, whether a first-born who died before the father (the latter was in fact succeeded by Akurgal, shown in second position), a daughter or a priestess. The figures are reduced to mere stereotypes, designed according to the conventions of combining front and side views, and scaled according to rank. This is more like pictograph or picture writing than figurative art. The intention is clearly utilitarian and informative; little attention is given to even the most elementary requirements of composition, and writings fill the voids in disorderly fashion, even covering the figures themselves.

Votive Tablet of Urnanshe
Sumeric art of the predynastic epoch
Ur I phase: circa 2630 B.C.
Limestone; 15 3/5″ high, 18 1/2″ wide.
From Tello (ancient Girsu).

Gudea
High-dynastic epoch, period of late Sumerian princedoms, Gudea phase (circa 2290–2255 B.C.) Statuette without inscriptions. Diorite, 41 1/3″ high. From Lagash; to the Louvre in 1953.

GUDEA. *Third Millennium B.C.*
Late Sumerian sculpture continued along the same lines followed in the Akkadian period, except that historical reliefs disappear from the scene. There are numerous statues of pious local nobles and princes in the act of praying. Gudea alone dedicated some thirty monuments. The well-dressed Sumerian here wears a large mantle with a fringed border and a cap which appears to be of lambskin. The figure is still frontal, with a stylized rotundity accented by the smooth surface of the drapery. This last feature may result from the artist's confrontation with an especially hard stone (diorite) or from some Egyptian influence. The proportions of the figure are typically Sumerian, in the compact solidity of the body and in the comparatively large head, hands and feet. Like the priest Abihil, the eyes are unnaturally large, and although the inlay is now missing, at one time he, too, had the singularly intense stare so characteristic of the Sumerian style.

VASE FROM SUSA. *Circa 2000 B.C.*
In comparison with the statue of Gudea, the Susa vase is "minor art." Yet the richness of the incisions, encrusted with a white paste, the balance between the central scene of bird and fish and the design as a whole, and the pleasing rhythm of the various subsidiary geometric motifs reflect a highly developed artistic sensibility.

Vase from Susa
Circa 2000 B.C.
Terra cotta with incised decoration and encrusted with white paste; 7 1/2″ high. From Susa.

NAVAL EXPEDITION. *VIII Century B.C.*
The historical relief reappeared during the Late Assyrian period. The scene illustrated here represents the transportation of building materials destined for the royal palace at Khorsabad. The sculptor went into great detail. Several great beams are loaded on the decks of the ships, and others are being floated behind. The fleet passes in front of walled cities (the ports of Phoenicia). The whole scene is depicted from a bird's-eye view. The observer looks down onto the sea, its waves drawn in stylized spirals and striations. Interspersed among the ships appear fish, and genii in the form of human-headed bulls. Thus the viewer is asked to see beyond the ships and the surface of the water and look into another dimension, that of depth.

MAN–BULL AND INTERCEDING GODDESS. *End of the Second Millennium B.C.*
The Man-Bull and the goddess decorate a brick wall originally forming

Man-Bull and Interceding Goddess
Middle Elamite period; 1170–1151 B.C.
Brick relief; 54″ high.
From Susa.

Naval Expedition
Late Assyrian period. Reign of Sharruukin (Sargon) II: 721–705 B.C.
Alabaster; 115 1/4″ high.
From Dur Sharruukin (Khorsabad).

part of a building connected with a fertility cult. The goddess herself
has hooves rather than hands. It is impossible to decide whether this
slab formed part of a continuous frieze or if it alternated with pilasters.

DETAIL FROM A SACRIFICIAL SCENE. *Beginning of the Second Millennium B.C.*

During the Larsa Period (named after a city in Sumer), political power
in Sumer was divided among a number of bickering city-states. Then
Hammurabi of Babylon united the area under his rule after the fall of
his greatest rival, the city of Mari, in 1897 B.C. The paintings in the
palace of Mari, which was the home of the last king, Zimralim, appear to date from the period just before Hammurabi's conquest. Several
sacrificial scenes were reconstructed from tiny fragments found in one
of the two great courtyards of the palace. The detail illustrated here
shows a procession of men leading a bull to the sacrifice. A giant figure
of a god, king or priest leads a group of the devout. The design was executed in black outlines on a white background, with the addition of light
and burnt ocher. On other murals in the same palace the artists used, in
addition, red, yellow, blue and brown. While the artists are still conscious of principal views and registers of representation, they are not
as constricted by them as were the Egyptians. Thus their art seems freer,
less chained by convention and tradition. On the other hand, the strong
profiles of the men depicted are clearly related to the canon of features
developed already in Akkadian and Late-Sumerian sculpture and reliefs. This, the most ancient example of Mesopotamian wall painting
we possess, obviously reflects a tradition already centuries old.

CODE OF HAMMURABI. *Beginning of the Second Millennium B.C.*

Hammurabi's famous Code of Laws is carved on most of the surface
of this large basalt block. The discovery in Susa of the remains of a
second example leads one to think that the code was carved on a number
of such monuments and thus published among the principal cities of
the kingdom. On the upper portion of the stele, King Hammurabi stands
in front of a seated divinity and raises his right hand in a gesture of devotion. The god appears to be handing him a scepter, the sign of power.
This motif of adoration is common on seals and has numerous antecedents in Late Sumerian monuments. Hammurabi's artists pay due
homage to the culture he conquered, adopting the stylized schemes inherited from the monuments of the period of Gudea.

*Propitiatory Genius of a Hero, Usually
Identified as the Gilgamesh*
*Late Assyrian period; Reign of Sargon: 721–
705 B.C. Alabaster; 166 1/2"* high. From the
palace of Sargon II in Dur Sharruukin (Khorsabad): from the front of the throne room in one of
the inner courts.

PROPITIATORY GENIUS OF A HERO. *End of the 8th Century B.C.*
During the reign of Sargon II, Assyrian sculptors reached the height of their artistic expression in the powerful isolated figures of divinities, heroes, princes or genii. The genius illustrated here, linked by some with the hero Gilgamesh, exemplifies the massive strength of these figures. Although the figure is essentially geometric and frontal, it is animated by the coloristic carving of the hair (animal and human) and cloth, and the artist's feeling for expressive anatomical details.

ARCHERS OF THE PERSIAN GUARD. *V Century B.C.*
The ancient Mesopotamian tradition of enameled brick, used by the Late Babylonians in Nebuchadnezzar's monumental Ishtar gate, was resumed by the Persian kings in the decoration of their luxurious palaces. Here, in stylized repetition, are shown the archers of Susa, the famous "Immortals," carrying lances with gold and silver tips.

Archers of the Persian Guard
Achemenide age: V century B.C.
Enameled bricks; height of each archer 57 4/5".
Frieze from the Palace of Darius in Susa.

LION. *IV Century B.C.*

Although Imperial Persian art owed a great deal to Assyria and Babylonia, it was open to numerous external influences; in this lion, and in the liveliness of its step, one senses a debt to Greek art. Yet the rhythmic interplay of curves which gives the muzzle its characteristic stylization departs from Assyrian tradition and reflects the influence of a linear sensibility originating in Central Asia. And, in turn, several centuries later, Chinese sculpture of the Liang period will feel the influence of the Achaemenian models on its own stylized lions.

48

Lion
Achemenide Age: IV century B.C.
Detail. Enameled bricks; length of
the entire animal 145 2/5″. From Susa,
formerly part of a "continuous" frieze.

ANCIENT GREECE AND ROME

HEAD OF AN IDOL. *Circa 2000 B.C.*

In the Third and Second millennia B.C. the Cycladic Islands in the Aegean were inhabited by a civilization which preceded that of the Minoans in Crete. For the most part, the Cycladic culture belongs to the Bronze Age, but it does have close connections with the preceding Stone Age, from which it inherited the Mediterranean cult of the Mother-Goddess. In comparison with the opulent forms of the best-known of the Neolithic mother-goddesses, the Cycladic idols are distinguish by their severely geometric outlines, lack of plastic modeling and their schematization. At times a nascent naturalism appears to have been suppressed almost intentionally, as in the series of violin-shaped idols. The typical Cycladic figures are more related to relief sculpture than to statues. Their heads are in the shape of large shields, the long necks are rounded, the bodies are upside-down triangles, with the base at the shoulders and the tip at the ankles; their arms are simple crossed lines and breasts, just little dots. The separation of the legs is indicated by a line which does not pierce through the stone. The idols are usually quite small and cut out of white marble. Sometimes facial features were added in paint. The extreme stylization is perhaps more a matter of esthetic choice than the result of limits imposed by the artists' skills, for these figures have been found in tombs with idols of a much more substantial corporeality.

The head illustrated here, from Amorgos, belonged to a figurine of exceptional size and workmanship. Now that it is separated from its body, its abstractness becomes even more striking—pure form or pure symbol according to the taste and viewpoint of the observer. Perhaps a formalist approach is the more legitimate, for the real meaning lies buried with the civilization which created it, while the form is as apparent to us today as it was to the artist who made it so many millennia ago. Thus one can understand the influence this head had on the first post-Cubist generation of abstract sculptors, including Archipenko, Arp and Brancusi.

Head of an Idol
Circa 2000 B.C.
Marble; height of fragment: 10 1/2".
From the island of Amorgos, Cyclades.

50

SARCOPHAGUS FROM CERVETERI. *Circa 500 B.C.*

Found in the necropolis of ancient Caere, this painted terra-cotta sarcophagus is covered by a lid decorated with the figures of a wife and husband reclining on a Greek couch *(kline)*. The Etruscans saw these as representations of the deceased at an everlasting banquet since their idea of an afterlife was a prolongation of everyday life after death. The wife's brimmed hat and her shoes with their upturned toes *(calcei repandi)* are Etruscan. These figures can be related to elements of Greek art, but basically they are products of Etruria, if for no other reason than the masterful use of terra cotta on a monumental scale. Stylistically, the monument relates to Ionic art in the clean profiles, slanting, almond eyes and "archaic smile." (Compare with the "Rampin Head.") The particular strength of this group lies in the expression of a warm human relationship between man and wife, and the ease with which the viewer can relate it to the reality of everyday life.

Sarcophagus from Cerveteri
Circa 500 B.C.
Painted terra cotta; 78″ long, 46″ high.
From Cerveteri.

HEAD OF A HORSEMAN (RAMPIN HEAD). *VI Century B.C.*

Only in recent years was it recognized that this head belonged to fragments of an equestrian statue in the Akropolis Museum in Athens. The head is now mounted on a plaster copy of the original body and horse. It belongs to the time of the tyrant Pisistratus, when Athens was under heavy Ionic influence and hiring sculptors from Ionian areas, including the islands of Paros and Chios. The head turns slightly to the left, which has been considered an indication of naturalism, since the artist has progressed beyond the tradition of severe frontality. Still, this twist of the head is only a modest concession to naturalism, or actually a naturalism *sui generis,* which seeks intellectually to restore reality after it has transformed the human figure into a composite of geometric parts. The sculptor is more interested in depicting a plausible canon of proportions and in rendering an exemplary model of the human body than he is in showing a realistic figure. His attitude is expressed in the ornamental conventions he used to depict the beard and hair, which relate to the stylization seen in Persian and Achaemenid art and through these reach back to Mesopotamia, and in the precisely calculated volumetric structure of the face.

ETRUSCAN AMPHORA. *VI Century B.C.*

Beginning in the VI century B.C., Etruscan workshops produced large numbers of the so-called *bucchero* vases made out of clay darkened by the addition of lampblack. The Louvre example is among the finest of this type both for the beauty of its profile and the refinement of its incised decoration accentuated by a white filling. The artist enlivened the century-old tradition of geometric decoration by the addition of naturalistic elements and by his careful attention to the balance between the non-organic motifs and the swelling curves of the vase. An elegantly stylized marsh bird hops through a field of spirals with a grace and agility so real, so precisely rendered within the total linear structure, that it suggests the watery home of its flesh-and-blood counterpart. The bent vertical lines become cane swaying in the wind, the little geometric wheel becomes a veined waterlily leaf floating on the water, and the spirals become the concentric circles of water stirred up by the long-legged leaps and bounds of the bird.

Piombino Apollo
First half of V century B.C.
Bronze; 49 1/5″ high.
From Piombino, Italy.

PIOMBINO APOLLO. *V Century B.C.*
This famous bronze youth, retrieved from the sea off Piombino in 1832, appears to represent Apollo, as suggested by the left hand outstretched as if holding a bow and arrows. The eyesockets are now empty, but at one time they were inlaid with colored paste or hard stone. The eyebrows, lips and nipples are indicated in red copper. An inscription in Doric dialect written in silver under the right foot reports that the work was dedicated in Athens as part of a tithe. The Doric writing reminds one of the great centers of Doric sculpture and its first protagonists, in particular Kanachos of Sicyon, whose Apollo Philesios (made for the Didymaion of Miletus and appearing on Milesian coins) resembles the Piombino youth in pose and in movement. Compared to the Rampin Head, the Louvre bronze shows the progressive development of Greek art in representing the human body as naturalistically as possible. The bronze still participates in certain archaic conventions—frontality, symmetry, juxtaposition of parts separately conceived, then united to make a whole—but the consequent reduction to geometric terms is less drastic than 60 or 70 years earlier. The male nude has become by this time the fundamental expression of the Greek ideal of *kalokagathia* (nobility of character) and the modeling is softer and more credible, while a certain asymmetry and deviations from rigid frontality make themselves felt, although timidly. Although the statue is bound still by the four principal views familiar from Egyptian art, an attempt to mask this fact is apparent. Whether or not the artist worked from a living model, a man would have little difficulty imitating the statue's pose, which would have been impossible in Egyptian art.

BERLIN PAINTER—ATTIC KRATER. *V Century B.C.*
Over 200 vases are assigned to the Berlin Painter, named after an amphora now in the museum of Berlin. He belonged to the second generation of Red-Figure masters, when the influence of Ionic art was weakening and the growing naturalism of Attic sculpture was replacing it as an inspiration for vase-painting. The Berlin Painter does not hesitate to show figures in three-quarter view and is conscious of anatomy, carefully indicating it with fine red lines often diluted to achieve a certain subtlety in shading. The vivacity and movement of the youth rolling his hoop has been properly compared to the famous bronze statue of the Zeus from Artemision.

CUP OF THE BIRD–HUNTER. *VI Century B.C.*

The Cup of the Bird-Hunter is executed in black-figure (with details picked out in red) on a natural buff background, one of the most ancient techniques of Greek pottery. The cup has been assigned tentatively to an Ionian workshop. The representation shows a man in a conventional running pose who grasps the branches of a pair of trees which grow sideways in the tondo, their branches and foliage occupying nearly the whole field. It is difficult to decide exactly what the artist was attempting to represent here. Since a nest and birds are shown in the fork of the left tree, it has been suggested that the man is after them, grasping the branches in order to climb the tree. The artist may be showing just one tree. Since he could not solve the problem of showing it from the top or from the bottom, he decided to split it in half and show the two sides. This explanation is not impossible in comparison with other works of this period presenting similar problems. P. Devambez has offered an alternate explanation, suggesting that the man is simply dancing in the forest, full of joy in the midst of nature.

BERLIN PAINTER
Attic Red-Figure Krater
Circa 480–470 B.C.
The reproduction shows a young man rolling a hoop (Ganymede?) and holding a rooster in his left hand. 13″ high; diameter of krater's mouth 13″. From an Etruscan tomb.

Cup of the Bird-Hunter
Ionian Black-Figure Kylix.
Middle of VI century B.C. 6″ high, diameter 9″. From Etruria, formerly in Campana Collection.

WORKSHOP OF PHIDIAS—PANATHENAIC PROCESSION.
V Century B.C.

The continuous frieze which ran around the cella of the Parthenon (within the peristyle) was executed by a team of sculptors and craftsmen under the direction of Phidias. The marbles of the Parthenon represent the high point of Greek art, when a perfect balance had been achieved between realism and the architectonic elements. The artists were still working within the stylistic conventions developed in the Archaic period, but they were elaborating on their heritage. The Panathenaic frieze characterizes the Greek concept of relief, which is born of a graphic tradition and seeks to give itself sculptural rather than two-dimensional, linear forms. The relief field is only two figures deep. When the artists wished to enlarge this shallow field, they used the old convention of indicating a horizontal expansion rather than penetrating the background visually. This is evident in the thrones of the gods at

PHIDIAS (workshop)
Panathenaic Procession
447–432 B.C.
Pentelic marble; 41 1/3″ high.
Section from frieze of the eastern part of Parthenon with maidens giving two officials of the procession the official robes as an offering to Athena.

the east end of the frieze. Thus the background retains the same spatial value of every point in the frieze.

Every figure and every group has the same value in the balance between occupied and unoccupied spaces throughout the frieze. This harmony is exemplified by the magnificent series of *peplophoroi* (wearers of the ceremonial Panathenaean festival robes) and the strong verticals of their drapery, which mark the rhythm of the whole procession honoring Athens' Athena.

VENUS OF MILOS.　*II Century B.C.*
The Venus found on the island of Milos attests the vitality of Hellenistic art during the century which also saw the production of the Pergamum Altar masterpieces. Her stylized elegance can be called

Venus of Milos
Second half of II century B.C.
Detail. Parian marble; 80 1/3″ high.
From island of Milos, discovered in
1820 and in the Louvre since 1821.

57

manneristic in the intentional contrast of the softness of female flesh with the deep shadows and rich texture of her heavy drapery—a contrast also reminiscent of the Pergamum sculpture. The artist treated feminine beauty with great warmth and understanding, and worked easily within the concept of rounded three-dimensional rather than four-faced figures. The classical artists had striven to reach this point, and the Hellenistic master reaped the fruits of their struggle.

VICTORY OF SAMOTHRACE. *Circa 190 B.C.*

The Winged Victory of Samothrace was connected for a number of years with the naval victory of Demetrius Poliorcetes in 306, and then more persuasively to the Rhodian conquest of Antiochus III (222–187 B.C.). The style justifies the later dating. The Victory is a spectacular piece. Her body is thrust forward by the giant wings and the sea wind catches her drapery which, dampened by the salt spray, clings to her body. The light chiton adheres to her breasts, and her cloak, slipping from her shoulders, wraps around her legs and billows out behind her. The treatment of the cloth is related to the so-called 'wet drapery' of the post-Phidian period, but in its exaggerated curves and chiaroscuro effect it is almost baroque, which again justifies the later dating.

Victory of Samothrace
Circa 190 B.C.
Parian marble; 108 1/3″ high.
Discovered in Samothrace in 1863.

FEMALE PORTRAIT. *II Century A.D.*

The portraits from Fayum (which also have been found elsewhere in Egypt) are the only "easel paintings" preserved to us from classical antiquity. They date from the first to the fourth centuries A.D., and approximately 500 are extant, scattered in museums all over the world. Most of them belong to a current of expressionistic popular art which is Coptic rather than Greco-Roman. Although the portraits were used on sarcophagi, as in the old Egyptian tradition, they were probably painted during the owner's lifetime. For the most part, the paintings were executed on board in the encaustic technique, where melted colored bees wax was spread on the surface of the wood with a spatula (although there are a few instances in tempera, and on cloth). Colors in wax are difficult to manipulate and to dilute, so that the portraits compare unfavorably with works done in the more versatile water paint mediums. The artists had to work in dabs and short strokes, creating forms without an outline in a technique which particularly lends itself to luministic effects.

This delicate portrait of a girl dates no earlier than the reign of Hadrian (if it really comes from Antinoë), and is related to the Hellenistic tradition of portraying the middle class along with philosophers, poets and statesmen. The highlights in the eyes, along the nose and on the upper lip as well as the shimmer of gold in the hair remind one of the delicate lighting and the golds in a Titian, a Velazquez or a Goya.

On page 60

Female Portrait
II century A.D.
Detail. Encaustic; 16 1/2″ high, 9 2/5″ wide. From Fayum, Egypt, more accurately, probably from the excavations at Antinoöpolis: acquired by the Louvre in 1953.

PERSIA
CHRISTIAN EGYPT
BYZANTIUM

BYZANTINE ART IN ROME. *The Story of Jonah.*
According to the Bible, Jonah was cast into the sea to placate the tempest which God had raised against him, whereupon he was swallowed by a marine monster in whose stomach he stayed for three days before being vomited up on a beach. According to the interpretation of early Christians, this story prefigured the death and resurrection of Christ in particular and of all the Christians in general. The Byzantine representation in this gold-leaf design on a fragment of a ritual cup is enclosed by a stylized frame symbolizing a great wave (following a similar convention for decorating the insides of pots). Within, a Roman ship with a large square rig appears in the upper zone; and below is shown the whale swallowing the prophet, the curve of his body echoing that of the keel and emphasizing the curve of the cup. Iconographically the representation is very close to that of the Lateran *Jonah Sarcophagus,* which dates from the end of the third-century A.D.

SASSANIAN ART. *Horse's Head.*
The silver horse's head is characteristic of third to fourth-century art—the interest in animal motifs, the liveliness and vitality of their execution, a quasi-calligraphic pleasure in geometric design and the taste for trappings covered with ornament of Oriental derivation. A certain Greek, or Western influence is also apparent in the corporeality of the horse's head.

SASSANIAN ART
Head of a Horse (4th–5th century)
Relief and incised silver, gilt with mercury; 5 1/2″ × 7 3/4″. Fragment from Kirman.

BYZANTINE ART IN ROME
Jonah (3rd–4th century)
Diameter; 4 1/4″. Incised gold sheet between two sheets of glass. Its circular, concave shape shows it to have belonged originally to a cup, used for ritual purposes. From a cemetery in Rome. The Greek inscription, "Zesis," is frequently found on glassware of this type.

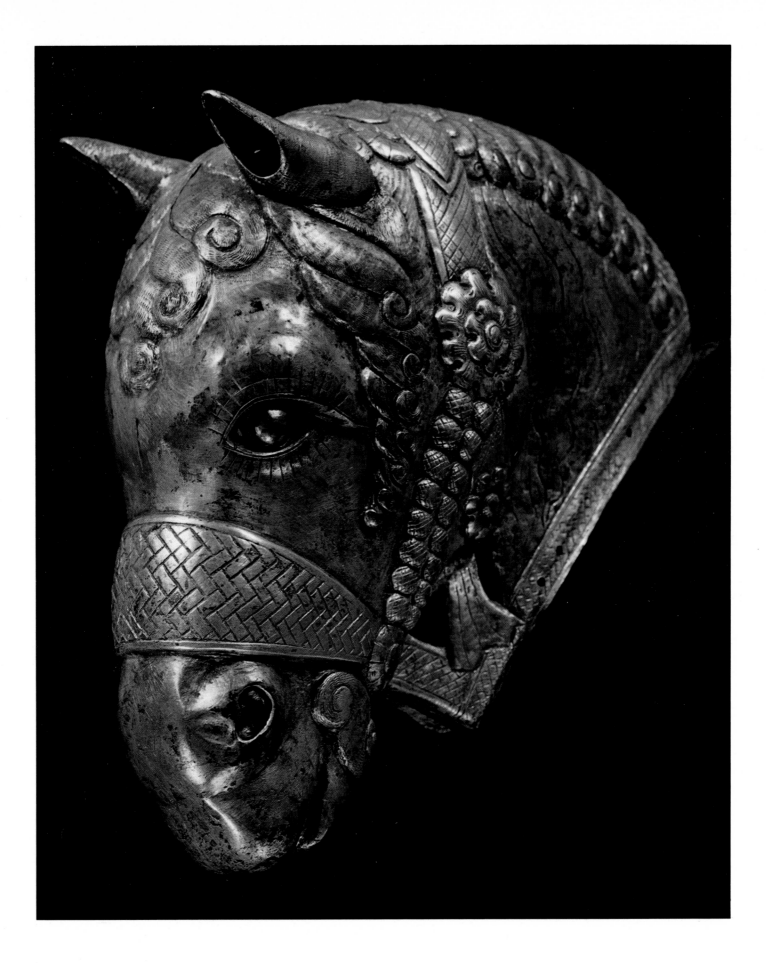

BYZANTINE ART. *Hunting Scene.*

While the subject and the technique of this Byzantine plaque are common, it has a special freshness, particularly in the attention paid to the detail of its lively tri-colored composition. Three hunters, two mounted and one on foot, all armed with lances, pursue several wild beasts.

One of them, a lion in the center of the composition, turns on a horseman. The hunter pivots about with the impetuous courage of those heroes depicted in the reliefs on Hellenistic sarcophagi. The movement of the composition follows an ideal structure in the shape of a sigma, and the representation is characterized by the artist's keen sense for the play of light, as seen in his use of gold and silver. The plaque illustrates the exquisite late Alexandrian taste of artist and patron.

BYZANTINE ART
Hunting Scene (5th–6th century)
Small rectangular plaque, gilt bronze with silver inlays drilled and punched, 7 1/4″ × 6″. The holes at the corners and the traces of a frame show it was originally an ornamental appliqué, probably for some piece of furniture.

COPTIC ART
Daphne (5th–6th century)
Marble relief, 10 1/4″ × 8 1/4″.
Fragment from *Sheh Abahd*. The figure orig-
inally seems to have worn a ribbon on its head.
The hands held the ends of a ribbon; the arms
were outstretched.

COPTIC ART. *Daphne (?).*

The identification of this figure as Daphne is suggested by the leaves
which frame her bust. The monument is part of a group of Coptic
sculptures found in centers far from Alexandria and characterized by
traces of Indian, Syrian, Armenian and Persian influences—that is,
those cultures which are considered in general as contributing to the
formation of Coptic art. Although this relief has obvious ties with
Western art, the artist's attitude was basically anti-classical, as is evident
in his use of Near-Eastern canons of proportion. The figure is inscribed
in a pentagon, whose axes control the placement and detail of the
woman's body. At the center of the pentagon glitters the large pendant
of her necklace. The relief probably was placed somewhat above the
observer's head since it looks best when viewed from below. The ideal
center of the composition is the face, remarkable for its serenity and
sweetness.

COPTIC ART. *Sea Goddess and Water Games.*

At the center of the textile appears a sea goddess (Venus?) framed by a
wave motif done in perspective, suggesting the movement of the sea.
Her head is set against a nimbus and crowned with a diadem. Outside
the central medallion four nereids are depicted playing in the sea,
accompanied by sea lions and fish. The whole is more decorative than
narrative. Both the composition and the colors relate to the monumental
elegance of mosaic floors. The classical themes, transmitted by Alex-

andria and frequent in Coptic art, are reinterpreted with lively imagination. They lasted well beyond the coming of Christianity to Egypt.

COPTIC ART. *Dionysos, with Motifs from the Cult of Isis.*
A giant Dionysos appears on the left side of the composition, carrying his thyrsus and surrounded by vines. He stands rather casually watching a ritual of the mysteries of Isis, as the symbol of the moon would indicate. Both the episodic character of the design, not easily explained as it stands alone, and the asymmetry of the representation suggest that this is only a portion of a more complex composition.

COPTIC ART. *Portrait of a Young Girl.*
A young girl is represented lying on her coffin. In her left hand she holds the symbol of Isis, which has become a Christian emblem, and it reappears by her feet. Her right hand is raised in a gesture of leave-taking. The realism of the head recalls that of the famous Fayum series. Here, however, the facial expression is distinguished by its greater composure and even resignation. The rest of the body is as stylized as a mummy. This shroud had to cover the sides of the corpse as well as the top, and the artist modified the decoration accordingly. We see the body from above, in a bird's eye view, while the sides are depicted flattened out, showing peacocks—symbol of immortality—and a row of leaves decorating the borders.

Above:
COPTIC ART
Dionysos, with Motifs from the Cult of Isis
(6th century)
Woven cloth, wool on linen, probably from Antinoë, 22 3/4″ × 21 3/4″.

Left:
COPTIC ART
Sea Goddess and Water Games
V century. Textile panel; 11 3/4″ wide.
From the von Clédat Collection.

COPTIC ART
Portrait of Young Girl Lying Down
(second half of 3rd century)
Fragment of a sheet painted in encaustic. From the excavations at Gayel. 85″ × 35 3/4″.

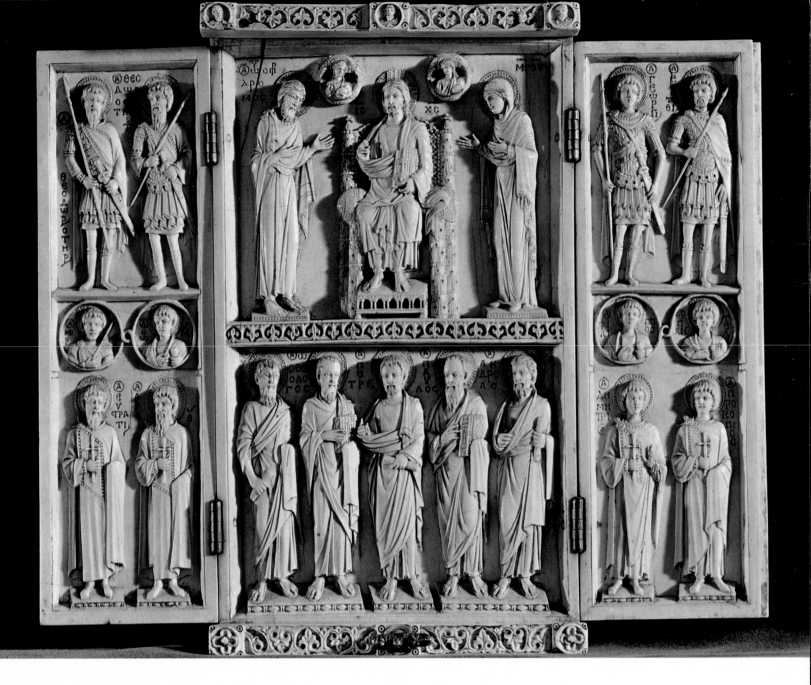

BYZANTINE ART. *The Harbaville Triptych.*

The Harbaville Triptych is a miniature portable icon. The central panel is divided into two superimposed registers by an ornament which is repeated with the addition of rosettes at the lower edge and of three little heads at the top. In the center of the upper register, Christ is shown seated on an ivory throne flanked by the Virgin and St. John standing in attitudes of worship. Above, on either side of Christ's head are a pair of medallions out of which peer angels holding the symbols of the sun and the moon, typical of imperial iconography. In the lower register stand five Apostles, dressed in classical togas. The shutters at left and right are perfectly symmetrical, with four warriors in the two upper registers, and eight saints below, four in medallions and four full-length wearing the dress of civilian dignitaries. The triptych exemplifies the revival of the ancient art of ivory carving; it has been assigned to the fifth century A.D., although a more acceptable date would be the tenth century, judging from the style of the Deisis.

BYZANTINE ART
Harbaville Triptych (10th century)
Small portable altar, ivory. Central panel, 9 1/2″ × 5 1/2″; side panels, 8 1/2″ × 2 3/4″. The name refers to the collection to which it belonged, in Arras, before coming to the Louvre.

SYRIAN ART
Christ Blessing (5th–6th century)
Silver relief, partly gilt tondo. Diameter 6″.
Crowning element of a cross. (?)

SYRIAN ART. *Christ Blessing.*

This silver tondo depicts the beardless Christ Pantocrator, following the Syrian tradition, according to which the book should be inscribed with the phrase *"Ego sum lux mundi, qui sequitur me non ambulat in tenebris."* The frame of pearls is probably a stylized representation of clouds, out of which Christ emerges clad in a toga. This type becomes canonical for centuries, an expression of geometric severity and majesty. The only element in motion is Christ's hand, curved into a stylized gesture of benediction.

OTTONIAN ART (?). *Binding for a Gospel Book.*

The origins of sumptuous objects of this type, with their mixed techniques, are difficult to determine: this Gospel Book binding has been alternately assigned to a Byzantine workshop of the Macedonian school and to Ottonian studios. In the central panel the theme of the Crucifixion is depicted with the Virgin and St. John at either side of the cross, above which appear the symbols of the sun and the moon. This central theme is framed by recessed planes in perspective, surrounded by a wide band of ornamentation, including the symbols of the Evangelists with their names in each corner. The binding is related to the Reliquary of St. Foy at Conques or the Portable Altar of S. Andrea at Treviri, both of which embody the major characteristics of the brilliant Ottonian school of goldsmiths.

OTTONIAN ART
Binding for a Gospel Book
(circa 9th century)
Gold relief, decorated with inset glass, stones, enamel, filigree and cameos. 15 3/4″ × 13″. From the Abbey of St. Denis. It was perhaps a gift from Beatrice, daughter of Hugues Capet. The inscription, restored and damaged, along the outer border reads as follows: "Beatrix me in onore Dei omnipotentis et omnium sanctorum eius fieri precepi."

BYZANTINE ART. *Transfiguration.*

The rigid iconography of the Transfiguration, from the Dalmatian Carolingian epoch to Raphael, demanded that the representation be organized according to the axial coordinates of the miraculous appari-

69

BYZANTINE ART
Transfiguration (12th century)
Mosaic of stones and glass paste on wax base;
20 1/2″ × 14″. Can be dated 12th century, but
with later restorations.

tion. In this miniature mosaic, stylization of the accessory details—
landscape, drapery, gestures, the frozen symbolism of the mandorlas
and rays—when fused with the realism of the facial expressions heighten
the sense of pathos and place the work among the ideal prototypes for
Trecento painting and Cimabue. The icon, intended for domestic use,
probably came from Constantinople.

RUSSIAN ART. *Last Judgment.*

The detail illustrated here is part of a large panel representing the Last
Judgment, Paradise, Hell and the Militant and the Triumphant Church,
all according to medieval Byzantine iconography. This detail shows an
angel thrusting aside the firmament which bears the symbol of the sun,
accompanied by the angelic host. Flanked by the symbol of the Holy
Spirit, God the Father is shown seated in the tondo, calling His Son
to sit at His side. Below, Christ sits on His throne in judgment, surrounded by the Tetramorphs (symbols of the Four Evangelists) and
flanked by Mary and the Precursor John the Baptist, who present to
him the kneeling Adam and Eve. The painting, in keeping with the
rigid orthodox liturgy, typifies conservative religious art in its iconography as well as in its five centuries of Byzantine style.

RUSSIAN ART
Last Judgment (17th century)
Detail. Tempera and oil on panel. Entire panel
measures 77″ × 57″. Probably from Moscow.

ISLAMIC ART. *Cup with Female Busts.*
The cup is decorated in a style of quiet refinement. The pale brown figures stand out against the opaline background, which otherwise is left largely bare of ornament. The two figures, both female, are depicted in half-moons and possess a rather ghostly quality which would have been heightened when they were seen through clear liquids. This aqueous character is emphasized by a wave design at the rim.

ISLAMIC ART
Cup with Female Busts (10th–11th century)
Diameter 7 3/4". Faïence with lustre decoration, found in Egypt.

FRANCE

BURGUNDIAN ART. *Descent from the Cross.*

The figure of Christ illustrated here originally formed part of a sculptural ensemble representing the Deposition. Although we know of no other examples in France itself, a number occur in Italy and these divide into two distinct types, one characterized by its realism (as at Norcia, Pescia, Tivoli and Volterra) and the other by its use of symbolism and by the appearance of the Virgin and St. John only (as at S. Miniato al Tedesco). In general the Italian examples are somewhat later than the French. Christ's elongated, almost serpentine body was the focal point in a composition remarkable for its refined, attenuated elegance. The effect is enhanced by the decorative quality of the hair framing the face and ending in curls on the shoulders, the wavy strands of the beard, and the carefully indicated folds of the drapery. Originating from the region of Burgundy, this figure is more closely related to the Last Judgment on the portal at Autun than to the Christ of the narthex at Vezelay. The drapery of the latter gives the figure a restless movement, similar to some of the more poignant *Pietà* representations. Whereas in the Autun Christ as well as the sculpture illustrated here the folds simply outline and accentuate the body, giving through their rhythms a note of serenity to the pathos of this image of divine lamentation.

HENRI BELLECHOSE (?). *Last Communion and Martyrdom of St. Denis.*
This painting is a typical example of "mixed" narrative, or, following Wickhoff's definition, a "continuous narrative." It consists of the repetition of the same figure in the same surroundings taking part in diverse situations. Although thus broken down, the narrative maintains an emphasis on a central sacred theme, which in size and importance overshadows all the others, thus becoming, in a sense, "discontinuous." Finally, both the continuous and discontinuous are united in symbolical function through the addition of certain attributes—such as that of the angelic host—which stem from the identification in medieval France of the St. Denis, who was first bishop of Paris and protector of France, with Denis the Areopagite, a disciple of St. Paul and a theological interpreter of the nature of angels.

To the left, St. Denis receives communion from the hand of Christ. On the right side, he is beheaded along with Saints Rusticus and Eleutherius, and in the center is shown the Trinity. The composition borrows its structure from the iconography of the Crucifixion. It is bathed in golden sunbeams streaming down from heaven, giving it the aura of a miraculous vision. A marked interest in the psychology of the facial expression, together with a certain sweetness point to a possible influence from the North Italian Trecento.

74

BURGUNDIAN ART
Descent from the Cross
(12th century)
Painted and gilt wood. The left arm is a modern restoration. 61" × 66 1/4".

HENRI BELLECHOSE
Brabant (?)—Dijon 1440–1444
Last Communion and Martyrdom of St. Denis
(between 1398 and 1416)
Tempera on panel, 63 1/2″ × 82 3/4″.
From the Charterhouse of Champmol.

SCHOOL OF AVIGNON. *Pietà*.

Despite its fame, this Pietà remains of uncertain attribution and date; it
it is assigned by some to a Spanish or Portuguese painter, by others to
an Italianate artist working in the tradition of Rogier van der Weyden.
Ragghianti and Sterling assign it to Enguerrand de Charrenton. The
painting has been dated by some to the 1470's; others consider 1457 a
date *ante quem,* since the Pietà of Tarragon, which included the same
detail of St. John removing the thorns from Jesus' head, was completed
that year. The praying figure at the left belongs to the Flemish tradition
of incisive portraiture. The figures of the mourners stand out as if
carved in ivory against an immense sky of gold, and the outlines of a
dream city, with a distinctly Islamic appearance, arise on the far horizon.
In their architectonic lines, these figures descend from a long tradition
of Pietàs in sculpture. They bend over Christ to form a sort of living
canopy, while the praying donor is set off from the group by the unyielding verticality of his genuflection. Christ's body, a long fluid
silhouette whose pallor stands in striking contrast to the dark background
of cloth, lies on His mother's knees as in a *Vesperbild,* the lines of its
pathetic abandon accentuated by the long inscription.

77

JEAN FOUQUET. *Charles VII, King of France.*

The king is depicted in kneeling attitude looking out of a chapel window whose curtains are pulled aside, as if he were participating in a religious ceremony. Although at first sight the painting appears to be a votive portrait, the inscription written on the frame (which imitates the window jambs) refers to the king as *"très victorieux."* Thus it appears to be a commemorative portrait, probably commissioned after the Truce of Arras in 1444 or after the battle of Formigny, both being events which would justify calling him "victorious." In all probability, the portrait was executed after Fouquet's voyage to Italy between 1444 and 1447.

The painting marks the debut of this portrait type in France. It harks back to prototypes in the circle of van Eyck, with some concessions to the Bohemian tradition, especially in the three-quarter position of the body on a light background and in the king's rich attire (compare for example the portrait of the Emperor Sigismund in the Vienna Museum, attributed to Pisanello), and to late Treccento Italy. During his trip to Italy, Fouquet must have visited Verona, where the memory of a great courtly tradition still survived, as in the works of Altichiero, who had a particular influence on Fouquet's miniatures, and of Pisanello.

ANONYMOUS FRENCH MASTER. *The Beautiful Gabrielle and the Maréchale de Balagny.*

During the 16th century in France, portrait painting enjoyed a special favor in court circles. Portraits were sent as gifts on numerous occasions, above all for weddings. In this painting, Gabrielle d'Estrée and her sister are shown taking a bath together, a fashionable theme at the time. The picture probably contains an allusion to the fertility of Gabrielle and her projected marriage with Henry IV. The ivory-like figures are framed by the curtains held back over their heads. A domestic scene in the background shows a woman sewing, seated in the warmth of a fireplace.

The influence of Clouet is strong in this work, which belongs to the later years of the School of Fontainebleau, perhaps around 1596, when Gabrielle, the king's mistress, was expecting a baby. At the latest, the picture could date from 1599, when she died in childbirth. The portrait is more interesting perhaps from the point of view of cultural history than of art, and projects a sense of intimacy, allowing an insight into the lives of these elegant French ladies.

JEAN FOUQUET
Tours 1420—died between 1477 and 1481
Charles VII, King of France
Panel, 33 3/4" × 28 1/4".
From the Ste. Chapelle of Bourges.

GERMAIN PILON. *Statue of the Cardinal de Birague.*
By the time he was commissioned to do this statue, Pilon had already enjoyed a certain vogue at court during his youth. Along with other works, he executed the statues for the tomb of Henry II and Catherine de' Medici at the cathedral of St. Denis, under the direction of Primaticcio. The memorial statue of Cardinal de Birague represents a turning point in Pilon's art. He abandoned the Mannerism of his earlier works and attempted a more realist approach. The deceased cardinal is shown on his knees, enveloped in the heavy folds of his garments. His attitude of intense devotion is emphasized by the inflexibility of his posture. The artist devoted most of his attention to a profound analysis of the man's physiognomy, as detailed and as precise as a life mask.

80

ANONYMOUS FRENCH
The Beautiful Gabrielle and the Maréchale de Balagny (circa 1596)
Panel, 37 3/4″ × 49 1/4″.

GERMAIN PILON
Paris 1537—1590
Statue of Cardinal de Birague (1584–85)
Detail. Bronze, 56 1/4″ × 76 3/4″.
Cardinal René de Birague, who was Chancellor of France, died in 1583; his tomb was commissioned by his daughter, the Marquise de Nesle.

BAUGIN
Documented circa 1630
Still-life with Pastries
(circa 1630) 20 1/2″ × 15 3/4″.

GEORGES DE LA TOUR. *Mary Magdalene with Oil Lamp.*
Georges de La Tour painted two pictures of the saint, the one illustrated here and *Mary Magdalene at Her Mirror* in the Fabius Collection. Both pictures show a woman absorbed in meditation, with hand resting on a skull by the light of a lamp which just barely illuminates a darkly shadowed space. The use of the same model and the very slight variation in subject matter suggest a close relation between the pictures.

The art of La Tour is nostalgically reminiscent of the Quattrocento in the sculptural compactness of its forms and in its restrained luminosity. More decisive, however, was the influence of Caravaggio, which according to some, La Tour felt during a trip to Rome around 1612–13. According to others, it came to him through the Flemish and Lorraine Caravaggesques (like Le Clerc), also from Honthorst, whom La Tour might have met on a trip to Holland. His acquaintance with the latter's work is reflected principally in the manipulation of light, which springs from a source within the picture itself and thus participates more naturalistically in the representation of a whole. Finally, the works of Terbrugghen were an important influence on La Tour.

In the painting of Mary Magdalene, as in all La Tour's canvases, there is a sense of cheerless solitude and despondent immobility which is in keeping with the morose and withdrawn nature of the artist.

GEORGES DE LA TOUR
Vic 1593—Lunéville 1652
Mary Magdalen with Oil Lamp
(1635–1640)
Detail. Oil on canvas; 50 1/2″ × 37″.

BAUGIN. *Still-life with Pastries.*
Baugin signed a group of still-lifes among which is included the Louvre example. During the reigns of Henry IV and Louis XIII, a colony of

83

Dutch artists living in St.-Germain-des-Près exerted a certain influence on French culture, and their effect is illustrated by this painting, which reflects contact with Northern taste. The composition is simple and disciplined. A platter full of pastries rolled up like sheets of parchment rests on the small table, while the flask and glass stand out against the dark background of the wall. The artist has limited his colors to a few basic tints. A golden tone highlighting the objects in sharp contrast to the dark background gives to the picture a sense of warm intimacy, as if the table stood in a room with the curtains pulled close.

LOUIS LE NAIN. *Peasant Family in an Interior*.
This is the most famous of Louis Le Nain's rustic scenes in which he specialized. The painting represents the interior of a peasant's home

LOUIS LE NAIN
Laon 1593—Paris 1648
Peasant Family in an Interior (1642)
Oil on canvas; 44 1/2″ × 62 1/2″.

just before the family sits down to dinner, its members having gathered together from various tasks. The old man has left off cutting the bread for a moment, his wife holds the glass of wine she has just poured from the jug resting on her lap, a child plays a few notes on a shepherd's pipe, and the other figures have momentarily paused, all intent on looking toward the entrance of the room, with an air of mild diffidence, of gentle surprise. In the background, two people preoccupied by the fire do not participate in the main scene. The balanced disposition of the figures, the suspended movement and the serenity of the scene clearly relate it to still-life compositions. Also evident is the poetic influence of Caravaggesque painters—Guercino, Reni, the Bamboccianti. In contrast to its genre character, however, is the poetic, almost Virgilian sense of tenderness and bucolic melancholy.

PHILIPPE DE CHAMPAIGNE.   *Portrait of Sister Catherine de Champaigne when She Was Ill and Sister Catherine Agnes Arnaud.*
Philippe de Champaigne painted the picture in honor of the miraculous healing of his daughter, Sister Catherine de Champaigne, following a novena said for her by Sister Catherine Agnes. The sick woman is shown half-prone, her reliquary purse on her knees and her face alight with pious inspiration as she gazes at Sister Catherine Agnes, who kneels next to her chair. On the left, a Latin inscription describes the incident. Heavenly rays pour into the top of the picture. The composition is based on the old iconographic scheme of ex-votos.
Philippe de Champaigne, although Flemish in origin, moved to France when he was still very young. There his painting was influenced by the School of Bologna and by Poussin. He also came into contact with the Jansenists of Port-Royal. He numbers among the great portraitists of the seventeenth century in France, as is immediately apparent in the animated, spiritual faces of the nuns.

PHILIPPE DE CHAMPAIGNE
Brussels 1602—Paris 1647
Portraits of Sister Catherine Susanne de Champaigne, when She Was Ill, and Sister Catherine Agnes Arnaud (1662)
Ex-voto. 65″ × 90″.

NICOLAS POUSSIN. *The Inspiration of the Poet.*
Although the subject of this painting is difficult to interpret, it concerns an allegorical celebration of epic poetry, as suggested by the presence of the muse Calliope, recognizable through her resemblance to her description in Father Ripa's treaty on iconography, and by the titles of the books in the foreground—the *Odyssey,* the *Iliad* and the *Aeneid.* The painting can hardly have been executed in honor of a contemporary poet as the inspired mortal bears no resemblance to any writers dear to the artist or to any of his friends, such as Ariosto, Tasso or Marino. The subject might be Apollo crowning Virgil, since the poet in the painting resembles a figure which appears on the frontispiece of the Virgil published by the *Imprimerie Royale* in 1641, an engraving by Claude Mellan after Poussin. The date of the picture too has caused some problems, although that proposed by Blunt—before 1630—seems likely. Poussin painted another picture with the same theme, with Euterpe, the muse of lyric poetry, and a poet identifiable as Anacreon. These depictions of the varieties of classical poetry go back iconographically and stylistically—in the evocation of mythology as well as in pictorial tradition—to Paolo Veronese, Titian and above all to Raphael, whose *Parnassus* in the Vatican furnished a striking precedent. Poussin's work is reminiscent of Raphael's, possessing the same quality of revery and exaltation. Apollo, crowned with a laurel wreath, sits in the center, his arm resting on his cithara. He is making a slow, solemn gesture as he dictates to the inspired poet, reflecting the theories of Plato's *Phaedrus.* At the god's side stands the muse, a flute in hand. Above and below, a pair of putti distribute wreaths. This painting, justly considered one of Poussin's finest, is dominated by the poetic exaltation of the figures, heightened by an ample, almost epic landscape of heaven and earth framing god, man and muse.

NICOLAS POUSSIN
Les Andelys 1594—Rome 1665
The Inspiration of the Poet (before 1630)
Oil on canvas; 72 1/2″ × 84 1/4″. The painting can be identified with the one formerly in Mazarin's collection, admired by Bernini in 1665, as mentioned by Chantelou.

NICOLAS POUSSIN. *Self-Portrait.*   p. 88
Poussin painted two self-portraits, probably planned together and executed at about the same time. One, painted in 1649 for Pointel, is now in the Museum of East Berlin, while a copy (?) is in the Gimpel Collection, London. The Louvre picture, begun in September of the same year and finished in 1650, was painted for the artist's friend and patron Paul Fréart de Chantelou. While the Berlin example is romantic, even Baroque, the Louvre painting, with a corner of the artist's studio and a pile of his works appearing in the background, is more severely classic.

NICOLAS POUSSIN
Les Andelys 1594—Rome 1665
Self-Portrait (1650)
Oil on canvas; 38 1/2″ × 18 1/2″. Bears the
following inscription: "Effigies Nicolai Pous-
sini Andelyensis pictoris. Anno aetatis 56.
Romae anno jubilei 1650."

Although the artist's position before his mirror is the same in both pictures, in the first Poussin shows himself more animated and elegantly dressed. He rests his hand on a book titled *De lumine et colore*. In the background there appears a frieze decorated in relief with putti and laurel festoons. The Louvre portrait is more purely documentary, showing the artist's studio with his pictures leaning against each other in a beautifully geometric pattern. The artist's clothing is simpler, instead of a book he holds a portfolio of sketches and his face has a solemn, impassive expression. Poussin probably intended to offer two examples of "modes" or manners of painting, chosen by the artist according to the requirements of the occasion. Here he uses the so-called "Phrygian" and "Doric" mode. The choice of mode for a portrait probably depended on the sitter's interests and taste. As a matter of fact, Poussin consigned this picture to Chantelou probably because it seemed to him a truer likeness.

CLAUDE LORRAIN.   *Ulysses Returning Chryseis to Her Father.*
The mythological subject of this picture is simply a pretext for a landscape of immense proportions, its vastness emphasized by the small scale of the figures. The scene of the reconciliation takes place at the left, on the stairs leading to a classical palace, reminiscent of Pietro da Cortona. Beyond a large Mediterranean pine appears a Roman villa,

CLAUDE GELÉE
(CLAUDE LORRAIN)
Chamagne 1600—Rome 1682
Ulysses Returns Chryseis to Her Father
(circa 1644)
Detail. Oil on canvas.
47″ × 59″.

then a medieval port tower. The whole gives the impression of a mythic townscape permeated with seventeenth-century buoyancy. In the harbor, a galleon rides at anchor, casting a long shadow on the water. To the right is a building remarkable for its gigantic orders, crowded together in a manner reminiscent of Bernini. A strip of light divides the background from the foreground, where the artist shows the activity characteristic of a port—boats, merchants, goods and sailors.

Although a contemporary of Poussin, Lorrain reverses the latter's vision and sentiment. He raised landscape to the level of a protagonist, reduced the importance of the human figure and abandoned himself to a dream of utopian surroundings, the thought of a golden age, without Poussin's Cartesian discipline, without his melancholy or restlessness.

ETIENNE–MAURICE FALCONET. *Bather.*
The *Bather* is a typical example of Rococo decorative statuary, destined to adorn the boudoirs of ladies and cardinals. The girl stepping into a pool is more a nymph than a real figure, inspired by the mythological imagination of the period, as in the poetics of Boucher. Already, however, one can sense a breath of cool Neo-Classicism.

In the year he finished this famous statue, Falconet found his true vocation. He became the director of the celebrated porcelain factory at Sèvres. His patroness was Mme. de Pompadour, whom he once portrayed as Venus Anadyomene. His works of this type, although drawing-room frivolities, are distinguished by their harmonious elegance and poetic delicacy.

FRANÇOIS BOUCHER. *Diana Resting.*
A pupil of Watteau, Boucher was a highly gifted, hard-working painter, a virtuoso of the brush. Five years after Diana was exhibited at the Salon, he was granted the patronage of Mme. de Pompadour, and to a certain extent became the paradigm of the Louis XV style. Diderot was his only opponent, expressing a preference for Chardin.

Diana Resting appears to reflect Boucher's Italian visit, especially in the goddess's golden nudity, of an impalpable softness inspired by Correggio and of a delicate fantasy inspired by Ricci's Arcadian visions.

ANTOINE WATTEAU. *The Embarkation for Cythera.*
With this picture Watteau was admitted to the Royal Academy of Painting and Sculpture in 1717. For this honor, he had waited since his original application in 1712. It took him five years to present this work to the Academy, and even then it had not assumed its final form. A little after 1717, resuming this same theme, he created a more finished work which was purchased by Julienne (it is in Berlin). The picture has enjoyed wide fame, as echoed in the words of the Goncourts, who in their book on eighteenth-century art called it the masterpiece of French masterpieces.

In this picture, Watteau reveals that he has matured through a study of

ETIENNE–MAURICE FALCONET
Paris 1716–1791
Bather (1756–57)
Marble. 32″ high. Once thought to have been sculpted for Tiroux d'Epersenne (allegedly exhibited in the *Salon* in 1757), it is now believed to have belonged to the Countess du Barry and to have come to the Louvre after the confiscation of her property during the Revolution.

FRANÇOIS BOUCHER
Paris 1703–1770
Diana Resting (1742)
Detail. 22 1/2″ × 28 3/4″.

90

Rubens, whose influence is evident in the thick brushstrokes, and of the drawings of Bassano, Titian and van Dyck. The theme was perhaps based on a comedy by Dancourt. Watteau always retained a taste for the theater, which he learned from Gillot, a painter of scenes from the *Commedia Italiana* and one of his first teachers, according to Caylus in his biography of Watteau.

Watteau painted with a light brush, as is particularly noticeable in the foliage, while the figures are drawn and emphasized with a slightly heavier touch.

JEAN–BAPTISTE–SIMÉON CHARDIN. *Self-Portrait.*
One of Chardin's late works, the self-portrait is signed and dated 1775. The artist began to use pastels around 1770, when he was an old man. This picture shows no sign of senility, however; his delicate colors soften and modulate the shadows, while the areas struck by light are emphasized by fine white strokes. Although he is best known as a painter of still-lifes and bourgeois scenes, Chardin shows here his extraordinary ability as a portraitist through this frank and sensitive exploration of his own character. Refusing fine clothing and elegant poses, he wears the cap of a common man, as if in protest against all pretension. His introspective candor here and the honesty of his other works show his determination to be free of any preconceptions.

JEAN–BAPTISTE–SIMÉON CHARDIN. *Still-life with Pipe.*   *p. 94*
Chardin's still-lifes were a complete novelty in 18th-century painting. He dedicated himself obstinately to this genre which the Academy despised, and which he had cultivated out of necessity, in painting screens and door panels. Diderot, one of Chardin's greatest supporters, wrote what is perhaps one of the best definition of his painting: "The magic of his work is difficult to grasp. He uses thick layers of color, one over the other, with the final effect filtering through from underneath.

ANTOINE WATTEAU
Valenciennes 1684–1721
The Embarkation for Cythera
(circa 1717)
Detail. Oil on canvas; 50″ × 75 1/2″.

JEAN–BAPTISTE SIMÉON CHARDIN
Paris 1699–1779
Self-Portrait (1775)
Pastel; 18″ × 15″

At times it looks as if a cloud of steam has blown across the canvas, at others as if light foam has been tossed at it . . . If you go close, everything becomes confused, flattens out, disappears; when you back off, the forms reappear and come to life."

JEAN-BAPTISTE-SIMÉON CHARDIN.   *Back from Market.*
Back from Market and other works by Chardin were exhibited at the Louvre Salon of 1739, and show us how Chardin had by that time created a style all his own, emphasizing domestic interiors, everyday objects, the middle class. In 1881, the Goncourts wrote "He limits his painting to the humble world to which he belongs, and to which belong his habits, his thoughts, his affections . . . he adheres to the illustration and representation of those scenes which touch him and which move him . . ." In the Louvre painting, Chardin treats his subject with a liberty which seems to foreshadow the realism of the 19th century. He worked outside the fashionable currents of his day, and actually belonged to the trend of French realism which persists from Le Nain to Courbet.

JEAN-BAPTISTE SIMÉON CHARDIN
Paris 1699–1779
Back from Market (1739)
Oil on canvas; 18″ × 14 1/2″.

JEAN-BAPTISTE SIMEON CHARDIN
Paris 1699–1779
Still-life with Pipe (1760–63)
Oil on canvas; 12 1/2″ × 16 1/2″.

JEAN-HONORÉ FRAGONARD. *The Music Lesson.*
The Music Lesson appears to be a sketch rather than a finished picture.
Fragonard's usually lively style is rather perfunctory in this work. A
generation younger than Watteau, Boucher and Chardin, he was an
unsuccessful pupil of the last. Subsequently he studied under Boucher,
who at first made a great impression on him. In 1756 he won a Prix de
Rome and went to Italy, where he studied Baroque painting and Pietro
da Cortona in particular. From that time on his work became more
animated and he developed a rapid, sure brilliant touch. He is the
typical representative of the Rococo in France, even in his most conservative phase, and was deaf to the first notes of Neo-Classicism in the
second half of the eighteenth century.

JEAN-HONORÉ FRAGONARD
Grasse 1732—Paris 1806
The Music Lesson (circa 1769)
Oil on canvas; 43 1/4″ × 47 1/4″.

NINETEENTH CENTURY FRANCE

JACQUES–LOUIS DAVID. *Portrait of Madame Récamier.*

This painting belongs to David's high period, when he was the official painter to the Napoleonic age. It dates sixteen years after his famous *Oath of the Horatii* which was immediately recognized as a masterpiece with a message, an invitation to esthetic and political revolt, and later as one of the main documents of Neo-Classicism. By 1800 the revolutionary thrust of the new style was but a memory, and David's big mythological works, magnificent and brilliant as they may be, are considered by some critics to be overly doctrinaire. The portraits, on the other hand, remain among the highest products of his personality and style. The *Portrait of Madame Récamier* is one of the most significant, together with those of Count Potocki, the architect Desmaison, the Lavoisiers and the two magisterial self-portraits of 1790 and 1794. The delicate, soft figure—which offers a glimpse of what would be the fluid line of Ingres—turns a sensitive head toward the spectator. In the purity and sharpness of space (the tripod at the left is an important compositional element) there is a vibrant pictorial harmony, far removed from that "frigid execution" for which Delacroix reproached David. Note the touches of color on the cushions, on the gown, on the braided hair, scattered with quick glimpses of light.

JACQUES–LOUIS DAVID. *The Coronation of Napoleon.*

Immediately following the opening of the nineteenth century, David was commissioned by the Emperor to execute a number of large canvases to illustrate the major events of the time, including his own coronation. We know from documents that he was influenced by Rubens,

JACQUES–LOUIS DAVID
Paris 1748—Brussels 1825
Portrait of Madame Recamier (1800)
Oil on canvas; 59 × 94 1/2".

JACQUES–LOUIS DAVID
Paris 1748—Brussels 1825
The Coronation of Napoleon (1805–1807)
Detail.
Oil on canvas; 240″ × 367″.
Signed and dated.

but it is also amply proved by the quality of the painting, which establishes an imposing synthesis of David's art and style. Our detail of the enormous composition furnishes additional evidence of David's genius as a portraitist. The head of the figure at the right certainly reminds us of his youthful passion for classical Roman sculpture.

EUGENE DELACROIX. *Liberty Leading the People.*
Like many of Delacroix's paintings, this one was inspired by a current political event, the 1830 insurrection of Paris. Almost to emphasize his enthusiasm as a liberal, the artist identified himself with the man brandishing a gun on the overturned barricade, while the armed mob is glimpsed through the smoke of the explosions that veil the city. (Six years earlier, Delacroix had painted, with parallel force, and on the same politically liberal theme, *Massacre of Chios,* inspired by the Greek struggle for independence.) Delacroix's rhetorical tone is compelling and the movements, the settings of the figures and, above all, the two bodies that almost completely dominate the foreground, reveal his emphasis on the theatrical. But the deep passion that motivated the artist more than redeems the violence of the scene. Two years later Delacroix made a long voyage to Morocco and Spain, a trip that proved crucial to his future.

EUGENE DELACROIX
Charenton-Saint-Maurice 1798—Paris 1863
Liberty Leading the People (1830)
Oil on canvas; 102 1/2″ × 128″; exhibited at the
Salon of 1831, the painting was acquired by the
French Government.

EUGENE DELACROIX. *Women of Algiers.*
"Here fame is a word without meaning: everything turns to a sweet laziness and it cannot be said that this is not the most desirable condition in the world." These words by Delacroix were written in a letter of 1832 from Tangier, and they explain the atmosphere of this masterpiece, deservedly among the most famous of the nineteenth century. It opens the long series of his paintings inspired by Oriental life, including lion hunts, Arabian horses, musicians and actors. The scene shows the interior of a harem, probably one visited by the artist during his African sojourn. It is evident that his first-hand observations left a deep mark, but above all they conditioned the development of his painting, as demonstrated in this luxurious setting where tiles, curtains, silks and jewels complement each other and yet each is painted with extraordinary precision. There is already a hint of that freedom of form which characterizes the later Delacroix, and of his complex compositional ideas which made him a rebel against the rules and doctrines of official art.

JEAN–AUGUSTE–DOMINIQUE INGRES. *The Turkish Bath.*

The Turkish Bath was to have been the property of Prince Napoleon, but his wife considered the work immoral, so the Bonapartes bought a self-portrait instead. Ingres, after recovering the painting, altered the format to its circular shape and made a number of changes in the figures at the edges. Before coming to the Louvre, the painting was owned by the Turkish Ambassador to France and later by Prince Amédée de Broglie. Ingres had the theme of *The Turkish Bath* in mind for years. Jean Alazard has pointed out that in one of his notebooks the artist cites a few sentences from the letters of Lady Mary Wortley Montagu (published in 1764): "There were 200 women . . . The sofas were covered with cushions and rich carpets, on which sat the ladies, all being in the state of nature, that is, in plain English, stark naked . . . yet there was not the least wanton smile or immodest gesture among them." Ingres' *Bathers* of 1828 is an early statement of the idea. But

EUGENE DELACROIX
Charenton-Saint-Maurice 1798—Paris 1863
Women of Algiers (1834)
Oil on canvas; 71″ × 90″. Signed and dated.
Exhibited at the Salon of 1834; bought by
French Government for 3,000 francs.

JEAN–AUGUSTE–DOMINIQUE INGRES
Montauban 1780—Paris 1867
The Turkish Bath (1826) Oil on canvas; diameter 41 1/2″—Signed and dated. Before entering the Louvre, it was owned by the Turkish Ambassador to Paris and later the Prince de Broglie.

the definitive version of *The Turkish Bath* dates from about 1860 and was finally finished in 1863, when the artist was 84. It can be considered his purest masterpiece; a sort of summation of the subject matter, content and problems he had treated many times before. The artist reveals himself, as always, conscious of the history of his own long artistic development. And it is extraordinary that none of this feeling of recapitulation detracts from the freshness of his inspiration. Many drawings show how specifically Ingres studied each figure, experimenting with them and visualizing them separately and in groups. The creative process was therefore long, and the power of abstract expression can be called absolute. The artist was completely immersed in his search for that depth and mastery of image to which he subordinated all other values. In this work are revealed some of his clearest and most daring intuitions, like that of "distorting" anatomy, and not losing himself in details, but forcing a central idea. The nude in the right foreground shows how Ingres found harmony in "deformation." **103**

THEODORE GERICAULT. *The Raft of the Medusa,* (preliminary study).
The Raft of the Medusa was to have been the first of a series of large
paintings and was preceded by some 50 studies, of which this is probably one of the last. The studies have noticeable differences: missing
in this one, for instance, are the body thrown overboard (foreground)
and the dying man on the edge of the raft (left). Although incomplete,
the composition of the central figures is already evident, and this sketch
is considered by some authorities to be superior to the huge masterpiece that derives from it.

THEODORE GERICAULT. *The Raft of the Medusa.*
In 1816 Géricault, barely 25 years old, went to Italy, where he became
fascinated with the works of the Classical and Renaissance masters.
Upon his return to Paris in 1817, it was clear how deeply his visit to
Italy had affected him when he undertook his most famous single
canvas, *The Raft of the Medusa.* Many suggestions have been made as
to which artists most influenced Géricault; from Michelangelo to
Guercino, Gros to Prud'hon. B. Nicholson feels that a number of
English and American painters of the late eighteenth century, especially Copley, left their impress on the artist. The *Raft,* according
to Ragghianti, demonstrates the possibilities of "majestic historic continuity," without diminishing originality. In spite of its complex movements, intense passions and the gesticulations, violent foreshortenings
of the limbs and bodies, the whole composition has a severe pyramidal
structure that was roundly denounced by many contemporaries. Particularly objectionable were the shrouds (not shown in the sketch).
The scene is foreshortened, receding swiftly to the horizon, but the
vast dimensions of the canvas compel you to look and think, which
104 was the intention of the artist who conceived of the painting as a "public"

THEODORE GERICAULT
Rouen 1791—Paris 1824
The Raft of the Medusa (1818)
Study. Oil and pen on canvas;
25 1/2" × 32 1/2".

THEODORE GERICAULT
Rouen 1791—Paris 1824
The Raft of the Medusa (1818–1819)
Oil on canvas; 193 1/2″ × 282″—Exhibited at
the Salon of 1819, then in England for two
years, the painting remained unsold until the
artist died. Auctioned in November 1824, it
was bought by Gericault's friend Dedreux-
Dorcy, who a few months before had helped
the dying artist.

message. Rejecting other episodes of the scandalous event (the ship-
wrecked seamen of the Medusa were set adrift on a raft in the Mediterranean and there were rumors of cannibalism), Géricault picked
the moment when the survivors catch sight of the gunboat Argus that
rescued them. Aside from the inevitable controversy it aroused in its
time, the *Raft* immediately became famous, evoking enthusiastic praise
from both critics and public.

CAMILLE COROT
Paris 1796—1875
Souvenir of Mortefontaine (1864)
Oil on canvas; 25 1/2″ × 35″.

CAMILLE COROT.   *Souvenir of Mortefontaine.*

A look at Corot's major paintings makes *Souvenir of Mortefontaine*
and similar works seem a bit sketchy and ordinary. But in any one of
his masterly Italian scenes, bright French landscapes, portraits or
figures, from the young nude of Mariette to the old *Woman at the Well*
(Kröller-Müller Museum), you see an artist completely wrapped up in
himself, completely oblivious to the life around him—artistic, social
or political. Until about 1850 Corot's masterpieces were unknown:
public recognition finally came to him through a series of large compositions. In this romantic *Souvenir,* the artist evokes the imaginative
re-creation of an atmosphere which remembers the eighteenth century.
Freshness catches your eye in the foreground touches of light, the
transparency of the shadows, the delicacy of the background passages.
A lofty tree dominates the rectangle and conceals most of the horizon,
creating a mild effect of crosslighting, echoed in the small figures
silhouetted against the clear, still waters.

FRANCOIS MILLET
Gruchy 1814—Barbizon 1875
The Gleaners (1848)
Oil on canvas; 21 1/4″ × 26″.

FRANÇOIS MILLET. *The Gleaners.*

The Angelus, 1859, and *The Gleaners,* 1857, continue to move the public today just as they did when they were executed. They are typical of the struggling Millet, who grew up on a farm in Normandy, and who, until he was almost 35, could not find his artistic direction. He hated the noise and frantic atmosphere of Paris and found a refuge in the little village of Barbizon in 1849. There he met, among other painters, Théodore Rousseau, whose friend he became. This was a happy and active time for Millet. He followed the style of rural Realism introduced in *The Gleaners,* especially in the three figures that stand out against the deep expanse of mowed fields. Note the firmness of the simple design, the absence of anecdote and details not essential to the dignity of the scene. The tiny figures in the background—wagon, horses, houses, trees, hay stacks—are an integral part of the wide landscape where man wears himself out in toil and suffering. In Millet's art, man is almost always in the center, and in this he distinguishes himself from his Barbizon friends, who were trying to understand "the language of the forest." It is indicative that, much later, van Gogh admired and copied Millet.

GUSTAVE COURBET. *The Artist's Studio.*

When this painting and his *Burial at Ornans* were rejected by the Universal Exposition of 1855, Courbet built his own "Pavilion of Realism," and organized an exhibition of 40 of his paintings. The detail illustrated here is the central section of the great composition in which he portrayed artists and writers sharing "the common action" for Realism. Also included are a proletarian and an Irishwoman. The symmetrical dignity of *Burial at Ornans* is a simply articulated scene, even though the figures are spread out across the composition. It can be called a synthesis of his cultural and formal experiences up to that time and in it we still find traces of his romantic and literary youth. His study of Velázquez and Ribera, of the seventeenth-century Dutch, of Caravaggio are evident in *The Studio;* yet all is converted to a style that separates Courbet from the past as well as from his contemporaries. The artist's strength and vitality hide but at the same time reveal his process of selection and comprehension, accomplished intelligently and with a precise purpose. Culture and a sense of reality—a passion for generous and fervid living—are united. Courbet was anything but "naive," ingenuous, or lacking in intellect; he would never submit to rules or participate in programs; he was a rebel, yet not without tenderness. We sense him here, too, in the figure of the child and in the nude who personifies Courbet's ideal woman. We see him in the entire group, and in the center, alone at his easel, in a world of illusion, but still close to the values and to the eternal allegories of life.

EDOUARD MANET. *Olympia.*   *p. 110*

"The flesh tone is dirty, the model is nothing"; "This brunette is thoroughly ugly: her face is stupid, her skin cadaverous . . . all this clash of colors, of impossible shapes, is stupefying." These are two of the many negative opinions and "savage reviews" which appeared in Paris newspapers between May and June of 1865 (the first is by none other than the lapidary poet Théophile Gautier). Manet was hurt, as he was pained by the violence of visitors who wanted to attack the canvas itself. "Insults rain on me like hail," he wrote his friend the poet Baudelaire a short time later. And the malicious Degas, almost spitefully remarked, "Now you are as famous as Garibaldi!" It is difficult today when *Olympia* is considered one of the masterpieces of nineteenth-century painting to understand why it caused such a scandal and was so scorned. Robert Rey has noted that Manet rediscovered "a forgotten alphabet," and that it was his radical invocation of art history that was beyond the understanding of his contemporaries. *Olympia* lies on a silk shawl, resting on her right elbow, with raised head gazing at you, completely aloof. Her figure breathes light, and shadows frown subtly in the gray outlines. Her white flesh stands out vividly against the dark

GUSTAVE COURBET
Ornans 1819—La Tour-de-Peilz 1877
The Artist's Studio (1855)
Detail. Oil on canvas; 141 1/4″ × 235 1/2″. The work, together with *Burial at Ornans,* was rejected by the Universal Exposition of 1855. The artist then built his own shed, "Pavilion of Realism" in the center of Paris and there exhibited 40 of his paintings.

background from which emerges the pale gray-rose of the dress of the Negress bringing in a bouquet of flowers. *Olympia* represents, says critic Marangoni, "all Manet's aversion to the clever and superficial and is a challenge to the bad taste and spiritual baseness of the official painters and of the 'bourgeoisie.'" With exceptional simplicity, Manet accomplished his ideal of "a genuine vision pursued as far as brutality."

ÉDOUARD MANET. *The Balcony.*
Our detail reproduction is of the left-hand figure of a group of three leaning over the balcony, while a fourth is glimpsed inside a dimly lit room; she is Manet's friend, the painter Berthe Morisot. Her comment on the painting was that *The Balcony* had turned out "more strange than ugly." Like *Olympia,* it caused a minor scandal when it was exhibited. The detail, about actual size, reveals how intelligently the artist used quick, brilliant strokes to achieve his image.

EDOUARD MANET
Paris 1832–1883
The Balcony (1868)
Detail.
Oil on canvas; 65 7/8″ × 29 1/8″.

EDOUARD MANET
Paris 1832–1883
Olympia (1863)
Oil on canvas; 51″ × 74 3/4″. The work was shown at the 1865 Salon, and caused an unprecedented scandal. *Olympia* did not enter the Louvre until the beginning of this century.

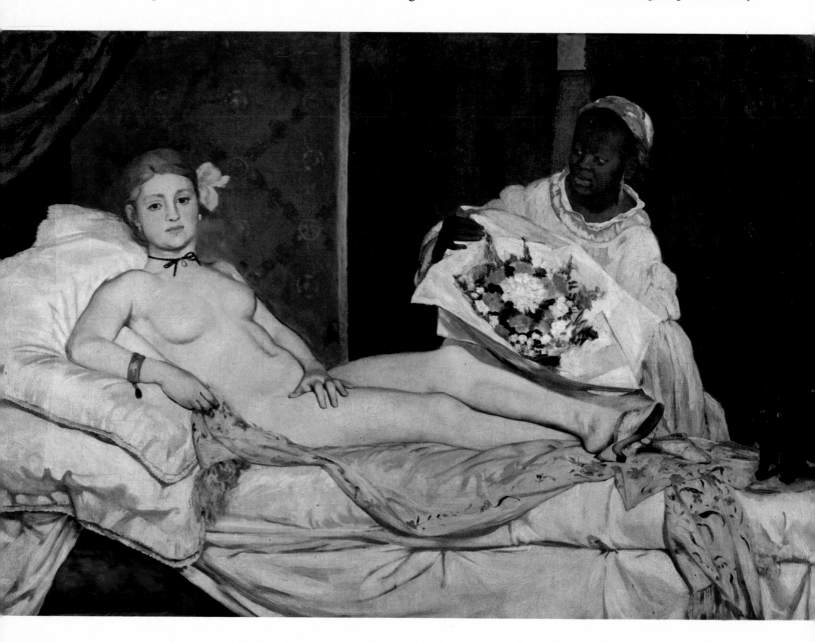

CAMILLE PISSARRO. *The Red Roofs.*

In 1874–75, at Pontoise, and then again in 1877, Pissarro and Cézanne worked side by side. It is almost certain that their close association and friendship contributed much to Pissarro's development, while Cézanne, on the other hand, recognized that he owed a good deal of his own growth to his older friend. This landscape is among the most representative of Pissarro's relationship with Cézanne between 1875 and 1880. With the help of Sisley and Monet, Pissarro, through selfless exertion, was mainly responsible for maintaining the cohesion of the Impressionist group and participated in all their shows from 1874 on. He had a sense for construction and felt that likenesses should develop slowly. Here you see, for example, his method of drawing with color, systematically superimposing dabs of color to create a mellow density and richness of tone. Émile Zola emphasized the "heroic simplicity" of Pissarro's art when he wrote: "It is enough to glimpse such works to understand that behind them is a man, an honest and vigorous personality, incapable of lying."

CLAUDE MONET. *Rouen Cathedral in Full Sunlight.*

During the winter months of 1892 and 1893, Claude Monet visited Rouen and, working with his characteristic energy, painted a series on the cathedral as he saw it from a window on the rue du Grand Pont at

CAMILLE PISSARRO
Saint-Thomas (Antilles) 1832—Paris 1903
The Red Roofs (1877)
Oil on canvas; 24 1/4″ × 25 1/2″.

CLAUDE MONET
Paris 1840—Giverny 1926
Rouen Cathedral in Full Sunlight
(1892–1893)
Oil on canvas; 42″ × 24 3/4″.

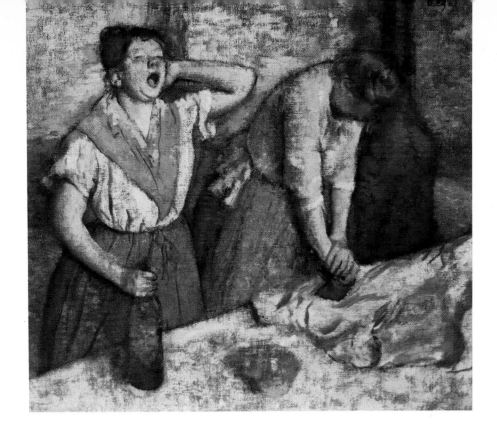

different hours of the day. Twenty of the 50 pictures, many of which he completed in his studio at Giverny, were exhibited in 1895 at Durand-Ruel's gallery. The cathedral's façade is always in the foreground and fills the whole rectangle. Light plays on the complex shapes, modifies and transposes the relationships between masses, continually altering the tones and local colors. Monet often complained of losing his youthful ability, of no longer being able to capture the fleeting instant, the momentary glimpse. But his Rouen Cathedral cycle comes closest to the modern vision, even if the happiest balance in Monet's art appears in the decade of 1870–80.

PIERRE–AUGUSTE RENOIR. *Moulin de la Galette.*

Moulin de la Galette, along with *The Luncheon of the Boating Party,* which he painted five years later, are shining examples of Renoir's genius, his innate talent for painting, his indifference to any form of intellectualism. Most interesting in this large composition, beautifully executed with an exact sense of space and with a marvellous impression of a crowd given by the superimposition of the faces, is the kaleidoscopic sparkling of color that filter unevenly through the leafy trees. The scene is lively. The daily life of Paris in the second half of the nineteenth century could not have found a more lyric and human interpreter. Rarely has painting made it possible to grasp so much of the contemporaneous poetic spirit.

EDGAR DEGAS. *Two Laundresses.*

The most commonplace, insignificant aspects of life and things attracted Edgar Degas, because for him they were the most suitable to "embody a clear vision." Here it is two laundresses at their daily work. What could have been a sketch of sorts, became under Degas' brush a wonderfully designed painting with rhythmic arrangements of contrasts and

115

dislocations of form. The most habitual, banal and private gestures are turned into admirable compositional instruments. A flat table establishes a downward diagonal movement opposing a movement from the opposite direction in the yawning figure. By such formal means and through Degas' rejection of any sentimentality about the laundress' sore arms, her bearing is presented in an absolute and dignified manner. The delicate, almost velvety color underlines the originality of one of the most coherent and forceful visions of any time.

RAYMOND HENRI DE TOULOUSE–LAUTREC. *The Clowness Cha-U-Kao.*
This is one of the most intense and vigorous paintings of Toulouse-Lautrec, whose best works were produced in the last ten years of the nineteenth century. The figure is almost monumental, and yet it has new motifs and forms and a new conception of space that shows the influence

HENRI RAYMOND DE
TOULOUSE–LAUTREC
Albi 1864—Malrome 1901
The Clowness Cha-U-Kao (1895)
Gouache on board;
22 1/2″ × 16 1/2″.

116

PAUL CEZANNE
Aix-en-Provence 1839–1906
The Card Players (1890–92)
Oil on canvas; 17 3/4″ × 22 1/2″.

of Degas, whom Lautrec admired and who was his true teacher. The focal point is the yellow skirt that spirals around the heavy figure of the clowness. Despite her swelling, spilling form, she is invested with a stupendous energy, which depends on the quick impression, or what can be called the lightning-like style so unique to Lautrec. Notwithstanding the explosive passage of yellow, Lautrec was intolerant of "beautiful" painting and unwilling to go back and repaint what he had already done. Thus his corrections and deletions add to the total effect of the image.

PAUL CÉZANNE. *The Card Players.*
There are several studies and versions of this picture; one of them contains four figures, but this famous painting probably best reflects Cézanne's conception and his aspiration to solemnity. It reveals, among

117

other things, an exceptional composition, on a level with the best works of this great master. The symmetrical organization gains intensity from a use of delicate, sensitive variations on divided and related colors. The background in itself is a comment on the figures—it is completely harmonious but implies a different emotion. The controlling colors suggest a timeless dignity. Light, almost fluid, flows with sudden movements and vibrations that suggest an incisive, subtle handwriting. Cézanne continued to accent this more sensitive style in his later works, creating a cornerstone for modern art.

PAUL GAUGUIN. *The White Horse.*
The taste and decorative instinct of Gauguin, and the new idea of color he evolved even before he went to Tahiti, are exemplified in this painting where he seems to overcome any and all programmatic esthetics. Here oranges, blues, reds, greens are used with a surprising liberty that later was to become the banner of the Fauves. The perspective he employed is based on the Japanese prints that had become known in Paris before Gauguin's Brittany period. Whether because of the way the horses moved, or because of the stream opening into the bottom of the picture, or because of the more broadly painted forms at the edges of the canvas, the total effect of the painting appears very personal. In such values as these are caught the contributions of a master who was erroneously judged as either savage or primitive by critics of the times.

VINCENT VAN GOGH. *Self-Portrait.*
Two months after finishing this masterpiece, Vincent van Gogh shot himself through the chest. His final letters expressed terror, then resignation. However, he worked incessantly up to the end. He painted landscapes and portraits, among them the magnificent one of the Impressionists' friend Dr. Gachet and this equally great self-portrait. His will and psychological insight and passionate concentration did not stop him from spreading rhythmic brushstrokes in tortuous waves on the canvas and into his torrential cascades of man, earth, sky. The background of this self-portrait could easily have been the sky that rose over the yellow fields of the Oise. From this background, which the jacket re-echoes and almost seems to turn into folds of cloth, Vincent's head boldly detaches itself, seemingly lost in the knowledge of his destiny.

PAUL GAUGUIN
Paris 1848—Atuana (Marquesas Islands) 1903
The White Horse (1898)
Oil on canvas; 55 1/2″ × 35 3/4″.

See p. 120
VINCENT VAN GOGH
Groot Zundert 1853—Auvers-sur-Oise 1890
Self-Portrait (1890)
Oil on canvas; 25 3/5″ × 21 1/4″.

ITALY

CIMABUE. *Madonna in Majesty.*

The painting was commissioned for the Church of St. Francis in Pisa; it remained there until the nineteenth century. The Virgin sits on a decorated throne set at a slant so that the line of her body follows that of the steps and the throne. Marking the planes in depth are the great golden nimbus inserted between her body and the back of the throne and the three pairs of angels set up against the throne to which their bodies and hook-like fingers cling in precise columnar arrangement.

The gold background here no longer serves as metallic curtain, screen or backdrop. It becomes real space. A limited space, to be sure, stretching out into a supernatural dimension: but nevertheless a space, structured by elements which subdivide it. Smaller areas are carefully blocked out, as for example the folds on the Virgin's sides, arms and knees. Her head is enclosed in an oval frame like those of Arnolfo di Cambio. After the tormented, ornamented linear style of the artist's *Christ* in Arezzo and the fantastic visions of the frescoes in Assisi (for example the *Crucifixion* where the medieval transcendental ideal still caused the works to vibrate with tensions and contrasts), Cimabue here seems to want to express himself in a more peaceful settled way. He avoids both the exalted and the dramatic style with its anxieties and high emotions. He seems to be attempting to communicate his own serene affirmation of faith to the visitors of the Church of St. Francis in Pisa.

SIMONE MARTINI. *Christ on the Road to Calvary.*

This small panel was once part of an altarpiece representing the *Passion of Christ* which is today divided between the Louvre and the Antwerp and Berlin museums. In spite of its size, the picture is extremely concentrated. Its structure is formed by the contrast between the geometric, block-like shape of the city, seen in perspective from the lower left, and the mob accompanying Christ. This brightly-colored group, irregularly subdivided, comes down from above, almost bursting forth from the narrow opening, then bearing to the right so that the rapid upward movement is braked and interrupted. The space, both within the walls and outside, is airless. The slope is lighted only in the background, where the figure of Christ with his bright red mantle carrying the Cross forms the focus of the composition. Such a composition, intensely personal and not to be translated into "normal" objective dimensions, expresses the sure style of Simone Martini, who matches in his painting the aims and literary achievements of his friend Petrarch. Both artists were conscious of taking part in an enormously creative period of European civilization, and indeed, Simone Martini was himself responsible for many elements of one of its most successful creations, the so-called "International Gothic" style.

CIMABUE
Florence 1240 (?)—Pisa 1302 (?)
Madonna in Majesty (1295–1300)
Tempera on panel; 167″ × 108 1/2″. Executed for the Church of St. Francis in Pisa, where it remained until 1882, when it was taken as part of Napoleon's booty.

SIMONE MARTINI
Siena 1284 (?)—Avignon 1344
Christ on the Road to Calvary (1335–40)
Tempera on panel; 9 1/2″ × 6 1/4″.
This small panel was once part of an altarpiece depicting the *Passion* of Christ. Other panels, representing *the Archangel Gabriel, The Annunciation, The Crucifixion* and *The Deposition* are in the Antwerp Museum, while *The Entombment* is in the Berlin Museum.

PISANELLO. *Portrait of a Princess of the House of Este.*
The princess is either Margherita Gonzaga, wife of Lionello d'Este, or Ginevra d'Este, wife of the notorious Sigismondo Malatesta. She wears on her sleeve the arms of the Este family, a vase or amphora. Her portrait is an example of Pisanello's intellectual style, of his aristocratic avoidance of the natural in favor of the sophisticated taste of the courtly world within which he moved so gracefully. His painting portrays acutely, often sympathetically, characteristic motifs from this world: animals in gardens or at the hunt, for instance, or the fashionable dress and decorations of lords and ladies. Here he shows the lady with every hair painstakingly, remorselessly drawn back, tightly bound by a ribbon. Her bosom is forced in a rigid bodice. Far from hiding the weakness of the profile, he emphasizes the roundness of the forehead and the bare neck. This delicate, vulnerable, asexual nakedness fits into a background of flowers and butterflies, represented like so many crystals and precious stones. As her skin and dress are transformed into marble, so, too, the sky is changed into lapis-lazuli by the artist's marvelous alchemy.

PAOLO UCCELLO. *The Rout of San Romano.*   *p. 126*
Paolo Uccello painted, in three panels, the battle fought in June 1432 near San Romano by the Florentine and Sienese armies under the *"condottieri"* Niccolò da Tolentino, Micheletto Attendolo da Cotignola on one side, and Bernardino della Carnia on the other. Today the panels are divided among the Uffizi Gallery in Florence, the National Gallery in London and the Louvre. Neither side is favored by the artist: the victorious Florentines cannot be distinguished from the losing Sienese. We have an immobile, enclosed, complex composition of white, bluish brown and rose-toned horses champing at the bit and stamping their powerful hoofs, horsemen shut into the shining anonymity of their silver-painted steel armor, and an intricate pattern of clubs, lances and pennants. Each element is reduced to a blind and splendid instrument of death. The artist, avoiding narration, created a kind of mysterious and frighteningly still masquerade, with all the figures caught in the instant just before the final catastrophe.

p. 127
DOMENICO GHIRLANDAIO. *Francesco Sassetti with His Grandson.*
Ghirlandaio, who often showed an interest in factual description, executed portraits in one of two ways. Most frequent is the type emphasizing learned allusions and details of dress which result in an "official" identification of a person. At times, however, as here, he concentrated on emotional relationships which allowed him to reveal the inner character of the people involved. In this painting of the famous Florentine banker Francesco Sassetti, Ghirlandaio is less concerned with his position in society than with the vigor and robustness of his old age, with all its faults, such as the growth on his large nose. Most important is the way in which the old man reacts to his grandson, who moves affectionately toward him. This relationship is echoed in the red color of the old man's dress, repeated in the boy's hat and jacket as though to underline the intimate relationship and continuity of these two, the oldest and

124   youngest members of the family.

PISANELLO
Verona (?) c. 1395—Verona 1455
Portrait of a Princess of the House of Este
(1435–40) Tempera on panel; 17″ × 11 3/4″.

ALESSIO BALDOVINETTI. *Madonna and Child.*
The artist's goal seems to have been to co-ordinate the structural elements of the composition in space through a use of perspective of color
rather than of geometric lines, in a way already worked out by Domenico
Veneziano. With this ideal in mind, he enlarged certain areas and reduced others, forming the surface into an irregularly articulated whole
over which plays the diffused cold, early-morning sun, alternately creating areas of light and shadow. In accordance with this system, the halo
is not shown as a line, but as a large mirror-like disk; the child is like a
wax model whose cylindrical volume is emphasized by the ribbon-like
band tied around his waist; the pillow marks the depth of the balustrade;
and the Virgin holds her hands before her in an opposed direction from
that of the arms of the chair, thus emphasizing the space before her,
which balances the space which extends behind her in the sloping,
deserted landscape. Such a static composition brings out the precious
quality of all colors and textures, such as the delicacy of veils and velvets, of ivory-colored skin, shiny metallic cloths and variegated marble. **127**

ANDREA MANTEGNA. *Parnassus.*

Parnassus, the traditional title for this work, is today recognized to be based on an erroneous interpretation of the painting. Scholars have repeatedly attempted, without ever agreeing, to work out the iconography of this painting and of the other four pictures of a group painted by Mantegna and Perugino, then at the height of their careers, and Lorenzo Costa, for Isabella of Este's *studiolo* around the end of the fifteenth century. The subject was chosen by the learned Isabella and her intellectual humanist friends. In any case, this work is of interest as an example of Mantegna's purist "classical" style, a style which often coexists with his other complex and heroic manners. Here we can clearly distinguish the three sections of the composition: Vulcan pointing towards Venus and Mars, shown serenely embracing each other; the women dancing, accompanied by Orpheus; and, finally, the enigmatic couple on the right. Tying these three elements together are the spaces and the converging and parallel lines of the limbs of the figures, the floating scarves, the lances, rocks and foliage. Such a clear sym-

ANDREA MANTEGNA
Isola di Cartura 1431—Mantua 1506
Parnassus (1495–97)
Tempera on canvas; 63″ × 75 1/2″. In the Louvre are also the three paintings of the *Myth of Comus,* by Mantegna and Lorenzo Costa, Costa's *Allegory* and Perugino's *Triumph of Chastity,* all painted like *Parnassus,* for the study of Isabella d'Este in her palace at Mantua.

PIETRO PERUGINO
Citta della Pieve 1445—Fontignano 1524
Apollo and Marsyas (1490–1500)
Oil on panel; 15 1/4″ × 11 1/2″.

metry, both in depth and on the plane, exemplifies that classical tradition which would continue from Poussin to Ingres.

PIETRO PERUGINO. *Apollo and Marsyas.*
Art historians have not always appreciated the importance of the inner structure of Perugino's altarpieces. But such works as this, in which the human figure is freed from the conventional restrictions of "official" painting, have always been popular with critics and public alike. The figure becomes a part of the landscape, and enters into close relationship with trees, rivers, hills, streets and castles. The relationship is an unexpected one, however. On the one hand, nature is relaxed; humanized and good-natured, but not completely taken over by cultivation. On the other hand, in a kind of contrast, the forms of Apollo and Marsyas are carefully and consciously modeled and controlled. Marsyas appears neither as satyr nor hairy shepherd, but as a handsome, polished youth. Their fixed poses which form the backbone of the composition are regulated according to an intellectual ideal, a mathematical, musical harmony. **129**

LEONARDO DA VINCI (?). *The Annunciation.*

Critics have repeatedly discussed the problem of this picture's attribution: is it by Leonardo or Lorenzo di Credi? In favor of Leonardo are the complex levels of meaning, the character of the brushstroke and the sure touch of color relationships, with reddish-brown tones prevailing. In favor of a different attribution, however, is the manner in which areas are defined, the painstaking divisions between garden, neighboring lawns, path and corner of the wall, as well as the rigorous symmetry of the plane within which the two figures have been placed in a curved composition. The lack of care given to details and dress also points to someone other than Leonardo, possibly Lorenzo di Credi, who had studied with Leonardo under Verrocchio.

LEONARDO DA VINCI
Vinci 1452—Amboise 1519
Portrait of Mona Lisa (circa 1505)
Oil on panel; 30 1/4″ × 20 3/4″.

LEONARDO DA VINCI. *Portrait of Mona Lisa (La Gioconda).*

The surface of the picture has suffered from overpainting. The paint has oxidized and today we see the figure through a greenish haze, completely altering the original colors. The significance of the figure, too, has suffered from over-interpretation and false interpretations. Yet somehow the Mona Lisa has, almost miraculously, survived all these vicissitudes. Its meaning is not easy to understand; but neither is it impenetrable, if one studies Leonardo's figurative motifs in the context of his scientific interests. In painting the Mona Lisa, Leonardo was reacting against a fifteenth-century concept of space which, after having been the focus of scientific and esthetic investigation during the whole of the century, was tied to a rigid Aristotelian classification. He has swept aside the traditional division of the horizontal plane by converging radial lines and the subordination of the single elements to a single vanishing point, and substituted, in their stead, a gradation of light and color. The frame no longer limits the figure; even the wooden panel loses its solidity. The viewer finds himself before an open window, as Alberti said, or as Leonardo himself put it, "a glass wall"; just beyond is the figure, placed in three-quarter profile, with hands together, the arm of the chair at a slant. There is movement in the evanescent, crinkly folds of the dress, the veil, the hair. A barely perceptible smile touches the curve of the mouth and the eyelids. Everything breathes and trembles imperceptibly: the waves of the water, the mist, the clouds, even the scaly rocks in the infinite, vaporous landscape.

LEONARDO DA VINCI (?)
The Annunciation (1480–85)
Tempera on panel; 5 1/2″ × 28 3/4″. It was originally the central panel of an altarpiece representing a "Sacred Conversation," executed by Lorenzo di Credi, in the Cathedral of Pistoia.

RAPHAEL. *Madonna and Child and St. John The Baptist.*
This is perhaps the work which best reveals the influence on Raphael of
Leonardo's mature work, as represented, for example, by the Louvre
cartoon for *St. Anne.* Raphael painted this *Madonna* during his stay in
Florence, in 1504–09. He deliberately chose certain Leonardesque
motifs, and discarded others. Leonardo fragments matter and brings
movements into it in an attempt to represent the dynamic aspect of the
cosmos, with its infinite possibilities for transformation; Raphael insists
instead on a clearly defined articulation of objects represented in their
immutable, crystalline interrelationships. This is why the fluid, descending pyramidal structure of Leonardo's *St. Anne,* which was the
pattern Raphael was following, is here completely changed. The re-
splendent colors form a measured, clear space. Within this space the
lines of limbs and garments, uninterrupted by jewels or other decorative
motifs, form a clear pattern.

RAPHAEL. *Portrait of Baldassarre Castiglione.*
The structure of the figure is not only pyramidal, but almost prismatic,
worked out in depth. This prism leads the eye from the hands at the
lower left, along the diagonal lines of the forearms to the elbows, and
from there in depth, back from each of the successive levels outlined
in turn by fold, shoulder and collar. The solid frame of the body is
emphasized with its wide shoulders and deep chest. Above it, the face

RAPHAEL
Urbino 1483—Rome 1520
Madonna and Child and St. John the Baptist
(1507) Oil on panel 48″ × 31 1/2″. The work is
signed and dated; it can be identified with a
Madonna which Vasari says Raphael painted
in Florence for Filippo Sergardi.

RAPHAEL
Portrait of Baldassarre Castiglione (1515–16)
Oil on panel, transferred to canvas;
29 1/2″ × 25 1/2″.

stands out, reflecting the whiteness of the shirt, and framed by the brim of the wide hat, whose dark outline adds to the stability of the form. The artist here is deeply interested in the character of his subject, the author of a famous book of manners, *The Courtier*. He seems, indeed, to be translating Castiglione's intellectual and moral character into pictorial terms by means of three-dimensional geometric, architectural forms, covered with luxurious furs and velvets in greenish yellows and browns.

GIORGIONE. *The Concert.*

The attribution of this work has been the subject of spirited debate: today the chief competitors are Giorgione and Titian. The painting's most striking quality is the stillness and isolation of the figures. There seems to be no communication between them, and one is aware of the fixity of their gazes. The nude about to fill the pitcher at the fountain bends forward languidly in precarious balance, her thoughts far removed from the present movement. As she turns she shows, only momentarily and incompletely, her naked flank; her breasts are hidden by the curve of her arm. What a world of difference there is between the classical model of this figure, doubtless a statue like the Venus of Milos, and this pictorial rendering, all lights and shadows, the solid forms lost in the brightly lit folds of the drapery which is just barely held in place by the knees. Within the soft curve of the landscape can almost be heard the sound of the lute, the breathing of human figures and flocks, the rustle of leaves and of the grasses. It is late afternoon; as in some of Virgil's poems, the artist tries to recapture the nostalgic moods and movements of nature at sunset. Yet the consciously intellectual sophistication of the Renaissance man is clearly shown by the studied harmony of silks and velvets, contrasting with the magnificent naked forms of the women. Is this Giorgione, or Titian painting like Giorgione? The intensity and rhythm of the whole work speak in favor of its attribution to Giorgione.

GIORGIONE
Castelfranco 1477 (?)—Venice 1510
The Concert (1505–10)
Oil on canvas; 43 1/4″ × 54 1/4″.

134

TITIAN. *Man with a Glove*.

Already in this work, one of his earliest portraits, Titian shows his
originality. The placement of the figure is typical of the artist. The
figure is seen to the waist. The body is simply formed, included within
repeated angles—the bent arm, the crossed leg. A few bright spots
attract the eye: the open hand, laid easily on the lap, the opening of
the jacket revealing the white cloth of the shirt, the clear-cut line of the
nose. The youth who commissioned the portrait belonged no doubt to
the upper classes of the Venetian Republic, perhaps even to the narrow
circle of its ruling aristocracy. He sits quietly but not stiffly, looking at
something we cannot see. The glove he holds, expensive, but soft and
wrinkled from daily use, has rightly been chosen to characterize him.
It tells us more about this anonymous young man and his place in
society than do either the narrow, carelessly fluttering lace borders or
the gold chain almost hidden on his chest. The focus of the whole
picture leads to this glove, by the downward direction of the lighted
features, the sloping lines of the shoulders and the pointing fingers.

TITIAN
Pieve di Cadore 1477 (?)—Venice 1576
*Portrait of an Unknown Gentleman,
Man with a Glove* (circa 1510)
Oil on canvas; 39 1/4″ × 34 1/4″.

TITIAN. *Woman at the Mirror*.

The woman has been identified as either Titian's mistress or Laura
Dianti, mistress of Alfonso d'Este. She was certainly Titian's favorite
model and appears in his pictures again and again, probably not for

TITIAN
Woman at the Mirror (circa 1515)
Oil on canvas; 37 3/4″ × 30″.

sentimental reasons, but rather because her physical type was well adapted to his style. The broad, fluid planes of her face and shoulders allowed him to express those gradations of tone which were his specialty. Her crisply curled hair could reflect the light either in bright sparkling spots or in luminous waves. Over her broad breasts he could widen the neckline of the finely pleated blouse and, under her rounded arms, form deep shadows in the openings of the sleeves. The figure of the model here provides the focus for an intricate, irregular rhythm of concentric forms, starting from the surface of the head of her lover, who adjusts the mirror, leaning over the girl. Her gaze turns elsewhere; and the rhythm is then taken up by the forms of her body and dress: the neckline of her blouse, slipping off her shoulders, the rounded forms within the open bodice, and the diagonal *contrapposto* of her arms, as she turns to adjust her hair, while the other arm closes off the composition on the right, the hand resting on the solid form of the little vase.

TITIAN
Deposition (circa 1525)
Oil on canvas; 58 1/4″ × 88 1/2″. This is the first of a series of works commissioned by the Marquis of Mantua, Federico Gonzaga, nephew of Alfonso d'Este.

TITIAN. *Deposition.*
The influence of Michelangelo is visible in the weight of the bodies and in the opposition of forces in the foreground, as well as the sweeping movement with which Mary Magdalen supports the weeping Virgin.

137

This influence also explains the powerful frame of the body of Christ, hidden in the shadows except for the bony hands and pointed knees. Nevertheless, the artist, who is conscious of this influence, turns it to new uses. The essential structure is, to be sure, sculptural; a central group based on a solid human form. Tensions resulting from its insertion in an architectural composition, however, are exploited by the painter, who is here showing the Deposition not directly, as something which is being re-lived in the present, but rather as a reenacted scene. Even the artist's own emotional participation is overwhelmed by the epic proportions of the drama and by the splendid colors—golden reds, blues and yellows—lit by the dark splendor of a stormy twilight.

PAOLO VERONESE. *The Wedding at Cana.*
Veronese liked the theme of the banquet or supper. Many of his pictures show this motif, the best-known being the famous *Feast in the*

House of Levi in the Accademia, Venice. He always transformed the theme, setting the various episodes of the religious story into the luxurious surroundings of sixteenth-century Venice, with its colorful, cosmopolitan crowds of lords and ladies, servants, buffoons, exotic animals and pets, precious silverware and plate, embroidered table-cloths, all within architectural frames—colonnaded porticos, staircases, terraces—triumphantly open to the light of day. The background is Venice, with marble palaces reminiscent of the local architectural tradition following Coducci, and also of the contemporary classical architecture of Andrea Palladio.

It is within such a context that we must look at this painting. It has been compared unfavorably to other works of the artist, especially to his *Feast in the House of Levi*. It is true that the *Marriage at Cana* is less grandiose compressed as it is between the two rows of huge columns. There are too many different types of guests—Venetians, Turks,

PAOLO VERONESE
Verona 1528—Venice 1588
The Wedding at Cana (1562–64)
Detail. Oil on canvas; 259 3/4″ × 389 3/4″.
Painted for the Refectory of the Convent of
S. Giorgio Maggiore, Venice.

139

Easterners, variously identified by their dress and features—of servants, musicians and paraphernalia in general. Yet the painting is of interest precisely for its experimental quality. It marks a moment of change, after which Veronese expressed himself in a different way, extending the use of quiet, white architectural frames to contrast with the bright colors of human figures.

JACOPO TINTORETTO. *Paradise.*

The subject is similar to that of the huge canvas painted for the Great Council Hall in the Doge's Palace in 1590. This smaller work cannot, however, be considered to be a sketch for the mural: at least it is not its preparatory study. Certain differences in style show that it probably should be dated 30 years earlier, to coincide with Tintoretto's work in the church of the Madonna dell'Orto. Perhaps it was a project for a commission which was never carried out, or perhaps the artist simply painted it for himself. The latter seems probable in view of the free flowing style. Groups of saints and of the blessed are placed within the rolling hemicycles, illuminated by a great light. We watch from below, while above, at a dizzying height, in the center of the "mystic rose," Christ is crowning the Virgin. In the "petals" of the rose all is transformed by color: clouds, figures and drapery are expressed in rapid strokes which define neither by outline nor by shadow, but by bright touches of gold on the rose and red colors, on the greens, above all on the predominant light blue and white. Tintoretto, who never pays too much attention to the solidity of his forms, here surpasses himself in the imaginative, fantastic reconstruction of the heavenly crowds, where any corporeal reality is denied and destroyed. All plastic values evaporate in this world where the successive widening of the "eternal circles" extends to the infinity of time and space.

JACOPO TINTORETTO
Venice 1518 (?)—Venice 1594
Paradise (1565–70)
Detail of left side.
Oil on canvas; 56 1/4″ × 14 1/2″.
Subject and composition are similar to that of the huge *Paradise* painted by Tintoretto in 1590 for the Great Council Hall of the Doge's Palace in Venice, but scholars agree this work is some twenty years earlier.

MICHELANGELO. *Bound Slave.*   *p. 142*

The figure was executed for the base of the Tomb of Pope Julius II, an ambitious project, several times interrupted and reduced in scale by those who had commissioned the work. Michelangelo struggled with it for forty years. It was never completed; but the magnificent figures of the *Bound Slaves* bear witness to the incredible effort, both intellectual and physical, which Michelangelo expended upon it. It is in these figures that we can see the concentration he put into this work and the sense of commitment with which he carried it out. In fact, it is just in this instant when he applies himself to hew the human form out of the raw block of marble that we can sense the basic theme of his creative process. The long, almost serpentine, sinuous figure is blocked out by three angles— the elbows, and the knee bent forward, expressing extension in height,

width and depth. The figure suffers, in a long, slow spasm, constrained as it is by tight bonds and almost, it would seem, by the unyielding marble itself. Yet the artist in effect has conquered the material, transforming it by means of subtle modeling, lovingly emphasizing the swelling forms of the muscles, and achieving thereby luminous effects reminiscent of Praxiteles.

CORREGGIO. *Antiope.*

This composition was designed to be the first of a series of paintings representing the loves of Jupiter; others include the stories of Danaë, Leda, Io and Ganymede. The god, shown here in the form of a satyr, sees Antiope sleeping, with Eros at her side; he stops to admire her, lifting the drapery which covered her body. The painting is an excellent example of the artist's mature style. To his interest in Giorgione, an influence which reached him originally by way of Dosso Dossi, has been added the influence of Leonardo da Vinci. He adopts the results of Leonardo's style without accepting its origin, Leonardo's interest in the relationship between science and painting. Correggio uses the smoky tones of Leonardo, but uses them to enrich the sentimental, nostalgic, bucolic mood of the idyll. The forms are daringly foreshortened, curved in soft lines which lead to the face of Antiope. These lines are not constructed on an abstract, geometric pattern: they expand, they flow out of an open, asymmetric space, and run diagonally along the grassy slope. The group has been caught in an instant of immobility; but the figures already seem to glow with desire and the sensuous movement of dreams. Almost magically, they seem to have been called forth, out of the dark shadows of the forest, by the warm afternoon light. This light casts a golden glow on the flesh tones, and is reflected by the bright hair and by the flame of the thyrsus; at the same time it further dematerializes the already delicate grass, the spotted animal tail used as a quiver, and the lion skin on which is lying the little winged Eros.

BENVENUTO CELLINI. *The Nymph of Fontainebleau.* p. 144

Cellini went to France in 1540, invited by Francis I. He could not have found a climate more favorable to his tastes than the School of Fontainebleau. There Rosso Fiorentino together with Primaticcio and others were giving a new impetus to the local school; their taste, as a result of both classical and of persistent late Gothic influence, ran to imaginative, sometimes deformed or grotesque forms. It is in such an ambience that we can understand the elongated silhouette of the Nymph, with crescent-shaped forms echoing each other across the bronze plaque: the curved border of the mantle and the curve of the stag's horns. The decorative quality of the background—thickly dotted with animals, flowers, leaves, fruits and waving water transformed into a soft resting-place—can only be explained within this same context in which spatial problems were sacrificed to decoration.

MICHELANGELO
Caprese 1475—Rome 1564
Bound Slave (circa 1513)
Marble sculpture; 90 1/4″ high. Originally
planned for the base of the Tomb of Pope
Julius II. It was given by the artist to Roberto
Strozzi, then living as an exile in France, along
with the other *Slave* in the Louvre, at the time
of one of the numerous interruptions and
changes in the Pope's monument.

CORREGGIO (ANTONIO ALLEGRI)
Correggio 1489—Correggio 1534
Antiope (1524–25)
Oil on canvas; 74 3/4″ × 48 3/4″.
This is the first of a series of paintings repre-
senting the *Loves of Jupiter,* apparently
executed for Federico Gonzaga, who planned
to present them as a gift to Charles V.

BENVENUTO CELLINI
Florence 1500—Florence 1571
The Nymph of Fontainebleau (1543–44)
Bronze relief; 80 3/4″ × 161″.

ROSSO FIORENTINO
Florence 1495—Paris 1540
Pietà (1537–40)
Oil on panel, transferred to canvas;
62 1/2″ × 96 1/2″.

ROSSO FIORENTINO. *Pietà*.

The work, executed for Anne de Montmorency, is one of the few surviving documents of the artist's activity in France between 1530 and
1540, when he was painter to the king and in charge of the decoration
of the palace at Fontainebleau. It has been criticized for its excessively
formal tone and for the absence of that artistic rebellion which characterizes the paintings he did in Tuscany and Umbria. There, he had made
it a point to avoid traditional motifs, and had reacted against the "classical" Florentine manner, especially that of Andrea del Sarto. But these
criticisms are unjust: the *Pietà* is actually a product of the artist's mature
style, when he is no longer rebelling, and when even the influence of
Michaelangelo, which in his youth he had over-emphasized, has now
been absorbed more quietly and on a deeper level.

The figures are closely bound together within a rocky hollow, the edges
of which are barely suggested by a jagged border. The forms of limbs
and bodies, touched by the light, determine an asymmetric composition
within a narrow frame. The eye moves along the wavering form of
St. John, tightly enclosed within sheets of yellow and reddish color,
and stops at the head of the Saint, prematurely grey, with its thick heavy
locks. This form is included within the double diagonals formed by the
livid body of Christ on the swelling, red pillow, and the open arms of
the Virgin, who, like the figure beside her, is thickly wrapped in a
purplish brown mantle. The diagonal opens, scissors-like, to contain
Mary Magdalen: her form, advancing towards the foreground, is made
up of broken folds, flesh and thick hair, over which there plays an ever-
changing pattern of rose, yellow, green and wine-dark colors.

CARAVAGGIO. *The Fortune-Teller*.   *p. 146*

According to tradition, this is one of the first paintings of Caravaggio
executed in Rome. It is said, indeed, to be the one he painted to demonstrate his own anti-Academic bent, when he was advised to study Classical models. "He called in a gypsy who happened to be passing by in
the street and painted her as she was telling the future . . . He also painted
a young man with his gloved hand on his sword, holding out toward her

the other hand, bared, while she holds it and looks into it; and in these two half-length figures Michele [Caravaggio] represented reality directly from nature, which he did to prove what he had said." Whether this anecdote told by Mancini is true or not, the painting is certainly one of the most typical examples of that peculiarity of Caravaggio's style called "direct painting." This implies that traditional "set" compositions are ignored and that the setting, point of view and lighting are handled in a free, revolutionary manner. His education at Brescia and contact with "genre painting" in the style of Giorgione may well have served to emphasize these tendencies. We must not, however, deny the originality of his compositions, in which he does away with planes defining space. The figure of the young man extends diagonally in space by means of the thrust of this sword and plumes. The figure of the gypsy, on the other hand, is more compact and solidly enclosed in space: the circle of her arms comes to a point in the three-dimensional knot of her hands. The three dominant colors—white, brown and ocher—are not simply added to a pre-determined structure, but rather belong to the most basic expression of the figure itself, which has, from the first, been imagined in these very colors.

146

CARAVAGGIO
(MICHELANGELO MERISI)
Caravaggio 1573—Porto Ercole 1610
The Fortune-Teller (1590–93)
Oil on canvas; 39″ × 51 1/2″.

FLANDERS
HOLLAND
GERMANY
SPAIN

ROGIER VAN DER WEYDEN. *The Annunciation.*

The artist's career is hard to reconstruct in detail since we have no dated works, and the existing documents do not give much information. *The Annunciation,* however, must be one of his relatively early works. It clearly shows the influences of Jan van Eyck and of the Master of Flémalle. The latter's work has sometimes wrongly been identified with that of Rogier himself before 1430; actually, the Master of Flémalle was Rogier's teacher. In this painting we find objects and descriptive passages from his master's repertory. These are, however, no longer placed in a set, sometimes awkward, logical relationship; rather, they are secondary elements in a unified image, within an almost atmospheric space. The whole is fused by a late Gothic style, emotional and linear. The main figures are placed within the silent interior in a conscious rhythmic pattern. Light, entering from the window at the right, quietly brings out large surfaces of walls and hangings; it casts delicate shadows, modeling the faces and draperies; and it shines forth with sudden, dazzling gem-like brilliance on the rich ornaments. There is an obvious resemblance to works by van Eyck, but the feeling of envelopment and penetration is even stronger. Within Rogier's complex style, traditional motifs are refined, so that they take on an inimitable, unique quality. The angel floats in precarious equilibrium, the Virgin is firmly enclosed in a sophisticated arabesque. Angel and Virgin are worked into the background, to form, with only a few other three-dimensional elements, a space which is full of life. Figures and atmosphere represent specific, religious symbols; yet they are also interpreted within a human, contemporary reality which goes beyond dogma and iconography to participate in the artist's personal, intimately religious feeling.

HIERONYMUS BOSCH. *The Ship of Fools.*   *p. 150*

The painting is certainly a rather early work of the artist; this can be seen not only by the style, but also by the relatively simple allegorical meaning, which gradually becomes more and more complicated and crowded in the works of Bosch. His freedom with the iconographic traditions is surprising. Within this remarkably narrow, vertical frame, the crowded grouping in the lower zone, full of nightmare images, startling forms and eccentric symbols, marks the characteristic *horror vacui* of many of the artist's most famous works, as it marks also his typical conscious exclusion of physical space, of a third dimension, of visual perspective. The bush, crackling with bright sparks, isolates the scene and closes it off as it ascends to the spacious upper zone (where narrative and symbolic elements are almost non-existent) and recedes to a magnificent seascape, airy, deep and spacious. The empty, silent sunset, suffused with a golden light, brings to mind the eternal loveliness of the world when it is not corrupted by the presence of man's folly and chaos.

ROGIER VAN DER WEYDEN
Tournai 1399—Brussels 1464
The Annunciation (circa 1430–35)
Panel; 33 3/4″ × 36 1/4″. Central part of a triptych; the doors, perhaps painted with the help of assistants, certainly overpainted, are in the Turin Pinacoteca.

QUENTIN METSYS. *The Moneychanger and His Wife.* p. 151
This is one of the best and most characteristic examples of the influence of early Flemish painting which is such a typical element in the style of Metsys. Here he almost exactly repeats a painting of Jan van Eyck (which is lost, but known to us from the description of Michiel). At the same time the work harks back to Petrus Christus' *St. Eligius,* similar in its detailed, almost precious rendering of the background, contrasting with the monumental detachment of the figures. Metsys combines with delicate grace a variety of stylistic elements taken from Gothic miniatures, from Memling, Gérard David (the great German artist of his time) and Italian art. He uses these elements with critical understanding, disciplining contrasting features within a unified vision, and so removing any literal meaning, by adopting them into his own coherent style.

HIERONYMUS BOSCH
's Hertogenbosch circa 1450—circa 1516
The Ship of Fools (circa 1490)
Panel; 22 3/4″ × 12 3/4″. The motif of folly is
here represented by the shipful of merry-makers
—a motif quite common, especially in literature, in the 15th century—and connected to
contemporary satire on the corruption of the
clergy (indicated by the monk and the nun).

QUENTIN METSYS
Louvain 1466—Antwerp 1530
The Moneychanger and His Wife (1514)
Panel; 28″ × 26 3/4″. Signed and dated, "Quin-
ten matsyss schilder 1514." This is doubtless
the signed original which was the model for an
enormous series of replicas and copies. It re-
states a convention, current in 15th-century
Flemish painting, and became widely used in
treating this popular theme.

PETER PAUL RUBENS. *The Arrival of Marie de' Medici at Marseilles.*
In spite of the enormity of the task and the speed of its execution, the entire series celebrating the Queen is from the artist's own hand; so, too, are the sketches, most of which are in Munich. Only minor help from assistants could have been contributed towards the final completion of the paintings. In this picture of the young Queen's disembarkation on French soil, Rubens has clearly divided the story into two horizontal zones, marked off by the diagonal line of the gangplank connecting the ship's deck with the not yet visible shore. Above, in the background—composed of fluctuating and intersecting decorative elements—can be seen foreshortened, the group of ladies-in-waiting and attendant mythological subjects, their figures softened by the pearly glow of the delicate colors and made even more lyrical by the rhythmic pattern of their gestures. The main episode below has far more emphasis. Rubens has used the mythological group of sea-divinities emerging from the glassy waves of an impossible sea, to realize one of the most daring, remarkable compositions of his career. We see bursting forth opulent naked forms, intertwined in incredible contortions, hurled forward by agitated waves of violent rhythms, of blazing colors occasionally frozen in sudden crystal light. The ornate, shining section of the ship on the left connects the two scenes with a solid, vertical movement. The immobile, static figure of the gentleman on deck, aloof from both action and participation in the scene, is almost a personification or symbol of detachment from any kind of engagement and of the emotional and formal control the artist, apparently so magnificently spontaneous and impulsive, constantly exercises in his paintings.

REMBRANDT VAN RIHN. *The Supper at Emmaus.*   *p. 154*
The architectural setting of the composition, bare but monumental, with its few elements—the door, the engaged pillars, the niche framing and symbolically containing Christ—at once forms the background and suggests its structure, based on an internal diagonal axis moving from the foreground on the right towards the back on the opposite side. The figures gathered around the table form a vertical diagonal pattern which is varied internally by triangular patterns on the surface and in depth. This constant interplay of converging and diverging directions, of parallels and contrasts, is so skillfully carried out as to be noticed only by careful observation. The figure of Christ, the spiritual center, is the source of the light which radiates forth, resulting in sudden, daring illuminations of the faces and the hands of the pilgrims, permeating the surrounding darkness with soft evocative light and creating a climate of imaginative thoughtfulness, mysterious and solemn at the same time. The extreme simplicity of the outward reality, crystallized in the immobility of the moment, underlines and parallels the intense but restrained, almost hidden life. In this self-contained expression of a complete organic unity, the artist, certain of the reality he has reconstructed, asks for neither understanding nor participation on the part of the viewer.

PETER PAUL RUBENS
Siegen 1577—Antwerp 1640
The Arrival of Marie de' Medici at Marseilles (1622–25) Panel; 155 1/2″ × 116 1/4″. It is one of the twenty-one historical-mythological scenes on the *Life of Marie de' Medici* commissioned from the artist by the Queen of France for the Luxembourg Palace in 1622, all of them completed within four years, in an almost miraculous burst of activity.

Above:

FRANS HALS
Antwerp circa 1581–85—Haarlem 1666
The Gypsy (circa 1630)
Panel: 22 3/4″ × 20 1/2″.

Right:

JOHANNES VERMEER
Delft 1632–1675
The Lace Maker (circa 1665)
Panel; 9 1/2″ × 8 1/4″.
Signed at the upper right on the very light
background with a slightly darker color.

Left:

REMBRANDT VAN RIJN
Leyden 1606—Rozengracht 1669
The Supper at Emmaus (1648)
Panel; 26 3/4″ × 25 1/2″.

FRANS HALS. *The Gypsy.*

This is one of the gayest and most lively characters of that every-day
world of the people and of the middle classes which Hals has set down
for us: a variety of commonplace scenes expressed with the precipitous
force of his imagination, with a boldness of form which seems almost
fantastically modern. The brushstroke, itself modeled with skillful
variations of thickness and width, impetuous yet fluid, forms the charm-
ing figure with only a few simple touches. This portrait is one of the
best and most successful examples of the real character of Hals' painting. A clear, sharp light illuminates the figure from the front. The shape
is formed by color relationships rather than by light and shade; each
stroke expresses at the same time depth, luminosity, movement and
material (this is the way Manet understood the use of the brushstroke).
The laughing girl, clear and sharp as the light, seems to turn to the
viewer with a spontaneity which parallels the artist's own; a spontaneity
which is, however, firmly controlled by the artist's sure hand.

JOHANNES VERMEER. *The Lace Maker.*

The figure is placed in the foreground, together with all the secondary
elements; it is so close to the viewer that it is difficult to pick out the
forms. This is a rare type of composition for the artist, who liked to
put large, empty, airy spaces between the viewer and his subject. The

ALBRECHT DÜRER
Nuremberg 1471–1528
Self-Portrait
Transferred from parchment to canvas, 22 1/4″ × 17 1/2″. Dated at top, 1493, and inscribed "Myn sach dy gat als es oben schtat," words perhaps in the dialect of Strasburg, meaning, "My life will go as ordered above." The flower —the "Eryngium amethystinum" —signifies loyalty and success in love. The unusual shape of the hat can be recognized in a print of the House-Book Master. Quite probably this splendid youthful self-portrait was painted during a stay in Strasburg (the artist arrived there in November, 1493) and sent to Nuremberg, where Dürer married Agnes Fry the following year, on July 7. There are two drawings which seem to be vaguely related, in Lemberg and Erlangen.

LUCAS CRANACH,
THE ELDER
Kronach 1472—Weimar 1553
Venus in a Landscape (1529)
Detail
Panel; 15″ × 10 1/4″.
Signed and dated in the
lower right hand corner.

placement of the light source to the right is also rare. On the other hand, the low angle of vision, here emphasized by the way the figure is cut off and fitted into the frame, was frequently used by the artist. Both theme and subject are from contemporaneous or earlier genre painters. The extraordinarily "impressionistic" technique and the formal technique in general point to a familiarity with earlier and contemporaneous figurative traditions (for example, Velazquez). But every historical reference, every traditional element, immediately loses its identity in Vermeer's personality. He is always able to see and to record the un-changeable and inexpressible beauty in everything, the eternal delight of those moments of absolute reality which men are able to feel only rarely, and then never so clearly, strongly and permanently as in his work. In few other works are his exceptional sensibility so realized.

ALBRECHT DÜRER. *Self-Portrait.*
Students of iconology have long been interested in this painting because of the hat, the inscription and especially the jewel-like flower which the twenty-two year-old Dürer holds in his right hand. According to scholars, the fact that the picture was painted specifically as love-token explains its sensuous refinement and the absence of dramatics.

A certain softness still models the bony face and strong features. The hair falls in disordered locks; the beard is only a hint of thin, blond fuzz; the magnificent dress shows a desire to adopt exotic costumes. Yet in this youthful image there is already a remarkable impressiveness. The artist's self-assurance is underlined by his self-possessed posture, turned diagonally towards the dark background, as well as by the strength of a basic composition only superficially graceful and naturalistic, and by the force of a style which has already developed beyond the Italian and German tradition which first inspired it. The most interesting detail is that of the hands, which seem about to open, especially the right one, with a slow, unfolding movement like the opening of a flower. These are the powerful instruments of the artist.

LUCAS CRANACH, the Elder. *Venus in a Landscape.*
This is one of a number of paintings of a similar subject, varying only slightly the linear rhythm of the graceful body, twisting in a slow, spiral movement about its own axis, and the few, bright details, such as the border of the invisible veil, the hair and the necklace. Differences of background and of allegorical elements are more important. This Venus is not one of the most famous, but is certainly one of the most interest-ing, and one of the best examples of Flemish influence on the artist's style, an influence which is still evident after 20 year's absence. It can be seen not only in the weightlessness and lack of real movement of the body, in contrast to the classic or Italian volumetric style, and in the landscape to the right which looks logical and "real," but also in the minute, detailed rendering of the abstract arabesque of the pebbles, the metallic curls of her locks, the bright, sudden glints from the dark trees; and in the colors, too, even though they have been consciously kept down to a few basic tones. The influence of Italian art, perhaps Botticelli, though remote, is reflected in the rhythm of the silhouette. Here a feeling for nature and atmosphere, which caused Cranach to be

called a precursor of Brueghel, is emphasized. There is more life in this brief expanse of mournful forest, and in the representation of the background landscape than in the sinuous form of the central figure.

EL GRECO. *St. Louis, King of France, with a Page.*

There are mysterious elements in the figure of this ascetic monarch, identified by some scholars as the saintly King Ferdinand of Spain. The painting belongs to the most mature phase of the artist's activity in Spain. At this time the experience of his study in Italy, and especially his study of Titian and Tintoretto, had already long been incorporated in his painting after his arrival in Spain in 1577.

He has gone beyond all these influences, fusing them in what has been called Greco's a-naturalist, anti-naturalist or even supernatural style. This is a manner which, even in a limited and strictly defined subject like this portrait, manages to give to the image a profound spiritual meaning, detaching it from any reference to day-to-day existence. The artist achieves this more by reversing every law of geometry, of perspective and of gravity, by ignoring every system of proportions, than by the consciously ambiguous, enigmatic significance of his subject matter. The enormous shoulder and the arm held out on the left bring forward the whole weight of the main figure, which is placed on a slant. The page is simply fitted in, without either weight or relief, in order to complete a composition which avoids symmetric and emphatic structure. The painting is devoid of any indication of real space; the column in the background, with its very high base, does not, nor is it meant to, indicate any real building. It serves only to emphasize the descending and forward movement of the figures. Within this non-existent space, in the empty silence of the dark background, Greco's miraculous colors are as much an "internal" element as the light which falls on the group from the foreground. The colors sparkle, breathe, touch every form, as they create a vision beyond and above the reality of the story.

DIEGO VELAZQUEZ DE SILVA. *The Infanta Margarita.*

The age of the Infanta provides us with a precise date for this portrait, painted during Velazquez' most brilliant period at the Court in Madrid. There he was involved in an intense activity which inevitably led him to devote himself to official commissions, and which often forced him, overburdened as he was by commissions, to use assistants instead of carrying out all the work himself.

He did not use assistants for this painting, however. It is one of his most personal works, in which his painting is at its most spontaneous and has the immediacy and honesty characteristic of all the authentic work of this master. The lofty official subject has been transformed into this little princess, whose typical Bourbon features are intentionally played down. The figure is at once moving and imposing by the boldness of the brilliant effects of color on her dress and in the background, only barely hinted at, as well as by the atmosphere of fragile, childish softness which the vibrant, almost evanescent light brings to her face and to the shining, delicately soft, blond hair.

158

FRANCISCO DE GOYA Y LUCIENTES
Fuentedetodos 1764—Bordeaux 1828
*Doña Rita of Barrenechea, Marquesa de la
Solana and Condesa del Carpio* (circa 1794–95)
Oil on canvas; 72″ × 48 3/4″.

FRANCISCO DE GOYA Y LUCIENTES. *Doña Rita of Barranechea, Marquesa dela Solana and Condesa del Carpio.* *(See page 160)*

(See page 160)

Painted in the artist's mature period, this figure is outstanding in its simplicity and aloofness among the large series of splendid, very "Spanish" portraits which represent the more serene aspect of Goya's style. This is not the Goya involved with anguish, cruelty, misery and the injustice of life doubtless the basic themes of his work, to be found not only in his wonderful drawings and famous prints, but also in his painting. Yet, even in this other, calm view of the world, one which delights in beauty and delicacy, elegance and wit, Goya's strength affirms itself. All attention is centered on the slender figure, dominating an empty space with scarcely any background. The artist concentrates on the splendid, fantastic color contrast of the dress, the deep, intense black, as soft as a butterfly's wing, and of the veil and luminous hair-ribbon; a contrast effectively repeated by the black mass of unruly hair framing the pale face.

EL GRECO
(DOMENICO THEOTOCOPOULOS)
Crete 1531–Toledo 1614
St. Louis, King of France, with a Page
(1586–96)
Panel; 46″ × 37 1/2″

DIEGO VELAZQUEZ DE SILVA
Seville 1599—Madrid 1660
The Infanta Margarita (circa 1653)
Oil on canvas; 50 1/2″ × 39 1/4″.

HISTORY OF THE MUSEUM
AND ITS BUILDING

On July 27, 1793 the "Musée central des Arts" was established by decree of the Revolutionary Government and less than a month later it was open to the public in the Grande Galerie of the Louvre. Though it actually included only a small selection of paintings from the incredibly rich collection of the former king, it was greeted by the people with tremendous enthusiasm. It was carried out by the Convention, but plans for it had been under way long before, under the monarchy, influenced by new situations and points of view which had developed in the context of the culture of the Enlightenment. Such eighteenth-century projects are evidence of a new consciousness of the possible historical and educational importance of these collections, gathered together through hundreds of years by the kings of France, from whom they were now inherited, along with the palace that housed them. In tracing their formation, as objects were bought, received as gifts or confiscated, we trace also a pattern of the tastes which marked four hundred years of French, as well as European art.

The first nucleus of the collection can be traced back to Francis I (1515–1547), who gathered together paintings, sculptures and other objects which reflect the tone of his court, at once learned and sophisticated; almost pedantic, almost frivolous. At that time he, perhaps more than any other Northern ruler, was open to the currents of innovation coming in from the South. Upon his return from his military campaigns around Milan he chose Fontainebleau as his residence, and invited artists, such masters as Leonardo, Rosso Fiorentino and Benvenuto Cellini—the greatest of their time—to France. He added to his collection works by Titian, Fra' Bartolomeo, Raphael, Sebastiano del Piombo, and the last year of his life he had the construction of the Louvre begun on the Right Bank of the Seine on the site of a thirteenth-century fortress.

The building project was carried on during the rest of the century, but the royal collections did not grow much under the following kings. This fact reflects the grave political crisis France was undergoing in the second half of the sixteenth century. Louis XIII was not himself an enthusiastic collector, but he was fortunate in having as his minister Cardinal Richelieu, a true art lover and collector—an *amateur* in the seventeenth-century meaning of the word. Richelieu acquired for the king such works as Leonardo's *Madonna and St. Anne,* the huge *Supper at Emmaus* by Veronese and a ceiling panel by his friend Poussin representing the *Allegory of Time and Truth.* At this time the Queen Mother, Marie de' Medici, who was then involved in building her own palace in the Luxembourg Gardens, also commissioned various works, such as the well-known suite of canvases by Rubens, now on exhibit at the Louvre. In spite of this, according to Villot and Engerand, when Louis XIV came to the throne the whole collection amounted to only slightly over 200 paintings. But at the death of Louis XIV, the collection consisted of 2,000 paintings; a tremendous growth which marks the most brilliant half-century of French collecting. From the beginning of his long reign, the king and his minister, Cardinal Mazarin, planned a systematic development of the royal art treasures, and they were fortunate enough to be able to buy some very important private collections, including that of Charles I, King of England. His holdings already had been enriched by the acquisition, in 1627, of most of the paintings of the Gonzagas of Mantua, a treasury of Italian Renaissance art. When Charles's collection was dispersed, during Cromwell's revolution of 1649–50, a major part of it came into the hands of Mazarin and of Evrard Jabach, a German banker and a director of the East India Company. At Mazarin's death in 1650, Louis bought the best pieces; so Raphael's *Portrait of Baldassare Castiglione* and Correggio's *Antiope* came to the Louvre. The king bought more than 5,000 drawings and 100 paintings from Jabach, among these Giorgione's *Concert Champètre*, Caravaggio's *Death of the Virgin* and Titian's *Man with a Glove.* In 1665, too, Mazarin's grandson sold him 13 paintings by Poussin, and the same year Don Camillo Pamphili sent to Paris paintings by Albani, Annibale Carracci's *The Hunt* and *Fishing Party* and Caravaggio's *Fortune Teller.* Other gifts enriched his personal collection. From the Republic of Venice came the *Supper in the House of Simon* by Veronese, and from the collection of the landscape architect Le Nôtre came works by Claude Lorrain, Albani and Poussin.

In this way the royal gallery was filled with priceless paintings by Italian and French artists of the sixteenth and seventeenth centuries. Around the end of the century there was a renewed interest in Northern art, reflecting a new taste for intimate scenes and for domestic genre subjects, a taste which fitted into the then-modern Rococo style. All the Holbeins in the Louvre today had already been bought as part of the Jabach collection, but now Louis XIV bought such famous works as Rubens' *Kermesse* and *Self-Portrait as an Old Man.*

In the eighteenth century, the Regent, Philippe, Duc d'Orléans, was, like Louis XIV, a patron of the arts, but the collection he set up was a private one, and it was dispersed at auction after the Revolution. During the reign of Louis XV and Louis XVI the huge paintings of the previous century were less popular, because they did not fit into the delicate, intricately designed interior decoration currently fashionable. In this period the most important acquisition, in 1742, consisted of paintings from the collection of Amedeo of Savoia; these were for the most part seventeenth-century Italian paintings.

At the same time it was felt by influential people that arrangements should be made in order to organize, house and take proper care of the now huge royal collection. In 1747 a certain Lafont de Saint-Yenne passed around a petition asking for the establishment of a special gallery where young artists could study. Following this request, 110 masterpieces from the collection were exhibited in the Luxembourg in 1749: and so the first, though only temporary, public gallery in France came into being. The importance of museum studies in this period is well illustrated by Diderot's treatment of the principles underlying the organization of the collection in the Louvre, which he published in the famous *Encyclopedia* (1765).

The Count of Angivillier, who became "Directeur des Bâtiments" in 1774, was in a way the creator of the museum as we know it today. Under his guidance important progress was made in planning and building the "Grande Galerie" of the palace of the Louvre. The Count also ordered some necessary restoration work, and began a policy of systematic buying, like that of Louis XIV. In these twenty years were bought, for example, van Dyck's *Portrait of Charles I of England,* Rubens' *Portrait of Hélène Fourment and her Children,* Rembrandt's *Supper at Emmaus* and Ruisdael's *Sunset,* as well as works by the Le Nains, Philippe de Champaigne and the series on the *Life of St. Bruno* by Le Sueur.

It is clear that the Revolution of 1789, rather than destroying the projected museum, brought it into being. The creation took place at a time of confiscation of church property and of the aristocrats who fled the country. From private collections came Michelangelo's *Slave* and Mantegna's *Allegories,* while van Eyck's *Madonna and Chancellor Rolin* and Fra' Bartolomeo's *Marriage of St. Catherine* were taken from the church of Notre-Dame at Autun. The policy of confiscations assumed alarming proportions under Napoleon, who re-named the museum after himself in 1803. In the twenty years between the Convention and the fall of his Empire, he despoiled all the conquered lands of their masterpieces, especially Italy. Italy then lost, for example, Raphael's *The Betrothal of the Virgin* and Giovanni Bellini's *Pietà.* These were the years when the Early Renaissance was being rediscovered and thus Denon, the museum's director, brought to the museum Giotto's *St. Francis Receiving the Stigmata* and Cimabue's *Madonna in Majesty* from the church of St. Francis in Pisa, among many others. This was a period of great traveling about of works of art, and many works from the so-called "central Museum" went to enrich or re-establish provincial collections. Napoleon's plan, however, collapsed when he was defeated, and already by November of 1815 more than 5,000 works of art had been returned to their respective countries: but a hundred or so masterpieces, some of which have already been mentioned, remained in the Louvre and were never returned.

In the nineteenth century, the Louvre rearranged its collections as well as engaged in buying other works. The new enthusiasm for archeology, which had started in the eighteenth century, within the context of the Neo-Classic taste, and had been encouraged by Napoleon's campaign in Egypt, caused this department to grow to international importance. It was subdivided into various departments, and the archeological collection was reorganized under Charles X. After the revolution of 1848, the whole painting collection was reorganized by Villot, who arranged it chronologically. The new emperor, Napoleon III, was ambitious in this direction, and added considerably to the Museum's holdings. In 1863 the whole Campana Collection was bought. It consisted of a variety of objects and of paintings by Tura, Crivelli, Signorelli *(The Annunciation)* and Paolo Uccello *(The Battle of San Romano).* Five years later La Caze left the Louvre 800 paintings, including, among others, works by Ribera, Rembrandt, Rubens, Hals and a group of French eighteenth-century canvases (Watteau, Fragonard, Chardin) which filled an important gap, since the museum had few works of this period.

In the last hundred years, the Louvre has continued to develop. Important works such as Dürer's *Self-Portrait* and the *Pietà* of Villeneuve-les-Avignon have been bought, and to these have been added in the last six years, the *Crucifixion* by the Master of San Sebastiano, a triptych by Beccafumi, the *Flagellation* by Huguet, *Still-life with Turkey* by Ruisdael, the *Assassination of the Bishop of Liège* by Delacroix, *Young Woman with Pink* by Corot and a Turner *Landscape.* In this same period the Museum has received some splendid gifts, among them *The Card Game* by Lucas van Leyden. The Lebaudy estate and the "Amis du Louvre" have given the Museum Vouet's *Allegory: Prudence Bringing Peace and Abundance,* as well as *The Blessed Rainier Freeing the Poor from Prison in Florence* and *Young Choirboy* by Claude Vignon. Baroness Gourgaud's gift includes the *Young Woman with Mandolin* by Corot, *Don Quixote* by Daumier and *Abduction of a Young Woman* by Delacroix, as well as various Impressionist and modern works. And now that certain prejudices in taste have at last disappeared, works of the French schools of the nineteenth century and by Impressionist artists have come into the Museum through the De Béstegui, Moreau-Nélaton and Caillebotte collections.

THE COLLECTIONS

DEPARTMENT OF GREEK AND ROMAN ANTIQUITIES
DEPARTMENT OF EGYPTIAN ANTIQUITIES
DEPARTMENT OF ORIENTAL ANTIQUITIES
DEPARTMENT OF MEDIEVAL, RENAISSANCE AND MODERN SCULPTURE
DEPARTMENT OF MEDIEVAL, RENAISSANCE AND MODERN ART OBJECTS
DEPARTMENT OF PAINTINGS AND DRAWINGS
SECTION OF CHRISTIAN ANTIQUITIES

The present Museum is divided into six Departments and a Cabinet of Drawings which gradually became separated from the nucleus of the painting collection whose history has just been traced. The Department of Greek and Roman Antiquities was the first to become autonomous. It was created in 1800, and was given its present organization in 1846. It includes, among other objects, the important group of Greek vases of the Campana Collection, the so-called "Boscoreale Treasure," composed of more than 100 pieces of Roman jewelry, given to the Museum in 1895 by Baron Rothschild, and famous works of art such as the *Venus* of Milos and the *Victory of Samothrace,* both discovered in excavations in the nineteenth century. In 1954 a "Section of Christian Antiquities" was created in order to group together Early Christian, Byzantine and Coptic works which were scattered here and there in various other departments. Aside from its Early Christian sarcophagi, Byzantine ivories, ceramics, glass, gold work and important textile collections, this Section now has also benefited from recent gifts and acquisitions, among them Greek and Russian icons and Coptic textiles.

The Department of Egyptian Antiquities was established in 1826 in order to organize Napoleon's collections. Its first curator was Champollion who first deciphered the hieroglyphs, and in this context Egyptian studies flourished. That year, "Oriental Antiquities" already formed a separate section within the Museum of ancient sculpture; in 1881 this, too, became a separate department. Organized topographically, it is exceptionally rich in Mesopotamian art, which had been brought to the Museum from the excavations at Lagash and Mari.

The "Department of Medieval, Renaissance and Modern Sculpture" was organized around what remained of the Royal Academy and its collections, moved in the Louvre in the eighteenth century. It contains Michelangelo's *Slaves,* as well as works by Cellini, Goujon, Pilon and others. It is now being enlarged to include the French eighteenth and nineteenth-century sculpture until recently kept in the storerooms. In 1893 another Department, that of Medieval, Renaissance and Modern Art Objects, was separated from this one; it includes all the precious objects from the Royal wardrobe, as well as material confiscated during the Revolution (treasures of the Order of St. Esprit, of the Royal Abbey of St. Denis and of the Ste. Chapelle), as well as the National Museum of Furniture, added to the Louvre in 1901.

ADMINISTRATION

The enormous size of the Louvre and its collections requires a special kind of organization, one that will allow the material to be exhibited to the public and also preserved for the future in the best way possible. In the nineteenth century, the Museum became the property of the state. As part of the "Réunion des Musées Nationaux" (1896), it was run by a board, which since 1941 has been divided into two sections, financial and artistic. In this way the Museum is enriched by new acquistions, some of which are paid for by the government, others privately.

Also in the Museum are a department of restoration, a library, archives and the "Ecole du Louvre," which offers courses in art history and restoration. Attached to the Director's office is a "Service for Cultural Activities," which has, among its other responsibilities, that of organizing within the National Museums lecture tours conducted by graduates of the "Ecole du Louvre," who are selected by competitive examinations. In 1966, for example, 7,856 groups of about 25 persons visited the Louvre in this way. In 1966, again, there were 1,182,878 paying visitors, as against 589,000 in 1952. It is estimated that the number would be double if one took into account nonpaying Sunday visits and student groups. Aside from the catalogues published by the curators of the various departments, the Museum also puts out two magazines, *Le Bulletin du Laboratoire du Musée du Louvre* and *La Revue du Louvre et des Musées de France.* The Louvre regularly offers exhibitions of drawings organized by the Cabinet of drawings and also special exhibitions, like that in 1960, when 800 paintings, all of which came from the Museum's storerooms, were shown. The Department of Paintings has also, in the last few years, organized several important exhibitions abroad. In 1962, in Rome, there was "French Portraits from Clouet to Degas"; in 1965 in Canada, "Eighteenth-Century French Paintings from the Louvre"; also in 1965, in Russia, "Paintings in French Museums"; in 1966, in Japan, " 'The Grand Siècle' in French Public Collections."

THE BUILDING

Since 1939 a long-term plan has been under way to get the collections ready, so that over two hundred thousand objects can be exhibited in the Louvre. The building was certainly not constructed according to modern ideas of what a perfect museum should be; in fact, the building, like the collections, shows traces of almost four centuries of French kings, all of whom, almost without exception, made some additions to the enormous palace. The nucleus of the building goes back to Francis I. This is the south-west section of the "Square Court" or "Cour Carrée" (the plan was that of the fortress of Philippe-Auguste, which had been destroyed), designed by the architect Lescot and adorned by statues by Jean Goujon. At the beginning of the seventeenth century all the South wing of palace, along the Seine, was finished; it was planned to reach the new palace of the Tuileries on the west. In 1624 Louis XIII decided to carry out the original plan for the "Cour Carrée," to enclose it on four sides, according to plans by Lemercier. This new project was carried out from 1661–63. Then Louis XIV, who had torn down what remained of the old fortress, as well as many surrounding buildings, commissioned Le Vau to complete the "quadruplement," still basically in the style of Lescot.

These sixteenth-century plans, however, could not give the monumental effect called for by the new "Porte d'Honneur" of the east side. The minister Colbert, therefore, ignoring the plans of Le Vau, Lemercier and Mansart, called in Bernini from Rome. In 1665, Bernini presented a baroque plan for the long façade. This was never carried out, since the taste of Louis XIV's court was by this time more classical: the style which was typical of all the production of this artistic center in the second half of the seventeenth century was already flowering. The suggestion put forward by a committee, Perrault, Le Vau and Le Brun, to have a long, continuous colonnade with a single row of columns, was taken up, and the façade was carried out along the south side of the palace as well. The decorations Le Brun executed for the "Petite Galerie" and in the rooms of the "Colonnade" also belong to this period.

When Louis XIV settled permanently in Versailles in 1678 the work had not yet been finished, and the palace was nearly abandoned. It was used only for meetings of the Academy, as a residence for members of the court, for offices and storerooms. Only at the end of the century, with the future Museum in mind, work started again under the supervision of the architects Gabriel and Soufflot. It was left to Napoleon to complete Perrault's "Cour Carrée" and "Colonnade" in the early years of the nineteenth century, as well as a wing on the north, along the Rue de Rivoli. The latter was continued by Napoleon III, fifty years later. He hired the architects Le Fuel and Visconti in an effort to make the west side, at last, harmonize with the whole. But when the work of so many centuries was finished at last, the palace of the Tuileries, ironically enough, burned down in 1871; and the original plan, to have a single complex, tied to the façade of the palace in a unified perspective, was never realized.

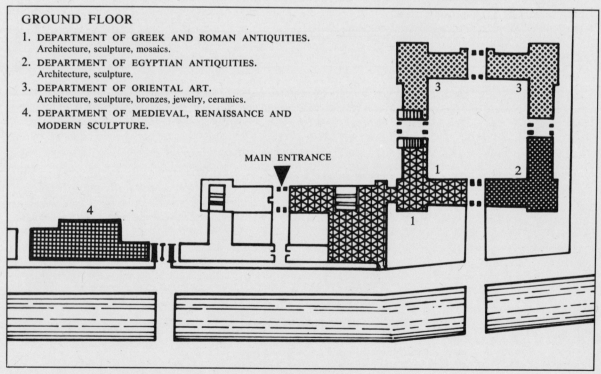

GROUND FLOOR

1. DEPARTMENT OF GREEK AND ROMAN ANTIQUITIES.
   Architecture, sculpture, mosaics.
2. DEPARTMENT OF EGYPTIAN ANTIQUITIES.
   Architecture, sculpture.
3. DEPARTMENT OF ORIENTAL ART.
   Architecture, sculpture, bronzes, jewelry, ceramics.
4. DEPARTMENT OF MEDIEVAL, RENAISSANCE AND
   MODERN SCULPTURE.

MAIN ENTRANCE

Plans of the Museum: Editions Musées Nationaux, Service des Activités Culturelles, Paris.

SECOND FLOOR

1. DEPARTMENT OF GREEK AND ROMAN ANTIQUITIES.
   Bronzes, jewelry, ceramics, Etruscan art.
2. DEPARTMENT OF EGYPTIAN ANTIQUITIES.
   Art objects.
3. DEPARTMENT OF ORIENTAL ART.
   Islamic Room.
4. DEPARTMENT OF MEDIEVAL, RENAISSANCE AND MODERN ART OBJECTS.
   Treasures of the French kings, furniture, bronzes, tapestries, porcelains, jewelry.
5. THE "GRANDE GALERIE."

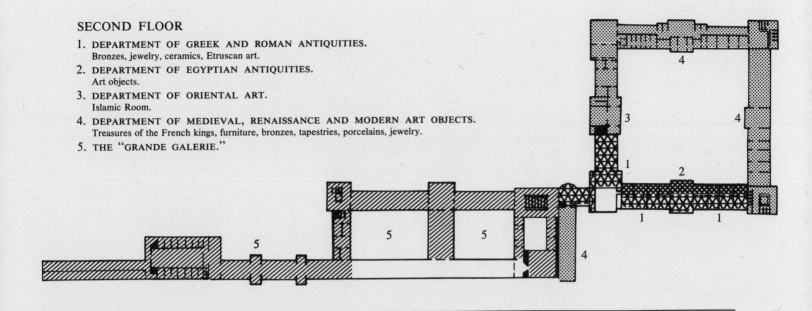

"GRANDE GALERIE"—FIRST FLOOR

DEPARTMENT OF PAINTING

1. Italy
2. France and Spain, 17th century
3. Flanders
4. Rubens (Life of Marie de' Medici)
5. France and Netherlands, from 14th to 16th centuries
6. Holland, 17th century.
7. France, 19th century

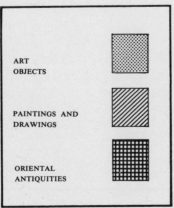

"GRANDE GALERIE"—SECOND FLOOR

1. 18th-century Painting
2. 19th-century Painting

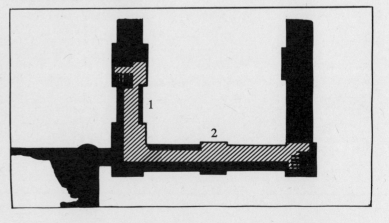

LEGEND

EGYPTIAN ANTIQUITIES	
ROMAN AND GREEK ANTIQUITIES	
SCULPTURE	

ART OBJECTS	
PAINTINGS AND DRAWINGS	
ORIENTAL ANTIQUITIES	

SELECTED BIBLIOGRAPHY

SMITH, WILLIAM STEVENSON: *The Art & Architecture of Ancient Egypt.* (Pelican History of Art, Penguin Books, Baltimore, 1958).

ALDRED, CYRIL: *Development of Ancient Egyptian Art, 3200–1315 B.C.* (Tiranti, London, 1952).

FRANKFORT, HENRI: *The Art and Architecture of the Ancient Orient.* (Pelican History of Art, Penguin Books, Baltimore, 1955).

CHAMOUX, FRANÇOIS: *Greek Art.* (In the Pallas Library of Art, New York Graphic Society, Greenwich, Connecticut).

BIEBER, MARGARETE: *The Sculpture of the Hellenistic Age.* (Columbia University Press New York).

VOLBACH, W. F.: *Early Christian Art, the Late Renaissance & Byzantine Empires from the 3rd to the 7th Centuries.* (Abrams, New York).

BURCKHARDT, JAKOB, C.: *The Civilization of the Renaissance.* (3rd rev. ed., Phaidon, London, 1950).

CHASTEL, ANDRÉ: *The Flowering of the Renaissance.* (Odyssey Press, New York).

DEWALD, ERNEST T.: *Italian Painting, 1200–1600.* (Holt, Rinehart & Winston, New York, 1961).

WATERHOUSE, ELIS: *Italian Baroque Painting.* (Phaidon, London & New York, 1961).

PANOFSKY, E.: *Early Netherlandish Painting.* (Harvard University Press, 1954).

FRIEDLÄNDER, MAX: *From Van Eyck to Brueghel.* (Phaidon, 1956).

BENESCH, OTTO: *The Art of the Renaissance in Northern Europe.* (Harvard University Press, 1945).

FROMENTIN, EUGÈNE: *The Masters of Past Times, Dutch and Flemish Painting.* (Phaidon, London, 1948).

BURCKHARDT, JAKOB C.: *Recollections of Rubens,* tr. By Mary Hottinger (Oxford University Press, New York, 1950).

WILENSKI, R. H.; *Dutch Painting.* (The Beechhurst Press, New York, 1955).

ROSENBERG, JAKOB: *Rembrandt.* (Harvard University Press, 1948).

JEDLICKA, GOTTHARD: *Spanish Painting.* (Viking Press, New York, 1963).

CHÂTELET, ALBERT AND THUILLIER, JACQUES: *French Painting, from Fouquet to Poussin.*

CHÂTELET, ALBERT AND THUILLIER, JACQUES: *French Painting from LeNain to Fragonard.*

JEAN LEYMARIE: *French Painting, the 19th Century.* (Skira, Geneva and New York).

FRIEDLAENDER, WALTER F.: *From David to Delacroix.* (Harvard University Press, 1952).

REWALD, JOHN: *History of Impressionism.* (Museum of Modern Art, New York 1946).

REWALD, JOHN: *Post-Impressionism from Van Gogh to Gauguin.* (Museum of Modern Art, New York, 1956).

For their courtesy in furnishing information relating to their departments we wish to thank Michel Lacotte, Head Curator of the Department of Paintings; Jean David Weill of the Moslem Art Section of the Department of Oriental Antiquities; Etienne Coche de la Ferté of the Section of Christian Antiquities; Pierre Amiet of the Department of Oriental Antiquities; R. Antelme of the Department of Egyptian Antiquities.

INDEX OF ILLUSTRATIONS

169

INDEX OF NAMES

Note: Italic numbers refer to names mentioned in captions.

GENERAL INDEX